SECOND EDITION

Making Embedded Systems
Design Patterns for Great Software

Elecia White

Beijing · Boston · Farnham · Sebastopol · Tokyo

Making Embedded Systems

by Elecia White

Copyright © 2024 Elecia White. All rights reserved.

Published by O'Reilly Media, Inc., 1005 Gravenstein Highway North, Sebastopol, CA 95472.

O'Reilly books may be purchased for educational, business, or sales promotional use. Online editions are also available for most titles (*http://oreilly.com*). For more information, contact our corporate/institutional sales department: 800-998-9938 or *corporate@oreilly.com*.

Acquisitions Editor: Brian Guerin	**Indexer:** Ellen Troutman-Zaig
Development Editor: Shira Evans	**Interior Designer:** David Futato
Production Editor: Katherine Tozer	**Cover Designer:** Karen Montgomery
Copyeditor: Penelope Perkins	**Illustrator:** Kate Dullea
Proofreader: Emily Wydeven	

October 2011:	First Edition
March 2024:	Second Edition

Revision History for the Second Edition

2024-03-01:   First Release

See *http://oreilly.com/catalog/errata.csp?isbn=9781098151546* for release details.

978-1-098-15154-6

LSI

Table of Contents

Preface

I love embedded systems. The first time a motor turned because I told it to, I was hooked. I quickly moved away from pure software and into a field where I can touch the world. Just as I was leaving software, the seminal work was done on design patterns.[1] My team went through the book, discussing the patterns and where we'd consider using them.

As I got more into embedded systems, I found compilers that couldn't handle C++ inheritance, processors with absurdly small amounts of memory in which to implement the patterns, and a whole new set of problems where design patterns didn't seem applicable. But I never forgot the idea that there are patterns to the way we do engineering. By learning to recognize the patterns, we can use the robust solutions over and over. Much of this book looks at standard patterns and offers some new ones for embedded system development. I've also filled in a number of chapters with other useful information not found in most books.

About This Book

After seeing embedded systems in medical devices, race cars, airplanes, and children's toys, I've found a lot of commonalities. There are things I wish I knew then on how to go about designing and implementing software for an embedded system. This book contains some of what I've learned. It is a book about successful software design in resource-constrained environments.

It is also a book about understanding what interviewers look for when you apply for an embedded systems job. Each section ends with an interview question. These are generally not language-specific; instead, they attempt to infer how you think. The most useful interview questions don't have a single correct answer. Instead of trying to document all the paths, the notes after each question provide hints about what an

---

1 Erich Gamma, et al., *Design Patterns: Elements of Reusable Object-Oriented Software* (Addison-Wesley).

interviewer might look for in your response. You'll have to get the job (and the answers) on your own merits.

One note, though: my embedded systems don't have operating systems (OS). The software runs on the bare metal. When the software says "turn that light on," it says it to the processor without an intermediary. This isn't a book about working with an embedded OS. But the concepts translate to processors running OSs, so if you stick around, you may learn about the undersides of OSs too. Working without one helps you really appreciate what an OS does.

This book describes the archetypes and principles that are commonly used in creating embedded system software. I don't cover any particular platform, processor, compiler, or language, because if you get a good foundation from this book, specifics can come later.

Who This Book Is For

I wrote this for some folks I've worked with in the past.

Sarah was a junior software engineer who joined my embedded systems team. She was bright and interested but didn't know how to handle hardware.

Josh was an experienced electromechanical engineer who needed to write software. He could power through some code but got stuck on designing the system, debugging memory issues, and reusing code.

Usually we only learn software or hardware in school; we don't learn how to make them work together. My goal is to cantilever off the knowledge you have to fill the gaps.

About the Author

In the field of embedded systems, I have worked on DNA scanners, inertial measurement units for airplanes and race cars, toys for preschoolers, a gunshot location system for catching criminals, and assorted medical, scientific, and consumer devices.

I have specialized in signal processing, hardware integration, complex system design, and performance. Having been through FAA and FDA certification processes, I understand the importance of producing high-quality designs and how they lead to high-quality implementations.

I've spent several years in management roles, but I enjoy hands-on engineering and the thrill of delivering excellent products. I'm happy to say that leaving management has not decreased my opportunities to provide leadership and mentoring.

After the first edition of this book, I started the Embedded.fm podcast to talk about embedded systems with other people. Through hundreds of episodes, I've learned how other engineers solve problems, about new technologies being developed, and other career paths.

Organization of This Book

I read nonfiction for amusement. I read a lot more fiction than nonfiction, but still, I like any good book. I wrote this book to be read almost as a story, from cover to cover. The information is technical (extremely so in spots), but the presentation is casual. You don't need to program along with it to get the material (though trying out the examples and applying the recommendations to your code will give you a deeper understanding).

This isn't intended to be a technical manual where you can skip into the middle and read only what you want. I mean, you can do that, but you'll miss a lot of information with the search-and-destroy method. You'll also miss the jokes, which is what I really would feel bad about. I hope that you go through the book in order. Then, when you are hip-deep in alligators and need to implement a function fast, pick up the book, flip to the right chapter, and, like a wizard, whip up a command table or fixed-point implementation of variance.

Or you can skip around, reading about solutions to your crisis of the week. I understand. Sometimes you just have to solve the problem. If that is the case, I hope you find the chapter interesting enough to come back when you are done fighting that fire.

The order of chapters is:

Chapter 1, *"Introduction"*
> This chapter describes what an embedded system is and how development is different from traditional software.

Chapter 2, *"Creating a System Architecture"*
> Whether you are trying to understand a system or creating one from scratch, there are tools to help.

Chapter 3, *"Getting Your Hands on the Hardware"*
> Hardware/software integration during board bring-up can be scary, but there are some ways to make it smoother.

Chapter 4, *"Inputs, Outputs, and Timers"*
> The embedded systems version of "Hello World" is making an LED blink. It can be more complex than you might expect.

Chapter 5, "Interrupts"

Interrupts are one of the most confusing topics in embedded systems: code that gets called asynchronously on events that happen inside the processor. A chicken is used to make this easier.

Chapter 6, "Managing the Flow of Activity"

This chapter describes methods for setting up the main loop of your system, where to use interrupts (and how not to), and how to make a state machine.

Chapter 7, "Communicating with Peripherals"

Different serial communication methods rule embedded systems: UART, SPI, I2C, USB, and so on. While you can look up the details for each, this chapter looks at what makes them different from each other and how to make them work more efficiently.

Chapter 8, "Putting Together a System"

Common peripherals such as LCDs, ADCs, flash memory, and digital sensors have common implementation needs such as buffer handling, bandwidth requirements, and pipelines.

Chapter 9, "Getting into Trouble"

Debugging is a skill every developer needs. Figuring out how to cause problems will teach you how to solve bugs, stack problems, hard faults, and cleverness.

Chapter 10, "Building Connected Devices"

Whether you have consumer IoT devices or industrial networked systems, managing many devices means dealing with firmware updates, security, and monitoring health.

Chapter 11, "Doing More with Less"

Optimization is not for the faint of heart. This chapter shows methods for reducing consumption of RAM, code space, and processor cycles.

Chapter 12, "Math"

Most embedded systems need to do some form of analysis. Understanding how mathematical operations and floating points work (and don't work) will make your system faster and more robust.

Chapter 13, "Reducing Power Consumption"

From reducing processor cycles to system architecture suggestions, this chapter will help you if your system runs on batteries.

Chapter 14, "Motors and Movement"

This chapter is a basic introduction to motors and movement. (Or possibly the introduction to an entirely new book.)

The information is presented in the order that I want my engineers to start thinking about these things. It may seem odd that architecture is first, considering that most people don't get to it until later in their career. But I want folks to think about how their code fits in the system long before I want them to worry about optimization.

Terminology

A *microcontroller* is a processor with onboard goodies like RAM, code space (usually flash), and various peripheral interfaces (such as I/O lines). Your code runs on a processor, or *central processing unit* (CPU). A *microprocessor* is a small processor, but the definition of "small" varies.

A DSP (*digital signal processor*) is a specialized form of microcontroller that focuses on signal processing, usually sampling analog signals and doing something interesting with the result. Usually a DSP is also a microcontroller, but it has special tweaks to make it perform math operations faster (in particular, multiplication and addition).

As I wrote this book, I wanted to use the correct terminology so you'd get used to it. However, with so many names for the piece of the system that is running your code, I didn't want to add confusion by changing the name. So, I stick with the term *processor* to represent whatever it is you're using to implement your system. Most of the material is applicable to whatever you actually have.

Conventions Used in This Book

The following typographical conventions are used in this book:

Italic
> Indicates new terms, URLs, email addresses, filenames, and file extensions.

`Constant width`
> Used for program listings, as well as within paragraphs to refer to program elements such as variable or function names, databases, data types, environment variables, statements, and keywords.

> This element signifies a tip or suggestion.

> This element signifies a general note.

This element indicates a warning or caution.

Using Code Examples

This book is here to help you get your job done. In general, you may use the code in this book in your programs and documentation. You do not need to contact us for permission unless you're reproducing a significant portion of the code. For example, writing a program that uses several chunks of code from this book does not require permission. Selling or distributing a CD-ROM of examples from O'Reilly books does require permission. Answering a question by citing this book and quoting example code does not require permission. Incorporating a significant amount of example code from this book into your product's documentation does require permission.

This book has a GitHub repository (*https://github.com/eleciawhite/making-embedded-systems*) for code, tools, and pointers to more information.

We appreciate, but do not require, attribution. An attribution usually includes the title, author, publisher, and ISBN. For example: "*Making Embedded Systems* by Elecia White (O'Reilly). Copyright 2024 Elecia White, 978-1-098-15154-6."

If you feel your use of code examples falls outside fair use or the permission given above, feel free to contact us at *permissions@oreilly.com*.

O'Reilly Online Learning

 For more than 40 years, *O'Reilly Media* has provided technology and business training, knowledge, and insight to help companies succeed.

Our unique network of experts and innovators share their knowledge and expertise through books, articles, and our online learning platform. O'Reilly's online learning platform gives you on-demand access to live training courses, in-depth learning paths, interactive coding environments, and a vast collection of text and video from O'Reilly and 200+ other publishers. For more information, visit *https://oreilly.com*.

How to Contact Us

Please address comments and questions concerning this book to the publisher:

O'Reilly Media, Inc.
1005 Gravenstein Highway North
Sebastopol, CA 95472
800-889-8969 (in the United States or Canada)
707-827-7019 (international or local)
707-829-0104 (fax)
support@oreilly.com
https://www.oreilly.com/about/contact.html

We have a web page for this book, where we list errata, examples, and any additional information. You can access this page at *https://oreil.ly/making-embedded-systems-2*.

For news and information about our books and courses, visit *https://oreilly.com*.

Find us on LinkedIn: *https://linkedin.com/company/oreilly-media*.

Watch us on YouTube: *https://youtube.com/oreillymedia*.

Acknowledgments

This book didn't happen in a vacuum. It started with a colleague who said, "Hey, do you know a book I can give to one of my junior engineers?" From that planted seed came months of writing; I learned to really appreciate understanding (and encouraging) friends. Then there were the engineers who gave their time to look at the technical material (any remaining issues are my fault, not theirs, of course). Finally, O'Reilly provided tremendous support through the whole process.

Thanking each person as they properly deserve would take pages and pages, so I will just go through them all in one breath, in no particular order: Phillip King, Ken Brown, Jerry Ryle, Matthew Hughes, Eric Angell, Scott Fitzgerald, John Catsoulis, Robert P. J. Day, Rebecca Demarest, Jen Costillo, Phillip Johnston, Rene Xoese Kwasi Novor, and Chris Svec. These folks made a difference in the flavor of this book. There are additional thank-yous spread throughout the book, where I got help from a particular person in a particular area, so you may see these names again (or a few different ones).

Finally, authors always give gushing thanks to their spouses; it is a cliché. However, having written a book, I see why. Christopher White, my favorite drummer, physicist, and embedded systems engineer, thank you most of all. For everything.

CHAPTER 1

Introduction

Embedded systems are different things to different people. To someone who has been working on servers, an application developed for a phone is an embedded system. To someone who has written code for tiny 8-bit microprocessors, anything with an operating system doesn't seem very embedded. I tend to tell nontechnical people that embedded systems are things like microwaves and automobiles that run software but aren't computers. (Most people recognize a computer as a general-purpose device.) Perhaps an easy way to define the term without haggling over technology is:

> An embedded system is a computerized system that is purpose-built for its application.

Because its mission is narrower than a general-purpose computer, an embedded system has less support for things that are unrelated to accomplishing the job at hand. The hardware often has constraints. For instance, consider a CPU that runs more slowly to save battery power, a system that uses less memory so it can be manufactured more cheaply, and processors that come only in certain speeds or support a subset of peripherals.

The hardware isn't the only part of the system with constraints. In some systems, the software must act deterministically (exactly the same each time) or in real time (always reacting to an event fast enough). Some systems require that the software be fault-tolerant, with graceful degradation in the face of errors. For example, consider a system in which servicing faulty software or broken hardware may be infeasible (such as a satellite or a tracking tag on a whale). Other systems require that the software cease operation at the first sign of trouble, often providing clear error messages (for example, a heart monitor should not fail quietly).

This short chapter goes over the high-level view of embedded systems. Realistically, you could read the Wikipedia article, but this is a way for us to get to know one another. Sadly, this chapter mostly talks about how difficult embedded systems are to develop. Between different compilers, debuggers, and resource constraints, the way we design and implement code is different from other varieties of software. Some might call the field a bit backward but that isn't true; we're focused on solving different problems, for the most part. And yet, there are some software engineering techniques that are useful but overlooked (but that's for the rest of the book).

One of the best things about embedded systems has been the maker movement. Everyone loves glowing lights, so people get interested in making a career of the lower-level software. If that is you, welcome. But I admit I'm expecting folks who have experience with hardware or software and need to know how to get the piece between them done well and efficiently.

At the end of every chapter, I have an interview question loosely related to the material. One of the leveling-up activities in my career was learning to interview other people for jobs on my team. Sorely disappointed that there wasn't a resource on how to do that, I'm putting in my favorite interview questions and what I look for as the interviewer. They are a bit odd, but I hope you enjoy them as much as I do.

Admittedly, I hope you enjoy all of embedded systems development as much as I do. There are challenges, but that's the fun part.

Embedded Systems Development

Embedded systems are special, offering unique challenges to developers. Most embedded software engineers develop a toolkit for dealing with the constraints. Before we can start building yours, let's look at the difficulties associated with developing an embedded system. Once you become familiar with how your embedded system might be limited, we'll start on some principles to guide us to better solutions.

Compilers and Languages

Embedded systems use *cross-compilers*. Although a cross-compiler runs on your desktop or laptop computer, it creates code that does not. The cross-compiled image runs on your target embedded system. Because the code needs to run on your embedded processor, the vendor for the target system usually sells a cross-compiler or provides a list of available cross-compilers to choose from. Many larger processors use the cross-compilers from the GNU family of tools such as GCC.

Embedded software compilers often support only C, or C and C++. In addition, some embedded C++ compilers implement only a subset of the language (multiple inheritance, exceptions, and templates are commonly missing). There is a growing popularity for other languages, but C and C++ remain the most prevalent.

Regardless of the language you need to use in your software, you can practice object-oriented design. The design principles of encapsulation, modularity, and data abstraction can be applied to any application in nearly any language. The goal is to make the design robust, maintainable, and flexible. We should use all the help we can get from the object-oriented camp.

Taken as a whole, an embedded system can be considered equivalent to an object, particularly one that works in a larger system (such as a remote control talking to a smart television, a distributed control system in a factory, or an airbag deployment sensor in a car). At a higher level, everything is inherently object-oriented, and it is logical to extend this down into embedded software.

On the other hand, I don't recommend a strict adherence to all object-oriented design principles. Embedded systems get pulled in too many directions to be able to lay down such a commandment. Once you recognize the trade-offs, you can balance the software design goals and the system design goals.

Most of the examples in this book are in C or C++. I expect that the language is less important than the concepts, so even if you aren't familiar with the syntax, look at the code. This book won't teach you any programming language (except for some assembly language), but good design principles transcend language.

Debugging

If you were to debug software running on a computer, you could compile and debug on that computer. The system would have enough resources to run the program and support debugging it at the same time. In fact, the hardware wouldn't know you were debugging an application, as it is all done in software.

Embedded systems aren't like that. In addition to a cross-compiler, you'll need a cross-debugger. The debugger sits on your computer and communicates with the target processor through a special processor interface (see Figure 1-1). The interface is dedicated to letting someone else eavesdrop on the processor as it works. This interface is often called JTAG (pronounced "jay-tag"), regardless of whether it actually implements that widespread standard.

The processor must expend some of its resources to support the debug interface, allowing the debugger to halt it as it runs and providing the normal sorts of debug information. Supporting debugging operations adds cost to the processor. To keep costs down, some processors support a limited subset of features. For example, adding a breakpoint causes the processor to modify the memory-loaded code to say "stop here." However, if your code is executing out of flash (or any other sort of read-only memory), instead of modifying the code, the processor has to set an internal register (hardware breakpoint) and compare it at each execution cycle to the code address being run, stopping when they match. This can change the timing of the code, leading to annoying bugs that occur only when you are (or maybe aren't) debugging. Internal registers take up resources, too, so often there are only a limited number of hardware breakpoints available (frequently there are only two).

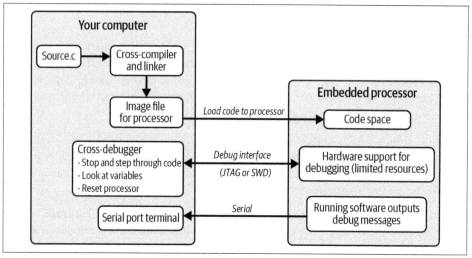

Figure 1-1. Computer and target processor

To sum up, processors support debugging, but not always as much debugging as you are accustomed to if you're coming from the non-embedded software world.

The device that communicates between your PC and the embedded processor is generally called a hardware debugger, programmer, debug probe, in-circuit emulator (ICE), or JTAG adapter. These may refer (somewhat incorrectly) to the same thing, or they may be multiple devices. The debugger is specific to the processor (or processor family), so you can't take the debugger you got for one project and assume it will work on another. The debugger costs add up, particularly if you collect enough of them or if you have a large team working on your system.

To avoid buying a debugger or dealing with the processor limitations, many embedded systems are designed to have their debugging done primarily via printf, or some sort of lighter-weight logging, to an otherwise unused communication port. Although incredibly useful, this can also change the timing of the system, possibly leaving some bugs to be revealed only after debugging output is turned off.

Writing software for an embedded system can be tricky, as you have to balance the needs of the system and the constraints of the hardware. Now you'll need to add another item to your to-do list: making the software debuggable in a somewhat hostile environment, something we'll talk more about in Chapter 2.

Resource Constraints

An embedded system is designed to perform a specific task, cutting out the resources it doesn't need to accomplish its mission. The resources under consideration include the following:

- Memory (RAM)
- Code space (ROM or flash)
- Processor cycles or speed
- Power consumption (which translates into battery life)
- Processor peripherals

To some extent, these are exchangeable. For example, you can trade code space for processor cycles, writing parts of your code to take up more space but run more quickly. Or you might reduce the processor speed in order to decrease power consumption. If you don't have a particular peripheral interface, you might be able to create it in software with I/O lines and processor cycles. However, even with trading off, you have only a limited supply of each resource. The challenge of resource constraints is one of the most pressing for embedded systems.

Another set of challenges comes from working with the hardware. The added burden of cross-debugging can be frustrating. During board bring-up, the uncertainty of whether a bug is in the hardware or software can make issues difficult to solve. Unlike your computer, the software you write may be able to do actual damage to the hardware. Most of all, you have to know about the hardware and what it is capable of. That knowledge might not be applicable to the next system you work on. You will need to learn quickly.

Once development and testing are finished, the system is manufactured, which is something most pure software engineers never need to consider. However, creating a system that can be manufactured for a reasonable cost is a goal that both embedded software engineers and hardware engineers have to keep in mind. Supporting manufacturing is one way you can make sure that the system that you created gets reproduced with high fidelity.

After manufacture, the units go into the field. With consumer products, that means they go into millions of homes where any bugs you created are enjoyed by many. With medical, aviation, or other critical products, your bugs may be catastrophic (which is why you get to do so much paperwork). With scientific or monitoring equipment, the field could be a place where the unit cannot ever be retrieved (or retrieved only at great risk and expense; consider the devices in volcano calderas), so it had better work. The life your system is going to lead after it leaves you is something you must consider as you design the software.

After you've figured out all of these issues and determined how to deal with them for your system, there is still the largest challenge, one common to all branches of engineering: change. Not only do the product goals change, but the needs of the project also change throughout its life-span. In the beginning, maybe you want to hack something together just to try it out. As you get more serious and better understand (and define) the goals of the product and the hardware you are using, you start to build more infrastructure to make the software debuggable, robust, and flexible. In the resource-constrained environment, you'll need to determine how much infrastructure you can afford in terms of development time, RAM, code space, and processor cycles. What you started building initially is not what you will end up with when development is complete. And development is rarely ever complete.

Creating a system that is purpose-built for an application has an unfortunate side effect: the system might not support change as the application morphs. Engineering embedded systems is not just about strict constraints and the eventual life of the system. The goal is figuring out which of those constraints will be a problem *later* in product development. You will need to predict the likely course of changes and try to design software flexible enough to accommodate whichever path the application takes. Get out your crystal ball.

Principles to Confront Those Challenges

Embedded systems can seem like a jigsaw puzzle, with pieces that interlock (and only go together one way). Sometimes you can force pieces together, but the resulting picture might not be what is on the box. However, we should jettison the idea of the final result as a single version of code shipped at the end of the project.

Instead, imagine the puzzle has a time dimension that varies over its whole life: conception, prototyping, board bring-up, debugging, testing, release, maintenance, and repeat. Flexibility is not just about what the code can do right now, but also about how the code can handle its life-span. Our goal is to be flexible enough to meet the product goals while dealing with the resource constraints and other problems inherent in embedded systems.

There are some excellent principles we can take from software design to make the system more flexible. Using *modularity*, we separate the functionality into subsystems and hide the data each subsystem uses. With *encapsulation*, we create interfaces between the subsystems so they don't know much about each other. Once we have loosely coupled subsystems (or objects, if you prefer), we can change one area of software with confidence that it won't impact another area. This lets us take apart our system and put it back together a little differently when we need to.

Recognizing where to break up a system into parts takes practice. A good rule of thumb is to consider which parts can change independently. In embedded systems, this is helped by the presence of physical objects that you can consider. If a sensor X talks over a communication channel Y, those are separate things and good candidates for being separate subsystems (and code modules).

If we break things into objects, we can do some testing on them. I've had the good fortune of having excellent QA teams for some projects. In others, I've had no one standing between my code and the people who were going to use the system. I've found that bugs caught before software releases are like gifts. The earlier in the process errors are caught, the cheaper they are to fix, and the better it is for everyone.

You don't have to wait for someone else to give you presents. Testing and quality go hand in hand. As you are thinking about how to write a piece of code, spend some time considering how you will test it. Writing test code for your system will make it better, provide some documentation for your code, and make other people think you write great software.

Documenting your code is another way to reduce bugs. It can be tough to know the level of detail when commenting your code:

```
i++; // increment the index
```

No, not like that. Lines like that rarely need comments at all. The goal is to write the comment for someone just like you, looking at the code a year from when you wrote it. By that time, future-you will probably be working on something different and have forgotten exactly what creative solution past-you came up with. Future-you probably doesn't even remember writing this code, so help yourself out with a bit of orientation. In general, though, assume the reader will have your brains and your general background, so document what the code does, not how it does it.

Finally, with resource-constrained systems, there is the temptation to optimize your code early and often. Fight the urge. Implement the features, make them work, test them out, and then make them smaller or faster as needed.

You have only a limited amount of time: focus on where you can get better results by looking for the bigger resource consumers *after* you have a working subsystem. It doesn't do you any good to optimize a function for speed if it runs rarely and is dwarfed by the time spent in another function that runs frequently. To be sure, dealing with the constraints of the system will require some optimization. Just make sure you understand where your resources are being used before you start tuning.

> We should forget about small efficiencies, say about 97% of the time: premature optimization is the root of all evil.
>
> —Donald Knuth

Prototypes and Maker Boards

"But wait," you say, "I already have a working system built with an Arduino or Raspberry Pi Pico. I just need to figure out how to ship it."

I get it. The system does nearly everything you want it to do. The project seems almost done. Off-the-shelf development boards are amazing, especially the maker-friendly ones. They make prototyping easier. However, the prototype is not the product.

There are many tasks often forgotten at this stage. How will the firmware update? Does the system need to sleep to lower power consumption? Do we need a watchdog in case of a catastrophic error? How much space and how many processing cycles do we need to save for future bug fixes and improvements? How do we manufacture many devices instead of one hand-built unit? How will we test for safety? Inexplicable user commands? Corner cases? Broken hardware?

Software aside, when the existing off-the-shelf boards don't meet your needs, custom boards are often necessary. The development boards may be too delicate, connected by fragile wires. They may be too expensive for your target market or take too much power. They may be the wrong size or shape. They may not hold up under the intended environmental conditions (like temperature fluctuations in a car, getting wet, or going to space).

Whatever the reason for getting a custom board, it usually means removing the programming (and debugging) hardware that are part of processor development boards.

Custom hardware will also push you out of some of the simplified development environments and software frameworks. Using the microprocessor vendor's hardware abstraction layers with a traditional compiler, you can get to smaller code sizes (often faster as well). The lack of anything between you and the processor allows you to create deterministic and real-time handling. You may also be able to use and configure an RTOS (real-time operating system). You can more easily understand the licensing of the code you are using in the libraries.

Adding in an external programmer/debugger gives you debugging beyond `printf`, allowing you to see inside your code. This feels pretty magical after doing it the hard way for so long.

Still, there is a chasm between prototype and shipping device, between supporting one unit on your desk and a thousand or a million in the field. Don't be lulled into believing the project is complete because all of the features finally worked (one time, in perfect conditions).

Development boards and simplified development environments are great for proto-types and to help select a processor. But there will be a time when the device needs to be smaller, faster, and/or cheaper. At that point, the resource constraints kick in, and you'll need a book like this one to help you.

Further Reading

There are many excellent references about design patterns. These are my favorites:

- First is *Design Patterns: Elements of Reusable Object-Oriented Software* by Erich Gamma, et al. (Addison-Wesley). Originally published in 1995, this book sparked the software design pattern revolution. Due to its four collaborators, it is often known as the "Gang of Four" book (or a standard design pattern may be noted as a GoF pattern).

- Second is *Head First Design Patterns* by Eric T. Freeman, et al. (O'Reilly). This book is far more readable than the original GoF book. The concrete examples were much easier for me to remember.

For more information about getting from prototype to shipping units, I recommend Alan Cohen's *Prototype to Product: A Practical Guide for Getting to Market* (O'Reilly).

Interview Question: Hello World

Here is a computer with a compiler and an editor. Please implement "hello world." Once you have the basic version working, add in the functionality to get a name from the command line. Finally, tell me what happens before your code executes—in other words, before the `main()` *function. (Thanks to Phillip King for this question.)*

In many embedded system projects, you have to develop a system from scratch. With the first part of this task, I look for a candidate who can take a blank slate and fill in the basic functionality, even in an unfamiliar environment. I want them to have enough facility with programming that this question is straightforward.

This is a solid programming question, so you'd better know the languages on your resume. Any of them are fair game for this question. When I ask for a "hello world" implementation, I look for the specifics of a language (that means knowing which header file to include and using command arguments in C and C++). I want the interviewee to have the ability to find and fix syntax errors based on compiler errors (though I am unduly impressed when they can type the whole program without any mistakes, even typos).

I am a decent typist on my own, but if someone watches over my shoulder, I end up with every other letter wrong. That's OK, lots of people are like that. So don't let it throw you off. Just focus on the keyboard and the code, not on your typing skills.

The second half of the question is where we start moving into embedded systems. A pure computer scientist tends to consider the computer as an imaginary ideal box for executing their beautiful algorithms. When asked what happens before the main function, they will tend to answer along the lines of "you know, the program runs," but with no understanding of what that implies.

However, if they mention "start" or "cstart," they are well on their way in the interview. In general, I want them to know that the program requires initialization beyond what we see in the source, no matter what the platform is. I like to hear mention of setting the exception vectors to handle interrupts, initializing critical peripherals, initializing the stack, initializing variables, and if there are any C++ objects, calling constructors for those. It is great if they can describe what happens implicitly (by the compiler) and what happens explicitly (in initialization code).

The best answers are step-by-step descriptions of everything that might happen, with an explanation of why these steps are important and how they happen in an embedded system. An experienced embedded engineer often starts at the vector table, with the reset vector, and moves from there to the power-on behavior of the system. This material is covered later in the book, so if these terms are new to you, don't worry.

An electrical engineer (EE) who asks this question gives bonus points when a candidate can, during further discussion of power-on behavior, explain why an embedded system can't be up and running 1 microsecond after the switch is flipped. The EE looks for an understanding of power sequencing, power ramp-up time, clock stabilization time, and processor reset/initialization delay.

CHAPTER 2

Creating a System Architecture

Even small embedded systems have so many details that it can be difficult to recognize where patterns can be applied. You'll need a good view of the whole system to understand which pieces have straightforward solutions and which have hidden dependencies. A good design is created by starting with an OK design and then improving on it, ideally before you start implementing it. And a system architecture diagram is a good way to view the system and start designing the software (or understanding the pile of code handed to you).

A product definition is seldom fixed at the start, so you may go round and round to hammer out ideas. Once the product functions have been sketched out on a whiteboard, you can start to think about the software architecture. The hardware folks are doing the same thing (hopefully in conjunction with you as the software designer, though their focus may be a little different). In short order, you'll have a software architecture and a draft schematic. Depending on your experience level, the first few projects you design will likely be based on other projects, so the hardware will be based on an existing platform with some changes.

In this chapter, we'll look at different ways of viewing the system in an effort to design better embedded software. We'll create a few diagrams to describe what our system looks like and to identify how we should architect our software. In addition to better understanding the system, the goal of the diagrams is to identify ways to architect the software to changing requirements and hardware: encapsulation, information hiding, having good interfaces between modules, and so on.

Embedded systems depend heavily on their hardware. Unstable hardware leaves the software looking buggy and unreliable. This is the place to start, making sure we can separate any changes in the hardware from bugs in the software.

It is possible (and usually preferable) to go the other way, looking at the system functions and determining what hardware is necessary to support them. However, I'm mostly going to focus on starting at the low-level, hardware-interfacing software to reinforce the idea that your product depends on the hardware features being stable and accessible.

When you do a bottom-up design as described here, recognize that the hardware you are specifying is archetypal. Although you will eventually need to know the specifics of the hardware, initially accept that there will be some hardware that meets your requirements (i.e., some processor that does everything you need). Use that to work out the system, software, and hardware architectures before diving into details.

Getting Started

There are two ways to go about architecting systems. One is to start with a blank slate, with an idea or end goal but nothing in place. This is *composition*. Creating these system diagrams from scratch can be daunting. The blank page can seem vast.

The other way is to go from an existing product to the architecture, taking what someone else put together to understand the internals. Reverse engineering like this is *decomposition*, breaking things into smaller parts. When you join a team, sometimes you start with a close deadline, a bunch of code, and very little documentation with no time to write more.

Diagrams will help you understand the system. Your ability to see the overall structure will help you write your piece of the system in a way that keeps you on track to provide good-quality code and meet your deadline.

You may need to consider formulating two architecture diagrams: one local to the code you are working on and a more global one that describes the whole product so you can see how your piece fits in.

As your understanding deepens, your diagrams will get larger, particularly for a mature design. If the drawing is too complex, bundle up some boxes into one box and then expand on them in another drawing.

Some systems will make more sense with one drawing or another; it depends on how the original architects thought about what they were doing.

In the next few sections, I'm going to ask you to make some drawings of a system from the ground up, not looking at an existing system for simplicity's sake (all good systems will be more complicated than I can show here).

I'm showing them as sketches because that is what I want you to do. The different diagrams are ways of looking at the system and how it can be (should be? is?) built. We are not creating system documentation; instead, these sketches are a way of thinking about the system from different perspectives.

Keep your sketches messy enough that if you have to do it all over again, it doesn't make you want to give up. Use a drawing tool if you'd like, but pencil and paper is my personal favorite method. It lets me focus on the information, not the drawing method.

Creating System Diagrams

Just as hardware designers create schematics, you should make a series of diagrams that show the relationships between the various parts of the software. Such diagrams will give you a view of the whole system, help you identify dependencies, and provide insight into the design of new features.

I recommend four types of diagrams: context diagrams, block diagrams, organigrams, and layering diagrams.

The Context Diagram

The first drawing is an overview of how your system fits into the world at large. If it is a children's toy, the diagram may be easy: a stick figure and some buttons on the toy. If it is a device providing information to a network of seismic sensors with an additional output to local scientists, the system is more complicated, going beyond the piece you are working on. See Figure 2-1.

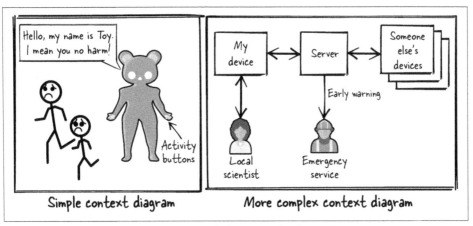

Figure 2-1. Two context diagrams with different levels of complexity

The goal here is a high-level context of how the system will be used by the customer. Don't worry about what is inside the boxes (including the one you are designing). The diagram should focus on the relationships between your device, users, servers, other devices, and other entities.

What problem is it solving? What are the inputs and outputs to your system? What are the inputs and outputs to the users? What are the inputs and outputs to the system-at-large? Focus on the use cases and world-facing interactions.

Ideally this type of diagram will help define the system requirements and envision likely changes. More realistically, it is a good way to remember the goals of the device as you get deeper into designing the software.

The Block Diagram

Design is straightforward at the start because you are considering the physical elements of the system, and you can think in an object-oriented fashion—no matter whether you are using an object-oriented language—to model your software around the physical elements. Each chip attached to the processor is an object. You can think of the wires that connect the chip to the processor (the communication methods) as another set of objects.

Start your design by drawing these as boxes where the processor is in the center, the communication objects are in the processor, and each external component is attached to a communication object.

For this example, I'm going to introduce a type of memory called *flash memory*. While the details aren't important here, it is a relatively inexpensive type of memory used in many devices. Many flash memory chips communicate over the SPI (Serial Peripheral Interface, usually pronounced "spy") bus, a type of serial communication (discussed in more detail in Chapter 7). Most processors cannot execute code over SPI, so the flash is used for off-processor storage. Our schematic, shown at the top of Figure 2-2, shows that we have some flash memory attached to our processor via SPI. Don't be intimidated by the schematic! We'll cover them in more detail in Chapter 3.

Ideally, the hardware block diagram is provided by an electrical engineer along with the schematics to give you a simplified view of the hardware. If not, you may need to sketch your own on the way to a software block diagram.

In our software block diagram, we'll add the flash as a device (a box outside the processor) and a SPI box inside the processor to show that we'll need to write some SPI code. Our software diagram looks very similar to the hardware schematic at this stage, but as we identify additional software components, it will diverge.

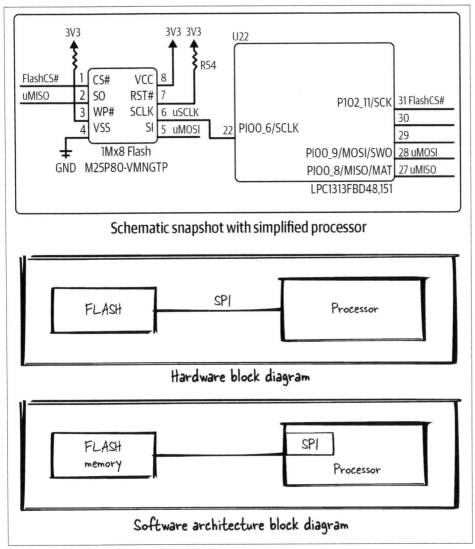

Figure 2-2. Comparison of schematic and initial hardware and software block diagrams

The next step is to add a flash box inside the processor to indicate that we'll need to write some flash-specific code. It's valuable to separate the communication method from the external component; if there are multiple chips connected via the same method, they should all go to the same communications block in the chip. The diagram will at that point warn us to be extra careful about sharing that resource, and to consider the performance and resource contention issues that sharing brings.

Figure 2-2 shows a snippet of a schematic and the beginnings of a software block diagram. Note that the schematic is far more detailed. At this point in a design, we want to see the high-level items to determine what objects we'll need to create and how they all fit together. Keep the detailed pieces in mind (or on a different piece of paper), particularly where the details may have a system impact, but try to keep the details out of the diagram if possible. The goal is to break the system down from a complete thing into bite-sized chunks you can summarize enough to fit in a box.

The next step is to add some higher-level functionality. What is each external chip used for? This is simple when each has only one function. For example, if our flash is used to store bitmaps to put on a screen, we can put a box on the architecture to represent the display assets. This doesn't have an off-chip element, so its box goes in the processor. We'll also need boxes for a screen and its communication method, and another box to convey flash-based display assets to the screen. It is better to have too many boxes at this stage than too few. We can combine them later.

Add any other software structures you can think of: databases, buffering systems, command handlers, algorithms, state machines, etc. You might not know exactly what you'll need for those (we'll talk about some of them in more detail later in the book), but try to represent everything from the hardware to the product function in the diagram. See Figure 2-3.

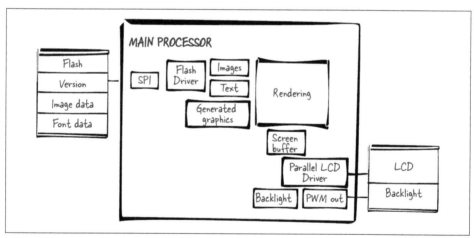

Figure 2-3. More detailed software block diagram

After you have sketched out this diagram on a piece of paper or a whiteboard (probably multiple times because the boxes never end up being big enough or in the right place), you may think you've done enough. However, other types of drawings often will give additional insight.

If you are trying to understand an existing codebase, get a list of the code files. If there are too many to count, use the directory names and libraries. Someone decided that these are modules, and maybe they even tried to consider them as objects, so they go in our diagram as boxes.

Where to put the boxes and how to order them is a puzzle, and one that may take a while to figure out.

Looking at other types of drawings may show you some hidden, ugly spots with critical bottlenecks, poorly understood requirements, or an innate failure to implement the product's features on the intended platform. Often these deficiencies can be seen from only one view or are represented by the boxes that change most between the different diagrams. By looking at them from the right perspective, ideally you will identify the tricky modules and also see a path to a good solution.

Organigram

The next type of software architecture diagram, *organigram*, looks like an organizational chart. In fact, I want you to think about it as an org chart. Like a manager, the upper-level components tell the lower ones what to do. Communication is not (should not be!) only one direction. The lower-level pieces will act on the orders to the best of their ability, provide requested information, and notify their boss when errors arise. Think of the system as a hierarchy, and this diagram shows the control and dependencies.

Figure 2-4 shows discrete components and which ones call others. The whole system is a hierarchy, with main at the highest level. If you have the device's algorithm planned out and know how the algorithm is going to use each piece, you can fill in the next level with algorithm-related objects. If you don't think they are going to change, you can start with the product-related features and then drop down to the pieces we do know, putting the most complex on top. Next, fill in the lower-level objects that are used by a higher-level object. For instance, our SPI object is used by our flash object, which is used by our display assets object, and so on. You may need to add some pieces here, ones you hadn't thought of before. You should determine whether those pieces need to go on the block diagram, too (probably).

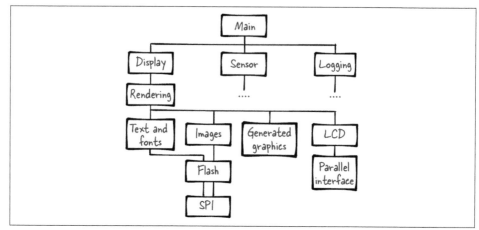

Figure 2-4. Organizational diagram of software architecture

However, as much as we'd like to devote a component to one function (e.g., the display assets in the flash memory), the limitations of the system (cost, speed, etc.) don't always support that. Often you end up cramming multiple, not particularly compatible functions into one component or communication pathway.

In the diagram, you can see where the text and images share the flash driver and its child SPI driver. This sharing is often necessary, but it is a red flag in the design because you'll need to take special care to avoid contention around the resource and make sure it is available when needed. Luckily, this figure shows that the rendering code controls both and will be able to ensure that only one of the resources—text or images—is needed at a time, so a conflict between them is unlikely.

Let's say that your team has determined that the system we've been designing needs each unit to have a serial number. It is to be programmed in manufacturing and communicated upon request. We could add another memory chip as a component, but that would increase cost, board complexity, and software complexity. The flash we already have is large enough to fit the serial number. This way, only software complexity has to increase. (Sigh.)

In Figure 2-5, we print the system serial number through the flash that previously was devoted to the display assets. If the logging subsystem needs to get the serial number asynchronously from the display assets (say I have two threads, or my display assets are used in an interrupt), the software will have to avoid collisions and any resulting corruption.

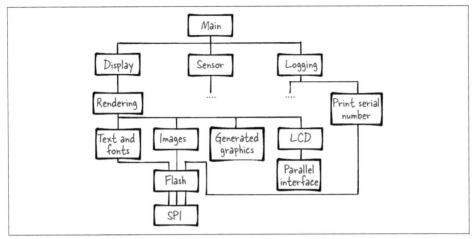

Figure 2-5. Organizational diagram with a shared resource

Each time something like this is added, some little piece where you are using A and B and have to consider a potential interaction with C, the system becomes a little less robust. This added awareness is very hard to document, and shared resources cause pains in the design, implementation, and maintenance phases of the project. The example here is pretty easily fixed with a flag, but all shared resources should make you think about the consequences.

Returning to the org chart metaphor, people managed by two entities will have conflicting instructions and priorities. While it's best to avoid the situation, sometimes you need to manage yourself a bit to handle the complexities of the job.

 If you are trying to understand an existing codebase, the organi-gram can be constructed by walking through the code in a debugger. You start in main() and step into interesting functions, trying not to get too lost in the details.

It might take a few repetitions, but the goal is to get a feel for where the flow of code is going and how it gets there.

Layering Diagram

The last architecture drawing looks for layers and represents objects by their estimated size, as in Figure 2-6. This is another diagram to start with paper and pencil. Start at the bottom of the page and draw boxes for the things that go off the processor (such as our communication boxes). If you anticipate that one is going to be more complicated to implement, make it a little larger. If you aren't sure, make them all the same size.

Next, add to the diagram the items that use the lowest layer. If there are multiple users of a lower-level object, they should all touch the lower-level object (this might mean making the lower-level component bigger). Also, each object that uses something below it should touch all of the things it uses, if possible.

That was a little sneaky. I said to make the object size depend on its complexity. Then I said that if an object has multiple users, make it bigger. As described in the previous section, shared resources increase complexity. So when you have a resource that is shared by many things, its box gets bigger so it can touch all of the upper modules. This reflects an increase in complexity, even if the module seems straightforward. It isn't only bottom layers that have this problem. In the diagram, I initially had the rendering box much smaller because moving data from the flash to the LCD is easy. However, once the rendering box had to control all the bits and pieces below it, it became larger. And sure enough, on the project that I took this snippet from, ultimately rendering became a relatively large module and then two modules.

Eventually, the layering diagram shows you where the layers in your code are, letting you bundle groups of resources together if they are always used together. For example, the LCD and parallel I/O boxes touch only each other. If this is the final diagram, maybe those could be combined to make one module. The same goes for the backlight and PWM output.

Also look at the horizontal groupings. Fonts and images share their higher-level and lower-level connections. It's possible they should be merged into one module because they seem to have the same inputs and outputs. The goal of this diagram is to look for such points and think about the implications of combining the boxes in various ways. You might end up with a simpler design.

Finally, if you have a group of several modules that try to touch the same lower-level item, you might want to take some time to break apart that resource. Would it be useful to have a flash driver that dealt only with the serial number? Maybe one that read the serial number on initialization and then never reread it, so that the display subsystem could keep control of the flash? Understand the complexity of your design and your options for designing the system to modify that complexity. A good design can save time and money in implementation and maintenance.

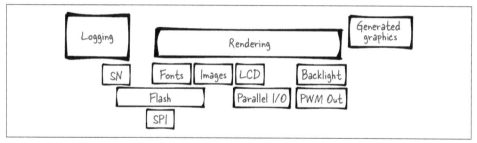

Figure 2-6. Software architecture layering diagram

Designing for Change

So now, sitting with the different architecture drawings, where do you go next? Maybe you've realized there are a few pieces of code you didn't think about initially. And maybe you have progressed a bit at figuring out how the modules interact. Before we consider those interactions (interfaces), there is one thing that is really worth spending some time on: *what is going to change?* At this stage everything is experimental, so it is a good bet that any piece of the system puzzle could change. However, the goal is to harden your initial architecture (and code) against the possible changes to the system features or actual hardware.

Given your product requirements, you may have confidence that some features of your system won't change. Our example, whatever it does, needs a display, and the best way to send bitmaps to it seems like flash. Many flash chips are SPI, so that seems like a good bet, too. However, exactly which flash chip is used will likely change. The LCD, the image, or font data also may change. Even the way you store the image or font data might change. The boxes in the diagram should represent the Platonic ideals of each thing instead of a specific implementation.

Encapsulate Modules

The diagramming process leads to interfaces that don't depend specifically on the content or behavior of the modules that they connect (this is encapsulation!). We use the different architecture drawings to figure out the best places for those interfaces. Each box will probably have its own interface. Maybe those can be mashed together into one object. But is there a good reason to do it now instead of later?

Sometimes, yes. If you can reduce some complexity of your diagrams without giving up too much flexibility in the future, it may be worth collapsing some dependency trees.

Here are some things to look for:

- In the organigram, look for objects that are used by only one other object. Are these both fixed? If they are unlikely to change or are likely to change together as you evolve the system, consider combining them. If they change independently, it is not a good area to consider for encapsulation.

- In the layering diagram, look for collections of objects that are always used together. Can these be grouped together in a higher-level interface to manage the objects? You'd be creating a hardware abstraction layer.

- Which modules have lots of interdependencies? Can they be broken apart and simplified? Or can the dependencies be grouped together?

- Can the interfaces between vertical neighbors be described in a few sentences? That makes it a good place for encapsulation to help you create an interface (for others to reuse your code or just for ease of testing).

In the example system, the LCD is attached to the parallel interface. In every diagram, it is simple, with no additional dependencies and no other subsystems requiring access to the parallel interface. You don't need to expose the parallel interface; you can encapsulate (hide) it within the LCD module.

Conversely, imagine the system without the rendering module to encapsulate the display subsystem. The layering diagram might show this best (Figure 2-5). The fonts, images, LCD, and backlight would all try to touch each other, making a mess of the diagram.

Each box you're left with is likely to become a module (or object). Look at the drawing. How can you make it simpler? Encapsulation in the software makes for a cleaner architecture drawing, and the converse is true as well.

Delegation of Tasks

The diagrams also help you divide up and apportion work to minions. Which parts of the system can be broken off into separate, describable pieces that someone else can implement?

Too often we want our minions to do the boring part of the job while we get to do all of the fun parts. ("Here, minion, write my test code, do my documentation, fold my laundry.") Not only does this drive away the good minions, it tends to decrease the quality of your product. Instead, think about which whole box (or whole subtree) you can give to someone else. As you try to describe the interdependencies to your imaginary minion, you may find that they become worse than you've represented in the diagrams. Or you may find that a simple flag (such as a semaphore) to describe who currently owns the resource may be enough to get started.

What if you have no chance of getting minions? It is still important to go through this thought process. You want to reduce interdependencies where possible, which may cause you to redesign your system. And where you can't reduce the interdependencies, you can at least be wary of them when coding.

Looking for things that can be split off and accomplished by another person will help you identify sections of code that can have a simple interface between them. Also, when marketing asks how this project could be made to go faster, you'll have an answer ready for them. However, there is one more thing our imaginary minion provides: assume they are slightly deficient and you need to protect yourself and your code from the faulty minion's bad code.

What sort of defensive structures can you picture erecting between modules? Imagine the data being passed between modules. What is the minimum amount of data that can move between boxes (or groups of boxes)? Does adding a box to your group mean that significantly less data is passed? How can the data be stored in a way that will keep it safe and usable by all those who need it?

The minimization of complexity between boxes (or at least between groups of boxes) will make the project go more smoothly. The more that your minions are boxed into their own sets of code, with well-understood interfaces, the more everyone will be able to test and develop their own code.

Driver Interface: Open, Close, Read, Write, IOCTL

The previous section used a top-down view of module interfaces to train you to consider encapsulation and think about where you can get help from another person. Going from the bottom up works as well. The bottom here consists of the modules that talk to the hardware (the drivers).

Top-down design is when you think about what you want and then dig into what you need to accomplish your goals. *Bottom-up design* is when you consider what you have and build what you can out of that.

Usually I end up using a combination of the two: *yo-yo design*.

Many drivers in embedded systems are based on the POSIX API used to call devices in Unix systems. Why? Because the model works well in many situations and saves you from reinventing the wheel every time you need access to the hardware.

The interface to Unix drivers is straightforward:

open
> Opens the driver for use. Similar to (and sometimes replaced by) init.

close
> Cleans up the driver after use.

read
> Reads data from the device.

write
> Sends data to the device.

ioctl *(pronounced "eye-octal" or "eye-oh-control")*
> Stands for input/output (I/O) control and handles the features not covered by the other parts of the interface. Its use is somewhat discouraged by kernel programmers due to its lack of structure, but it is still very popular.

In Unix, a driver is part of the kernel. Each of these functions takes an argument with a file descriptor that represents the driver in question (such as /dev/tty01 for the first terminal on the system). That gets pretty cumbersome for an embedded system without an operating system. The idea is to model your driver upon Unix drivers. A sample functionality for an embedded system device might look like any of these:[1]

- spi.open()
- spi_open()
- SpiOpen(WITH_LOCK)
- spi.ioctl_changeFrequency(THIRTY_MHz)
- SpiIoctl(kChangeFrequency, THIRTY_MHz)

This interface straightens out the kinks that can happen at the driver level, making them less specific to the application and creating reusable code. Further, when others come up to your code and the driver looks like it has these functions, they will know what to expect.

---

1 Style is very important. Coding guidelines will save you debugging time, and they won't quash your creativity. If you don't have a style guide, look at the ones Google suggests for open source projects (search for "Google Style Guides"). The explanations of why they chose what they did might help you formulate your own guide.

The driver model in Unix sometimes includes two newer functions. The first, select (or poll), waits for the device to change state. That used to be done by getting empty reads or polling ioctl messages, but now it has its own function. The second, mmap, controls the memory map the driver shares with the code that calls it.

If your round peg can't fit into this POSIX-compliant square hole, don't force it. But if it looks like it might, starting with this standard interface can make your design just a little better and easier to maintain.

Adapter Pattern

One traditional software design pattern is called *adapter* (or sometimes *wrapper*). It converts the interface of an object into one that is easier for a client to use (a higher-level module). Often, adapters are written over software APIs to hide ugly interfaces or libraries that change.

Many hardware interfaces are like ungainly software interfaces. That makes each driver an adapter, as shown in Figure 2-7. If you create a common interface to your driver (even if it isn't open, close, read, write, ioctl), the hardware interface can change without your upper-level software changing. Ideally, you can switch platforms altogether and need only to rework the underpinnings.

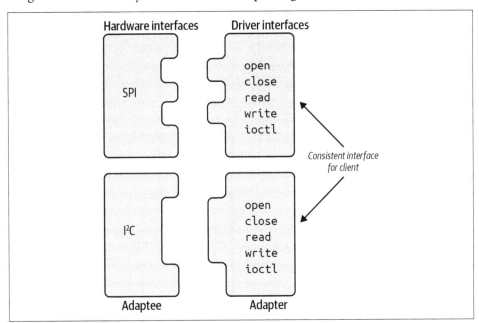

Figure 2-7. Drivers implement the adapter pattern

Note that drivers are stackable, as shown in Figure 2-7. In our example we have a display that uses flash memory, which in turn uses SPI communication. When you call open for the display, it will call its subsystems initialization code, which will call open for the flash, which will call open for the SPI driver. That's three levels of adapters, all for the cause of portability and maintainability.

The layers and the adapters add complexity to the implementation. They may also require more memory or add delays to your code. That is a trade-off. You can have simpler architectures with all of the good maintainability, testing, portability, and so on for a small price. Unless your system is very resource constrained, this is usually a good trade.

If the interface to each level is consistent, the higher-level code is pretty impervious to change. For example, if our SPI flash changes to an I²C EEPROM (a different communication bus and a different type of memory), the display driver might not need to change, or it might only need to replace flash functions with EEPROM (electrically erasable programmable read-only memory) ones.

In Figure 2-8, I've added a function called test to the interface of each of the modules. In Chapter 3, I'll discuss some strategies for choosing automated tests to make your code more robust. For now, they are just placeholders.

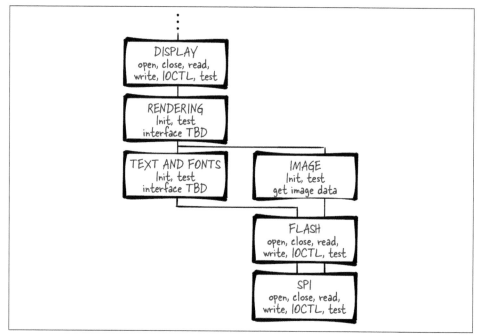

Figure 2-8. Interfaces for display subsystem and below

Creating Interfaces

Moving away from drivers, your definition of a module interface depends on the specifics of the system. It is pretty safe to say that most modules will also need an initialization function (though drivers often use open for this). Initialization may happen as objects are instantiated during start-up, or it may be a function called as the system initializes. To keep modules encapsulated (and more easily reused), high-level functions should be responsible for initializing the modules they depend upon. A good init function should be able to be called multiple times if it is used by different subsystems. A very good init function can reset the subsystem (or hardware resource) to a known good state in case of partial system failure.

Now that you don't have a completely blank slate anymore, it may be easier to fill in the interface of each of your boxes. Consider how to retain encapsulation for your module, your hypothetical minion's contribution, and the driver model, and then start working out the responsibilities of each box in your architecture diagrams.

Having created different views of the architecture, you probably won't want to maintain each one. As you fill in the interface, you may want to focus on whichever one is most useful to you (or clearest to your boss or minions).

Example: A Logging Interface

The goal of the logging module is to implement a robust and reusable logging system. In this section we'll start off by defining the requirements of the interface, and then explore some options for the interface (and the local memory). It doesn't matter what your communication method is. By coding to the interface in the face of limitations, you leave yourself open to reusing your code in another system.

Logging debug output can slow down a processor significantly. If your code behavior changes when you turn logging on and off, consider how the timing of various subsystems works together.

The implementation is dependent on your system. Sometimes the best you can do is toggle an I/O line attached to an LED and send your messages via Morse code (I kid you not). However, most of the time you get to write text debug messages to some interface. Making a system debuggable is part of making it maintainable. Even if your code is perfect, the person who comes after you might not be so lucky when they add a newly required feature. A logging subsystem will not only help you during development, it is an invaluable tool during maintenance.

A good logging interface hides the details of how the logging is actually accomplished, letting you hide changes (and complexity). Your logging needs may change with the development cycle. For example, in the initial phase, your development kit may come with an extra serial port and your logging information can go to a computer. In a later phase, the serial port might not be available, so you might have to pare your output back to an LED or two.

I have occasionally wished for a complete mind meld when a system is acting oddly. Sadly, there are never enough resources available to output everything you might want. Further, your logging methodology may change as your product develops. This is an area where you should encapsulate what changes by hiding its functions called from the main interface. The small overhead you add will allow greater flexibility. If you can code to the interface, changing the underlying pathway won't matter.

Commonly, you want to output a lot of information over a relatively small pipe. As your system gets bigger, the pipe looks smaller. Your pipe may be a simple serial port connecting to your computer, a pathway available only with special hardware. It may be a special debug packet that happens over your network. The data may be stored in an external RAM source and be readable only when you stop the processor and read via JTAG. The log may be available only when you run on the development kit, and not on the custom hardware. So the first big requirement for the module is this: the logging interface should be able to handle different underlying implementations.

Second, as you work on one area of the system at a time, you may not need (or want) messages from other areas. So the requirement is that logging methods should be subsystem-specific. Of course, you do need to know about catastrophic issues with other subsystems.

The third requirement is a priority level that will let you debug the minutiae of the subsystem you are working on without losing critical information from other parts of the code.

From requirements to an interface

Defining the main interface requirements of a module is often enough, particularly during design. However, those are a lot of words for something that can be summed up in one line of code:

```
void Log(enum eLogSubSystem sys, enum eLogLevel level, char *msg);
```

This prototype isn't fixed in stone and may change as the interface develops, but it provides a useful shorthand to other developers.

The log levels might include none, information only, debugging, warning, error, and critical. The subsystems will depend on your system but might include communications, display, system, sensor, updating firmware, etc.

Note that the log message takes a string, unlike `printf` or `iostream`, which take variable arguments. You can always use a library to provide similar formatting and even variable argument functionality if you need to. However, the `printf` and `iostream` family of functions is one of the first things cut from a system that needs more code space and memory. If that is the case, you'll probably end up implementing what you need most on your own, so this interface should have the bare minimum of what you'll need. In addition to printing strings, usually you'll need to be able to print out at least one number at a time:

```
void LogWithNum(enum eLogSubSystem sys, enum eLogLevel level, char *msg,
int number);
```

Using the subsystem identifiers and the priority levels allows you to change the debug options remotely (if the system allows that sort of thing). When debugging something, you might start with all subsystems set to a verbose priority level (e.g., debug), and once a subsystem is cleared, raise its priority level (e.g., error). This way, you get the messages you want when you want them. So we'll need an interface to allow this flexibility on a subsystem and priority level:

```
void LogSetOutputLevel(enum eLogSubSystem sys, enum eLogLevel level)
```

Because the calling code doesn't care about the underlying implementation, it shouldn't have direct access to it. All logging functions should go through this log interface. Ideally, the underlying interface isn't shared with any other modules, but your architecture diagram will tell you if that isn't true. The log initialization function should call whatever it depends on, whether it's to initialize a serial port driver or set up I/O lines.

Because logging can change the system timing, sometimes the logging system needs to be turned off globally. This allows you to say with some certainty that the debugging subsystem is not interfering in any way with any other part of the code. Although it might not be used often, an on/off switch is an excellent addition to the interface:

```
void LogGlobalOn();
void LogGlobalOff();
```

Version Your Code

At some point, someone will need to know exactly what revision of code is running. In the application world, putting a version string in the help/about box is straightforward. In the embedded world, the version should be available via the primary communication path (USB, WiFi, UART, or other bus). If possible, this should print out automatically on boot. If that is not possible, try to make it available through a query. If that is not possible, it should be compiled into its own object file and located at a specific address so that it is available for inspection.

Consider *semantic versioning*, where the version is in the form *A.B.C.*:

- *A* is the major version (1 byte).
- *B* is the minor version (1 byte).
- *C* is a build indicator (2 bytes).

If the build indicator does not increment automatically, you should increment it often (numbers are cheap). Depending on your output method and the aesthetics of your system, you may want to add an interface to your logging code for displaying the version properly:

```
void LogVersion(struct sFirmwareVersion *v)
```

The runtime code is not the only piece of the system that should have a version. Each piece that gets built or updated separately should have a version that is part of the protocol. For example, if an EEPROM is programmed in manufacturing, it should have a version that is checked by the code before the EEPROM is used. Sometimes you don't have the space or processing power to make your system backward compatible, but it is critical to make sure all of the moving pieces are currently compatible.

Designs of the other subsystems do not (and should not) depend on the way that logging is carried out. If you can say that about the interface to your modules ("The other subsystems do not depend on the way XYZ is carried out; they just call the given interface"), you've successfully designed the interfaces of the system.

State of logging

As you work on the architecture, some areas will be easier to define than others, especially if you've done something similar before. And as you define interfaces, you may find that ideas come to you and implementation will be easy (even fun), but only if you start *right now*.

Hold back a bit when you get this urge to jump into implementation; try to keep everything at the same level. If you finish gold-plating one module before defining the interface to another, you may find that they don't fit together very well.

Once you've gotten a little further with all the modules in the system, it may be time to consider the state associated with each module. In general, the less state held in the module, the better (so that your functions do the same things every time you call them). However, eliminating all state is generally unavoidable (or at least extremely cumbersome).

Back to our logging module: can you see the internal state needed? The LogGlobalOn and LogGlobalOff functions set (and clear) a single variable. LogSetOutputLevel needs to have a level for each subsystem.

You have some options for how to implement these variables. If you want to eliminate local state, you could put them in a structure (or object) that every function calling into the logging module would need to have. However, that means passing the logging object to every function that might possibly need logging and passing it to every function that has a function that needs to log something.

 You may think passing around the state like that is convoluted. And for logging, I'd agree. However, have you ever wondered what is in the file handler you get back when your code opens a file? Open files embody lots of state information including the current read and write positions, a buffer, and a handle to where the file is on the drive.

Maybe passing all these parameters around isn't a good idea. How can every user of the logging subsystem get access to it? As noted in the "Object-Oriented Programming in C" sidebar, with a little extra work, even C can create objects that make this parameter-passing problem simpler. Even in a more object-oriented language, you could have a module where the functions are globally available and the state is kept in a local object. However, there is another way to give access to the logging object without opening up the module completely.

Object-Oriented Programming in C

Why not use C++? Most systems have pretty good embedded C++ compilers. However, there is a lot of code already written in C, and sometimes you need to match what is already there. Or maybe you just like C for its speed. That doesn't mean you should leave your object-oriented principles behind.

One of the most critical ideas to retain is *data hiding*. In an object-oriented language, your object (class) can contain private variables. This is a polite way of saying they have internal state that no one else can see. C has different kinds of global variables. By scoping a variable appropriately, you can mimic the idea of private variables (and even friend objects). First, let's start with the C equivalent of a public variable, declared outside a function, usually at the top of your C file:

```
// Anyone can see this global if they have
// "extern tBoolean gLogOnPublic;"
tBoolean gLogOnPublic;
```

These are the global variables upon which spaghetti code is built. Try to avoid them. A private variable is declared with the static keyword and is declared outside a function, usually at the top of your C file:

```
// file variables are globals with some encapsulation
static tBoolean gLogOnPrivate;
```

The static keyword means different things in different places; it's actually kind of annoying that way. For functions and variables outside functions, the keyword means "hide me so no other files can see" and limits scope. For variables within a function, the static keyword maintains the value between calls, acting as a global variable whose scope is only the function it is declared in.

A set of loose variables is a little difficult to track, so consider a structure filled with the variables private to a module:

```
// contain all the global variables into a structure:
struct {
  tBoolean logOn;
  enum eLogLevel outputLevel[NUM_LOG_SUBSYSTEMS];
} sLogStruct;
static struct sLogStruct gLogData;
```

If you want your C code to be more like an object, this structure would not be part of the module, but would be created (malloc'd) during initialization (LogInit, for the logging system discussed in this chapter) and passed back to the caller like this:

```
struct sLogStruct* LogInit(){
  int i;
  struct sLogStruct *logData = malloc(sizeof(*logData));
  logData->logOn = FALSE;
  for (i=0; i < NUM_LOG_SUBSYSTEMS; i++) {
    logData-> outputLevel[i] = eNoLogging;
  }
  return logData;
}
```

The structure can be passed around as an object. Of course, you'd need to add a way to free the object; that just requires adding another function to the interface.

Pattern: Singleton

Another way to make sure every part of the system has access to the same log object is to use another design pattern, this one called the *singleton*.

When it is important that a class have exactly one instance, the singleton pattern is commonly seen. In an object-oriented language, the singleton is responsible for intercepting requests to create new objects in order to preserve its solitary state. The access to the resource is global (anyone can use it), but all access goes through the single instance. There is no public constructor. In C++ this would look like:

```
class Singleton {
public:
  static Singleton* GetInstance() {
```

```
    if (instance_ == NULL) {
      instance_ = new Singleton;
    }
    return instance_;
  }
protected:
  Singleton(); // no one can create this except itself

private:
  static Singleton* instance_; // the one single instance
};

// Define the one and only Singleton pointer
Singleton* Singleton::instance_ = nullptr;
```

For logging, the singleton lets the whole system have access to the logging subsystem with only one instantiation. Often when you have a single resource (such as a serial port) that different parts of the system need to work with, a singleton can come in handy to avoid conflicts.

In an object-oriented language, singletons also permit lazy allocation and initialization so that modules that are never used don't consume resources.

Sharing private globals

Even in a procedural language like C, the concept of the singleton has a place. The data-hiding goodness of object-oriented design was noted in "Object-Oriented Programming in C" on page 31. Protecting a module's variables from modification (and use) by other files will give you a more robust solution.

However, sometimes you need a back door to the information, either because you need to reuse the RAM for another purpose (Chapter 8) or because you need to test the module from an outside agency (Chapter 3). In C++, you might use a friend class to gain access to otherwise hidden internals.

In C, instead of making the module variables truly global by removing the static keyword, you can cheat a little and return a pointer to the private variables:

```
static struct sLogStruct gLogData;
struct sLogStruct* LogInternalState() {
  return &gLogData;
}
```

This is not a good way to retain encapsulation and keep data hidden, so use it sparingly. Consider guarding against it during normal development:

```
static struct sLogStruct gLogData;
struct sLogStruct* LogInternalState() {
#if PRODUCTION
  #error "Internal state of logging protected!"
#else
```

```
    return &gLogData;
#endif /* PRODUCTION */
}
```

As you design your interface and consider the state information that will be part of your modules, keep in mind that you will also need methods for verifying your system.

A Sandbox to Play In

That pretty much covers the low- and mid-level boxes, but we still have some algorithm boxes to think about. One goal of a good architecture is to keep the algorithm as segregated as possible. The common pattern of *model-view-controller* (MVC) is an excellent one to apply here. The purpose of the pattern is to isolate the gooey center of the application from the user interface so they can be developed and tested independently.

Usually MVC is used to allow different displays, interfaces, and platform implementations. However, it can also be used to allow the application and algorithms to be developed separately from the hardware. In this pattern, the *view* is the interface to the user, both input and output. In our device, the user might not be a person; it could be hardware sensors (input) and a screen (output). In fact, if you have a system without a screen but that sends data over a network, the view may have no visual aspect, but it is still a part of the system as the form of input and output. The *model* is the domain-specific data and logic. This is the part that takes raw data from the input and creates something useful, often using the algorithm that makes your product special. The *controller* is the glue that works between the model and the view: it handles how to get the input to the model for processing and the data from the model for display or outside communication. There are standard ways for these three elements to interact, but for now it is enough to understand the separation of functions.

Different Aspects of the Model-View-Controller

The good news about MVC is that nearly everyone agrees that there are three parts to it. The bad news is that this might be the only thing everybody agrees on.

The *model* holds the data, state, and application logic. If you are building a weather station, the model has the temperature monitoring code and predictive models. For an MP3 player, the model consists of a database of music and the codec necessary to play it.

Traditionally thought of in contexts where there is a screen, the *view* represents the display-handling functions. The view is what the user sees of the model. A view could be a picture of a sun or a detailed readout of the statistics from a weather service. Those are both views of the same information.

The *controller* is the somewhat nebulous cloud that sits between (or near) the model and view to help them work together. The goal of the controller is to make the view and model independent of each other so that each can be reused. For that MP3 player, your company may want a consistent interface even when your audio-playing hardware is revamped. Or maybe it is the same hardware but marketing wants to make the system look more child-friendly. How can you achieve both of these, while touching the smallest amount of code? The controller enables the model/view separation by providing services such as translating a user button press into an event for the model.

Figure 2-9 shows a basic interpretation of MVC and some common variants. There are a lot of different ways to put it together, some of them seemingly contradictory. The term "MVC" is kind of like the adjective "sanguine," which can mean either murderous or cheerfully optimistic. You may need some context clues to know which it is, but either way, you are probably talking about someone's mood.

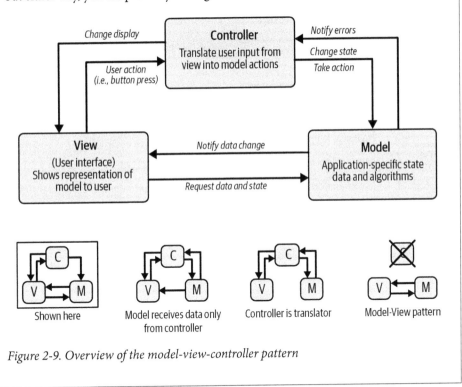

Figure 2-9. *Overview of the model-view-controller pattern*

There is another way to use the MVC pattern, which serves as a valuable way to develop and verify algorithms for embedded systems: use a *virtual box*, or *sandbox*. The more complex the algorithm, the more this is a necessity.

If you can make all of the inputs to an algorithm's box and put them through a single interface, you can switch back and forth between a file on a PC and the actual system.

Similarly, if you can redirect the output of the algorithm to a file, you can test the algorithm on a PC (where the debugging environment may be a lot better than an embedded system), and rerun the same data over and over again until any anomalous behavior can be isolated and fixed. This is a great way to do regression tests to verify that minor algorithm changes don't have unforeseen side effects.

In the sandbox environment, your files and the way you read the data in are the view part of MVC. The algorithm you are testing is the model, and this shouldn't change. The controller is the part that changes when you put the algorithm on a PC. Consider an MP3 player (Figure 2-10) and what the MVC diagram might look like with a sandbox. Note that both the view and controller will have relatively strict APIs because you will be replacing those as you move from virtual device to actual device.

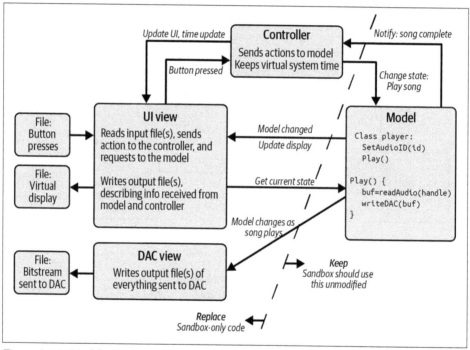

Figure 2-10. Model-view-controller in a sandbox

Your input view file might be like a movie script, directing the sandbox to act as the user might. The first field is a time when the second field, a method in your system, is fired:

```
Time, Action, Variable arguments // comment
00:00.00, PowerOnClean           // do all of the initialization
00:01.00, PlayPressed            // no action, no song loaded
00:02.00, Search, "Still Alive"  // expect list back based on available matches
00:02.50, PlayPressed            // expect song to be played
```

The output file can look however you want. For instance, you might have multiple output files, one to describe the state and the changes sent to the user interface from the controller and the model and another one to output what the model would send to the digital-to-analog converter (DAC). The first output file might look like this:

```
Time, Subsystem, Log message
00:00.01, System, Initialization: sandbox version 1.3.45
00:01.02, Controller, Minor error: no song loaded
00:02.02, Controller, 4 songs found for "Still Alive" search, selecting ID 0x1234
00:02.51, Controller, Loading player class to play ID 0x1234
```

Again, you get to define the format so that it meets your needs (which will probably change). For instance, if you have a bug where the player plays the wrong song, the sandbox could output the song ID in every line.

The Model-View-Controller here is a very high-level pattern, specifically a system-level pattern. Once you look at breaking up the system this way, you might find that it has fractal qualities. For instance, what if you only want to be able to test the code that reads a file from the memory and outputs it to a DAC? The filename and the resulting bitstream of information that would go to the DAC could be considered the view (which consists of inputs and outputs, even if no humans are involved), the logic and data necessary to convert the file would be the model, and the file handler may be the controller since that would have to change between platforms.

With this idea of separation and sandboxing in mind, take a look at the architecture drawings and see how many inputs the algorithm has. If there is more than one, does it make sense to have a special interface object? Sometimes it is better to have multiple files to represent multiple things going on. Looking further into the diagrams, does it make sense to incorporate the sandbox at a lower level than just the product feature algorithms? This expands your model and, more importantly, lets you test more of your code in a controlled environment.

Your sandbox could be expensive to develop, so you may not want to start implementation immediately. In particular, your sandbox may have different sizes for your variables and its compiler potentially could act differently, so you may want to hold off building it unless your algorithms are complex or your hardware is a long time in coming. There is a trade-off between time to develop the sandbox and its extraordinary powers of debuggability and testability. But identifying how to get to a sandbox from the design and keeping it in mind as you develop your architecture will give you leeway for when things go wrong.

Back to the Drawing Board

I asked you to make four sketches of your system. Remember, sketches are cheap! It's easy to try out different ideas and different options before committing. You can change sketches much more easily than you can change a system's worth of source code.

If you look at your sketches with a mind full of encapsulation, data hiding, interfaces, and design patterns, what do you see? The drawings I've chosen are intended to give you different perspectives about the system. Together they will ask questions about the architecture so you think about issues earlier in the process, during design instead of development.

No design will remain static. The goal of design is to understand things from the system perspective. This doesn't mean you need to update your diagrams with every change. Some of the diagrams may become part of the documentation and need to be maintained, but these sketches are for you, to improve your understanding of the system and your ability to communicate with your team.

The context diagram is a you-are-here map that keeps you on track for what you are supposed to be doing. This is likely to be useful when talking about what the system requirements are.

The block diagram shows the pieces of the hardware and software. The available resources are shown along with a box-sized description of how they are intended to be used. The whole-picture view helps with identifying the tasks that will need to be accomplished. I recommend starting out with nonspecific component boxes; the chips these represent will change, so how can you harden your code against those changes? The block diagram is the most common drawing and will likely be very useful when talking to colleagues.

The organigram shows where control flows and where there will be conflicts as multiple subsystems try to access the same resources. It can help with encapsulating modules that don't need to talk to each other (or that do need to talk to each other but shouldn't do so directly). This one may be hard to get your head around, but I find the manager relationship helps me think about it: who is bossing this component around? This diagram is most useful for understanding the details of the system and debugging weird errors.

The layering diagram shows how modules can be grouped to provide interfaces and abstraction layers. It helps with identifying what information can be hidden. It can also identify when modules are too big and need to be broken apart. This view can help you reduce complexity and reuse code (or understand those deep vendor-provided hardware abstraction layers).

Each of these diagrams were presented at the whole-system level. However, systems are made of subsystems, which are made of subsystems. Making the high-level diagram too detailed is a good way to lose the whole-system picture. Sometimes a large box needs to be moved to a new page for more detail (and more thought as you design and understand this subsystem).

If diagramming is useful but my diagrams don't work for you, look up the *C4 model* for visualizing software architecture or the *4+1 architectural view model*—both are excellent alternatives. For a drawing program, when I'm ready to formalize my sketches, I like to use mermaid.live, because it is based on written text and can be put into most Markdown documents.

Further Reading

This chapter touched on a few of the many design patterns. The rest of the book will as well, but this is a book about embedded systems, not about design patterns. Think about exploring one of these to learn more about standard software patterns:

- *Design Patterns: Elements of Reusable Object-Oriented Software.* This is the original, seminal work on design patterns. It uses C++ as the reference language.
- *Head First Design Patterns.* Using Java as the example language, this book gives great examples with an engaging style.
- Search in Wikipedia for "software design patterns."

I've given an overview of architecture and sketching it out, but if your system is more complex or your diagrams need to become part of a safety certification process, there are other good resources:

- *Documenting Software Architectures* by Len Bass, et al. (Addison-Wesley) is an excellent book that covers different architectural styles and the corresponding visual models.
- *Real-Time Software Design for Embedded Systems* by Hassan Gomaa (Cambridge University Press) discusses different models and diagrams you can create to sketch out your system.

While we'll be looking more at developing a module later, if you want to jump ahead or are interested in going beyond the short logging code I put here, take a look at Embedded Artistry's Arduino Logging Library (*https://embeddedartistry.com/arduino-logger*). The author goes through the process of development and ends up with code you can use. (While you are there, click the Welcome link (*https://oreil.ly/siMLU*) because Embedded Artistry has a wealth of code and information.)

Interview Question: Create an Architecture

Describe the architecture for this [pick an object in the room].

Looking around an interviewing area for a suitable object is usually fairly dicey because such places are devoid of most interesting things. The conference phone gets picked a lot because it is sometimes the most complicated system in the room. Another good target is the projector.

When asking this question, I want to know that the candidate can break a problem down into pieces. I want to see the process as they mentally deconstruct an object. In general, starting with the inputs and outputs is a safe bet. For a conference phone, the speaker and the display are outputs; the buttons and the microphone are inputs. I like to see these as boxes on a piece of paper. A candidate shouldn't be afraid to pick up the object and see the connections it has. Those are inputs and outputs as well. Once they have the physical hardware down, they can start making connections by asking (themself) how each component works: how does the power button work, and how might the software interface to it? How does the microphone work, and what does it imply about other pieces of the system (e.g., is there an analog-to-digital converter)?

A candidate gets points for mentioning good software design practices. Calling the boxes drivers for the lowest level and objects for the next level is a good start. It is also good to hear some noises about parts of the system that might be reused in a future phone and how to keep them encapsulated.

I expect them to ask questions about specific features or possible design goals (such as cost). However, they get a lot of latitude to make up the details. Want to talk about networking? Pretend it is a voice over internet protocol (VoIP) phone. Want to skip that entirely? Focus instead on how it might store numbers in a mini-database or linked list. I'm happy when they talk about things they are interested in, particularly areas that I've failed to ask about in other parts of the interview.

In that same vein, although I want to see a good overview of the whole system, I don't mind if a candidate chooses to dig deep into one area. This question gives a lot of freedom to expound on how their particular experience would help them design a phone. When I ask a question, I don't mind if they admit some ignorance and talks about something they know better.

Asking an interviewee about architecture is not about getting perfect technical details. It is crucial to draw something, even if it is only mildly legible. The intent of the question is about the candidate showing enthusiasm for problem solving and effectively communicating their ideas.

CHAPTER 3

Getting Your Hands on the Hardware

It can be tough to start working with embedded systems. Most software engineers need a crash course in electrical engineering, and most electrical engineers need a crash course in software design. Working closely with a member of the opposite discipline will make getting into embedded systems much easier. Some of my best friends are electrical engineers.

If you've never been through a development cycle that includes hardware, it can be a bit daunting to try to intuit your roles and responsibilities. In this chapter, I'll start out with an overview of how a project usually flows. Then I'll give you some more detailed advice on the skills you need to hold up your end of the team, including:

- Reading a datasheet
- Getting to know a new processor
- Unraveling a schematic
- Creating your own debugging toolbox
- Testing the hardware (and software)

Hardware/Software Integration

The product starts out as an idea or a need to be filled. Someone makes a high-level product design based on features, cost, and time to market. At this point, a schedule is usually created to show the major milestones and activities (see Figure 3-1).

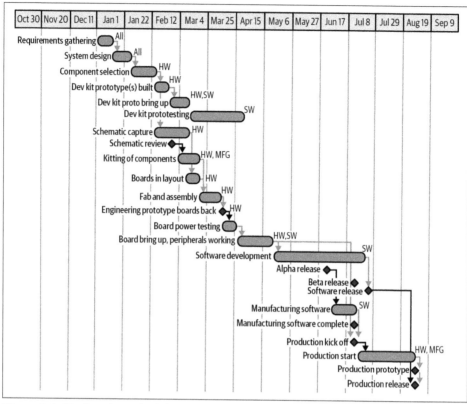

Figure 3-1. Ideal project schedule example

Ideal Project Flow

This sort of schedule is based on the engineering managers (or tech leads) talking about the goals and then estimating the time and resources the project will take. This is only part of the schedule; it doesn't include the mechanical engineering, server-side software, marketing launch, or a host of other activities. On the other hand, this is likely the part of the schedule that includes hardware and embedded software, so it likely shows your work and that of your immediate team.

The schedule in Figure 3-1 shows a waterfall type of development, where one activity flows into the next. It makes sense that a schematic review is necessary before the boards get created. Of course the boards are created before embedded software development has an alpha release.

But this won't be the actual schedule. It can be quite frustrating to spend a lot of time creating such a masterpiece only to have it be out of date before it is finished. The goal of planning is to identify dependencies. If it takes 12 weeks to make the boards and 14 weeks to create the embedded software, then the whole project can be done in

14 weeks, right? Well, no: the software likely needs more time with the completed boards. But hopefully the whole project doesn't need 26 weeks (12 + 14).

A large part of putting together a schedule is figuring out which tasks can be done in parallel versus those that must be done after hardware is complete. Too often the focus is on the end date, the all-important ship date, but there is more information in the schedule: dependencies, human resource needs, and when cash needs to be spent (aside from salaries).

Of course, no matter how much scheduling and planning you do, nothing ever goes according to plan. There will be overruns and backtracking. The act of planning helps you figure out where you need to be careful and which dependencies matter in the long run (and which don't).

Sadly, embedded software is often at the end, trying to make up for delays due to changing requirements or hardware fixes. You develop with partial hardware, with prototype boards, and will make good bring-up tests so you'll be ready when the boards finally arrive.

You may develop using Agile methods instead of waterfall, allowing for more and faster releases. But at some level, when creating physical, shippable products, you will likely need to look into the pieces your firmware depends upon and how they get developed.

Hardware Design

Once they know what they are building, the hardware team goes through datasheets and reference designs to choose components, ideally consulting the embedded software team. Often development kits are purchased for the riskiest parts of the system, usually the processor and the least-understood peripherals (more on processors and peripherals in a bit).

The hardware team creates schematics, while the software team works on the development boards. It may seem like the hardware team is taking weeks (or months) to make a drawing, but most of that time is spent wading through datasheets to find a component that does what it needs to for the product, at the right price, in the correct physical dimensions, with a good temperature range, and so on. During that time, the embedded software team is finding (or building) a toolchain with compiler and debugger, creating a debugging subsystem, trying out a few peripherals, and possibly building a sandbox for testing algorithms.

Schematics are entered using a schematic capture program (aka CAD package). These programs are often expensive to license and cumbersome to use, so the hardware engineer will usually generate a PDF schematic at checkpoints or reviews for your use. Although you should take the time to review the whole schematic (described in "Reading a Schematic" on page 58), the part that has the largest impact on you is the processor and its view of the system. Because hardware engineers understand that, most will generate an I/O map that describes the connection attached to each pin of the processor. (Chapter 4 suggests taking the I/O map and making a header file from it.)

The schematic shows the electrical connections but it doesn't specify exactly which parts need to be on the board. It may show a header with ten pins, but for the boards to be assembled, the manufacturer will need to know exactly what kind of header, usually with a link to a datasheet specifying everything about it. All of the components are on the *bill of materials* (BOM), something that is started during schematic capture.

Once the schematic is complete (and the development kits have shown that the processor and risky peripherals are probably suitable), the board can be laid out. In layout, the connections on the schematic are made into a drawing of physical traces on a board, connecting each component as it is in the schematic.

 Board layout is often a specialized skill, different from electrical engineering, so don't be surprised if someone other than your hardware engineer does the board layout.

After layout, the board goes to fabrication (fab), where the printed circuit boards (PCBs) are built. Then they get assembled with all of their components. Gathering the items on the BOM so you can start assembly is called putting together the *kits*. Getting the parts with long lead times can make it difficult to create a complete kit, which delays assembly. An assembled board is called a PCBA (printed circuit board assembly), or just a PCA, which is what will sit on your desk.

When the schematic is done and the layout has started, the primary task for the embedded software team is to define the hardware tests and get them written while the boards are being created. Working on the user-facing code may seem more productive, but when you get the boards back from fabrication, you won't be able to make progress on the software until you bring them up. The hardware tests will not only make the bring-up smoother, but they also will make the system more stable for development (and production). As you work on the hardware tests, ask your electrical engineer which parts are the riskiest. Prioritize development for the tests for those subsystems (and try them out on a development kit, if you can).

When the boards come back, the hardware engineer will power them on to verify there aren't power issues, possibly verifying other purely hardware subsystems. Then you get a board (finally!) and bring-up starts.

Board Bring-Up

This can be a fun time, one where you are learning from an engineer whose skill set is different from yours. Or it can be a shout-fest where each team accuses the other of incompetence and maliciousness. Your call.

The board you receive may or may not be full of bugs. Electrical engineers don't have an opportunity to compile their code, try it out, make a change, and recompile. Making a board is not a process with lots of iterations. Remember that people make mistakes, and the more fluffheaded the mistake, the more likely it will take an eternity to find and fix (what was the longest time you ever spent debugging an error that turned out to be a typo?).

Don't be afraid to ask questions, though, or to ask for help finding your problem (yes, phrase it that way). An electrical engineer sitting with you might be what you need to see what is going wrong.

Finding a hardware (or software) bug at an early stage of design is like getting a gift. The earlier you find a bug, the happier you'll be. Your product team's bugs reflect upon you, so be willing to give your time and coding skills to unravel a problem. It isn't just polite and professional; it is a necessary part of being on a team. If there is a geographic or organizational separation and getting the hardware engineer's help requires leaping through hoops, consider some back-channel communications (and trade in lunches). It might make you poor in the short term, but you'll be a hero for getting things done, and your long-term outlook will be good.

 Don't be embarrassed when someone points out a bug; be grateful. If that person is on your team or in your company, that bug didn't get out to the field where it could be seen by customers.

To make bring-up easier on both yourself and your hardware engineer, first make each component individually testable. If you don't have enough code space, make another software subproject for the hardware test code (but share the underlying modules as much as possible).

Second, when you get the PCBA, start on the lowest-level pieces, at the smallest steps possible. For example, don't try out your fancy motor controller software. Instead, set an I/O device to go on for a short time, and hook up an LED to make sure it flashes. Then (still taking things one step at a time), do the minimum necessary to make sure the motor moves (or at least twitches).

Finally, make your tools independent of *you* being present to run them, so that someone else is able to reproduce an issue. Once an issue is reproducible, even if the cause isn't certain, fixes can be tried. (Sometimes the fix will explain the cause.) The time spent writing good tests will pay dividends. There is a good chance that this hardware verification code will be around for a while, and you'll probably want it again when the next set of boards comes back. Also, these tests tend to evolve into manufacturing tests used to check the board's functionality during production.

How do you know what tests need to be written? It starts with an in-depth knowledge of the processor and peripherals. That leads to the topic of reading a datasheet.

Reading a Datasheet

With the pressure to get products released, it can be tough to slow down enough to read the component datasheets, manuals, and application notes. Worse, it can feel like you've read them (because you've turned all the pages), but nothing sticks, because it is a foreign language. When the code doesn't work, you're tempted to complain that the hardware is broken.

If you are a software engineer, consider each chip as a separate software library. Think of all the effort you would need to put into learning a software package (Qt, OpenCV, Zephyr, Unity, TensorFlow, etc.). That is about how long it will take to become familiar with your processor and its peripherals. The processors will even have methods of talking to the peripherals that are somewhat like APIs. As with libraries, you can often get away with reading only a subset of the documentation—but you are better off knowing which subset is the most important one for you before you end up down a rabbit hole.

Datasheets are the API manuals for peripherals. Make sure you have the latest version of your datasheet (check the manufacturer's site and do an online search just to be sure) before I let you in on the secrets of what to read twice and what to ignore until you need it.

 Unfortunately, some manufacturers release their datasheets only under NDA, so their websites contain only an overview or summary of their product.

Hardware components are described by their datasheets. Datasheets can be intimidating; they are packed densely with information. Reading datasheets is an art, one that requires experience and patience. The first thing to know about datasheets is that they aren't really written for you. They are written for an electrical engineer, more precisely for an electrical engineer who is already familiar with the component or its close cousin.

In some ways, reading a datasheet is like coming into the middle of a technical conversation. Take a look at Figure 3-2, which resembles a real datasheet, even though it's not a component you're likely to interface with in your software (it is a prehistoric gait controller for leg actuators).

Near the top of each datasheet is an overview or feature list. This is the summary of the chip, but if you haven't already used a component with a datasheet that is 85% the same as this one, the overview isn't likely to be very helpful. On the other hand, once you have used three or four analog triceratops (or accelerometers, or whatever you are really looking at), you can just read the overview of the next one and get an idea of how this chip is the same and different from your previous experience. If the datasheet took the time to explain everything a newcomer might want to know, each one would be a book (and most would have the same information). Additionally, it isn't the newcomers who buy components in volume; it is the experienced engineers who are already familiar with the devices.

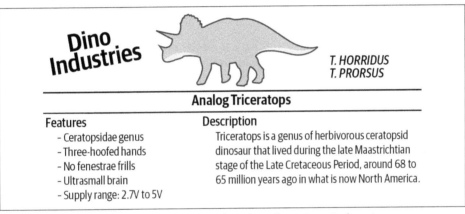

Dino Industries

T. HORRIDUS
T. PRORSUS

Analog Triceratops

Features
- Ceratopsidae genus
- Three-hoofed hands
- No fenestrae frills
- Ultrasmall brain
- Supply range: 2.7V to 5V

Description
Triceratops is a genus of herbivorous ceratopsid dinosaur that lived during the late Maastrichtian stage of the Late Cretaceous Period, around 68 to 65 million years ago in what is now North America.

Figure 3-2. Top of the Analog Triceratops datasheet from Dino Industries

So I say skip the overview header (or at least come back to it later).

I like the functional diagrams that are often on the first page, but they are a lot like the overview. If you don't know what you are looking for, the block diagram probably isn't going to enlighten you. So the place to start is the description. This usually covers about half the first page, maybe extending a little on to the second page.

The description is not the place to read a few words and skip to the next paragraph. The text is dense and probably less than a page long. Read this section thoroughly. Read it aloud, underline the important information (which could be most of the information), or try to explain it to someone else (I keep a teddy bear in my office for this purpose, but some people use their EEs).

Datasheet Sections You Need When Things Go Wrong

After the first page, the order of information in each datasheet varies. And not all datasheets have all sections. Nonetheless, you don't want to scrutinize sections that won't offer anything to help your software. Save time and mental fatigue by skipping over the absolute maximum ratings, recommended operating conditions, electrical characteristics, packaging information, layout, and mechanical considerations.

The hardware team has already looked at that part of the sheet; trust them to do their jobs.

Although you can skip the following sections now, remember that these sections exist. You may need them when things go wrong, when you have to pull out an oscilloscope and figure out why the driver doesn't work, or (worse) when the part seems to be working but not as advertised. Note that these sections exist, but you can come back to them when you need them; they are safe to ignore on the first pass.

Pinout for each type of package available

You'll need to know the pinout if you have to probe the chip during debugging. Ideally, this won't be important, because your software will work and you won't need to probe the chip.

The pin configuration shows some pin names with bars over them (Figure 3-3).

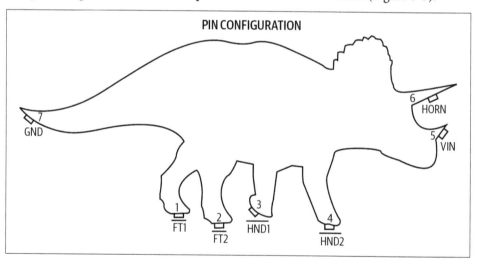

Figure 3-3. Analog Triceratops pinout

The bars indicate that these pins are *active low*, meaning that they are on when the voltage is low. In the pin description, active low pins have a slash before the name. You may also see other things to indicate active low signals. If most of your pins have a NAME, look for a modifier that puts the name in the format nNAME, #NAME, _NAME,

NAME*, NAME_N, etc. Basically, if it has a modifier near the name, look to see whether it is active low, which should be noted in the pin descriptions section.

If this is all brand new to you, consider picking up a beginner's guide to electronics, such as one of those listed in "Further Reading" on page 84.

Pin descriptions

This is a table that looks like Figure 3-4. Come back when you need this information, possibly as you look to see whether the lines should be active low or as you are trying to make your oscilloscope show the same image as the datasheet's timing diagrams.

Symbol name	Pin	Type	Description
/FT1	1	O	Four-hoofed foot channel 1
/FT2	2	O	Four-hoofed foot channel 2
/HND1	3	O	Three-hoofed hand channel 1
/HND2	4	O	Three-hoofed hand channel 2
VIN	5	I	Power supply
HORN	6	I	Mode setting
GND	7	I	Ground

Figure 3-4. Analog Triceratops pin descriptions

Performance characteristics

These tables and graphs, describing exactly what the component does, offer too much detailed information for your first reading. However, when your component communicates but doesn't work, the performance characteristics can help you determine whether there might be a reason (e.g., the part is rated to work in the range 0°C–70°C, but it's right next to your extremely warm processor, or the peripheral works when the input voltage is just right but falls off in accuracy when the input gets a little outside the specified range).

Sample schematics

Sometimes you get driver code, it works as you need it to, and you don't end up changing much, if anything. The sample schematics are the electrical engineering version of driver code. When your part is acting up, it can be reassuring to see that the sample schematics are similar to your schematics. However, as with vendor-provided driver code, there are lots of excellent reasons why the actual implementation doesn't match the sample implementation. If you are having trouble with a part and the schematic doesn't match, ask your electrical engineer about the differences. It may be nothing, but it could be important.

Datasheet Sections for Software Developers

Eventually, possibly halfway through the datasheet, you will get to some text (Figure 3-5). This could be titled "Application Information" or "Theory of Operation." Or possibly the datasheet just switches from tables and graphs to text and diagrams. This is the part you need to start reading. It is fine to start by skimming this to see where the information you need is located, but eventually you will really need to read it from start to end. As a bonus, the text there may link to application notes and user manuals of value. Read through the datasheet, considering how you'll need to implement the driver for your system. How does it communicate? How does it need to be initialized? What does your software need to do to use the part effectively? Are there strict timing requirements, and how can your processor handle them?

THEORY OF OPERATION

In normal mode, the triceratops has a phase shifted output where the opposite signal is synchronized (FT1 with HND2, FT2 with HND1). Each signal is high for approximately one quarter of the cycle.

In charge mode (HORN pulled low), all output pins are synchronized. When the triceratops is charging, it spends less time with its hands and feet in the ground state: each signal is low for approximately one quarter of each cycle. It also has a higher cycle rate which gets incrementally faster until it reaches its maximum charge speed. It maintains this output until the charge is ended (HORN pulled high) or until the triceratops encounters undue resistance (crashes) and boot mode is reinitiated. While not necessary, the HORN is generally pulled high after the crash to prevent overheating of the component.

Figure 3-5. Analog Triceratops theory of operation

As you read through the datasheet, mark areas that may make an impact on your code so you can return to them. Timing diagrams are good places to stop and catch your breath (Figure 3-6). Try to relate those to the text and to your intended implementation. More information on timing diagrams is provided in the sidebar "How Timing Diagrams Help Software Developers" on page 52.

In addition to making sure you have the latest datasheet for your component, check the manufacturer's web page for errata, which provide corrections to any errors in the datasheet. Search the web page for the part number and the word "errata" (Figure 3-7). Errata can refer to errors in the datasheet or errors in the part. Most parts have some sort of errata.

 Datasheets can have revisions, and components can have revisions. Get the latest datasheet for the component revision you are using.

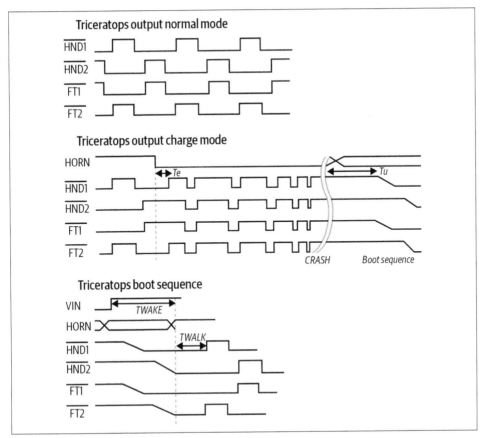

Figure 3-6. Analog Triceratops timing diagrams

When you are done, if you are very good or very lucky, you will have the information you need to use the chip. Generally, most people will start writing the driver for the chip and spend time re-reading parts as they write the interface to the chip, then the communication method, then finally actually use the chip. Reading datasheets is a race where the tortoise definitely wins over the hare.

Once you are all done with the driver and it is working, read through the feature summary at the top of the datasheet because now you have conquered this type of component and can better understand the summary. Even so, when you implement something similar, you'll probably still need to read parts of the datasheet, but it will be simpler and you'll get a much better overview from the summary on the datasheet's front page.

Dino Industries

Analog Triceratops

Analog Triceratops Datasheet Errata

Classifications/corrections to the datasheet

In the device datasheet listed below, the following clarifications and corrections should be noted. The component Triceratops may mature over time into the Torosaurus as light and temperature cycles cause the frills to develop fenestrae (holes). To work around the issue, the frill is not recommended for use in the Triceratops.

Device	Datasheet
T. horridus T. prorsus	Analog Triceratops
T. latus T. utahensis	Analog Torosaurus

Figure 3-7. Analog Triceratops errata

Other resources may also be available as you work with peripherals:

- If the chip has a user manual, be sure to look at that.

- Application notes often have specific use cases that may be of interest. These often have vendor example code associated with them. Also look for a vendor code repository.

- Search the part on GitHub or the web. Example code from other folks using the part can show you what you should be doing.

Look around before diving in; the answer to something you don't know yet may be out there.

How Timing Diagrams Help Software Developers

Timing diagrams show the relationship between transitions. Some transitions may be on the same signal, or the timing diagram may show the relationship between transitions on different signals. For instance, alternating states of the hands (HND1 and HND2) in normal mode at the top of Figure 3-6 show that one hand is raised shortly after the other is put down. When approaching a timing diagram, start on the left side with the signal name. Time advances from left to right.

Most timing diagrams focus on the digital states, showing you when a signal is high or low (remember to check the name for modifiers that indicate a signal is active low). Some diagrams include a ramp (such as hands and feet in the boot sequence in Figure 3-6) to show you when the signal is in a transitory state. You may also see signals that are both high and low (such as the horn in the boot sequence of Figure 3-6); these indicate the signal is in an indeterminate logical state (for output) or isn't monitored (for input).

The important time characteristics are highlighted with lines with arrows. These are usually specified in detail in a table. Also look for an indication of signal ordering (often shown with dashed lines) and causal relationships (usually arrows from one signal to another). Finally, footnotes in the diagram often contain critical information.

Evaluating Components Using the Datasheet

It may seem odd to have this section about evaluating a component after its implementation. That isn't the way it goes in projects. However, it is the way it goes in engineering life. Generally, before you get to the point where you choose pieces of the system, you have to cut your teeth on implementing pieces of systems designed by other people. So evaluating a component is a more advanced skill than reading the datasheet, a skill that electrical engineers generally develop before software engineers.

When you are evaluating a component, your goal is to quickly eliminate components that won't work. Don't waste valuable time determining precisely how a component does feature X if the component can't be used because it requires 120 V AC and your system has 5 V of DC. Start off with a list of must-haves and a list of wants. Then you'll want to generate your potential pool of parts that require further investigation.

Before you get too deep into that investigation, let's talk about the things that datasheets don't have. They usually don't have prices, because those depend on many factors, especially how many you plan to order. And datasheets don't have lead times, so be careful about designing around the perfect part; it may be available only after a six-month wait. Unless you are ordering online, you'll need to talk to your vendor or distributor.

Talking with your vendor is a good opportunity to ask whether they have any guidance for using the part, initialization code, application notes, whitepapers, forums, or anything that might get you a little further along. Vendors recognize that these can be selling points, and their application engineers are generally willing to help. Distributors might even help you compare and contrast the different options available to you.

Even when working with a distributor, DigiKey (*https://digikey.com*) is often a great way to get some idea of price and lead times.

Back to the datasheet. Some of those information-dense sections previously skipped are now important. Start with the absolute maximum ratings and electrical characteristics (see Figure 3-8). If they don't match (or exceed) your criteria, set the datasheet aside. The present goal is to wade through the pile of datasheets quickly; if a part doesn't meet your basic criteria, note where it fails and go on. (Keeping notes is useful; otherwise, you may end up rejecting the same datasheet repeatedly.) You may want to prioritize the datasheets by how far out of range they are. If you end up without any datasheets that meet your high standards, you can recheck the closest ones to see whether they can be made to work.

Once the basic electrical and mechanical needs are met, the next step is to consider the typical characteristics, determining whether the part is what you need. I can't help you much with specifics, as they depend on your system's needs and the particular component. Some common questions at this level are about your functional parameters: does the component go fast enough? Does the output meet or exceed that required by your system? In a sensor, is the noise acceptable?

Absolute maximum ratings
over operating free-air temperature range

Parameter	Rating	Units
VIN to GND	–0.3 to +6	V
Output current	100, momentary	mA
Input current	10, continuous	mA
Maximum junction temperature	150	C
Operating temperature range	–40 to +105	C
Storage temperature range	–60 to +150	C
Animation period	68 to 65	Mya
Top charge speed	24	km/h

Figure 3-8. Analog Triceratops absolute maximum ratings

Once you have two or three datasheets that pass the first round of checking, delve deeper into them. If there is an application section, that is a good place to start. Are any of these applications similar to yours? If so, carry on. If not, worry a bit. It is probably all right to be the first to use a peripheral in a particular way, but if the part is directed particularly to underwater sensor networks and you want to use it in your supersmart toaster, you might want to find out why they've defined the application so narrowly. More seriously, there may be a reason why the suggested applications don't cover all uses. For example, chips directed toward automotive use may not be available in small quantities. The goal of the datasheet is to sell things to people already using similar things, so there may be a good reason for a limited scope.

Next, look at the performance characteristics and determine whether they meet your needs. Often you'll find new requirements while reading this section, such as realizing your system should have the temperature response of part A, the supply voltage response of part B, and the noise resistance of part C. Collect these into the criteria, and eliminate the ones that don't meet your needs (but also prioritize the criteria so you don't paint yourself into a corner).

At this point, you should have at least two but no more than four datasheets per part. If you have more than four, ask around to see whether one vendor has a better reputation in your purchasing department, shorter lead times, or better prices. You may need to come back to your extras, but select four that seem good.

If you have eliminated all of your datasheets or you have only one, don't stop there. It doesn't mean that everything is unusable (or that only one is usable). Instead, it may mean that your criteria are too strict and you'll have to learn more about the options available to you. So choose the two best components, even if one or both fail your most rigorous standards.

For each remaining datasheet, you want to figure out the tricky pieces of the implementation and see how well the component will fare in your system. This is where some experience dealing with similar parts is useful. You want to read the datasheet as though you were going to implement the code. In fact, if you don't have experience with something pretty similar, you may want to type up some code to make it real. If you can prototype the parts with actual hardware, great! If not, you can still do a mental prototype, going through the steps of implementation and estimating what will happen.

Even though you will be doing this for two to four parts and probably using only one of them, this will give you a jump start on your code when the part is finally chosen.

Such in-depth analysis takes a significant amount of time but reduces the risk of the part not working. How far you take your prototype is up to you (and your schedule). If you still have multiple choices, look at the family of the component. If you run out of something (space, pins, or range), is there a pin-for-pin compatible part in the same family (ideally with the same software interface)? Having headroom can be very handy.

Finally, having selected the component, the feature summary is an exercise in comparative literature. Now that you have become that person who has already read several datasheets for similar components, the overview that starts the datasheet is for you. If you have any remaining datasheets to evaluate, start there. Compare the ones you've done against the new ones to get a quick feel for what each chip does and how different parameters interact (e.g., faster speed likely will be proportional to higher cost).

Your Processor Is a Language

The most important component is the one your software runs on: your processor.

Some vendors (ST, TI, Microchip, NXP, and so on) use a common core (i.e., Arm Cortex-M4F). The vendors provide different on-chip peripherals. How your code interfaces with timers or communication methods will change. Sharing a core will make the change less difficult than moving between a tiny 8-bit processor and a mighty 64-bit processor, but you should expect differences.

As you get to know a new processor, expect that it will take almost the same level of effort as if you were learning a new programming language. And, like learning a language, if you've already worked with something similar, it will be simpler to learn the new one. As you learn several programming languages or several processors, you will find that learning the new ones becomes easier and easier.

Although this metaphor gives you an idea of the scale of information you'll need to assimilate, the processor itself is really more like a large library with an odd interface. Talking to the hardware is a misnomer. Your software is actually talking to the processor software through special interfaces called *registers*, which I'll cover in more detail in Chapter 4. Registers are like keywords in a language. You generally get to know a few (`if`, `else`, `while`), and then later you get to know a few more (`enum`, `do`, `sizeof`), and finally you become an expert (`static`, `volatile`, `union`).

The amount of documentation for a processor scales with the processor complexity. Your primary goal is to learn what you need to get things accomplished. With a flood of information available, you'll need to determine which pieces of documentation get your valuable time and attention. Some documents to look for include:

User Manual (or User Guide or Reference Manual) from the processor vendor
> Often voluminous, the user manual provides most of what you'll need to know. Reading the introduction will help you get to know the processor's capabilities (e.g., how many timers it has and its basic memory structure).

 Why get the user manual from the vendor? Take for example the STM32F103 processor, which uses an Arm Cortex-M3 core. You don't want to read the Arm user manual if you are using the F103, because 88% of the information in the Arm manual is extraneous, 10% will be in the STM32F10x manual, and the last few percent you probably won't ever need.

Often these are written for families of processors, so if you want to use an STM32F103, you'll need to get an STM32F10x manual and look for the notes that differentiate the processors. Once you read the introduction, you'll probably want to skip to the parts that will be on your system. Each chapter usually has a helpful introduction of its own before moving into gritty details.

The user manual will have the information you need to work with the chip, though it may not help you get a system up and working.

Getting Started Guide or User Manual for the development kit
A development kit (dev kit) is often the place to start when working with a new processor. Using a dev kit lets you set up your compiler and debugger with confidence, before custom hardware comes in (and gives you something to compare against if your hardware doesn't work immediately). The dev kit is generally a sales tool for the processor, so it isn't too expensive and tends to have excellent documentation for setting the system up from scratch. The kit recommends compilers, debuggers, and necessary hardware, and even shows you how to connect all the cables. The development kit documentation is intended to be an orientation for programmers, so even if you don't purchase a kit, the associated documentation may help orient you to the processor's ecosystem.

Getting Started Guide (slides)
This document describes how to get started using the processor for both electrical engineers and software developers. Although interesting and fast to read, this slide deck generally won't answer questions about how to use the processor. It can be helpful when evaluating a processor for use in a project, as it does discuss what the processor is and common applications. Also, it might give you an idea of what dev kits are available.

Application Notes (App Notes)
That complicated thing you want to do with your system? It is quite possible that someone else has done it. Or even better, the vendor got tired of answering the same questions about how to do it, so they wrote up a description. App notes are like cheat codes for development. While the user manual will tell you everything about the processor, application notes are usually more tactical, describing how to accomplish different goals. They often have code associated with them.

Wikis and forums
While the main Wikipedia page for your processor probably won't have enough information to help you get code written, it may give you a high-level overview (though usually the user manual's introduction is more useful to you). The Wikipedia page may have valuable links to forums and communities using the processor where you can search for problems you might encounter and see how other people solved them.

The vendor may also have wiki pages or forums devoted to the processor. These can be valuable for another perspective on the information in the user manual or getting started guide. They are often easy to search, with links to lots of examples.

Vendor or distributor visits

Sit in on these. They may have little readily pertinent information, but the networking is useful later when you ask for code or support.

Processor datasheet

The datasheet for your processor is usually more focused on the electrical aspects. Since you'll be writing the software, you want something more software oriented. So for processors, unless you are looking up electrical spec, skip the datasheet and go to the user manual (or user guide).

Errata

Even more difficult to read than a very dense datasheet, you still need to skim the errata to know what parts of the chip have errors. For instance, if the errata mention seven separate I^2C bugs, you'll know to dig in further if you're using I^2C.

Most processors now come with many examples, including a ton of driver code. Sometimes this is good code, sometimes not. Even with the not-so-great code, it is nice to have an example to start from. Though the examples generally work as described, they probably won't be robust or efficient enough for your needs. If you are going to use the code, it becomes your code to own, so make sure you understand it.

Once you get oriented, preferably with a dev kit up and running, hunker down with the user manual and read the chapters for every interface you are using (even if your vendor gave you example code that does what you need). As we work through the specifics of an embedded system, there will be more details about what to expect from chapters in the user manual (inputs and outputs, interrupts, watchdogs and communications, etc.). For now, let's go back to the bigger picture of the system we are about to bring up.

Reading a Schematic

If you come from the traditional software world, schematics can seem like an eye chart with hieroglyphics, interspersed with strange boxes and tangled lines. As with a datasheet, knowing where to start can be daunting. Beginning on page one of a multipage schematic can be dicey because many electrical engineers put their power-handling hardware there, something you don't necessarily care about. Figure 3-9 shows you a snippet of one page of a schematic.

Some schematics have blocks of textual data (often in the corner of a page). Those are comments; read them carefully, particularly if the block is titled "Processor I/Os" or something equally useful. These are like block comments in code: they aren't always there, so you should take your electrical engineer out to lunch when their schematic is well commented.

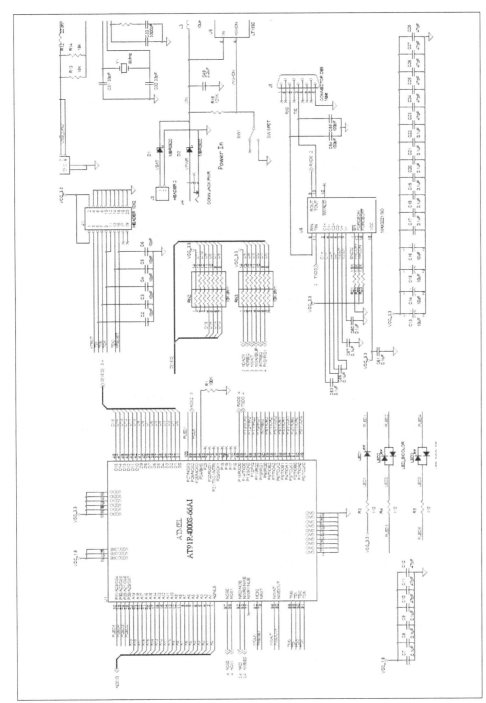

Figure 3-9. Example schematic snippet

Most of the time you'll get a hardware block diagram to help you decode a schematic. However, a question I've been asked in several interviews is, "What does this schematic do?" So this section gives you tips on getting through that as well as a more friendly schematic.

As you go through a schematic for the first time, start by looking for boxes with lots of connections. Often this can be simplified further because box size on the schematic is proportional to the number of wires, so look for the largest boxes. Your processor is likely to be one of those things. Because the processor is the center of the software world, finding it will help you find the peripherals that you most care about.

Above the box is the component ID (U1), often printed on the PCB. Inside or under the boxes is usually the part number. As shown in Figure 3-9, the part number might not be what you are used to seeing. For example, your processor manual may say Atmel AT91R40008, but the schematic may have AT91R40008-66AI, which is more of a mouthful. However, the schematic describes not only how to make the traces on the printed circuit board, but also how to put together the board with the correct components. The extra letters for the processor describe how the processor is packaged and attached to the board.

By now you've found two to four of the largest and/or most connected components. Look at their part numbers to determine what they actually are. Hopefully, you've found your processor. (If not, keep looking.) You may also have found some memory. Memory used to be on the address bus, so it would have almost as many connections as the processor, often with 8 or more address lines and 16 data lines, as in Figure 3-9. Many newer processors have enough embedded memory to alleviate the need for external RAM or flash, so you may not find any large components in addition to your processor.

Next, look at the connectors, which can look like boxes or long rectangles. These are labeled with a *J* instead of a *U* (e.g., J3). There should be a connector for power to the system (at least two pins: power and ground). There is probably a connector for debugging the processor (J1 in Figure 3-9). The other connectors may tell you quite a bit about the board; they are how the world outside sees the board. Is there a connector with many signals that could indicate a daughter board? Is there a connector with an RS-232 signal to indicate a serial port? A connector filled with *net labels* (the wire names) that start with USB or LCD? The names are intended to give you a hint.

With connectors and the larger chips identified, you can start building a mental model of the system (or a hardware block diagram if you don't already have one). Now go back to the boxes and see if you can use the names to estimate their function. Looking for names such as SENSOR or ADC might help. Chapter 7 will give you some other signal names that might help you find interesting peripherals.

In a schematic, wires can cross without connecting. Look for a dot to indicate the junction is connected. Schematics seldom have a dot at a four-way cross, as it can be difficult to tell if there is a dot there when the schematic is printed.

In all this time, we've been ignoring the non-box-shaped components. Although it is useful to be able to understand a resistor network, an analog filter, or an op-amp circuit, you don't need to know these right away. Figure 3-10 shows some common schematic components and their names, though they will be drawn a little differently in your schematic. This will let you express curiosity about the function of a particular resistor. "Further Reading" on page 84 gives you some suggestions on how to increase your hardware knowledge.

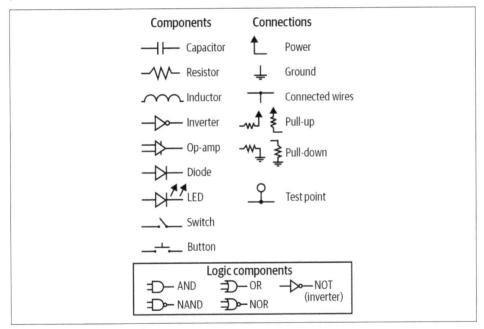

Figure 3-10. Common schematic components

There are two exceptions to my recommendation that you ignore everything but boxes. First, LEDs, switches, and buttons are often connected to the processor. The schematic will tell you the processor line this type of component is connected to so you know where to read the state of a switch or turn on an LED.

The other kind of components to pay attention to are resistors connected to the processor and power, known as *pull-ups* because they pull the voltage up (toward power). Usually, pull-ups are relatively weak (high amounts of resistance) so the processor can drive a pulled-up I/O line to be low. The pull-up means that the signal on that line is defined to be high when the processor isn't driving it. A processor may have internal pull-ups so that inputs to the processor have a default state even when unconnected.

Note that there are also *pull-downs*, which means resistors to ground. All of the pull-up information also applies to them, except that their default logic level is low instead of high. Inputs without a pull-up or pull-down are driven to neither a logical high nor low, so they are *floating* (they can also be called hi-Z, high impedance, or tri-stated).

Practice Reading a Schematic: Arduino!

Arduinos are awesome little boards, designed to be easy to use, to make electronics accessible to artists, students, and generally everyone. For many people, the Arduino is the gateway into embedded systems; it's the first hardware they ever program.

I want to show you how to go from looking at the Arduino as an opaque system to looking it as a board with a familiar schematic.

Figure 3-11 shows a hardware block diagram of the Arduino UNO schematic. On the bottom right is the microcontroller. This is the end-user feature of the board. The I/O pins come directly from the microcontroller but are kind of separate on the board (and are an important feature of this system) so they get their own box.

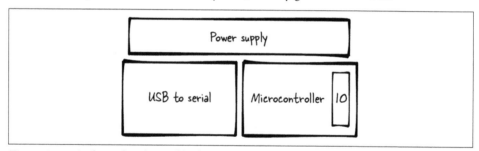

Figure 3-11. Arduino hardware block diagram

To the left of the microcontroller, there is a USB-to-UART (or USB-to-serial) box representing the hardware that translates from what your computer speaks to something the microcontroller understands. It is used for programming the board with new code as well as for printing out data as your code runs. On most block diagrams this piece would be a small box; it is a minor feature, sometimes part of a cable. However, I'm building up to a schematic so I'm keeping it about as large as the space it takes on the schematic.

The final box, on top, is the power subsystem. The Arduino board is a little odd because you can plug it into USB or into a 5 V DC wall wart. If you think about the electronic devices around you (phone, mouse, webcam), it is usually one or the other. But on this board you can plug into both and not blow anything up. The power subsystem is more complicated because of that flexibility.

Take a look at Figure 3-12. Even better, print out your own copy and get out some colored pencils.

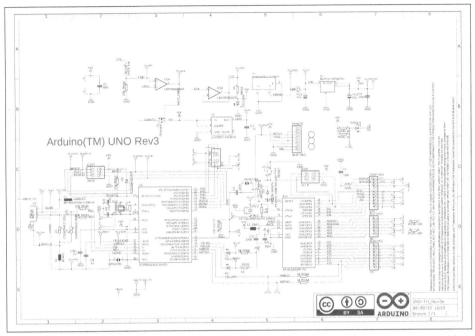

Figure 3-12. Arduino schematic, retrieved from https://content.arduino.cc/assets/UNO-TH_Rev3e_sch.pdf

Draw the hardware block diagram over the schematic. The microcontroller is on the bottom right with the I/O pins on the very right. Then there are some passive components (which we don't care about, so we'll just skip those pesky symbols). On the left of those is the USB-to-UART section (and to the left of that, more pesky passives as well as the USB connector on X2).

Over the top is the power subsystem. Find a connector marked with the word POWER. Everything above that is power-related stuff. In the end, your colored pencil diagram should look like Figure 3-11.

What else can you find on the schematic?

- If we go with the "larger things are more interesting" methodology, we'd find the ATMEGA16U2-MU(R) and the ATMEGA328P-PU are the two big chips. From the block diagram I gave you, the ATMEGA328P-PU is the microcontroller for the user. The other is the USB-to-UART section.

- Can you find the LEDs? Not only do the names include the color, look for the triangle symbol with arrows. These are useful on your schematics.

- Look for ICSP and ICSP1 (they are above the chips). These are connectors used to program the boards in manufacturing. If you have an Arduino UNO board, can you find these connectors? Are they different from the general I/O connectors?

If you take some time to look for the ATMEGA328 datasheet, you'll find it has two pages of dense, possibly impenetrable, summary information. Then it will show pin descriptions that look similar to the physical processor on your board. The datasheet has a comparison of different, but similar, processors. It will talk about the core of the processor (the AVRCore). This is an interesting view into microcontroller design, but the compiler will hide most of this behind the magic of our programming language. The datasheet will include a chapter about memories—Flash, RAM, EEPROM—and then chapters about each subsystem and communication protocol. It has all the basic information.

If you've been following along, you may have already noticed that Microchip is the vendor of this chip. If you find the processor on the Microchip site, you'll discover pages and pages of documents and application notes that dive deeper (ADC basics, reference manuals, errata, and dozens more). The vendors provide this information because they want to sell their chips.

Keep Your Board Safe

The datasheets, user manuals, and schematics are just paper (or electronic forms of paper). Let's get to the hardware. Wait: before you grab it, be aware that touching hardware can give it an electrostatic zap and damage it (especially if you've just taken off a fleece jacket on a dry day).

Ask your hardware engineer for the tools to keep your board safe. Try to be conscious of what your board is sitting on (standoffs keep your board off of coffee-carrying surfaces!). Always carry it around in the bag it came in; the bag is likely made from antistatic material to protect the board. Antistatic mats are cheap and force you to allocate a portion of your desk for hardware (even if you don't use the antistatic wrist band, it is still an improvement over crushing the hardware under a falling book or spilling coffee on it).

If possible, when any wires are added to the board, get them glued down as well as soldered. Many an hour has been lost to a broken rework wire. In that same vein, if the connectors are not keyed so that they can be inserted only one way, take a picture of the board or make notes about which way is the correct way to plug in a connector.

I like having my hardware connected to a power strip I can turn off (preferably one my computer is not connected to). It is really good to have an emergency stop-all plan. And note where the fire extinguisher is, just in case.

Seriously, the problem usually isn't flames but more like little puffs of smoke. Whatever you do to it, though, a damaged board is unlikely to win friends. When your manager or hardware engineer asks you how many boards you want allocated for the embedded software, always ask for a spare or two. Nominally this is so you can make sure the hardware tests work on more than one board. Once the system starts making baby steps, you are the person most likely to lose access to a board so it can be shown off to others. At least those are the reasons you should give for wanting a spare board and not because you may very well damage the first one (or two).

 Often there are also manufacturing errors, especially early on, in dense-board designs. The bare PCB will be tested for continuity, but there is only so much that can be done, especially with a new design, to test for proper solder connections with no breaks and no shorts. If something doesn't work on one piece of hardware, it is really useful to have a second to try it on, plus a third as a tie breaker if you get different results on two boards.

Creating Your Own Debugging Toolbox

I love my toolbox because it gives me some level of independence from my hardware engineer. With the toolbox on my desk, I can make small changes to my board in a safer way (using needle-nose pliers to move a jumper is much less likely to damage a board than using fingers). Not counting the detritus of assorted jumper wires, RS-232 gender changers, and half-dead batteries I've accumulated over the years, my toolbox contains the following:

- Needle-nose pliers
- Tweezers (one pair for use as mini-pliers, one pair for use as tweezers)
- Box cutter
- Digital multimeter (more on this in a minute)
- Electrical tape
- Wire cutters (or, even better, a wire stripper)
- Sharpies
- Assorted screwdrivers (or one with many bits)
- Flashlight
- Magnifying glass
- Safety glasses
- Cable ties (Velcro and zip ties)

If your company has a good lab with someone who keeps the tools in labeled areas, use those (but still have your own). If not, a trip to the hardware store may save some frustration in the future.

Digital Multimeter

Even if you opt not to get a more complete toolbox, I strongly suggest getting a digital multimeter (DMM).

You can get a cheap one that covers the basic functionality for about what you'd pay for a good lunch. Of course, you can blow your whole week's food budget on an excellent DMM, but you shouldn't need to. As an embedded software engineer, you need only a few functions.

First, you need the *voltage mode*. Ideally, your DMM should be able to read at least from 0–20 V with 0.1 V granularity and from 0–2 V with 0.01 V granularity. Usually the question you are looking to answer with the voltage mode of the DMM is simple: are any volts getting there at all? A DMM with 1 mV granularity might be nice occasionally, but 80% of your DMM use will be to answer this broader question: "Is the chip or component even powered?"

The second most important mode is the *resistance check mode*, usually indicated with the Ohm symbol (Ω) and a series of three arcs. You probably don't need to know what value a resistor is; the real use for this mode is to determine when things are connected to each other. Just as voltage mode tests whether something has power, this mode will answer the question, "Are these things even connected to each other?"

To determine the resistance between two points on the board, the DMM sends a small current through the test points. As long as the board is off, this is safe. Don't run it in resistance mode with a powered board unless you know what you are doing.

 Be careful to touch only the two points you are testing. The temptation to run the probe along a header to find the pin that beeps is really high (trust me, I know), but if you connect three points, then the small current may cause problems. Or you can damage a tiny processor leg with rough handling. Be gentle!

When the DMM beeps, there is no significant resistance between the two test probes, indicating they are connected (you can check whether the beep is on by just touching the two probes together). Using this mode, your DMM can be used to quickly determine whether a cable or a trace has broken.

Finally, you want a DMM with a current mode denoted with an amp or milliamp symbol (A or mA). This is for measuring how much power your system is taking. A good implementation of current mode can make a DMM a lot more expensive. Good news, though: if you need the fine granularity necessary for developing very low power products, you will need a tool that goes beyond the DMM. Get a DMM that can measure milliamps, but realize the nanoamp versions cost more and probably aren't worth it. More on low-power programming and the necessary tools are in Chapter 13.

Oscilloscopes and Logic Analyzers

Sometimes you need to know what the electrical signals on the board are doing. There are three flavors of scopes that can help you see the signals as they move:

Traditional oscilloscope
Measures analog signals, usually two or four of them at a time. A digital signal can be measured via analog, but it is kind of boring to see it in one of two spots. Of course, if your digital signal isn't high or low but somewhere in between, the oscilloscope will help you immensely.

Logic analyzer
Measures digital signals only, usually a lot of them at the same time (16, 32, or 64). At one time, logic analyzers were behemoth instruments that took days to set up, but generally found the problem within hours of setup being complete. Many modern logic analyzers hook to your computer and help you do the setup, so that this step takes only a little while. Additionally, many logic analyzers have *protocol analyzers* that interpret the digital bus so you can easily see what the processor is outputting. Thus, if you have a SPI communication bus and you are sending a series of bytes, a protocol analyzer will interpret the information on the bus. A *network analyzer* is a specific type of protocol analyzer, one that focuses on the complex traffic associated with a network. (However, an *RF network analyzer* is very different; it characterizes device response in the radio frequency range.)

Mixed signal oscilloscope
Combines the features of a traditional scope and logic analyzer with a couple of analog channels and 8 or 16 digital ones. A personal favorite of mine, the mixed signal scope can be used to look at different kinds of information simultaneously.

These scopes tend to be shared resources, as they are relatively expensive. You can buy reasonably priced ones that hook to your computer, but sometimes their feature sets are limited in nonobvious ways. Generally, you get what you pay for. The amount of debugging time they can save makes them a good investment.

Setting Up a Scope

Step one is to determine which signal(s) can help you figure out a problem. Next, you'll need to attach the scope's ground clip to ground. If you have more than one ground (AC ground, DC ground, analog ground) and you aren't sure which one to connect the scope to, ask your electrical engineer. Choosing the wrong one can be detrimental to the health of your oscilloscope.

Next, attach the probes to the signals of interest. Many processors have such tiny pins that they require specialized probes. On the other hand, many hardware engineers put test points on their board, knowing that the software team is likely to need access to particular signals for debugging. Alternatively, you can get wires soldered onto the board at the signals you need and hook a probe to those.

Using a scope can be a bit daunting if you've never set one up before. Oscilloscope manuals vary, but they are the best place to look for help (and most of them are online). There is no generic manual for all of them, so I can only tell you the words to look for as you page through the manual.

Figure 3-13 shows a representation of an archetypal oscilloscope screen. The most important point is that time moves along the x-axis and voltage varies along the y-axis. The scales of these axes are configurable.

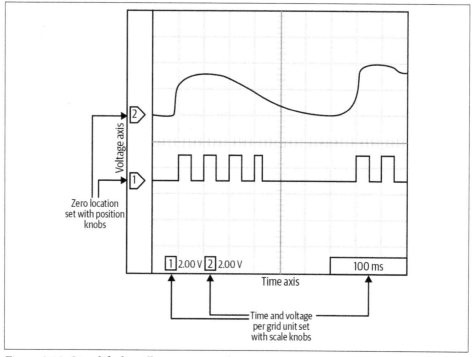

Figure 3-13. Simplified oscilloscope screenshot

Somewhere on the scope's interface, there should be a knob to make the time scale change. Move it to the right, and each horizontal tick goes from, say, 1 s to 0.5 s (and then down into the millisecond or microsecond range). This controls the time scale for the whole screen. For debugging, the goal is to start with the largest possible time base that shows what you are looking for.

If you zoom in too far, you'll see strange things as the supposedly digital signals show their true (and weird) analog colors.

Once you set the time base, you'll need to set the scale of the voltage axis. There could be one knob that accesses all channels (or probes), making you shift the channel some other way, or you might get one knob per channel. Either way, as you turn it to the right, each vertical block magnifies (5 V goes to 2 V, down to millivolts).

If you aren't sure, set the time scale to be about 100 ms/division and the voltage granularity to be about 2 V/block. You can zoom in (or out) from there if you need to.

A different knob will set where each channel is on the screen, in other words, where its zero line is. Figure 3-13 shows the zero line for each channel on the left side of the screen. There may be one knob per channel or a way to multiplex the knob between all the channels. Keep the channels a little offset from each other so you can see each one. (You can turn off the channels you don't need—probably with a button.)

Next, look for a knob to set the zero point of your time scale. This will cause a vertical line to wander across your screen. Set it near the middle. Alternatively, you can set it toward the left of your screen if you are looking for information that happens after an event, or toward the right if you want to know what goes on before an event.

At this point, you can probably turn on your system and see a line wiggle. It may go by so quickly that you don't see what it does, but it can be a start. If nothing happens, look for the buttons that say Run/Stop. You want the scope to be in Run mode. The Stop mode freezes the display at a single point in time, which gives you the opportunity to think about what you've discovered. Near Run/Stop may be a button that says Single, which waits for a trigger and then puts the system in Stop mode. There may also be an Auto button, which will let the system trigger continuously.

If there is an Auto button, be very careful about pushing it. Check to see whether the name means auto trigger or auto set. The former is useful, but the latter tries to configure your scope for you automatically. I find that this tends to reset the configuration to something completely random.

To set up a trigger, look for the trigger knob. This will put up a horizontal line to show where the trigger voltage level is. It is channel dependent, but unlike the other channel-dependent knob, you can't usually set a trigger for each channel. Instead, it requires additional configuration, usually via an on-screen menu and button presses. You want the trigger to be on the channel that changes just at the start (or end) of an interesting event. You'll need to choose whether the trigger is activated going up or going down. You'll also need to choose how often the scope will trigger. If you want to see the first time it changes, set a long timeout. If you want to see the last time it changes, set a short one.

There are a few other things to note. Unless you know what you are doing, you don't want the scope in AC mode. And there is the possibility that the probes are giving signals that are 10x (or 1/10) the size on the screen. This depends on the probe, so if you are off by an order of magnitude, look for a 10x marker and toggle its state.

If you've set up your scope according to my instructions (and the scope manual) and it still doesn't work the way you want it to, get someone with more experience to help you. Scopes are powerful and useful tools, but using one well requires a lot of practice. Don't get discouraged if it is a bit frustrating to start.

Testing the Hardware (and Software)

I strongly recommend being ready to pull out the toolbox, DMM, and scope, but that can reasonably be left to your hardware engineer if you aren't ready to do it alone. As a software person, it is more important that you get as far as possible in building software that will test the hardware in a manner conducive to easy debugging.

Three kinds of tests are commonly seen for embedded systems. First, the *power-on self-test* (POST) runs every time you boot the system, even after the code is released. This test verifies that all of the hardware components are in working order and whatever else is needed to run your system safely. The more the POST tests, the longer the boot time is, so there is a trade-off that might impact the customer. Once the POST completes, the system is ready to be used by the customer.

 Ideally, all POST debug messages printed out at boot time should be accessible later. Whether it is the software version string or the type of sensor attached, there will be a time when you require that information without power cycling.

The second kind of test is the *unit test*. Unit tests should be run before every software release, but they might not be suitable to run at every boot, perhaps because they take too long to execute, return the system to factory default, or put unsightly test patterns on the screen. These tests verify the software and hardware are working together as expected.

The words "unit test" mean different things to different people. To me, a unit test is automated test code that verifies a unit of source code is ready for use. Some developers want tests to cover all possible paths through the code. This can lead to unit test suites that are large and unwieldy, which is the argument used to avoid unit testing in embedded systems. My sort of unit tests are meant to test the basic functionality and the corner cases most likely to occur. This process lets me build testing into my development and keep it there, even after shipping.

 Find out what your industry (or your management) expects of your unit tests. If they mean for the tests to check all software paths, make sure you (and they) understand how much work and code that will take.

Some unit tests may be external to the hardware of the system (i.e., if you are using a sandbox to verify algorithms as suggested in Chapter 2). For the ones that aren't, I would encourage you to leave them in the production code if you can, making them accessible in the field upon some special set of criteria (for instance, "hold down these two buttons and cross your eyes as the system boots"). Not only will this let your quality department use the tests, but you may also find that using the unit tests as a first-line check in the field will tell you whether the system's hardware is acting oddly.

The third and final sorts of tests are those you create during bring-up, usually because a subsystem is not functioning as intended. These are sometimes throwaway checks, superseded by more inclusive tests or added to unit tests. Temporary bring-up code is OK. The goal of this whole exercise is not to write classic source code, but to build systems. And once you've checked such code into your version control system, deleting it is fine because you can always recover the file if you realize you need the test again.

Building Tests

As noted earlier, the code to control peripherals (and the associated tests) often is written while the schematic is being completed. The good news is that you've just spent time with the datasheets, so you have a good idea how to implement the code. The bad news is that while you wait for the boards to arrive, you may end up writing drivers for six peripherals before you get to integrate your software with the hardware.

In Chapter 2, we had a system that communicated to a flash memory device via the SPI communication protocol (a partial schematic is reproduced in Figure 3-14). What do we need to test, and what tools do we need to verify the results?

- I/O lines are under software control (external verification with a DMM).
- SPI can send and receive bytes (external verification with a logic analyzer).
- Flash can be read and written (internal verification; use the debug subsystem to output results).

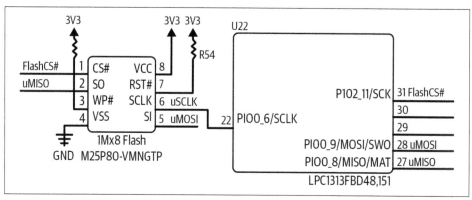

Figure 3-14. Flash memory schematic snippet

To make bring-up easy, you'll need to be able to do each of these. You might choose to run the all-inclusive flash test first. If that works, you know the other two work. However, if it doesn't, you'll need the others available for debugging as necessary.

Other chapters cover controlling I/O lines (Chapter 4) and a bit more about SPI (Chapter 7), so for now let's focus on the tests that we can write to test the flash memory. How flash works isn't critical, but you can test your skills with datasheets by looking over the Macronix MX25V8035 flash memory datasheet (search for the part number on Google, DigiKey, or the vendor's website).

Flash Test Example

Flash memory is a type of *nonvolatile memory* (so it doesn't get cleared when the power is turned off). Other types of nonvolatile memory include ROM (read-only memory) and electrically erasable programmable read-only memory (EEPROM).

Volatile memory doesn't retain its value after a power cycle. There are different kinds of volatile memory, but they are all one type of RAM or another.

Like an EEPROM, flash can be erased and written to. However, most EEPROMs let you erase and write a byte at a time. With flash, you may be able to write a byte at a time, but you have to erase a whole sector to do so. The sector size depends on the flash (usually the larger the flash, the larger each sector). For our test's component, a sector is 4 kilobytes (or 4,096 bytes), and the whole chip contains 8 Mb (1 MB or 256 sectors). Flash usually has more space than an EEPROM and is less power hungry. However, EEPROMs come in smaller sizes, so they are still useful.

When we write a bring-up test, nothing in the flash chip needs to be retained. For the POST, we really shouldn't modify the flash, as the system might be using it (for storing version and graphic data). For a unit test, we'd like to leave it the way we found it after testing, but we might be able to set some constraints on that.

Tests typically take three parameters: the goal flash address, so that the test can run in an unpopulated (or noncritical) sector; a pointer to memory; and the memory length. The memory length is the amount of data the flash test will store to RAM. If the memory is the same size as the sector, no data will be lost in the flash. The following prototypes illustrate three types of test: an umbrella test that runs the others (and returns the number of errors it encounters), a test that tries to read from the flash (returning the number of bytes that were actually read), and a test that tries to write to the flash (returning the number of bytes written):

```
int FlashTest(uint32_t address, uint8_t *memory, uint16_t memLength);
uint16_t FlashRead(uint32_t addr, uint8_t *data, uint16_t dataLen);
uint16_t FlashWrite(uint32_t addr, uint8_t *data, uint16_t dataLen);
```

We'll use the FlashTest extensively during bring-up, then put it in unit tests and turn it on as needed when things change or before releases. We don't want this test as part of the POST. Flash wears out after some number of erase and write cycles (often 100,000; this information is in the datasheet). Further, at least two of these tests have the potential to be destructive to our data.

Plus, we don't need to do this testing on boot. If the processor can communicate with the flash at all, then it is reasonable to believe the flash is working. (You can check basic communication by putting a header in the flash that includes a known key, a version, and/or a checksum.)

There are two ways to access this flash part: individual bytes and multibyte blocks. Later, when running the real code, you'll probably want to use the faster block access. During initial bring-up and testing, you might want to start out with the simpler byte method to ensure a good foundation for your driver.

Test 1: Read existing data

Testing that you can read data from the flash actually verifies that the I/O lines are configured to work as a SPI port, that the SPI port is configured properly, and that you understand the basics of the flash command protocol.

For this test, we'll read out as much data as we can from the sector so we can write it back later. Here is the start of `FlashTest`:

```
// Test 1: Read existing data in a block to make sure it's possible
dataLen = FlashRead(startAddress, memory, memLength);
if (dataLen != memLength) {
  // read less than desired, note error
  Log(LogUnitTest, LogLevelError, "Flash test: truncation on byte read");
  memLength = dataLen;
  error++;
}
```

Note that there is no verification of the data, since we don't know if this function is being run with an empty flash chip. If you were writing a POST, you might do this read and then check that the data is valid (and then stop testing, because that is enough for a power-on check).

Test 2: Byte access

The next test starts by erasing the data in the sector. Then it fills the flash with data, writing one byte at a time. We want to write it with something that changes so we can make sure the command is effective. I like to write it with an offset based on the address. (The offset tells me that I'm not accidentally reading the address back.)

```
FlashEraseSector(startAddress);

// want to put in an incrementing value but don't want it to be
// the address
addValue = 0x55;
for (i=0; i< memLength; i++) {
  value = i + addValue;
  dataLen = FlashWrite(startAddress + i, &value, 1);
  if (dataLen != 1) {
    Log (LogUnitTest, LogLevelError, "Flash test: byte write error.");
    error++;
  }
}
```

To complete this check, you need to read the data back, byte by byte, and verify the value is as expected at each address (`address + addValue`).

Test 3: Block access

Now that the flash contains our newly written data, confirm that block access works by putting back the original data. That means starting with an erase of the sector again:

```
FlashEraseSector(startAddress);
dataLen = FlashWrite(startAddress, memory, memLength);
if (dataLen != memLength) {
  LogWithNum(LogUnitTest, LogLevelError,
    "Flash test: block write error, len ", dataLen);
  error++;
}
```

Finally, verify this data using another byte-by-byte read. We know that works from test 2. If the results are good, then we know that block writes work from this test and that block reads work from test 1. The number of errors is returned to the higher-level verification code.

This tests the flash driver software. It doesn't check that the flash has no sticky bits (bits that never change, even though they should). A manufacturing test can confirm that all bits change, but most flash gets verified that way before it gets to you.

Test wrap-up

If the board passes these three tests, you can be confident that the flash hardware and software both work, satisfying your need for a bring-up test and a unit test.

For most forms of memory, the pattern we've seen here is a good start:

1. Read the original data.
2. Write some changing but formulaic data.
3. Verify the data.
4. Rewrite the original.
5. Verify the original.

However, there are many other types of peripherals—more than I can cover here. Although automated tests are best, some will need external verification, such as an LCD that gets a pattern of colors and lines to verify its driver. Some tests will need fake external inputs so that a sensing element can be checked.

For each of your peripherals and software subsystems, try to figure out which tests will give you the confidence that it is working reliably and as expected. It doesn't sound difficult, but it can be. Designing good tests is one of those things that can make your software great.

Command and Response

Let's say you take the advice in the previous section and create test functions for each piece of your hardware. During bring-up, you've made a special image that executes each test on power-up. If one of them fails, you and the hardware engineer may want to run just that test over and over. So you recompile and reload. Then you want to do the same thing for a different test. So you recompile and reload again. And then again for yet another test. This recompile–reload loop is getting old. Wouldn't it be easier to send commands to your embedded system and have it run the tests as needed?

Embedded systems often do not have the rich user interface experience found in computers (or even smartphones). Many are controlled through a command line. Even those with screens often use a command-line interface for debugging. The first part of this section describes how to send commands in C using function pointers in a command-handling jump table. This nifty problem-and-solution gives me an opportunity to show the standard command pattern, which is a useful pattern to know, whatever language you are using.

Figure 3-15 shows some high-level goals for our automated command handler, one that will let us send a command from a serial terminal on a PC and get a response from the unit under test.

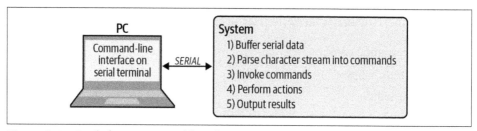

Figure 3-15. Goals for a command handler

Once you have some data read in, the code will need to figure out which function to call. A small interpreter with a command table will make the lives of those around you easier. By separating the interface from the actual test code, you will be able to extend it more easily in unforeseen directions.

Creating a command

Let's start with a small list of commands you want to implement:

Version of the code
> Outputs the version information

Test the flash
> Runs the flash unit test, printing out the number of errors upon completion

---

Blink LED
   Sets an LED to blink at a given frequency

Help
   Lists available commands with one-line descriptions

Once you have a few commands implemented, adding commands as you go along should be pretty easy.

I'm going to show how to do this in C because it is probably the scariest way you'd implement it. Object-oriented languages such as C++ and Java offer friendlier ways to implement this functionality using objects. However, the C method will often be smaller and generally faster, so factor that in when you are choosing how to implement this pattern. For readers unfamiliar with C's function pointers, the sidebar "Function Pointers Aren't So Scary" on page 78 provides an introduction.

Each command we can call will be made up of a name, a function to call, and a help string:

```
typedef void(*functionPointerType)(void);
struct commandStruct {
  char const *name;
  functionPointerType execute;
  char const *help;
};
```

An array of these will provide our list of commands:

```
const struct commandStruct commands[] ={
  {"ver", CmdVersion,
    "Display firmware version"},
  {"flashTest", CmdFlashTest,
    "Runs the flash unit test, prints number of errors upon completion"},
  {"blinkLed", CmdBlinkLed,
    "Sets the LED to blink at a desired rate (parameter: frequency (Hz))"},
  {"help", CmdHelp,
    "Prints out help messages"},
  {"",0,""} //End of table indicator. MUST BE LAST!!!
};
```

The command execution functions CmdVersion, CmdFlashTest, CmdBlinkLed, and CmdHelp are implemented elsewhere. The commands that take parameters will have to work with the parser to get their parameters from the character stream. Not only does this simplify this piece of code, but it also gives greater flexibility, allowing each command to set the terms of its use, such as the number and type of parameters.

Note that the list in the help command is a special command that prints out the name and help strings of all items in the table.

Function Pointers Aren't So Scary

Can you imagine a situation where you don't know what function you want to run until your program is already running? For example, say you want to run one of several signal-processing algorithms on some data coming from your sensors. You can start off with a switch statement controlled by a variable:

```
switch (algorithm) {
  case kFIRFilter:
    return fir(data, dataLen);
  case kIIRFilter:
    return iir(data, dataLen);
  ...
}
```

Now, when you want to change your algorithm, you send a command or push a button to make the algorithm variable change. If the data gets processed continually, the system still has to run the switch statement, even if you didn't change the algorithm.

In object-oriented languages, you can use a reference to an interface. Each algorithm object would implement a function of the same name (for this signal-processing example, we'd call it filter). Then, when the algorithm needed to change, the caller object would change. Depending on the language, the interface implementation could be indicated with a keyword or through inheritance.

C doesn't have those features (and using inheritance in C++ may be verboten in your system due to compiler constraints). So we come to function pointers, which can do the same thing.

To declare a function pointer, you need the prototype of a function that will go in it. For our switch statement, that would be a function that took a data pointer and data length and didn't return anything. However, it could return results by modifying its first argument. The prototype for one of the functions would look like this:

```
void fir(uint16_t* data, uint16_t dataLen);
```

Now take out the name of the function and replace it with a star and a generic name surrounded by parentheses:

```
void (*filter)(uint16_t* data, uint16_t dataLen);
```

Instead of changing your algorithm variable and calling the switch statement to select a function, you can change the algorithm only when needed and call the function pointer. There are two ways to do this, the implicit method (on the left here) and the explicit method (right). They are equivalent, just different forms of syntax:

```
filter = fir;            // or filter = &fir;
filter(data, dataLen);   // or (*filter)(data,dataLen);
```

Once you are comfortable with the idea of function pointers, they can be a powerful asset when the code needs to adapt to its environment. Some common uses for function pointers include the command structure described in this chapter, callbacks to indicate a completed event, and mapping button presses to context-sensitive actions.

One caution: egregiously excessive use of function pointers can cause your processor to be slow. Some processors try to predict where your code is going and load the appropriate instructions before execution. Function pointers inhibit branch prediction because the processor can't guess where you'll be after the call. On the other hand, if you are trying to optimize your code to this extent, perhaps skip to Chapter 11.

However, other methods of selecting on-the-fly function calls also interrupt branch prediction (such as the switch statement we started with). Unless you have reached the stage of hand tuning the assembly code, it generally isn't worth worrying about the slight slowdown caused by the awesome powers of the function pointer.

Invoking a command

Once the client on the command line indicates which command to run by sending a string, you need to choose the command and run it. To do that, go through the table, looking for a string that matches. Once you find it, call the function pointer to execute that function.

Compared to the previous section, this part seems almost too easy. That is the goal. Embedded systems are complex, sometimes hideously so, given their tight constraints and hidden dependencies. The goal of this (and many other patterns) is to isolate the complexity. You can't get rid of the complexity; a system that does nothing isn't very complex, but it isn't very useful either. There is still a fair amount of complexity in setting up the table and the parsing code to use it, but those details can be confined to their own spaces.

Command Pattern

What we've been looking at is a formal, classic design pattern. Where the command handler I've described is a tactical solution to a specific problem, the *command pattern* is the strategy that guides it and other designs like it.

The overarching goal of this pattern is to decouple the command processing from the actual action to be taken. The command pattern shows an interface for executing operations. Anytime you see a situation where one piece of a system needs to make requests of another piece without the intermediaries knowing the content of those requests, consider the command pattern. As Figure 3-16 shows, there are four pieces:

Client
> A table that maps the receivers onto commands. Clients create concrete command objects and create the association between receivers and command objects.

A client may run at initialization (as was done in our example by creating an array) or create the associations on the fly.

Invoker

Parser code that determines when the command needs to run and executes it. It doesn't know anything about the receiver. It treats every command the same.

Command

An item from the client table that is an interface for executing an operation. This is a C++ class, a Java interface, or a C structure with a function pointer. An instantiation of the command interface is called a concrete command.

Receiver

A function that knows how to service the request. Running the receiver code is the goal of the person (or other device) that sent the command.

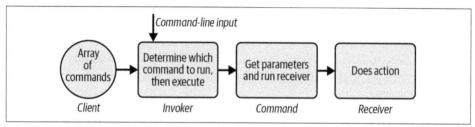

Figure 3-16. How the command handler works

Figure 3-17 shows the purpose of each element of the command pattern.

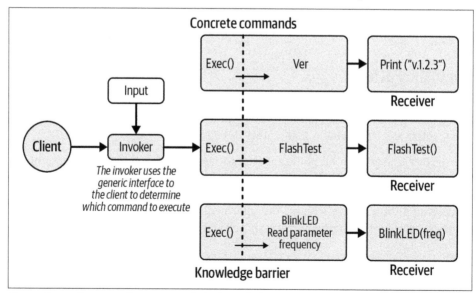

Figure 3-17. Command pattern and the knowledge barrier

Consider the client as protecting the secrets of the system by disguising all of the commands to look alike. This decouples the commands from your code, making it much easier to expand later (which you will need to do).

Dealing with Errors

The longevity of code shocks me. For all that it sometimes seems like we are rewriting the same old things in different ways, one day you may discover that a piece of code you wrote at a start-up over a decade ago is being used by a Fortune 500 company. Once it works well enough, why fix the depths of code?

It only makes it scarier to know that at some point your code will fail. An error will occur, either from something you wrote or from an unexpected condition in the environment. There are two ways to handle errors. First, the system can enter a state of *graceful degradation*, where the software does the best it can. Alternatively, the system could fail loudly and immediately. Long-term, sensor-type systems require the former, whereas medical systems require the latter. Either way, a system should fail safely.

But how to implement either one? More importantly, what criteria should be used to determine which subsystems implement which error-handling method? What you do depends on your product; my goal is to get you to think about error handling during design.

Consistent Methodology

Functions should handle errors as best they can. For example, if a variable can be out of range, the range should be fixed and the error logged as appropriate. Functions can return errors to allow a caller to deal with the problems. The caller should check and deal with the error, which may mean passing it further upstream in a multilayered application. In many cases, if the error is not important enough to check, it is not important enough to return. On the other hand, there are cases where you want to return a diagnostic code that is used only in testing. It can be noted in the comments that the returned error code is not for normal usage or should be used only in `assert()` calls.

`assert()` is not always implemented in embedded systems, but it is straightforward to implement in a manner appropriate to the system. This might be a message printed out on the debugger console, a print to a system console or log, a breakpoint instruction such as `BKPT`, or even an I/O line or LED that toggles on an error condition. Printing changes the embedded system's timing, so it is often beneficial to separate the functions for error communications to allow other methods of output (e.g., an LED).

A breakpoint instruction tells the processor to stop running if the debugger is attached. A *programmatic breakpoint* can be compiled into your code. Usually it is an assembly function, often hidden by a macro:

```
#define BKPT() __asm__("BKPT")
#define BKPT() __asm__("bkpt #0")
#define BKPT() __asm__("break")
```

These breakpoints get compiled into your code (they don't count against your limited hardware breakpoint budget!). This can make it easier to walk through code, particularly if you are seeing errors only upon certain conditions.

Error return codes for an application or system should be standardized over the codebase. A single high-level *errorCodes.h* file (or some such) can be created to provide consistent errors in an enumerated format. Some suggested error codes are:

- No error (should always be 0)
- Unknown error (or unrecognized error)
- Bad parameter
- Bad index (pointer outside range or null)
- Uninitialized variable or subsystem
- Catastrophic failure (this may cause a processor reset unless it is in development mode, in which case it probably causes a breakpoint or spin loop)

There should be a minimum number of errors (generic errors) so that the application can interpret them. While you could use something like UART_FAILED_TO_INIT_SEC OND_PARAM_TOO_HIGH, generalization makes error handling easier. If the error PARAME TER_BAD occurs in a subsystem, you have a good place to start to look for it. Essentially, by keeping it simple, you make sure to hand the developer the important information (the existence of a bug), and additional debugging can dig into where and why.

Error Checking Flow

Returning errors doesn't do anyone any good if the errors aren't handled. Too often we code for the working case, ignoring the other paths. Are we hoping that the errors just never occur? That's silly.

On the other hand, it gets pretty tedious to handle individual errors when the function should skip to the end and return its own error, bubbling up the problem to a higher level. While some folks use a nested `if`/`else` statement, I usually prefer to flow through the function, trying to keep the error redundant enough that it is generally ignorable in the good path flow:

```
error = FunctionSay();
if (error == NO_ERROR) {
  error = FunctionHello();
}
if (error == NO_ERROR) {
  error = FunctionWorld();
}
if (error != NO_ERROR) {
  // handle error state
}
return error;
```

This allows you to call several functions at a time, checking the error at the end instead of at each call.

Error-Handling Library

An error-handling library is another option:

```
ErrorSet(&globalErrorCode, error);
```

or

```
ErrorSet(&globalErrorCode, FunctionFoo());
```

The ErrorSet function would not overwrite a previous error condition if this function returned without a failure. As before, this allows you to call several functions at a time, checking the error at the end instead of at each call.

In such an error-handling library, there would be four functions, implemented and used as makes sense for the application: ErrorSet, ErrorGet, ErrorPrint, and Error Clear. The library should be designed for debugging and testing, though the mechanism should be left in place, even when development is complete. For example, ErrorPrint may change from writing out a log of information on a serial port to a small function that just toggles an I/O line. This is not an error for the final user to deal with; it is for a developer confronted with production units that do not perform properly.

 If this sounds vaguely familiar, it may be because this is what standard C/C++ libraries do. If your file fails to open with fopen, not only does it return NULL to tell you that an error occurred, fopen also puts an error code into errno with more information about what went wrong. Even for most embedded systems, you can use perror and strerror to get text versions of the error codes. Of course, as with my version above, if you don't clear errno, you may be looking at old errors.

Debugging Timing Errors

When debugging hardware/software interactions (or any software that is time critical), serial output such as logging or `printf` can change the timing of the code. In many cases, a timing problem will appear (or disappear) depending on where your output statements and/or breakpoints are located. Debugging becomes difficult when your tools interfere with the problem.

One of the advantages to using an error library (or a logging library, as described in Chapter 2) is that you don't have to output the data; you can store it locally in RAM, which is usually a much faster proposition. In fact, if you are having trouble with timing, consider making a small buffer (4–16 bytes, depending on your RAM availability) to contain signals from the software (one or two bytes). In your code, fill the buffer at interesting trigger points (e.g., an `ASSERT` or `ErrorSet`). You can dump this buffer when the code exits the time-sensitive area. If you are most interested in the last error, use a circular buffer to continually capture the last few events (circular buffers are discussed in more detail in Chapter 7).

Alternatively, if you have some input into the board design, I highly recommend pushing for spare processor I/Os to be available on the board and easily accessible with a header. They will come in handy for debugging (especially tricky timing issues, where serial output breaks the timing), showing the status of the system in testing and profiling processor cycles. These are called *test points*. The best EEs will ask you how many you need as they work on the schematic. There will be more on their usage in Chapter 11.

Further Reading

If you want to learn more about handling hardware safely, reading schematics, and soldering, I suggest getting the latest edition of *Make: Electronics* by Charles Platt (O'Reilly). This step-by-step introduction is an easy read, though better if you follow along with components in hand.

For more information about getting from prototype to shipping units, I recommend Alan Cohen's *Prototype to Product: A Practical Guide for Getting to Market* (O'Reilly). It goes through all of the steps needed to go from a napkin sketch to a product.

Along those lines, but more focused on your personal career, is Camille Fournier's *The Manager's Path: A Guide for Tech Leaders Navigating Growth & Change* (O'Reilly). Even if you aren't a manager, this book talks about the things managers need to know, which will give you insight into how to present your work. This is the sort of book I read for a few chapters then put on my shelf until I receive a promotion, then read the next few chapters.

Adafruit and SparkFun are amazing resources, filled with well-documented tutorials combining hardware and software. Even better, their extensive GitHub repositories have *good* code. If they have code for a part similar to the one you're using, their code may hold the key to getting your driver to work.

Interview Question: Talking About Failure

Tell me about a project that you worked on that was successful. Then, tell me about a project that you worked on that was not so successful. What happened? How did you work through it? (Thanks to Kristin Anderson for this question.)

The goal of this question is not really about judging an applicant's previous successes and failures. The question starts there because the processes that lead to success (or failure) depend on knowledge, information, and communication. By talking about success or failure, the applicant reveals what they learn from available information, how they seek out information, and how they communicate important information to others on the team. If they can understand the big picture and analyze the project's progress, they're more likely to be an asset to the team.

The successful half of the question is interesting to listen to, particularly when the interviewee is excited and passionate about their project. I want to hear about their part in making it successful and the process they used. However, like many of the more technical questions, the first half of the question is really about getting to the second half of the question: failure.

Did they understand all the requirements before jumping into the project, or were there perhaps communication gaps between the requirements set by the marketing group and the plans developed by the engineers? Did the applicant consider all the tasks and even perhaps Murphy's Law before developing a schedule and then add some time for risk?

Did they bring up anything relative to any risks or issues they faced and any mitigation strategies they considered? Some of these terms are program management terms, and I don't really expect the engineers to use all the right buzzwords. But I do expect them to go beyond talking about the technical aspects and be able to tell me other factors in successful projects.

Often, in talking about successful projects, an applicant will say they understood the requirements and knew how to develop the right project and make people happy. That is enough to go on to the next question.

Then, when I ask what went wrong, I really want to hear how the applicant evaluated the factors involved in trying for a successful project and whether they can tell me why they thought the project failed (poor communication, lack of clear goals, lack of clear requirements, no management support, etc.). There is no right or wrong answer; what I'm interested in is how they analyze the project to tell me what went wrong. (Though if they only take the time to blame everyone around them, I do get worried.)

I am disappointed by the interviewees who cannot think of an unsuccessful project, because no project goes perfectly, so I tend to think they weren't paying attention to the project as a whole. Understanding more than just what technical work they have to do makes an engineer a much better engineer.

CHAPTER 4

Inputs, Outputs, and Timers

Inputs, outputs, and timers form the basis for almost everything embedded systems do. Even the communication methods to talk to other components are made up of these (see bit-bang drivers in Chapter 7). In this chapter, I'm going to walk through a product development example. The goals will constantly change so it will feel like real life. That also lets us explore how to go from a simple system of a blinking light to debouncing buttons and dimming LEDs. Along the way, we'll see a lot about timers and how they do much more than measure time.

However, before we get started with world domination, err, I mean product development, you need to know a bit about registers, the interface from your software to the processor.

Handling Registers

To do anything with an I/O line, we need to talk to the appropriate register. As described in "Your Processor Is a Language" on page 56, you can think of registers as an API to the hardware. Described in the chip's user manual, registers come in all flavors to configure the processor and control peripherals. They are memory-mapped, so you can write to a specific address to modify a particular register. Often each bit in the register means something specific, which means we need to start using binary numbers to look at the values of specific bits.

Binary and Hexadecimal Math

Becoming familiar with basic binary and hexadecimal (hex) math will make your career in embedded systems far more enjoyable. Shifting individual bits around is great when you need to modify only one or two places. But if you need to modify the whole variable, hex comes in handy because each digit in hex corresponds to a nibble (four bits) in binary (see Table 4-1). (Yes, of course a nibble is half of a byte. Embedded folks like their puns.)

Table 4-1. Binary and hexadecimal math

Binary	Hex	Decimal	Remember this number
0000	0	0	This one is easy.
0001	1	1	This is (1 << 0).
0010	2	2	This is (1 << 1). Shifting is the same as multiplying by $2^{shiftValue}$.
0011	3	3	Notice how in binary this is just the sum of one and two.
0100	4	4	(1 << 2) is a 1 shifted to the left by two zeros.
0101	5	5	This is an interesting number because every other bit is set.
0110	6	6	See how this looks like you could shift the three over to the left by one? This could be put together as ((1 << 2)|(1 << 1)), or ((1 << 2) + (1 << 1)), or, most commonly, (3 << 1).
0111	7	7	Look at the pattern of binary bits. They are very repetitive. Learn the pattern, and you'll be able to generate this table if you need to.
1000	8	8	(1 << 3). See how the shift and the number of zeros are related? If not, look at the binary representation of 2 and 4.
1001	9	9	We are about to go beyond the normal decimal numbers. Because there are more digits in hexadecimal, we'll borrow some from the alphabet. In the meantime, 9 is just 8 + 1.
1010	A	10	This is another special number with every other bit set.
1011	B	11	See how the last bit goes back and forth from 0 to 1? It signifies even and odd.
1100	C	12	Note how C is just 8 and 4 combined in binary? So of course it equals 12.
1101	D	13	The second bit from the right goes back and forth from 0 to 1 at half the speed of the first bit: 0, then 0, then 1, then 1, then repeat.
1110	E	14	The third bit also goes back and forth, but at half the rate of the second bit.
1111	F	15	All of the bits are set. This is an important one to remember.

Note that with four bits (one hex digit) you can represent 16 numbers, but you can't represent the number 16. Many things in embedded systems are zero-based, including addresses, so they map well to binary or hexadecimal numbers.

A byte is two nibbles, the left one being shifted up (left) four spaces from the other. So 0x80 is (0x8 << 4).

A 16-bit word is made up of two bytes. We can get that by shifting the most significant byte up 8 bits, then adding it to the lower byte:

```
0x1234 = (0x12 << 8) + (0x34)
```

A 32-bit word is 8 characters long in hex, but 10 characters long in decimal. While this dense representation can make debug prints useful, the real reason we use hex is to make binary easier.

 Since memory is generally viewed in hex, some values are used to identify anomalies in memory. In particular, expect to see (and to use) 0xDEADBEEF or 0xDEADC0DE as an indicator (they are a lot easier to remember in hex than in decimal). Two other important bytes are 0xAA and 0x55. Because the bits in these numbers alternate, they are easy to see on an oscilloscope and good for testing when you want to see a lot of change in your values.

Bitwise Operations

As you work with registers, you will need to think about things at the bit level. Often, you'll turn specific bits on and off. If you've never used bitwise operations, now is the time to learn. Where the logical operator && commonly means AND, ! means NOT, and || means OR, these work on the idea that anything zero is false, and anything nonzero is true.

Bitwise operations operate on a bit-by-bit basis (see Table 4-2). For bitwise AND, if the two inputs have a bit set, then the output will as well. Other bits in the output will be zero. For OR, if either of the two inputs has a bit set, then the output will as well.

Table 4-2. Bitwise operations

Bitwise operation	Meaning	Syntax	Examples
AND	If both of the two inputs have a bit set, the output will as well.	&	0x01 & 0x02 = 0x00 0x01 & 0x03 = 0x01 0xF0 & 0xAA = 0xA0
OR	If either of the two inputs has a bit set, the output will as well.	|	0x01 | 0x02 = 0x03 0x01 | 0x03 = 0x03 0xFF | 0x00 = 0xFF
XOR	If only one of the two inputs has a bit set, the output will as well.	^	0x01 ^ 0x02 = 0x03 0x01 ^ 0x03 = 0x02 0xAA ^ 0xF5 = 0x5F
NOT	Every bit is set to its opposite.	~	~0x01 = 0xFE ~0x00 = 0xFF ~0x55 = 0xAA

XOR

XOR (exclusive or) is a somewhat magical bitwise operation. It doesn't have a logical analog and isn't used as much as the others we've seen, so remembering it can be tough.

Imagine your nemesis puts on his blog that he is going to the movies this evening, which is just what you had planned to do. If you both avoid going, the movie won't play, because there won't be an audience. One of you can go to see the movie. But if you both go, the movie won't play (the theater is still not happy about the fuss you caused last time). This is the XOR operator in action.

XOR is often represented as a Venn diagram, as shown in Figure 4-1. Note that XOR is true inside each circle, but not where they overlap.

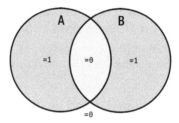

Figure 4-1. XOR Venn diagram

XOR has some nifty applications in computer graphics and finding overflows (math errors).

If it is Input A, we are using only the bottom half of the Table 4-3. If the register (Input B) already has that pin set, what would the output be?

Table 4-3. The truth table of XOR

Input A	Input B	Output
0	0	0
0	1	1
1	0	1
1	1	0

Test, Set, Clear, and Toggle

Hex and bitwise operations are only a lead-up to being able to interact with registers. If you want to know if a bit is set, you need to bitwise AND with the register:

```
test = register & bit;
test = register & (1 << 3); // check 3rd bit in the register
test = register & 0x08;     // same, different syntax
```

Note that the `test` variable will either equal zero (bit is not set in the register) or `0x08` (bit is set). It isn't true and false, though you can use it in normal conditionals as they only check for zero or nonzero.

If you want to set a bit in a register, OR it with the register:

```
register = register | bit;
register = register | (1 << 3); // turn on the 3rd bit in the register
register |= 0x08;               // same, different syntax
```

Clearing a bit is quite a bit more confusing because you want to leave the other bits in the register unchanged. The typical strategy is to invert the bit we want to clear using bitwise NOT (~). Then AND the inverted value with the register. This way, the other bits remain unchanged:

```
register = register & ~bit;
register = register & ~(1 << 3); // turn off the 3rd bit in the register
register &= ~0x08;               // same, different syntax
```

If you wanted to toggle a bit, you could check its value and then set or clear it as needed. For example:

```
test = register & bit;
if (test) {                        // bit is set, need to clear it
    register = register & ~bit;
} else {                           // bit is not set, need to set it
    register = register | bit;
}
```

However, there is another way to toggle a bit using the XOR operation:

```
register = register ^ bit;
register = register ^ (1 << 3);
```

If the register has the `0x08` bit set, XOR will see two ones and will output zero for that bit. If the register didn't have the bit set, the XOR will see a one and a zero, outputting a one for that bit. The other bits in the register won't be changed because only the single bit is set in the second input, and the others are zero.

Enough review. You will need to know these operations to use registers. If this isn't something you are comfortable with, there are resources at the end of the chapter for you to learn more or practice.

Toggling an Output

Marketing has come to you with an idea for a product. When you see through the smoke and mirrors, you realize that all they need is for a light to blink.

Most processors have pins whose digital states can be read (input) or set (output) by the software. These go by the name of I/O pins, general-purpose I/O (GPIO), digital I/O (DIO), and, occasionally, general I/O (GIO). The basic use case is usually straightforward, at least when an LED is attached:

1. Initialize the pin to be an output (as an I/O pin, it could be input or output).

2. Set the pin high when you want the LED on. Set the pin low when you want the LED off. (Although the LED can also be connected to be on when the pin is low, this example will avoid inverted logic.)

Throughout this chapter, I'll give you examples from three different user manuals so you get an idea of what to expect in your processor's documentation. Microchip's ATtiny AVR microcontroller manual describes an 8-bit microcontroller with plenty of peripherals. The TI MSP430x2xx user's guide describes a 16-bit RISC processor designed to be ultra low power. The STMicroelectronics STM32F103xx reference manual describes a 32-bit Arm Cortex microcontroller. You won't need these documents to follow along, but I thought you might like to know the processors that the examples are based upon.

Setting the Pin to Be an Output

Getting back to marketing's request to toggle an LED, most I/O pins can be either inputs or outputs. The first register you'll need to set will control the direction of the pin so it is an output. First, determine which pin you will be changing. To modify the pin, you'll need to know the pin name (e.g., "I/O pin 2," not its number on the processor (e.g., pin 12). The names are often inside the processor in schematics, while the pin number is on the outside of the box (as shown in Figure 4-2).

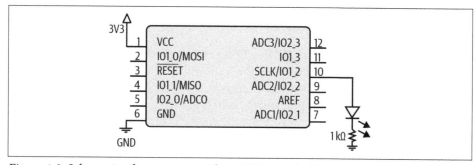

Figure 4-2. Schematic of a processor with an LED attached

The pins may have multiple numbers in their name, indicating a port (or bank) and a pin in that port. (The ports may also be letters instead of numbers.) In the figure, the LED is attached to processor pin 10, which is named "SCLK/IO1_2." This pin is shared between the SPI port (remember, this is a communication method, which we'll discuss in Chapter 7) and the I/O subsystem (IO1_2). The user manual will tell you whether the pin is an I/O by default or a SPI pin (and how to switch between them). Another register may be needed to indicate the purpose of the pin. Most vendors are good about cross-referencing the pin setup, but if it is shared between peripherals, you may need to look in the peripheral section to turn off unwanted functionality. In our example, we'll say the pin is an I/O by default.

In the I/O subsystem, it is the second pin (2) of the first bank (1). We'll need to remember that and to make sure the pin is used as an I/O pin and not as a SPI pin. Your processor user manual will describe more. Look for a section with a name like "I/O Configuration," "Digital I/O Introduction," or "I/O Ports." If you have trouble finding the name, look for the word "direction," which tends to be used to describe whether you want the pin to be an input or an output.

Once you find the register in the manual, you can determine whether you need to set or clear a bit in the direction register. In most cases, you need to set the bit to make the pin an output. You could determine the address and hardcode the result:

```
*((int*)0x0070C1) |= (1 << 2);
```

However, please don't do that.

The processor or compiler vendor will almost always provide a header file or a *hard-ware abstraction layer* (*HAL*, which includes a header file) that hides the memory map of the chip so you can treat registers as global variables. If the vendor didn't give you a header file, make one for yourself, so that your code looks more like one of these lines:

STM32F103 processor
```
GPIOA->CRL |= 1 << 2;   // set IOA_2 to be an output
```

MSP430 processor
```
P1DIR |= BIT2;          // set IO1_2 to be an output
```

ATtiny processor
```
DDRB |= 0x4;            // set IOB_2 to be an output
```

Note that the register names are different for each processor, but the effect of the code in each line is the same. Each processor has different options for setting the second bit in the byte (or word).

In each of these examples, the code is reading the current register value, modifying it, and then writing the result back to the register. This read-modify-write cycle needs to happen in *atomic* chunks, meaning they need to execute without interruptions or any other processing between steps. If you read the value, modify it, and then do some other stuff before writing the register, you run the risk that the register has changed and the value you are writing is out of date. The register modification will change the intended bit, but also might have unintended consequences.

Turning On the LED

The next step is to turn on the LED. Again, we'll need to find the appropriate register in the user manual:

STM32F103 processor

```
        GPIOA->ODR |= (1 << 2);      // IOA_2 high
```

MSP430 processor

```
        P1OUT |= BIT2;               // IO1_2 high
```

ATtiny processor

```
        PORTB |= 0x4;                // IOB_2 high
```

The GPIO hardware abstraction layer header file provided by the processor vendor shows how the raw addresses get masked by some programming niceties. In STM32F103x6, the I/O registers are accessed at an address through a structure (I've reorganized and simplified the file):

```
typedef struct
{
  __IO uint32_t CRL;  // Port configuration (low)
  __IO uint32_t CRH;  // Port configuration (high)
  __IO uint32_t IDR;  // Input data register
  __IO uint32_t ODR;  // Output data register
  __IO uint32_t BSRR; // Bit set/reset register
  __IO uint32_t BRR;  // Bit reset register
  __IO uint32_t LCKR; // Port configuration lock
} GPIO_TypeDef;

#define PERIPH_BASE         0x40000000UL
#define APB2PERIPH_BASE     (PERIPH_BASE + 0x00010000UL)
#define GPIOA_BASE          (APB2PERIPH_BASE + 0x00000800UL)
#define GPIOA               ((GPIO_TypeDef *)GPIOA_BASE)
```

The header file describes many registers we haven't looked at. These are also in the user manual section, with a lot more explanation. I prefer accessing the registers via the structure because it groups related functions together, often letting you work with the ports interchangeably.

Once we have the LED on, we'll need to turn it off again. You just need to clear those same bits, as shown in "Test, Set, Clear, and Toggle" on page 91:

STM32F103 processor

```
        GPIOA->ODR &= ~(1 << 2);      // IO1_2 low
```

MSP430 processor

```
        P1OUT &= ~(BIT2);              // IO1_2 low
```

ATtiny processor

```
        PORTB &= ~0x4;                 // IOB_2 low
```

Blinking the LED

To finish our program, all we need to do is put it all together. The pseudocode for this is as follows:

```
main:
    initialize the direction of the I/O pin to be an output
loop:
    set the LED on
    do nothing for some period of time
    set the LED off
    do nothing for the same period of time
    repeat loop
```

Once you've programmed it for your processor, you should compile, load, and test it. You might want to tweak the delay loop so the LED looks about right. It will probably require several tens of thousands of processor cycles, or the LED will blink faster than you can perceive it.

Troubleshooting

If you have a debugging system such as JTAG set up, finding out why your LED won't turn on is likely to be straightforward. Otherwise, you may have to use the process of elimination.

First, double-check your math. Even if you are completely comfortable with hex and bit shifting, a typo is always possible. In my experience, typos are the most difficult bugs to catch, often harder than memory corruptions. Check that you are using the correct pin on the schematic. And make sure there is power to the board. (You may think that advice is funny, but you'd be surprised at how often this plays a role!)

Next, check to see whether a pin is shared between different peripherals. While we said that the pin was an I/O by default, if you are having trouble, check to see if there is an alternate function that may be set in the configuration register.

As long as you have the manual open, verify that the pin is configured properly. If the LED isn't responding, you'll need to read the peripherals chapter of the user manual. Processors are different, so check that the pin doesn't need additional configuration (e.g., a power control output) or have a feature turned on by default (do not make the GPIO an interrupt by accident).

Most processors have I/O as a default because that is the simplest way for their users (us!) to verify the processor is connected correctly. However, particularly with low-power processors, you will want to keep all unused subsystems off to avoid power consumption. (And other special-purpose processors may have other default functionality.) The user manual will tell you more about the default configuration and how to change it. There are often other registers that need a bit set (or cleared) to make a pin act as an I/O.

Sometimes the clocks need to be configured to let the I/O subsystem work correctly (or to make a delay function go slow enough that you can see the toggling). If you still have trouble, look for the vendor's examples and identify any differences.

Next, make sure the system is running your code. Do you have another way to verify that the code being run is the code that you compiled? If you have a debug serial port, try incrementing the revision to verify that the code is getting loaded. If that doesn't work, make sure your build system is using the correct processor for the target.

Make the code as simple as possible to be certain that the processor is running the function handling the LEDs. Eliminate any noncritical initialization of peripherals in case the system is being delayed while waiting for a nonexistent external device. Turn off interrupts and asserts, and make sure the watchdog is off (see "Watchdog" on page 164).

With many microcontrollers, pins can sink more current than they can source (provide). Therefore, it is not uncommon for the pin to be connected to the cathode rather than the anode of the LED. In these instances, you turn on an LED by writing a zero rather than a one. This is called *inverted logic*. Check your schematic to see if this is the case.

If the output still doesn't work, consider whether there is a hardware-related issue. First, double-check that the LED is connected to the chip pin that you think it is. Then, if possible, run your software on multiple boards to rule out an assembly-related defect. Even in hardware, it can be something simple (installing LEDs backward is pretty easy). It may be a design problem, such as the processor pin being unable to provide enough current to drive the LED; the datasheet (or user manual) might be able to tell you this. There might be a problem on the board, such as a broken component or connection. With the high-density pins on most processors, it is very easy to short pins together. Ask for help, or get out your multimeter (or oscilloscope).

Separating the Hardware from the Action

Marketing liked your first prototype, though it may need to be tweaked a bit later. The system went from a prototype board to a PCB. During this process, somehow the pin number changed (to IO1_3). Both systems need to be able to run.

It is trivially simple to fix the code for this project, but for a larger system, the pins may be scrambled to make way for a new feature. Let's look at how to make modifications simpler.

Board-Specific Header File

Using a board-specific header file lets you avoid hardcoding the pin. If you have a header file, you just have to change a value there instead of going through your code to change it everywhere it's referenced. The header file might look like this:

```
#define LED_SET_DIRECTION  (P1DIR)
#define LED_REGISTER       (P1OUT)
#define LED_BIT            (1 << 3)
```

The lines of code to configure and blink the LED can be processor-independent:

```
LED_SET_DIRECTION |= LED_BIT; // set the I/O to be output
LED_REGISTER |= LED_BIT;      // turn the LED on
LED_REGISTER &= ~LED_BIT;     // turn the LED off
```

That could get a bit unwieldy if you have many I/O lines or need the other registers. It might be nice to be able to give only the port (1) and position in the port (3) and let the code figure it out. The code might be more complex, but it is likely to save time (and bugs). For that, the header file would look like this:

```
// ioMapping_v2.h
#define LED_PORT 1
#define LED_PIN 3
```

If we want to recompile to use different builds for different boards, we can use three header files. The first is the old board pin assignments (*ioMapping_v1.h*). Next, we'll create one for the new pin assignment (*ioMapping_v2.h*). We could include the one we need in our main *.c* file, but that defeats the goal of modifying that code less. If we have the main file always include a generic *ioMapping.h*, we can switch the versions in the main file by including the correct header file:

```
// ioMapping.h
#if COMPILING_FOR_V1
#include "ioMapping_v1.h"
#elif COMPILING_FOR_V2
#include "ioMapping_v2.h"
#else
#error "No I/O map selected for the board. What is your target?"
#endif /* COMPILING_FOR_*/
```

Using a board-specific header file hardens your development process against future hardware changes. By sequestering the board-specific information from the functionality of the system, you are creating a more loosely coupled and flexible codebase.

Keeping the I/O map in Excel is a pretty common way to make sure the hardware and software engineers agree on the pin definitions. With a little bit of creative scripting, you can generate your version-specific I/O map from a CSV file to ensure your pin identifiers match those on the schematic.

I/O-Handling Code

Instead of writing directly to the registers in the code, we'll need to handle the multiple ports in a generic way. So far we need to initialize the pin to be an output, set the pin high so the LED is on, and set the pin low so the LED is off. Oddly enough, we have a large number of options for putting this together, even for such a simple interface.

In the implementation, the initialization function configures the pin to be an output (and sets it to be an I/O pin instead of a peripheral if necessary). With multiple pins, you might be inclined to group all of the initialization together, but that breaks the modularity of the systems.

Although the code will take up a bit more space, it is better to have each subsystem initialize the I/Os it needs. Then, if you remove or reuse a module, you have everything you need in one area. However, we've seen one situation where you should *not* separate interfaces into subsystems: the I/O mapping header file, where all of the pins are collected together to make the interface with the hardware more easily communicated.

Moving on with the I/O subsystem interface, setting a pin high and low could be done with one function: IOWrite(port, pin, high/low). Alternatively, this could be broken out so that there are two functions: IOSet(port, pin) and IOClear(port, pin). Both methods work. Imagine what our main function will look like in both cases.

The goal is to make the LED toggle. If we use IOWrite, we can have a variable that switches between high and low. In the IOSet and IOClear case, we'd have to save that variable and check it in the main loop to determine which function to call. Alternatively, we could hide IOSet and IOClear within another function called IOToggle. We don't have any particular constraints with our hardware, so we don't need to consider optimizing the code in this example. For education's sake, however, consider the options we are giving ourselves with these potential interfaces.

The IOWrite option does everything in one function, so it takes less code space. However, it has more parameters, so it takes more stack space, which comes out of RAM. Plus, it has to keep around a state variable (also RAM).

With the IOSet/IOClear/IOToggle option, there are more functions (more code space), but fewer parameters and possibly no required variables (less RAM). Note that the toggle function is no more expensive in terms of processor cycles than the set and clear functions.

This sort of evaluation requires you to think about the interface along another dimension. Chapter 11 will go over more details on how to optimize for each area. During the prototyping phase, it is too soon to optimize the code, but it is never too soon to consider how the code can be designed to allow for optimization later.

Main Loop

The modifications in the previous sections put the I/O-handling code in its own module, though the basics of the main loop don't change. The implementation might look like the following:

```
void main(void){
  IOSetDir(LED_PORT, LED_PIN, OUTPUT);
  while (1) {     // spin forever
    IOToggle(LED_PORT, LED_PIN);
    DelayMs(DELAY_TIME);
  }
}
```

The main function is no longer directly dependent on the processor. With this level of decoupling, the code is more likely to be reused in other projects. In (a) of Figure 4-3, the original version of software architecture is shown, with its only dependency being the processor HAL. The middle, labeled (b), is our current version. It is more complicated, but the separation of concerns is more apparent. Note that the header files are put off to the side to show that they feed into the dependencies.

Our next reorganization will create an even more flexible and reusable architecture, illustrated by (c).

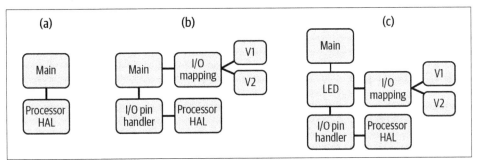

Figure 4-3. Comparison of different architectures in order of increasing abstraction

Facade Pattern

As you can imagine, our I/O interface is going to get more complex as the product features expand. (Currently we have only one output pin, so it can't really get any simpler.) In the long run, we want to hide the details of each subsystem. There is a standard software design pattern called *facade* that provides a simplified interface to a piece of code. The goal of the facade pattern is to make a software library easier to use. Along the lines of the metaphor I've been using in this book, that interfacing to the processor is similar to working with a software library, it makes sense to use the facade pattern to hide some details of the processor and the hardware.

In "Designing for Change" on page 21, we saw the adapter pattern, which is a more general version of the facade pattern. Whereas the adapter pattern acted as a translation between two layers, the facade does this by simplifying the layer below it. If you were acting as an interpreter between scientists and aliens, you might be asked to translate "x = y + 2, where y = 1." If you were an adapter pattern, you'd restate the same information without any changes. If you were a facade pattern, you'd probably say "x = 3" because it's simpler and the details aren't critical to using the information.

Hiding details in a subsystem is an important part of good design. It makes the code more readable and more easily tested. Furthermore, the calling code doesn't depend on the internals of the subsystem, so the underlying code can change, while leaving the facade intact.

A facade for our blinking LED would hide the idea of I/O pins from the calling code by creating an LED subsystem, as shown in the right side of Figure 4-3. Given how little the user needs to know about the LED subsystem, the facade could be implemented with only two functions:

LEDInit()
    Calls the I/O initialization function for the LED pin (replaces IOSetDir(…))

LEDBlink()
    Blinks the LED (replaces IOToggle(…))

Adding a facade makes your code easier to extend and change when requirements inevitably change.

The Input in I/O

Marketing wants to change the way the system blinks in response to a button. Now, when the button is held down, the system should stop blinking altogether.

Our schematic is not much more complex with the addition of a button (see Figure 4-4). Note that the button uses IO2_2 (I/O port 2, pin 2), which is denoted in the schematic with S1 (switch 1). The icon for a switch makes some sense; when you push it in, it conducts across the area indicated. Here, when you press the switch, the pin will be connected to ground.

Many processor I/O pins have internal pull-up resistors. When a pin is an output, the pull-ups don't do anything. However, when the pin is an input, the pull-up gives it a consistent value (1), even when nothing is attached. The existence and strength of the pull-up may be configurable, but this depends on your processor (and possibly on the particular pin). Most processors even have an option to allow internal pull-downs on a pin. In that case, our switch could have been connected to power instead of ground.

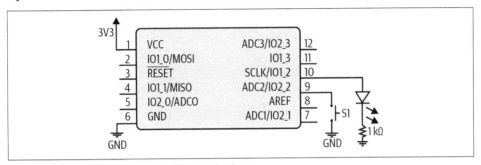

Figure 4-4. *Schematic with an LED and a button*

 Inputs with internal pull-ups take a bit of power, so if your system needs to conserve a few microamps, you may end up disabling the unneeded pull-ups (or pull-downs).

Your processor user manual will describe the pin options. The basic steps for setup are these:

1. Add the pin to the I/O map header file.
2. Configure it to be an input. Verify that it is not part of another peripheral.
3. Configure a pull-up explicitly (if necessary).

Once you have your I/O pin set up as an input, you'll need to add a function to use it—one that can return the state of the pin as high (true) or low (false):

```
boolean IOGet(uint8_t port, uint8_t pin);
```

When the button is pressed, it will connect to ground. This signal is *active low*, meaning that when the button is actively being held down, the signal is low.

To keep the details of the system hidden, we'll want to make a button subsystem that can use our I/O-handling module. On top of the I/O function, we can put another facade, so that the button subsystem will have a simple interface.

The I/O function returns the level of the pin. However, we want to know whether the user has taken an action. Instead of the button interface returning the level, you can invert the signal to determine whether the button is currently pressed. The interface could be:

void ButtonInit()
    Calls the I/O initialization function for the button

boolean ButtonPressed()
    Returns true when the button is down

As shown in Figure 4-5, both the LED and button subsystems use the I/O subsystem and I/O map header file. This is a simple illustration of how the modularization we did earlier in the chapter allows reuse.

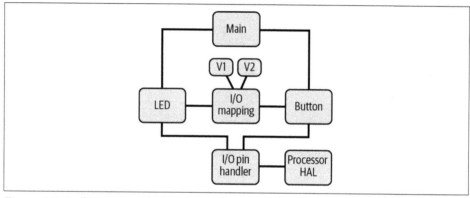

Figure 4-5. Architecture with the newly added button

At a higher level, there are a few ways to implement the main function. Here is one possibility:

```
main:
  initialize LED
  initialize button
loop:
  if button pressed, turn LED off
  else toggle LED
  do nothing for a period of time
  repeat
```

With this code, the LED won't go off immediately, but will wait until the delay has expired. The user may notice some lag between pushing the button and the LED turning off.

 A system that doesn't respond to a button press in less than a quarter of a second (250 ms) feels sluggish and difficult to use. A response time of 100 ms is much better, but still noticeable to impatient people. A response time under 50 ms feels very snappy.

To decrease the response time, we could check constantly to see whether the button was pressed:

```
loop:
  if button pressed, turn LED off
  else
    if enough time has passed,
      toggle LED
      clear how much time has passed
  repeat
```

Both of these methods check the button to determine whether it is pressed. This continuous querying is called *polling* and is easy to follow in the code. However, if the LED needs to be turned off as fast as possible, you may want the button to interrupt the normal flow.

Wait! That word (*interrupt*) is a really important one. I'm sure you've heard it before, and we'll get into a lot more detail soon (and again in Chapter 5). Before that, look at how simple the main loop can be if you use an interrupt to capture and handle the button press:

```
loop:
  if button not pressed, toggle LED
  do nothing for a period of time
  repeat
```

The interrupt code (aka *ISR*, or *interrupt service routine*) calls the function to turn off the LED. However, this makes the button and LED subsystems depend on each other, coupling the systems together in an unobvious way. There are times where you'll have to do this so an embedded system can be fast enough to handle an event.

Chapter 5 will describe how and when to use interrupts in more detail. This chapter will continue to look at them at a high level only.

Momentary Button Press

Instead of using the button to halt the LED, marketing wants to test different blink rates by tapping the button. For each button press, the system should decrease the length of the delay by 50% (until it gets to near zero, at which point it should go back to the initial delay).

In the previous assignment, all you had to check was whether the button was pressed down. This time you have to know both when the button will be pressed and when it will be released. Ideally, we'd like the switch to look like the top part of Figure 4-6. If it did, we could make the system note the rising edge of the signal and take an action there.

Interrupt on a Button Press

This might be another area where an interrupt can help us catch the user input so the main loop doesn't have to poll the I/O pin so quickly. The main loop becomes straightforward if it uses a global variable to learn about the button presses:

```
interrupt when the user presses the button:
  set global button pressed = true

loop:
  if global button pressed,
    set the delay period (reset or decrease it)
    set global button pressed = false
    turn LED off
  if enough time has passed,
    toggle LED
    clear how much time has passed
  repeat
```

The input pins on many processors can be configured to interrupt when the signal at the pin is at a certain level (high or low) or has changed (rising or falling edge). If the button signal looks like it does in the ideal button signal at the top of Figure 4-6, where would you want to interrupt? Interrupting when the signal is low may lead to multiple activations if the user holds the button down. I prefer to interrupt on the rising edge so that when the user presses the button down, nothing happens until they release it.

 To check a global variable accurately in this situation, you'll need the volatile C keyword, which perhaps you've never needed before now when developing software in C and C++. This keyword tells the compiler that the value of the variable or object can change unexpectedly and should never be optimized out. All registers and all global variables shared between interrupts and normal code should be marked as volatile. If your code works fine without optimizations and then fails when optimizations are on, check that the appropriate globals and registers are marked as volatile.

Configuring the Interrupt

Configuring a pin to trigger an interrupt is usually separate from configuring the pin as an input. Although both count as initialization steps, we want to keep the interrupt configuration separated from our existing initialization function. This way, you can save the complexity of interrupt configuration for the pins that require it (more in Chapter 5).

Configuring a pin for interrupting the processor adds three more functions to our I/O subsystem:

IOConfigureInterrupt(*port, pin, trigger type, trigger state*)
> Configures a pin to be an interrupt. The interrupt will trigger when it sees a certain trigger type, such as edge or level. For an edge trigger type, the interrupt can occur at the rising or falling edge. For a level trigger type, the interrupt can occur when the level is high or low. Some systems also provide a parameter for a callback, which is a function to be called when the interrupt happens; other systems will hardcode the callback to a certain function name, and you'll need to put your code there.

IOInterruptEnable(*port, pin*)
> Enables the interrupt associated with a pin.

IOInterruptDisable(*port, pin*)
> Disables the interrupt associated with a pin.

If interrupts are not per-pin (they could be per-bank), the processor may have a generic I/O interrupt for each bank, in which case the ISR will need to untangle which pin caused the interrupt. It depends on your processor. If each I/O pin can have its own interrupt, the modules can be more loosely coupled.

Debouncing Switches

Many buttons do not provide the clean signal shown in the ideal button signal in the top part of Figure 4-6. Instead, they look more like those labeled "Bouncy digital button signal." If you interrupted on that signal, your system could waste processor cycles by interrupting on the glitches at the start and end of the button press. *Switch bouncing* can be due to a mechanical or electrical effect.

Figure 4-6 also shows an analog view of what could happen when a button is pressed and only slowly goes into effect. (What really happens can be a lot more complicated, depending on whether the bouncing is due primarily to a mechanical or electrical cause.) Note that there are parts of the analog signal where the signal is neither high nor low, but somewhere in between. Since your I/O line is a digital signal, it can't represent this indeterminate value and can behave badly. A digital signal full of edges would cause the code to believe multiple presses happened per user action. The result would be inconsistent and frustrating to the user. Worse, interrupting on such a signal can lead to processor instability, so let's go back to polling the signal.

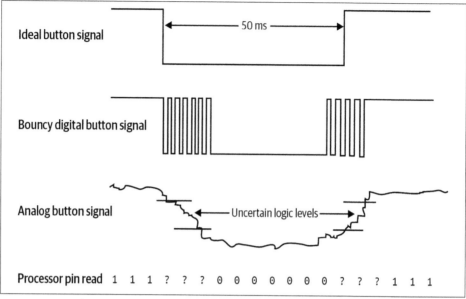

Figure 4-6. Different views of button signals

Debouncing is the technique used to eliminate the spurious edges. Although it can be done in hardware or software, we'll focus on software. See Jack Ganssle's excellent web article on debouncing (in "Further Reading" on page 123) for hardware solutions.

Many modern switches have a very short period of uncertainty. Switches have datasheets, too; check yours to see what the manufacturer recommends. Beware that trying to empirically determine whether you need debouncing might not be enough, as different batches of switches may act differently.

You still want to look for the rising edge of the signal, where the user releases the button. To avoid the garbage near the rising and falling edges, you'll need to look for a relatively long period of consistent signal. How long that is depends on your switch and how fast you want to respond to the user.

To debounce the switch, take multiple readings (aka samples) of the pin at a periodic interval several times faster than you'd like to respond. When there have been several consecutive, consistent samples, alert the rest of the system that the button has changed. See Figure 4-6; the goal is to read enough that the uncertain logic levels don't cause spurious button presses.

You will need three variables:

- The current raw reading of the I/O line
- A counter to determine how long the raw reading has been consistent
- The debounced button value used by the rest of the code

How long debouncing takes (and how long your system takes to respond to a user) depends on how high the counter needs to increment before the debounced button variable is changed to the current raw state. The counter should be set so that the debouncing occurs over a reasonable time for that switch.

If there isn't a specification for it in your product, consider how fast buttons are pressed on a keyboard. If advanced typists can type 120 words per minute, assuming an average of five characters per word, they are hitting keys (buttons) about 10 times per second. Figuring that a button is down half the time, you need to look for the button to be down for about 50 ms. (If you really are making a keyboard, you probably need a tighter tolerance because there are faster typists.)

For our system, the mythical switch has an imaginary datasheet stating that the switch will ring for no more than 12.5 ms when pressed or released. If the goal is to respond to a button held down for 50 ms or more, we can sample at 10 ms (100 Hz) and look for five consecutive samples.

Using five consecutive samples is pretty conservative. You may want to adjust how often you poll the pin's level so you need only three consecutive samples to indicate that the button state has changed.

 Strike a balance in your debouncing methodology: consider the cost of being wrong (annoyance or catastrophe?) and the cost of responding more slowly to the user.

In the previous falling-edge interrupt method of handling the button press, the state of the button wasn't as interesting as the change in state. To that end, we'll add a fourth variable to simplify the main loop:

```
read button:
  if raw reading is the same as debounced button value,
    reset the counter
  else
    decrement the counter
    if the counter is zero,
      set debounced button value to raw reading
      set changed to true
      reset the counter
```

```
main loop:
  if time to read button,
    read button
    if button changed and button is no longer pressed,
      set button changed to false
      set the delay period (reset or halve it)
  if time to toggle the LED,
    toggle LED
  repeat
```

Note that this is the basic form of the code. There are many options that can depend on your system's requirements. For example, do you want it to react quickly to a button press but slowly to a release? There is no reason the debounce counter needs to be symmetric.

In the preceding pseudocode, the main loop polls the button again instead of using interrupts. However, many processors have timers that can be configured to interrupt. Reading the button could be done in a timer to simplify the main function. The LED toggling could also happen in a timer. More on timers soon, but first, marketing has another request.

Runtime Uncertainty

Marketing has a number of LEDs to try out. The LEDs are attached to different pins. Use the button to cycle through the possibilities.

We've handled the button press, but the LED subsystem knows only about the output on pin 1_2 on the v1 board or 1_3 on the v2 board. Once you've initialized all the LEDs as outputs, you could put a conditional (or switch) statement in your main loop:

```
if count button presses == 0, toggle blue LED
if count button presses == 1, toggle red LED
if count button presses == 2, toggle yellow LED
```

To implement this, you'll need to have three different LED subsystems, or (more likely) your LED toggle function will need to take a parameter. The former represents a lot of copied code (almost always a bad thing), whereas the latter means the LED function will need to map the color to the I/O pin each time it toggles the LED (which consumes processor cycles).

Increasing Code Flexibility

Our goal here is to create a method to use one particular option from a list of several possible objects. Instead of making the selection each time (in the main loop or in the LED function), you can select the desired LED when the button is pressed. Then the LED toggle function is agnostic about which LED it is changing:

```
main loop:
  if time to read button,
    read button
    if button changed and button is no longer pressed,
      set button changed to false
      change LED variable

  if time to toggle the LED,
    toggle LED
  repeat
```

By adding a state variable, we use a little RAM to save a few processor cycles. State variables tend to make a system confusing, especially when the change LED variable section of the code is separated from toggle LED. Unraveling the code to show how a state variable controls the option can be tedious for someone trying to fix a bug (commenting helps!). The state variable simplifies the LED toggle function considerably, so there are times where a state variable is worth the complications it creates.

Dependency Injection

However, we can go beyond a state variable to something even more flexible. Earlier we saw that abstracting the I/O pins from the board saves us from having to rewrite code when the board changes. We can also use abstraction to deal with dynamic changes (such as which LED is to be used). For this, we'll use a technique called *dependency injection*.

Before, we were hiding the I/O pin in the LED code (creating a hierarchy of functions that depend only on the lower levels). With dependency injection, we'll remove that dependency by passing an I/O handler as a parameter to the LED initialization code. The I/O handler will know which pin to change and how to change it, but the LED code will know only how to call the I/O handler. See Figure 4-7.

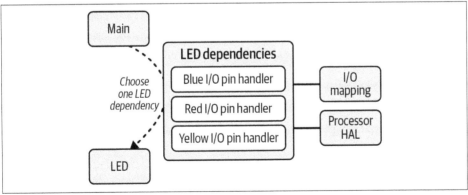

Figure 4-7. Dependency injection architecture for runtime uncertainty

An oft-used example to illustrate dependency injection relates engines to cars. The car, the final product, depends on an engine to move. The car and engine are made by the manufacturer. Though the car cannot choose which engine to install, the manufacturer can inject any of the dependency options that the car can use to get around (e.g., the 800-horsepower engine or the 20-horsepower one).

Tracing back to the LED example, the LED code is like the car and depends on the I/O pin to work, just as the car depends on the engine. However, the LED code may be made generic enough to avoid dependence on a particular I/O pin. This allows the main function (our manufacturer) to install an I/O pin appropriate to the circumstance instead of hardcoding the dependency at compile time. This technique allows you to compose the way the system works at runtime.

In C++ or other object-oriented languages, to inject the dependency, we pass a new I/O pin handler object to the LED whenever a button is pressed. The LED module would never know anything about which pin it was changing or how it was doing so. The variables to hide this are set at initialization time (but do remember that these are variables, consuming RAM and cluttering the code).

 A structure of function pointers is often used in C to achieve the same goal.

Dependency injection is a very powerful technique, particularly if your LED module were to do something a lot more complicated, for instance, output Morse code. If you passed in your I/O pin handler, you could reuse the Morse code LED output routine for any processor. Further, during testing, your I/O pin handler could print out every call that the LED module made to it instead of (or in addition to) changing the output pin.

However, the car engine example illustrates one of the major problems with dependency injection: complexity. It works fine when you only need to change the engine. But once you are injecting the wheels, the steering column, the seat covers, the transmission, the dashboard, and the body, the car module becomes quite complicated, with little intrinsic utility of its own.

The aim of dependency injection is to allow flexibility. This runs contrary to the goal of the facade pattern, which reduces complexity. In an embedded system, dependency injection will take more RAM and a few extra processor cycles. The facade pattern will almost always take more code space. You will need to consider the needs and resources of your system to find a reasonable balance.

Using a Timer

Using the button to change the blinking speed was helpful, but marketing has found a problem in the uncertainty introduced into the blink rate. Instead of cutting the speed of the LED in half, marketing wants to use the button to cycle through a series of precise blink rates: 6.5 times per second (Hz), 8.5 Hz, and 10 Hz.

This request seems simple, but it is the first time we've needed to do anything with time precision. Before, the system could handle buttons and toggle the LED generally when it was convenient. Now the system needs to handle the LED in real time. How close you get to "precise" depends on the parameters of your system, mainly on the accuracy and precision of your processor input clock. We'll start by using a timer on the processor to make it more precise than it was before, and then see if marketing can accept that.

Timer Pieces

In principle, a timer is a simple counter measuring time by accumulating a number of clock ticks. The more deterministic the master clock is, the more precise the timer can be. Timers operate independently of software execution, acting in the background without slowing down the code at all. To be technical, they are happening in the silicon gates that are part of the microcontroller.

To set the frequency of the timer, you will need to determine the clock input. This may be your processor clock (aka the *system clock*, or *master clock*), or it may be a different clock from another subsystem (for instance, many processors have a peripheral clock).

System Statistics

When embedded systems engineers talk about the stats of our systems to other engineers, we tend to use a shorthand consisting of the vendor, the processor (and its core), the number of bits in each instruction, and the system clock speed. Earlier in this chapter, I gave register examples from the STM32F103xx, MSP430, and ATtiny processor families. Systems with these processors could have stats like this:

- STM32F103 (Cortex-M3), 32-bit, 72 MHz
- Texas Instruments MSP430 G2201, 16-bit, 16 MHz
- Atmel ATtiny45, 8-bit, 4 MHz

That last number is the processor clock, which describes the theoretical number of instructions the processor can handle per second. The actual performance may be slower if your memory accesses can't keep up, or faster if you can use processor features to bypass overhead. The system clock is not the same as the oscillator on the

---

board (if you have one). Thanks to an internal PLL circuit, your processor speed might be much faster than an onboard oscillator. PLL stands for *phase lock loop* and denotes a way that a processor can multiply a slower clock (i.e., a slow oscillator) to get a faster clock (a processor clock). Because slower oscillators are generally cheaper (and consume less power) than faster ones, PLLs are ubiquitous.

Many small microcontrollers use an internal RC oscillator as their clock source. Although these make life easier for the hardware designer, their accuracy leaves a lot to be desired. Considerable drift can accumulate over time, and this can lead to errors in communication and in some real-time applications.

For example, the ATtiny45 has a maximum processor clock of 4 MHz. We want the LED to be able to blink at 10 Hz, but that means interrupting at 20 Hz (interrupt to turn it on, interrupt again to turn it off). This means we'll need a division of 200,000. The ATtiny45 is an 8-bit processor; it has two 8-bit timers and a 16-bit timer. Neither timer will count up that high (see the sidebar "System Statistics" on page 111). However, the chip designers recognized this issue and gave us another tool: the *prescaler register*, which divides the clock so that the counter increments at a slower rate.

 Many timers are zero-based instead of one-based, so for a prescaler that divides by 2, you put a 1 in the prescaler register. This whole timer thing is complicated enough without carrying it through the math above. Look in your processor manual to see which timer registers are zero-based.

The effect of the prescaler register is seen in Figure 4-8. The system clock toggles regularly. With a prescaler value of two, the prescaled clock (the input to our timer subsystem) toggles at half the system clock speed. The timer counts up. The processor notes when the timer matches the *compare register* (set to 3 in the diagram). When the timer matches, it may either continue counting up or reset, depending on the processor and the configuration settings.

Before getting back to the timer on the ATtiny45, note that the registers needed to make a timer work generally consist of the following:

Timer counter
  This holds the changing value of the timer (the number of ticks since the timer was last reset).

Compare register (or capture compare register or match register)
  When the timer counter equals this register, an action is taken. There may be more than one compare register for each timer.

Action register (or auto-reload register)

This register sets up an action to take when the timer and compare register are the same. (For some timers, these actions are also available when the timer overflows, which is like having a compare register set to the maximum value of the timer counter.) There are four types of possible actions to be configured (one or more may happen):

- Interrupt
- Stop or continue counting
- Reload the counter
- Set an output pin to high, low, toggle, or no change

Clock configure register (optional)

This register tells a subsystem which clock source to use, though the default may be the system clock. Some processors have timers that even allow a clock to be attached to an input pin. You can often choose whether to count up or down; I'll be using count-up with these examples but the process is similar for count-down.

Prescaler register

As shown in Figure 4-8, this reduces the fast incoming clock so that it runs more slowly, allowing timers to happen for slower events.

Control register

This sets the timer to start counting once it has been configured. Often the control register also has a way to reset the timer.

Interrupt register (may be multiple)

If you have timer interrupts, you will need to use the appropriate interrupt register to enable, clear, and check the status of each timer interrupt.

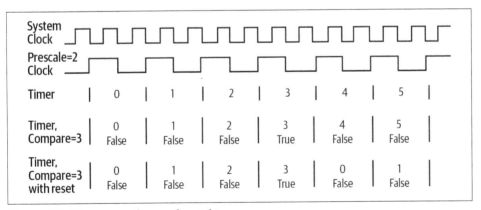

Figure 4-8. Timer prescaling and matching

Setting up a timer is processor-specific; the user manual generally will guide you through setting up each of these registers. Your processor user manual may give the registers slightly different names. A good way of understanding how to use a timer is to look at a chip vendor's sample code: it usually includes a few examples that configure timers in various ways. You should walk through the example code line-by-line, with the datasheet in front of you, to make sure you understand how the timer is configured.

 Instead of a compare register, your processor might allow you to trigger the timer actions only when the timer overflows. This is an implicit match value of two to the number of bits in the timer register, minus 1 (e.g., for an 8-bit timer, $(2^8) - 1 = 255$). By tweaking the prescaler, most timer values are achievable without too much error.

Doing the Math

I'm about to show the math needed to configure a timer. Feel free to skim or skip ahead to "Using Pulse-Width Modulation" and come back when you need the math. Also, check out this book's GitHub repository (*https://github.com/eleciawhite/making-embedded-systems*) for some calculators that let you go through this math without following my algebra here.

Timers are made to deal with physical time scales, so you need to relate a series of registers to an actual time. Remember that the frequency (e.g., 10 Hz) is inversely proportional to the period (e.g., 0.1 seconds).

The basic equation for the relationship between the interrupt frequency, clock input, prescaler, and compare register is:

```
interruptFrequency = clockIn / (prescaler * compare)
```

This is an optimization problem. You know the `clockIn` and the goal, `interruptFre quency`. You need to adjust the prescaler and compare registers until the interrupt frequency is close enough to the goal. If there were no other limitations, this would be an easy problem to solve (but it isn't always so easy).

How Many Bits in That Number?

Better than counting sheep, figuring out powers of two is often how I fall asleep. If you don't share the habit, you really should memorize some powers of two.

The number of different values a variable can have is 2 to the power of the number of bits it has (e.g., 8 bits offers 2^8, so 256 different values can be in an 8-bit variable). However, that number has to hold a 0 as well, so the maximum value of an 8-bit variable is 2^8-1, or 255. Even that is true only for unsigned variables. A signed variable

---

uses one bit for the sign (+/−), so an 8-bit variable would have only seven bits available for the value. Its maximum would be 2^7-1, or 127. Zero has to be represented only once, so the minimum value of a signed 8-bit variable is −128.

Bits	Power of two	Maximum value	Significance
4	$2^4 = 16$	15	A nibble
7	$2^7 = 128$	127	Signed 8-bit variable
8	$2^8 = 256$	255	Byte and an unsigned 8-bit variable
10	$2^{10} = 1{,}024$	1,023	Many peripherals are 10-bit
12	$2^{12} = 4{,}096$	4,095	Many peripherals are 12-bit
15	$2^{15} = 32{,}768$	32,767	Signed 16-bit variable
16	$2^{16} = 65{,}536$	65,535	Unsigned 16-bit variable
24	$2^{24} = 16{,}777{,}216$	~1.6 million	Color is often 24-bit
31	$2^{31} = 2{,}147{,}483{,}648$	~2 billion	Signed 32-bit variable
32	$2^{32} = 4{,}294{,}967{,}296$	~4 billion	Unsigned 32-bit variable

I usually fall asleep before 2^{20}, so I remember the higher-order numbers as estimates only. There will be times when a 32-bit number is too small to hold the information you need. Even a 64-bit number can fall down when you build a machine to do something as seemingly simple as shuffling cards.

Remember that variables (and registers) have sizes and that those sizes matter.

Returning to the ATtiny45's 8-bit timer, 4 MHz system clock, and goal frequency of 20 Hz, we can export the constraints we'll need to use to solve the equation:

- These are integer values, so the prescaler and compare register have to be whole numbers. This constraint is true for any processor.
- The compare register has to lie between 0 and 255 (because the timer register is eight bits in size).
- The prescaler on the ATtiny45 is 10 bits, so the maximum prescaler is 1,023. (The size of your prescaler may be different.)

The prescaler for this subsystem is not shared with other peripherals, so we don't need to be concerned about this potential constraint for our solution (yet).

There are several heuristics for finding a prescaler and compare register that will provide the interrupt frequency needed (see Figure 4-9).

I asked two math professors how to solve this problem in a generic manner. The answers I got back were interesting. The most interesting part was learning that this problem is NP-complete for two reasons: integers are involved, and it is a nonlinear, two-variable problem. Thanks, Professor Ross and Professor Patton!

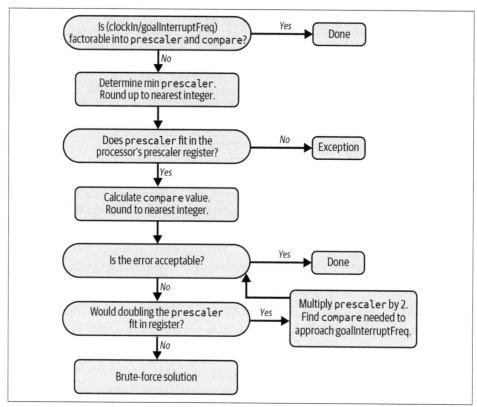

Figure 4-9. Heuristic for finding the register values for a goal interrupt frequency

We can determine the minimum prescaler by rearranging the equation and setting the compare register to its maximum value:

```
prescaler = clockIn / (compare * interruptFrequency)
          = 4 MHz / (255 * 20 Hz)
```

Unfortunately, the resulting prescaler value is a floating-point number (784.31). If you round up (785), you end up with an interrupt frequency of 19.98 Hz, which is an error of less than a tenth of a percent.

If you round down on the prescaler (784), the interrupt frequency will be above the goal, and you may be able to decrease the compare register to get the timer to be about right. With prescaler = 784 and compare = 255, the error is 0.04%. However,

---

marketing asked for high precision, and there are some methods to find a better prescaler.

First, note that you want the product of the prescaler and compare register to equal the clock input divided by the goal frequency:

```
prescaler * compare = clockIn / interruptFrequency = 4 MHz/20 Hz = 200,000
```

This is a nice, round number, easily factored into 1,000 (prescaler) and 200 (compare register). This is the best and easiest solution to optimizing the `prescaler` and `compare`: determine the factors of (`clockIn/interruptFrequency`) and arrange them into `prescaler` and `compare`. However, this requires the (`clockIn/interrupt Frequency`) to be an integer and the factors to split easily into the sizes allowed for the registers. It isn't always possible to use this method.

More Math: Difficult Goal Frequency

As we move along to another blink frequency requested by marketing (8.5 Hz, or an interrupt frequency of 17 Hz), the new target is:

```
prescaler * compare = clockIn / interruptFrequency = 4 MHz/17 Hz = 235294.1
```

There is no simple factorization of this floating-point number. We can verify that a result is possible by calculating the minimum prescaler (we did that earlier by setting the compare register to its maximum value). The result (923) will fit in our 10-bit register. We can calculate the percent error using the following:

```
error = 100 * (goal interrupt frequency - actual) / goal
```

With the minimum prescaler, we get an error of 0.03%. This is pretty close, but we may be able to get closer.

Set the prescaler to its maximum value, and see what the options are. In this case, a prescaler of 1,023 leads to a compare value of 230 and an error of less than 0.02%, which is a little better. But can we reduce the error further?

For larger timers, you might try a binary search for a good value, starting out with the minimum prescaler. Double it, and then look at the prescaler values that are +/– 1 to find a compare register that is the closest whole number. If the resulting frequency is not close enough, repeat the doubling of the modified prescaler. Unfortunately, with our example, we can't double our prescaler and stay within the bounds of the 10-bit number.

Finally, another way to find the solution is to use a script or program (e.g., MATLAB or Excel) and use brute force to try out the options, as shown in the procedure below. Start by finding the minimum and maximum prescaler values (by setting the compare register to 1). Limit the minimum and maximum so they are integers and fit into the correct number of bits. Then, for each whole number in that range, calculate the compare register for the goal interrupt frequency. Round the compare register to the nearest whole number, and calculate the actual interrupt frequency. This method led to a prescaler of 997, a compare register of 236, and a tiny error of 0.0009%. A brute-force solution like this will give you the smallest error, but will probably take the most developer time. Determine what error you can live with, and go on to other things once you've met that goal.

Brute-force method for finding the lowest error interrupt frequency register value:

1. Calculate the minimum and maximum prescaler values:

$$minPrescaler = \frac{clockInput}{goalFrequency \times maxCompare}$$

$$= \frac{4MHz}{17Hz \times 255} = 922$$

$$maxPrescaler = \frac{clockInput}{goalFrequency \times maxCompare}$$

$$= \frac{4MHz}{17Hz \times 1} = 235{,}294 \rightarrow \text{exceeds max}$$

$$= 2^{10} - 1 = 1{,}023$$

2. For each prescaler value from 922 to 1,023, calculate a compare value:

$$compare = \frac{clockInput}{goalFrequency \times prescaler} = \frac{4MHz}{20Hz \times 922} = 255.2$$

$$= round(255.2) \Rightarrow 255$$

Use the calculated compare value to determine the interrupt frequency with these values:

$$interruptFrequency = \frac{clockInput}{prescaler * compare} = \frac{4mHz}{923 * 255} = 17.013Hz$$

Calculate the error:

$$error\% = 100 \times \frac{abs(goalFrequency - interruptFrequency)}{goalFrequency}$$

$$= 100 \times \frac{abs(17Hz - 17.013)}{17Hz}$$

$$= 0.08\%$$

3. Find the prescaler and compare registers with the least error.

A Long Wait Between Timer Ticks

Brute force works well for 17 Hz, but when you get the goal output of 13 Hz (marketing's new 2 × 6.5 Hz goal), the minimum prescaler that you can calculate is more than 10 bits. The timer cannot fit in the 8-bit timer. This is shown as an exception in the flowchart (Figure 4-9). The simplest solution is to use a larger timer if you can. The ATtiny45's 16-bit timer can alleviate this problem because its maximum compare value is 65,535 instead of the 8-bit 255, so we can use a smaller prescaler.

If a larger timer is unavailable, another solution is to disconnect the I/O line from the timer and call an interrupt when the timer expires. The interrupt can increment a variable and take action when the variable is large enough. For example, to get to 13 Hz, we could have a 26 Hz timer and toggle the LED every other time the interrupt is called. This method is less precise because there could be delays due to other interrupts.

Using a Timer

Once you have determined your settings, the hard part is over, but there are a few more things to do:

- Remove the code in the main function to toggle the LED. Now the main loop will need only a set of prescaler and compare registers to cycle through when the button is pressed.
- Write the interrupt handler that toggles the LED.
- Configure the pin. Some processors will connect any timer to any output, whereas others will allow a timer to change a pin only with special settings. For the processor that doesn't support a timer on the pin, you will need to have an interrupt handler in the code that toggles only the pin of interest.
- Configure timer settings and start the timer.

Using Pulse-Width Modulation

Market research has shown that potential customers are bothered by the brightness of the LED, saying its laser-like intensity is blinding them. Marketing wants to try out different brightness settings (100%, 80%, 70%, and 50%), using the button to switch between the options.

This assignment gives us a fine opportunity to explore *pulse-width modulation* (PWM), which determines how long a pin stays high or low before toggling. PWMs operate continuously, turning a peripheral on and then off on a regular schedule. The cycle is usually very fast, on the order of milliseconds (or hundreds of Hz).

PWM signals often drive motors and LEDs (though motors require a bit more hardware support). Using PWM, the processor can control the amount of power the hardware gets. Using some inexpensive electronics, the output of a PWM pin can be smoothed to be the average signal. For LEDs, though, no additional electronics are necessary. The brightness is relative to the amount of time the LED is on during each cycle.

A timer is a set of pulses that are all alike, so the timer signal is 50% high and 50% low (this is known as a 50% *duty cycle*). In PWM, the pulses' widths change depending on the situation. So a PWM can have a different ratio. A PWM with a 100% duty cycle is always on, like a high level of an output pin. And a 0% duty cycle represents a pin that has been driven (or pulled) low. The duty cycle represents the average value of the signal, as shown by the dashed line in Figure 4-10.

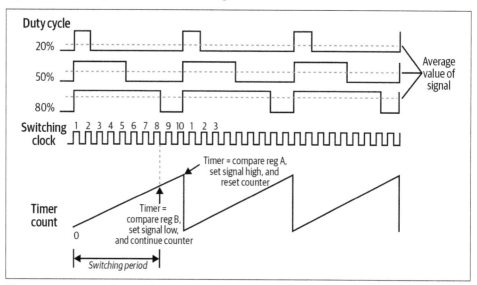

Figure 4-10. PWM duty cycles: 20%, 50%, and 80%

Given the timer from "Using a Timer" on page 119, we could implement a PWM with an interrupt. For our 20 Hz LED example, we had a compare register of 200, so that every 200 ticks, the timer interrupt would do something (toggle the LED). If we wanted the LED to be on 80% of the time with a 20 Hz timer (instead of the 50% we were doing earlier), we could ping-pong between two interrupts that would set the compare register at every pass:

- Timer interrupt 1
  - — Turn LED on.
  - — Set the compare register to 160 (80% of 200).
  - — Reset the timer.
- Timer interrupt 2
  - — Turn LED off.
  - — Set the compare register to 40 (20% of 200).
  - — Reset the timer.

With a 20 Hz timer, this would probably look like a very quick series of flashes instead of a dim LED. The problem is that the 20 Hz timer is too slow. The more you increase the frequency, the more the LED will look dim instead of blinking. However, a faster frequency means more interrupts.

There is a way to carry out this procedure in the processor. In the previous section, the configurable actions included whether to reset the counter as well as how to set the pin. Many timers have multiple compare registers and allow different actions for each one. Thus, a PWM output can be set with two compare registers, one to control the switching frequency and one to control the duty cycle.

For example, the bottom of Figure 4-10 shows a timer counting up and being reset. This represents the *switching frequency* set by a compare register. We'll name this compare register A and set it to 100. When this value is reached, the timer is reset and the LED is turned on. The duty cycle is set with a different register (compare register B, set to 80) that turns the LED off but allows the timer to continue counting.

Which pins can act as PWM outputs depends on your processor, though often they are a subset of the pins that can act as timer outputs. The PWM section of the processor user manual may be separate from the timer section. Also, there are different PWM controller configurations, often for particular applications (motors are often finicky about which type of PWM they require).

For our LED, once the PWM is set up, the code only needs to modify the duty cycle when the button is pressed. As with timers, the main function doesn't control the LED directly at all.

Although dimming the LED is what marketing requested, there are other neat applications you can try out. To get a snoring effect, where the LED fades in and out, you'll need to modify the duty cycle in increments. If you have tricolor LEDs, you can use PWM control to set the three LED colors to different levels, providing a whole palette of options.

Shipping the Product

Marketing has found the perfect LED (blue), blink rate (8 Hz), and brightness (100%), and is ready to ship the product as soon as you set the parameters.

It all seems so simple to just set the parameters and ship the code. However, what does the code look like right now? Did the timer code get morphed into the PWM code, or is the timer interrupt still around? With a brightness of 100%, the PWM code isn't needed any longer. In fact, the button code can go. The ability to choose an LED at runtime is no longer needed. The old board layout can be forgotten in the future. Before shipping the code and freezing development, let's try to reduce the spaghetti into something less tangled.

A product starts out as an idea and often takes a few iterations to solidify into reality. Engineers often have good imaginations for how things will work. Not everyone is so lucky, so a good prototype can go a long way toward defining the goal.

However, keeping around unneeded code clutters the codebase (see the left side of Figure 4-11). Unused code (or worse, code that has been commented out) is frustrating for the next person who doesn't know why things were removed. Avoid that as much as possible. Instead, trust that your version control system can recover old code. Don't be afraid to tag, branch, or release a development version internally. It will help you find the removed features after you prune the code for shipment.

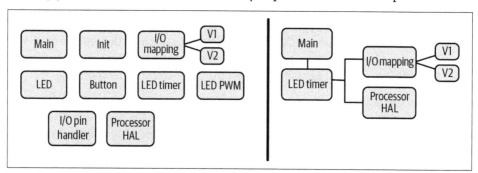

Figure 4-11. Comparing spaghetti prototyping code with a simpler design

In this example, many things are easy to remove because they just aren't needed. One thing that is harder to decide about is the dependency injection. It increases flexibility for future changes, which is a good reason for leaving it in. However, when you have to allocate a specific timer to a specific I/O pin, the configuration of the system becomes more processor-dependent and rigid. The cost of forcing it to be flexible can be high if you try to build a file to handle every contingency. In this case, I considered the idea and weighed the cost of making a file I'd never want to show anyone with the benefit of reducing the chance of writing bugs in the I/O subsystem. I chose to make more readable files, even if it means a few initial bugs, but I respect either option.

On the right side of Figure 4-11, the codebase is trimmed down, using only the modules it needs. It keeps the I/O mapping header file, even with definitions for the old board because the cost is low (it is in a separate file for easy maintenance and requires no additional processor cycles). Embedded systems engineers tend to end up with the oldest hardware (karmic payback for the time at the beginning of the project when we had the newest hardware). You may need the old board header file for future development. Pretty much everything else that isn't critical can go into version control and then be removed from the project.

It hurts to see effort thrown away. But you haven't! All of the other code was necessary to make the prototypes that were required to make the product. The code aided marketing, and you learned a lot while writing and testing it. The best part about developing the prototype code is that the final code can look clean *because* you explored the options.

You need to balance the flexibility of leaving all of the code in with the maintainability of a codebase that is easy to understand. Now that you've written it once, trust that your future self can write it again (if you have to).

Further Reading

- A Guide to Debouncing (*http://ganssle.com/debouncing.htm*) on Jack Ganssle's website (*http://ganssle.com*) offers mechanics, real-world experimentation, other methods for implementing your debouncing code, and some excellent methods for doing it in the hardware and saving your processor cycles for something more interesting. His whole website is worth some of your time.

- STM32F101xx, STM32F102xx, STM32F103xx, STM32F105xx, and STM32F107xx Reference Manual (RM0008) (*https://oreil.ly/PMKTr*), Rev 21, February 2021

- MSP430F2xx, MSP430G2xx Family User's Guide (*https://oreil.ly/6tqZE*) (SLAU144K), August 2022

- Atmel user manual: 8-bit Microcontroller with 2/4/8K Bytes In-System Programmable Flash (*https://oreil.ly/ziPWV*) (ATtiny25/V, ATtiny45/V, ATtiny85/V), Rev. 2586Q–AVR–08/2013.

- Atmel application note: AVR 130: Setup and Use the AVR Timers (*https://oreil.ly/Jhfyh*)

- If bitwise operations are new to you, there are several games that can give you a more intuitive feel for how these work. Turing Complete is my current favorite. Look in this book's GitHub repository (*https://github.com/eleciawhite/making-embedded-systems*) for other suggestions.

Interview Question: Waiting for a Register to Change

What is wrong with this piece of code?

```
void IOWaitForRegChange(unsigned int* reg, unsigned int bitmask){
  unsigned int orig = *reg & bitmask;
  while (orig == (*reg & bitmask)) { /* do nothing */ ; }
}
```

"What's wrong with this code?" is a tough question because the goal is to figure out what the interviewer thinks is wrong with the code. For this code, I can imagine an interviewee wondering about a comment block for the function. And whether there really should exist a function that waits forever without any sort of timeout or error handling.

If an interviewee flails, pointing out noncritical things, I would tell them that the function never returns, even though the register changes, as observed on an oscilloscope. If they continue to flounder, I would tell them that the code compiles with optimizations on.

In the end, this is not a see-how-you-think question, but one with a single correct answer: the code is missing the volatile keyword. To succeed in an embedded systems interview, you have to know what that keyword does (it is similar in C, C++, and Java).

Interrupts

Interrupts can be scary. They are one of the things that make embedded systems different from traditional application software. Interrupts swoop in from out of nowhere to change the flow of the code. They can safely call only certain functions (and usually not the debug functions). Interrupts need to be fast, so fast that they are a piece of code that is still occasionally written in assembly language. And bugs in interrupts are often quite difficult to find because, by definition, they occur asynchronously (outside the normal flow of execution).

However, interrupts are not the bogeymen they've been made out to be. If you understand what happens when an interrupt occurs, you'll find where they can be a useful part of your software design.

A Chicken Presses a Button

Consider interrupts as a Rube Goldberg machine[1] with the goal of telling your software that something happened outside the normal flow of code. Let us consider the chicken in Figure 5-1.

---

1 A Rube Goldberg machine is an overly complex contraption used to do something relatively simple. Such machines (real and metaphorical) often consist of a series of simple, unrelated elements, with the action of each element triggering the start of the next until the goal action occurs.

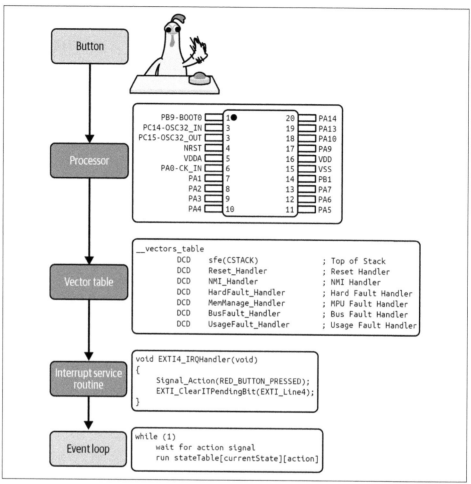

Figure 5-1. A chicken presses a button leading to a cascade of actions ending with the code in the event loop taking an action

The chicken presses a button. The interrupt signal goes to the processor. The processor saves where it is and then looks up what code to call. It calls that code, which does something (maybe sets a variable). The interrupt ends, the processor returns to where it was before all this happened. The normal code continues but now there is a variable change or other signal that seemingly appeared from nowhere.

Let me put it another way. First, I want you to remember that processors and interfaces are like software APIs (see "Reading a Datasheet" on page 46) and that function pointers aren't scary (see the sidebar "Function Pointers Aren't So Scary" on page 78). You'll need both of those ideas in your head as we walk through what happens when an interrupt occurs:

1. An interrupt request (IRQ) happens inside the processor, triggered by an external component, the software, or a fault in the system.
2. The processor saves the context, which includes where it was and the local variables.
3. The processor finds the function associated with the interrupt in the vector table.
4. The callback function runs (aka interrupt service routine or ISR or interrupt handler).
5. The processor restores the saved context, returning to the point before the interrupt occurred, and the program continues to run.

Let's go through the process of interrupt handling in more detail. Then we'll talk about how to set up these interrupts to work the way you want.

An IRQ Happens

Some interrupts are like small high-priority tasks. Once their ISR is complete, the processor restores the context it saved and continues on its way as though nothing had happened. Most peripheral interrupts are like that: input lines, communication pathway, timers, peripherals, ADCs (analog-to-digital converters), etc.

Other interrupts are more like exceptions, handling system faults and never returning to normal execution. For example, an interrupt can occur when there is a memory error, a divide-by-zero error, the processor tries to execute an invalid instruction, or the power level is not quite sufficient to run the processor properly (brownout detection). These errors mean something is seriously wrong and the processor can't run properly. Usually when this happens the interrupt puts the system into an infinite loop or resets the processor.

Most interrupts you need to handle will be more like tasks than exceptions. They will let your processor run multiple tasks, seemingly in parallel.

Usually an interrupt request happens because you've configured the interrupt. If it wasn't you, then your vendor's startup code probably did the work. While often invisible to high-level language programmers, the startup code configures some hardware-oriented things (such as setting up the default interrupts, usually the fault interrupts, and configuring system clocks).

For task-like interrupts, your initialization code can configure them to occur under the conditions you specify. What exactly those conditions are depend on your processor. Your processor's user manual will be critical to setting up interrupts. (More on configuration in "Configuring Interrupts" on page 140 later in this chapter, after we go through the parts of the interrupt itself.)

Because processors are different, I'll focus on the STM32F103xx processor, which is middle-of-the-road in its interrupt-handling complexity (Microchip's ATtiny AVR is much simpler, and the TI MSP430x2xx is more complex).

Nonmaskable Interrupts

Some processors define certain interrupts as so important that they can't be disabled; these are called *nonmaskable interrupts* (NMIs). (I suppose not-disable-able interrupts was a little unwieldy to say.)

The processor faults noted earlier are one form of NMI. Often there is one I/O pin that can be linked to an NMI, which usually leads to an "on" button on the device. These interrupts cannot be ignored at any time and must be handled immediately, even in critical sections of code.

Interrupt Priority

Getting back to our "chicken presses a button" example, we haven't really talked about why a chicken has a button. Say the button is for when a fox has been spotted and the farmer needs to be informed. Say that there is also a timer interrupt that automatically feeds the chicken.

If the feed-timer and fox-button occur at precisely the same time (as improbable as that is), which one should the processor handle? Obviously, reducing the danger from predators outranks feeding the chicken. Interrupts can have different priorities.

Some processors handle interrupt priority by virtue of the peripherals themselves (so timer 1 has a higher priority than timer 2, which in turn is more important than timer 3). Other processors allow you to configure the priority on a per-interrupt basis.

Nested Interrupts

Some processors allow interrupts to be interrupted by another interrupt. Instead of priority being important only when an ISR is called, the priority is used to determine whether a new interrupt can preempt the one currently running.

This is a powerful tool that is likely to cause unnecessary complexity. Unless nested interrupts solve a clear problem particular to your system, it is customary to disable other interrupts while in an ISR. Most processors that allow nested interrupts give you a method for disabling them at system initialization.

Stacks (and Heaps)

A stack is a data structure that holds information in a LIFO (last in, first out) manner, as shown in Figure 5-2. You push data onto the stack (adding it to the stack's memory and increasing the pointer to where the next set of data will go). To get the last piece of data out, you pop the stack (which decreases the pointer).

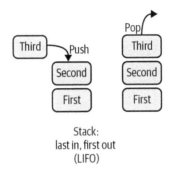

Figure 5-2. Stack basics

A stack is a simple data structure any developer can implement, but *the stack* (note the definite article "the") refers to the system call stack that lies behind every running program in a designated section of RAM. For each function called, the compiler creates a stack frame that contains the local variables, parameters, and the address to return to when the function is finished. There is a stack frame for every function call, starting with the reset vector, then the call to main, and then whatever you call after that. (Or if you have multiple threads, each one will have its own stack.)

A *heap* is a tree data structure. *The heap* is where dynamically allocated memory comes from (so named because it can be implemented as a heap data structure).

Usually the heap grows up (see Figure 5-3), whereas the stack grows down. When they meet, your system crashes. Well, actually your system will probably crash before they meet because there may be other things between them (global and static variables and possibly code). (More about this in Chapter 11.)

If the stack gets too large, it can grow into other areas of memory, for example, where a global array is located. If the stack overwrites the memory of the array, the corrupt data in the array is likely to give you incorrect results. This is called a *stack overflow*. On the other hand, if the global array overwrites the stack, the function return address may be corrupted. When the function returns, the program will return to a bogus address and crash (usually due to an inappropriate instruction).

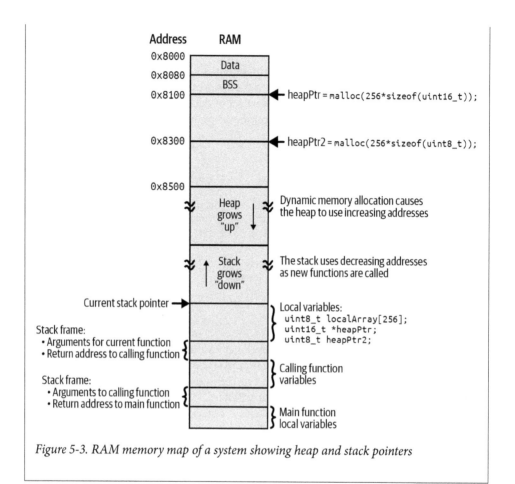

Figure 5-3. RAM memory map of a system showing heap and stack pointers

Save the Context

After the interrupt request happens, the processor saves where it was before it finds the appropriate function handler. Like a bookmark saving your spot, the processor saves the context to the stack; see "Stacks (and Heaps)" on page 129. The context includes the program counter (which points to the next instruction to execute) and a subset of the processor registers (which are like the processor's own cached local RAM). The register contents are saved so that the interrupt code can use them in its execution without corrupting the state of the primary code path.

These steps don't come for free. The amount of time it takes between the IRQ and the ISR is the processor's *interrupt latency*, usually advertised in the user manual as taking a certain number of processor cycles.

The *system latency* is the worst-case amount of time it takes from when an interrupt event happens to the start of the ISR. It includes the processor's interrupt latency and the maximum amount of time interrupts are ever disabled.

 If interrupt nesting is disallowed, then new interrupts are disabled while an interrupt is being handled. The largest contributor to system latency may be the time spent in the longest interrupt. Keep interrupts short!

The interrupt latency processor cycles are lost. If you had a processor that could do a hundred instructions a second (100 Hz) with an interrupt latency of 10 cycles, and you set up a timer that interrupted every second, you'd lose 10% of your cycles to context switching. Actually, since you have to restore the context, it could be worse than that. Even though 10 cycles is a decent interrupt latency (not great, but not bad), 100 Hz systems are rare. However, doing this math with a 30 MHz processor, handling audio in an interrupt at 44,100 Hz with a 10-cycle latency uses 1.47% of the processor's cycles simply calling the interrupt handler. That doesn't even include the time spent executing the ISR or returning from it.

Processor designers work to keep the interrupt latency low. One way to do that is to store the minimum amount of context. This means that instead of saving all of the processor registers, the processor will save only a subset, requiring the software to store the other ones it needs. This is usually handled by the compiler, increasing the effective system latency.

Calculating System Latency

Calling lots of functions while in an interrupt is discouraged. Each function call has some overhead (discussed more fully in Chapter 11), so function calls make your interrupt take longer. If you have other interrupts disabled during your interrupt, your system latency increases with each function call.

As your system latency increases, its ability to handle events in real time decreases. Consider the aforementioned 30 MHz processor with a 44,100 Hz interrupt. If each interrupt uses 10 cycles for interrupt overhead and 10 cycles calling five short functions (each) that collectively use 275 cycles actually processing information, no other interrupt can be handled for at least 335 cycles ($10 + 5 \times 10 + 275$). The time consumed by this is 11 μs (335/30 MHz). Also note that the system spends nearly 50% of its time in the interrupt (44,100 Hz × 11 micros = 0.492 s). Reducing the overhead of the interrupt will free up processor cycles for other tasks.

Retrieve the ISR from the Vector Table

After the IRQ happens and the context is saved, the third step for handling an interrupt is to determine which ISR to call by looking in the *interrupt vector table* (IVT). This table is located at a specific area of memory on your processor. When an interrupt occurs, the processor looks in the table to call the function associated with the interrupt.

The IVT is a list of callback functions, one for each type of interrupt. Secretly, the vector table is a list of function pointers, though the code for it is often implemented in assembly.

Initializing the Vector Table

The startup code (which probably came with your compiler or processor vendor HAL) sets up the vector table for you, usually with placeholder interrupt handlers. When debugging, you probably want your unhandled interrupts to go into an infinite loop so that you find them and turn off the interrupt or handle it properly.

When the product hits the market, having an unhandled interrupt handler go into an endless loop will cause your system to become unresponsive. You may want unhandled interrupts to simply return to normal execution. It wastes processor cycles and is still a bug, but at least the bug's effect on the customer is a slight slowdown instead of a system that needs a reboot.

In some cases, if you name your handler function the same as the one in the table, some tools' magic will make the linker use yours in the IVT. With other processors and compilers, though, you will need to insert your ISR into the function table at the correct slot for your interrupt.

In the STM32F103xx processor, using the STM32Cube HAL, we'd only need to name the ISR `TIM2_IRQHandler`, and the linker will put the correct function address in the vector table. In some processors, such as Microchip's AT91SAM7S, you have to create a function and put it in the table manually:

```
interrupt void Timer1ISR(){
  …
}

void FoodTimerInit(){
  …
  AT91C_BASE_AIC->AIC_SVR[AT91C_ID_TC1] = // Set TC1 IRQ handler
                                          // address in the IVT
      (unsigned long)Timer1ISR;  // Source Vector Register,
                                 // slot AT91C_ID_TC1 (12)
  …
}
```

This has to occur when the interrupt is initialized and before the interrupt is enabled.

Looking Up the ISR

The vector table is located at a particular address in memory, set by the linker script. Since this is probably done for you in the startup code, you usually don't need to know how to do it. However, in case you are curious, let's dig into the startup code for the STM32F103xx for a moment:

```
__attribute__ ((section(".isr_vector")))
void (* const g_pfnVectors[])(void) = {
  // Core Level - CM3
  &_estack,              // The initial stack pointer
  Reset_Handler,         // This is the very beginning of running
  NMI_Handler,           // Nonmaskable fault handler

  ...
  TIM2_IRQHandler,  // 28, TIM2 global interrupt
  TIM3_IRQHandler,  // 29,
  TIM4_IRQHandler,  // 30,
  ...
}
```

First in the listing is a nonstandard line that communicates to the compiler that the following variable needs to go someplace special and that the linker script will indicate where this is (at the location specified by .isr_vector). We'll talk more about linker scripts later (see "Intro to Linker Scripts" on page 257), but right now it is safe to say that the .isr_vector linker variable is located where the user manual says the vector table should be (0x00000000).

Inside the array of void * elements, there is the location for the stack, also set in the linker script. After that is the reset vector, which is the address of the code that is called when your system boots up or resets for another reason. It is one of the exception interrupts mentioned earlier. Most people don't think of turning on the power or pushing the reset button as an interrupt to their code. However, the processor responds to a reset by loading a vector from the table, in the same way that it responds to an interrupt by loading a vector. Later in the table, there are the peripheral interrupts, such as our timer. Figure 5-4 shows how this would look in the processor's memory.

Each interrupt has an interrupt number. For our timer 3 interrupt, it is 50. When the interrupt happens, it is signaled by just this number, and the part of the processor that generates the IRQ sends it to the part of the processor that looks up the handler in the vector table as the number. The processor uses the interrupt number and the structure of the vector table to look up the address to call when the interrupt arrives.

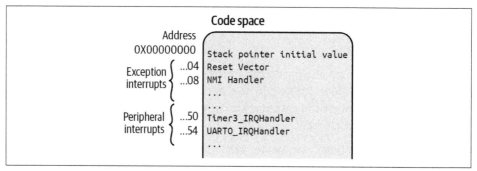

Figure 5-4. Vector table in memory

Reentrant Functions

A *reentrant function* is one that can be safely called multiple times while it is running. The following garden-variety swap function, for instance, is nonreentrant because it has a temporary variable t whose value must not change before it is used to set the final y variable:

```
int t;

void swap(int* x, int* y) {
  t = *x;
  *x = *y;
  // hardware interrupt might invoke isr() here while
  // the function has been called from main or other
  // non-interrupt code
  *y =  t;
}

void isr {
  int x=1, y=2;
  swap(&x, &y);
}
```

Functions that use static or global variables are nonreentrant. Many C++ objects are nonreentrant by virtue of their private data. Worse, some standard library calls are nonreentrant, including malloc (or new) and printf (any I/O or file function).

When the system saves the context, it does the bare minimum. The compiler can do more, but even that does not give you an entirely clean slate to work with. That is actually a good thing, because you usually want a global variable or two to signal the noninterrupt code that the interrupt occurred. However, when writing an ISR, you should be extremely wary about functions that use global variables without protecting them against interrupts.

Count on interrupts to occur at the worst time. That way, you can design your system to minimize the havoc they can cause.

Call the ISR

So far we've gone through what you need to know about the workings of an ISR and how to set it up. Now we'll get to the meaty part of actual ISR, the part that you'll need to implement. We've already seen the most important rules surrounding ISRs:

- Keep ISRs short because longer ones increase your system latency. Generally avoid function calls, which may have hidden depths and increase overhead.

- Don't call nonreentrant functions (such as `printf`), because global variables can be corrupted by interrupts.

This gives us the design guidelines to implement an ISR. Our timer interrupt is easy to implement because all we need to do is set a flag indicating it is time to feed the chicken:

```
volatile tBoolean gFeedChicken= FALSE; // global variable set by the interrupt
                                       // handler, which is cleared by normal
                                       // code when event handled
void TIM2_IRQHandler(void){
  __disable_irq();        // disallow nesting of interrupts
  gFeedChicken = TRUE;
  __enable_irq();
}
```

The interrupt doesn't print out a debug message or drive the feed mechanism. As much as it seems to make sense to do that, keeping it short means we need to let other parts of the system take care of these things. This keeps system latency to a minimum.

Interrupts can do more than set flags and unblock communications drivers. Adding longer code to make the system safer is a worthy trade-off. Otherwise, keep interrupts short!

Many processors require that you acknowledge (or clear) the interrupt. Usually this is accomplished by reading a status register. As noted in "Writing an Indirect Register" on page 136, this may have the side effect of clearing the bit.

Writing an Indirect Register

Memory-mapped registers can have some interesting properties. Registers don't always act like variables.

If you want to modify a normal variable, the steps hidden in your `memoryReg |= 0x01` line of code are:

1. Read the current value of the memory into a processor register.
2. Modify the value.
3. Write the variable back into memory.

However, for a register that sets interrupt handling, this multistep process can cause problems if an interrupt occurs between any two of these steps. To prevent this race condition—where an interrupt occurs during an inconsistent state—actions on registers must be atomic (executing in a single instruction).

This is accomplished by having a set of *indirect* registers: a register that can set bits and a register that can clear bits, each of which acts on a third functional register that may not be directly writable (nor memory mapped). To indirectly set a bit, you have to write the bit in the set register. To indirectly clear a bit, you write that bit in the clear register. In either register (set or clear), the unset bits don't do anything to the functional register. (Part B of Figure 5-5 gives an example of setting and clearing bits and the contents of the functional register at each step.)

Sometimes the functional register is reflected in the set and clear registers, so if you read either one of those, you can see the currently set bits. It can be confusing, though, to read something that is not what you have written to the same register.

A functional register also can be write-only without any way to be read. Some processors save memory space by having a register act as a functional register when it is written but a status register when it is read. In that case, you'll need to keep track of the bit set in the functional register using a *shadow variable*, a global variable in your code that you modify whenever you change the register. Instead of setting and clearing intermediate registers, you'll need to modify your shadow and then write the register with the shadow's value.

There are also registers where the act of reading the register modifies its contents. This is commonly used for status registers, where the pending status is cleared by the processor once your code reads the register (see part C of Figure 5-5). This can prevent a race condition from occurring in the time between the user reading the register and clearing the relevant bit.

Your user manual will tell you which types of registers exhibit special behaviors.

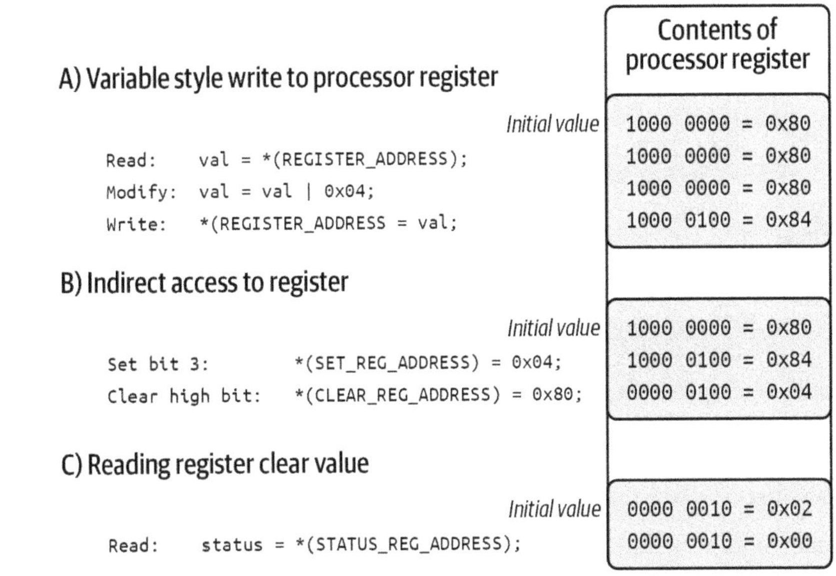

Figure 5-5. Methods for setting register values

In the figure:

Contents of processor register

A) Variable style write to processor register

	Initial value	`1000 0000 = 0x80`
Read:	`val = *(REGISTER_ADDRESS);`	`1000 0000 = 0x80`
Modify:	`val = val	0x04;`	`1000 0000 = 0x80`
Write:	`*(REGISTER_ADDRESS = val;`	`1000 0100 = 0x84`

B) Indirect access to register

	Initial value	`1000 0000 = 0x80`
Set bit 3:	`*(SET_REG_ADDRESS) = 0x04;`	`1000 0100 = 0x84`
Clear high bit:	`*(CLEAR_REG_ADDRESS) = 0x80;`	`0000 0100 = 0x04`

C) Reading register clear value

	Initial value	`0000 0010 = 0x02`
Read:	`status = *(STATUS_REG_ADDRESS);`	`0000 0010 = 0x00`

Multiple Sources for One Interrupt

Some processors have only one interrupt. The machinery necessary to stop the processor takes up space in the silicon, and a single interrupt saves on cost (and power). When this interrupt happens, the ISR starts by determining which of the peripherals activated the interrupt. This information is usually stored in a *cause* or *status* register, where the ISR looks at each bit to separate out the source of the interrupt ("Timer 1, did you trigger an interrupt? No? What about you, timer 2?").

Having an interrupt for each possible peripheral is a luxury of many larger processors. When there are many possible sources, it is inefficient to poll all of the options. However, even when you have identified a peripheral, there is still a good chance you'll need to unravel the real source of the interrupt. For example, if your timer 3 is used for multiple purposes, the chicken feeder timeout may be indicated when timer 3 matches the first match register. To generate the appropriate event when the interrupt happens, you'll need to look at the peripheral's interrupt register to determine why the timer 3 interrupt occurred:

```
if (TIM3->SR & 0x1) { // interrupt occurs when timer's counter
                      // is updated
```

Most peripherals require this second level of checking for the interrupt. To look at another example, in a specific communication mechanism such as SPI, you'll probably get a single interrupt to indicate that something interesting happened. Then you'll need to check the SPI status register to determine what it was: it ran out of bytes to send, it received some bytes, the communication experienced errors, etc.

 For GPIOs, there may be one interrupt for a bank of pins, and you'll need to determine the specific pin that caused the interrupt.

Whether you have one interrupt with many sources or many interrupts with even more sources, don't stop looking at the cause register when you find the first hit. There could be multiple causes. That leads us back to the question of priorities: which interrupt source will you handle first?

Disabling Interrupts

Nested interrupts are allowed on the STM32F103xx, but we don't want to deal with the complexity of interrupts within interrupts. The __disable_irq() and __enable_irq() macros come from the compiler vendor HAL and insert a single instruction, so the overhead to prevent nesting is minimal.

Critical Sections

Race conditions can happen in critical sections. To avoid that, we'll need to turn off interrupts there as well. We could disable a particular interrupt, but that might lead to the priority inversion (we'll talk more about that in Chapter 6). Unless you have a good reason for your particular design, it is usually safer to turn off all interrupts.

There are two methods for disabling interrupts. The first method uses the macros we've already seen. However, there is one problem with those: what if you have critical code inside critical code? For example:

```
HandyHelperFunction:
   disable interrupts
   do critical things
   enable interrupts

CriticalFunction:
   disable interrupts
   call HandyHelperFunction
   do supposedly critical things  // unprotected!
   enable interrupts
```

Note that as soon as interrupts are enabled in HandyHelperFunction, they are also enabled in the calling function CriticalFunction, which is a bug. Critical sections should be short (to keep system latency at a minimum), so you could avoid this problem by not nesting critical sections, but this is something easier said than done.

 Because some processors won't let you nest critical pieces of code, you'll need to be sure to avoid doing it accidentally. To avoid this issue, I recommend naming the functions in a way that indicates they turn off interrupts.

Alternatively, if your processor allows it, implement the global disable and enable functions (or macros) a little differently by returning the previous status of the interrupts in the code that disables them:

```
HandyHelperFunction:
  interrupt status  = disable interrupts()
  do critical things
  enable interrupts(interrupt status)

CriticalFunction:
  interrupt status = disable interrupts()
  call HandyHelperFunction
  do critical things
  enable interrupts(interrupt status)
```

Here the helper function gets an interrupt status indicating the interrupts are already off. When the helper function calls the method to enable the interrupts, the interrupt status parameter causes no action to be taken. The critical code remains safe throughout both functions. Also important, if the helper is called by a different function, the helper's critical area is still protected.

Restore the Context

After your ISR has finished, it is time to return to normal execution. Some compilers extend C/C++ to include an `interrupt` keyword (or `__IRQ`, or `_interrupt`) to indicate which functions implement interrupt handlers. The processor gives these functions special treatment, both when they start (some context is saved before the ISR starts running) and when they return.

As noted in "Save the Context" on page 130, the program counter points to the machine instruction you are about to run. When you call a function, the address of the next instruction (program counter + 1 instruction) is put on the stack as the return address. When you return from the function (`rts`), the program counter is set to that address.

It is not unusual for different assembly languages to have similar opcodes. However, rts and rti tend to be pretty common. They stand for "ReTurn from Subroutine" and "ReTurn from Interrupt," respectively.

However, the interrupt isn't a standard function call; it is a jump to the interrupt handler caused by the processor. If the interrupt simply returned as though it were a function, the things that the processor did to store the context would not get undone. So interrupts have a special assembly instruction (rti) to indicate that they are returning from an interrupt. This lets the processor know that it must restore the context to its state prior to the function call before continuing on its way.

If your C/C++ compiler doesn't require you to indicate that a function is an interrupt, you can rest assured it is finding some other way to make the return from interrupt happen. That is, the compiler is probably wrapping the interrupt function in assembly code that merely calls your function. Once your handler returns from the function call, the assembly wrapper returns from the interrupt. The processor resets the stack the way it was, and program execution continues from exactly the point it left off.

Until the chicken presses the button again.

Configuring Interrupts

Handling interrupts is a matter of an ISR called from the vector table when the processor gets an appropriate IRQ. While there are exceptions automatically set up in case of fault conditions, most interrupts from buttons and peripherals need to be configured before the interrupt can happen.

The first step to setting up an interrupt is often, somewhat oddly, disabling the interrupt. Even though part of the power-on sequence is to disable and clear all interrupts, it is sensible to take the precaution anyway. If the interrupt is enabled, it might fire before the initialization code finishes setting it up properly, possibly leading to a crash.

Setting up interrupts uses registers that are memory mapped, similar to those we saw in "Function Pointers Aren't So Scary" on page 78. As noted in that sidebar, accessing the memory address directly will make for illegible code. Most processor and compiler vendors will give you a header file of #define statements, often allowing you to access individual registers as members of structures. Let's take apart a typical line of code:

```
NVIC->ICER[0] = (1<<2); // disable timer 2 interrupt
```

Many things are going on in that one line. First, NVIC is a pointer to a structure located at a particular address. The header file from the compiler vendor unravels the hard-coded memory-mapped address:

```
#define SCS_BASE  (0xE000E000UL)       /*!< System Control Space Base Addr */
#define NVIC_BASE (SCS_BASE + 0x0100UL) /*!< NVIC Base Address  */
#define NVIC   ((NVIC_Type *)NVIC_BASE) /*!< NVIC configuration struct */
```

The same header file defines the structure that holds the registers and where they are in the address space, so we can identify the next element in our line of code, ICER[0]:

```
typedef struct{
  __IO uint32_t ISER[8]; /*!< Offset: 0x000  Interrupt Set Enable Register */
       uint32_t RESERVED0[24];
  __IO uint32_t ICER[8];/*!< Offset: 0x080  Interrupt Clear Enable Register*/
...
} NVIC_Type;
```

 This header file structure can be built by reading the user manual if you can't find where someone else has done it for you.

This processor has separate clear and set registers, as described in "Writing an Indirect Register" on page 136, so what our code does is set a bit in the clear (ICER) register that disables the timer interrupt. This is known as *masking* the interrupt. Once the interrupt is disabled, we can configure it to cause an IRQ when the timer has expired. (Timer configuration was covered in Chapter 4). All operations use the structure that points to the memory map of the processor registers for this peripheral (TIM2). The user manual says that the match control register describes whether an interrupt should happen (yes) and whether the timer should reset and start again (no):

```
TIM2->DIER |= 0x01;              // interrupt definition reg, on update
TIM2->CR1  |= TIM_OPMODE_SINGLE; // stop incrementing after it expires
```

Even though the first line of this snippet sets the timer interrupt to occur when it modified the register, it didn't really turn on the interrupt. Many processors require two steps to turn on the interrupt: a peripheral-specific interrupt-enable like the one just shown, plus a global interrupt-enable like the following:

```
NVIC->ISER[0] = (1<<2);     // enable timer 2 interrupt
TIM2->CR1  |= TIM_CR1_CEN;  // start the timer counting
```

Note that the peripheral interrupt configuration is in the peripheral part of the user manual, but the other register is in the interrupts section. You need to set both so that an interrupt can happen. Before putting that line in our code, we might want to configure a few more things for our timer interrupt.

When and When Not to Use Interrupts

Now that we've set up our chicken's feed timer to use an interrupt and created the code to handle the interrupt, we need to backtrack. We forgot a design step: should the feed timeout be an interrupt?

There are many circumstances in which the simplest solution is an interrupt. Communication pathways often have buffers that need to be filled (or emptied). An interrupt can act as a background task to feed the buffers, while the foreground task generates (or uses) the data. Changes to input lines may need interrupts if they need to be handled quickly. The more real-time the requirement to handle a change on the line, the more likely an interrupt is appropriate for a solution. Also, if checking to see whether an interrupt-type event has occurred takes time from other activities, it is better to have an interrupt.

We've also seen that interrupts have some serious downsides. I already mentioned the overhead of each interrupt, which can add up if you have a lot of them. Interrupts also make your system less deterministic. One of the great things about not having an operating system[2] is being able to say that once instruction x happens, y will happen. If you have interrupts, you lose the predictability of your system. And because the code is no longer linear in flow, debugging is harder. Worse, some catastrophic bugs will be very difficult to track down if they depend on an interrupt happening at a very specific time in the code (i.e., a race condition). Plus, the configuration is largely compiler- and processor-dependent (and the implementation may be as well), so interrupts tend to make your code less portable.

In the end, the development cost of implementing (and maintaining) interrupts is pretty high, sometimes higher than figuring out how to solve the problem at hand without them. Save interrupts for when you need their special power: when a system is time-critical, when an event is expensive to check for and happens very rarely, and when a short background task will let the system run more smoothly.

How to Avoid Using Interrupts

So if you don't need their special power, how can you avoid interrupts? Some things can be solved in hardware, such as using a faster processor to keep up with time-critical events. Other things require more software finesse.

Returning to our chicken example, we've considered the fox button and feed timer as interrupts. The interrupts cause events to be communicated to the main loop code. Do these events need to be caused by interrupts?

---

2 Some real-time operating systems (RTOSs) are deterministic, usually the more expensive ones.

Let's assume the system doesn't do anything besides handle the events. It just waits for these events to happen. The implementation of the system could be much simpler to maintain if we can always see what the code is waiting for.

 When you get to Chapter 13, interrupts become a way to wake the processor from sleep, so you have to use them.

Polling

Asking a human "are you done yet?" is generally considered impolite after the fourth or fifth query, but the processor doesn't care if the code incessantly asks whether an event is ready. Polling adds processor overhead, even when there are no events to process. However, if you are going to be in a while loop anyway (i.e., an idle loop), there is no reason not to check for events.

Polling is straightforward to code. There's one subtlety worth mentioning: if you are polling and waiting for the hardware to complete something, you might want a time-out, just in case you happen to miss the event or the hardware didn't get your command properly.

For feeding the chicken, all we need to do is wait for a certain amount of time to pass. Even though embedded systems have a reputation for being fast, many systems spend an inordinate amount of their clock cycles waiting for time to pass.

System Tick

Like the sound you hear when the clock's second hand moves, many systems have a tick that indicates time is passing. The amount of time in that tick varies, but one millisecond tends to be a popular choice.

 Ticks don't have to be one millisecond. If you have a time that is important to your system for other reasons (e.g., you have an audio recording system that is running at 44,100 Hz), you might want to use that instead.

The tick is implemented with a timer interrupt that counts time passing. Yes, if we implemented the chicken feed timeout this way, we are still basing the solution on an interrupt, but it is a much less specific interrupt. The system tick solves a much broader range of problems. In particular, it lets us define this function:

```
void DelayMs(tTime delay);
```

This will wait for the amount of time indicated—well, for approximately the amount of time indicated (see the sidebar, "Fenceposts and Jitter"). Note that because of fenceposting and jitter, `DelayMs` isn't a good measure of a single millisecond. However, if you want to delay 10 or 100 milliseconds, the error becomes small enough not to matter. If your system depends on one-millisecond accuracy, you could use a shorter tick, though you'll need to balance the overhead of the timer interrupt with the processing needs of the rest of the system.

Fenceposts and Jitter

A fencepost error is an example of an off-by-one error, often illustrated with building materials:

If you build a straight fence 100 m long with posts 10 m apart, how many posts do you need?

The quick and wrong answer is that you need 10 posts, but you actually need 11 posts to enclose the 100 meters, as shown in Figure 5-6. The same is true of a system tick. To cover at least the number of milliseconds in question, you need to add one to the delay.

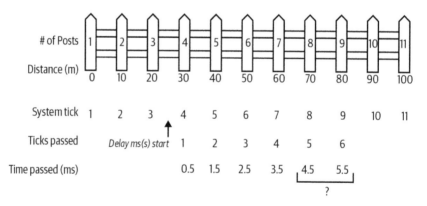

Figure 5-6. Fencepost example: looking at the spaces between system ticks

However, this calculation is complicated by *jitter*: your call to `DelayMs` is very unlikely to happen on a tick boundary. Instead, the delay will always start after a tick, so that `DelayMs` will always be longer than the number of ticks indicated.

You can choose whether you want to wait no more than the delay indicated (in which case, with a one millisecond delay, you may wait less than a processor cycle) or no less than the delay indicated (with a one millisecond delay, you may wait two milliseconds minus a processor cycle). You can make whatever choice leaves your application most robust, as long as the code is clear.

While waiting for the next feed time, we could call DelayMs and dispense food when it finishes. However, then we couldn't respond to any other commands.

If you want to keep track of time passing and do other things, add a few more functions to your system tick:

```
tTime TimeNow();
tTime TimePassed(tTime since);
```

The TimeNow function should return the tick counter. The code never looks at this directly, instead using the TimePassed function to determine whether enough time has passed. In fact, DelayMs can be implemented as a combination of these functions (getting the initial time and then waiting for the time passed to be greater than the delay). In between these functions, your system can do other things. In effect, this is a kind of polling.

Note that the TimeNow function gives the number of ticks since the system was booted. At some point this variable holding the number of ticks will run out of space and roll over to zero. If you used an unsigned 16-bit integer, a 1 ms tick would make the clock roll over every 65.5 seconds. If you need to use these functions to try to measure something that takes 70 seconds, you may never get there.

However, if you use an unsigned 32-bit integer, your system will roll over to zero in 4,294,967,296 ms, or about 49.7 days. If you use an unsigned 64-bit integer, your 1 ms tick won't roll over for half an eon (0.58 billion years). I'm impressed by this long-term thinking, but are you sure there won't be a power outage or system reboot before then?

So the size of your timekeeping variable determines the length of time you can measure. In many systems, instability can occur when the rollover happens. Protect against this by taking the rollover into account when you write the time-measuring function, to ensure the discontinuity does not cause a problem:

```
tTime TimePassed(tTime since) {
  tTime now = gSystemTicks;

  if (now >= since) {return (now - since);}

  // rollover has occurred
  return (now + (1 + TIME_MAX - since));
}
```

Time-Based Events

In our chicken example, the feed timer can use the system tick to create its time-based event. When the code finishes dispensing food, it sets a state variable:

```
lastFoodTime = TimeNow();
```

Then, when doing housekeeping, it checks for the completion of the event:

```
if (TimeSince(lastFoodTime) > CHICKEN_FEED_TIMEOUT)
  // dispense some food
```

Between those two times, the system can do whatever it needs to: listen for commands, check the chicken's panic button, play Tetris, and so on.

A Very Small Scheduler

For things that recur or need attention on a regular basis, you can use a timer as a mini-scheduler to fire off a callback function (a task).

 At this point, you are starting to re-create the functions of an operating system. If your mini-scheduler becomes more and more complicated, consider investing in an operating system. More about that in Chapter 6.

Feeding the chicken is a good example of something the scheduler can accomplish. But to make it interesting, let's add an egg check that causes a slowly blinking red light if there is an egg.

Although we could use the time-based event to check for eggs and then blink the red light, it might be a little simpler to make this a background task, something that the scheduler can accomplish.

So, before looking at the gory details, let's consider what the main loop needs to do to make all this work for a scheduler that runs about once a second, appropriate for our red light blinking state (but too sluggish for handling other events):

```
Run the scheduler after initialization is complete
LastScheduleTime = TimeNow()

Loop forever:
  if TimePassed(LastScheduleTime) > ONE_SECOND
    Run the scheduler, it will call the functions (tasks) when they are due
    LastScheduleTime = TimeNow()
```

We already worked out the time-based functionality in the previous section; now let's look at the scheduler in more detail.

When a task is allocated, it has some associated overhead, including the callback function that is the heart of the task. It also contains the next time the task should be run, the period (if it is a periodic task), and whether or not the task is currently enabled:

```
struct Task;                // forward declaration of the struct
typedef void (*TaskCallback)(struct Task *); // type of the callback function
```

```
typedef struct Task {
  tTime runNextAt;        // next timer tick at which to run this task
  tTime timeBetweenRuns;  // for periodic tasks
  TaskCallback  callback;
  int enabled;            // current status
};
```

The calling code should not know about the internals of the task management, so each task has an interface to hide those details:

```
void TaskResetPeriodic(struct Task *t);
void TaskSetNextTime(struct Task *t, tTime timeFromNow, tTime now);
void TaskDisable(struct Task *t);
```

(Yes, these could be methods in a class instead of functions; both ways work fine.)

The scheduler is straightforward and has only one main interface:

```
void SchedulerRun(tTime now);
```

When the scheduler runs, it looks through its list of tasks. Upon finding an enabled task, it looks to see whether the current time is later than runNextAt. If so, it runs the task by calling the callback function. The SchedulerRun function sits in the main loop, running whenever nothing else is.

These tasks are not interrupt-level, so they should not be used for activities with real-time constraints. Also, the tasks have to be polite and give up control relatively quickly, because they will not be preempted as they would be in typical operating systems.

There is one final piece to the scheduler: attaching the tasks to the scheduler so that they run. First, you'll need to allocate a task. Next, configure it with your callback function, the time at which the function should run, and the time between each subsequent run (for periodic functions). Finally, send it to the scheduler to put in its list:

```
void SchedulerAddTask(struct Task* t);
```

Publish/Subscribe Pattern

With the scheduler, we've built what is known as a *publish/subscribe* pattern (also called an *observer* pattern or *pub/sub* model). The scheduler publishes the amount of time that has passed, and several tasks subscribe to that information (at varying intervals). This pattern can be even more flexible, often publishing several different kinds of information.

The name of the pattern comes from newspapers, which is probably the easiest way to remember it. One part of your code publishes information, and other parts of your code subscribe to it. Sometimes the subscribers request only a subset of the information (like getting the Sunday edition only). The publisher is only loosely coupled to the subscribers. It doesn't need to know about the individual subscribers; it just sends the information in a generic method.

Our scheduler has only one type of data (how much time has passed), but the publish/subscribe pattern is even more powerful when you have multiple types of data. This pattern is particularly useful for passing messages, allowing parts of your system to receive messages they are interested in but not others. When you have one object with access to information that many others want to know about, consider the publish/subscribe pattern as a good solution.

Further Reading

If you are using an Arm Cortex processor, look into the series *The Definitive Guide to ARM Cortex-M* by Joseph Yiu (Newnes). The series includes volumes for the different processors, and each one looks deeply into the internals of the Cortex-M processors. The interrupts section is particularly good, though there is usually some example assembly code so you can see what the processor is really doing.

Interview Question: What Not to Do

Know any good jokes?

I love a terrible joke. But this is an awful interview question. It isn't as bad as asking about race, religion, gender, age, national origin, marital situation, disabilities, and so on. Many of the qualities above are *illegal* to ask about in the US. Worse than illegal, questions of these sorts are unprofessional.

The goal of an interview is to determine whether interviewees can do the job and you can work with them.

So many times, our goal in hiring is to hire another one of *me* so *I* have less work to do. It makes things faster if you can just hire a me-clone: someone who speaks the same language, has the same cultural background so the idioms and in-jokes are understood, and uses the same frame of reference.

This is shortsighted. While you may be completely awesome, in the long term, diversity pays huge dividends by providing more points of view to a problem.

We need the arguers and the mediators, we need the ones who think in a straight line and the ones who go in circles or jump around, we need people who grew up with a different idea of inexpensive, the person who travels at light speed, and the people who can make sure they are going in the right direction.

It isn't diversity of skin color, age, gender, or anything like that; it is diversity of thought that is critical. Funny thing though: the bodies get different experiences based simply on the bodies, so to get diversity of thought, you need diversity of everything else.

This is very hard in a small company. There is the need to move fast, and lacking diversity means maybe going faster (by not having to explain why something is important). But faster is not success. You can shoot yourself in the foot mighty quickly.

Back to bad questions. Many of the verboten topics can be boiled down to this: don't discriminate on things that aren't important to the job and/or things people can't control. If this was not a person sitting across from you but an intelligent mystery device, would you ask them the same question?

OK—I ask a lot of electronic devices to tell me jokes. But don't be a jerk. Even unintentionally.

When you are sitting in an interview room, it is pretty easy not to ask these questions. But when you head out to lunch as a group and ask, "So, do you have any kids?", well, don't.

Let them bring up things they want to talk about. "Do you have any interesting hobbies?" is fine. Or you can just talk about what makes you and your place of business so nifty.

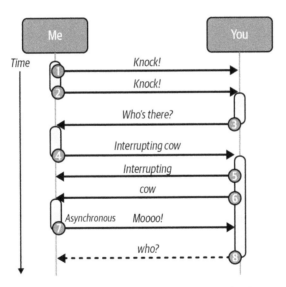

Figure 5-7. Sequence diagram of interrupting cow knock-knock joke

CHAPTER 6

Managing the Flow of Activity

In Chapter 2, we looked at different ways to break up a system into manageable chunks. That chapter described the what and why of design; this chapter covers the how. Once you've identified the pieces, getting them all to work together as a system can be daunting.

Scheduling and Operating System Basics

Structuring an embedded system without an operating system requires an understanding of some of the things that an operating system can do for you. I'm only going to give brief highlights; if any of this first section is brand new to you, you may want to review a book about operating systems (see "Further Reading" on page 177).

Tasks

When you turn on your computer, if you are like me, you load up an email client, web browser, and compiler. Several other programs start automatically (such as my calendar). Each of these programs runs on the computer, seemingly in parallel, even if you have only one processor.

 Three words that mean slightly different things, but that overlap extensively, are sometimes used interchangeably. While these definitions are the ones I was taught, some RTOSs may switch them around. A *task* is something the processor does. A *thread* is a task plus some overhead, such as memory. A *process* typically is a complete unit of execution with its own memory space, usually compiled separately from other processes. I'm focusing on tasks; threads and processes generally imply an operating system.

The operating system you are running has a *scheduler* that does the switching between active processes (or threads), allowing each to run in its proper turn. There are many ways to implement schedulers, a topic far beyond the scope of this book (let alone this small section). The key point is that a scheduler knows about all of the tasks/threads/processes/things your system should do and chooses which one to do *right now*.

Without an operating system, you are going to need to manage the scheduling yourself. The simplest scheduler has only one task. As with the blinking LED project in Chapter 4, you can do the same thing every time (on, wait, off, wait, repeat). However, things become more complex as the system reacts to changes in its environment (e.g., the button presses that change the LED timing).

Communication Between Tasks

The button-press interrupt and the LED-blinking loop are two tasks in the tiny system we have been examining. When we used a global variable to indicate that the button state changed, the two tasks communicated with each other. However, sharing memory between tasks is dangerous; you have to be careful about how you do it.

Figure 6-1 shows the normal course of events, where the interrupt sets the shared memory when a button is pressed. Then the main loop reads and clears the variable. The user presses the button again, which causes the interrupt to set the memory again.

Suppose that just as the main loop is clearing the variable, the interrupt fires again. At the very instant that the variable is being cleared, an interrupt stops the processing, swooping in to set the variable. Does it end up as set or cleared?

The answer depends on the precise timing of what happens. This uncertainty is a big problem. If it can be this complicated with a simple Boolean value, consider what could happen if the code needs to set two variables or a whole array of data.

This uncertainty about what will actually happen is called a *race condition*. Any memory shared between tasks can exhibit this uncertainty, leading to unstable and inconsistent behavior.

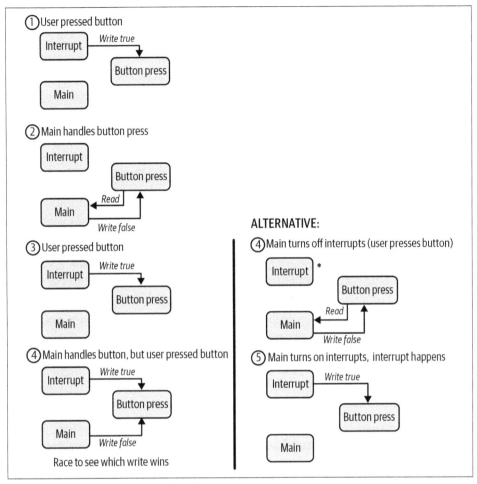

Figure 6-1. Race condition in shared memory

In this example, given the way the interrupt and button work together, it is likely that the system will miss a button press (if the interrupt wins the race to set the variable, the main function will clear it, even though it should be set). Though only a slight annoyance to a user in this particular system, race conditions can lead to unsafe conditions in more critical systems.

Avoiding Race Conditions

We need a way to prohibit multiple tasks from writing to the same memory. It isn't only writing that can be an issue; the main loop reads both the variable that says the button is changed and the value of the button. If an interrupt occurs between those two reads, it may change the value of the button between them.

Any time memory shared between tasks is read or written, it creates a *critical section* of code, meaning code that accesses a shared resource (memory or device). The shared resource must be protected so only one task can modify it at a time. This is called *mutual exclusion*, often shortened to *mutex*. Mutexes are sometimes implemented with *semaphores*, *mailboxes*, or *message queues*.

In a system with an OS, when two tasks are running but neither is an interrupt, you can use a mutex to indicate which task owns a resource. This can be as simple as a variable indicating whether the resource (or global variable) is available for use. However, when one of the two tasks is an interrupt, we have already seen that not even a Boolean value is safe, so this resource ownership change has to be *atomic*. An atomic action is one that cannot be interrupted by anything else in the system.

From here on, we are going to focus on systems where a task is interruptible but otherwise runs until it gives up control. In that case, race conditions are avoided by disallowing interrupts while accessing the shared global variables. This has a downside, though: when you turn off interrupts, the system can't respond as quickly to button presses, because it has to wait to get out of a critical section. Turning off interrupts increases the *system latency* (time it takes to respond).

Latency is important as we talk about *real-time systems*. A real-time system must respond to an event within a fixed amount of time. Although the required response time depends on the system, usually it is measured in microseconds or milliseconds. As latency increases, the time it takes before an event can be noticed by the system increases, and so the total time between an event and its response increases.

Priority Inversion

Some processors allow interrupts to have different priorities (like operating systems do for processes and threads). Although this flexibility can be very useful, it is possible to create a lot of trouble for yourself. Figure 6-2 shows a typical operating system's definition of priority inversion. It is OK for a high-priority process to stop because it needs access to something a low-priority process has. However, if a medium-priority process starts, it can block the low-priority process from completing its use of the resource needed by the high-priority task. The medium-priority task blocks the high-priority task.

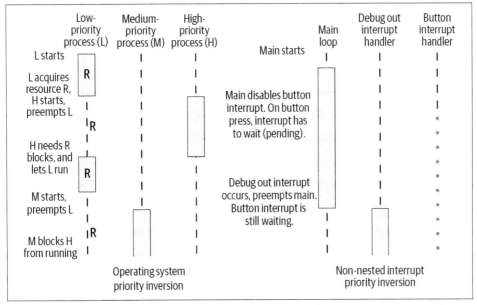

Figure 6-2. Priority inversion with an operating system and interrupts, competing for resource R

For example, say we have the high-priority, button-press interrupt and our low-priority main loop. When the main function accesses the button-press variable, it turns off the button-press interrupt to avoid a race condition. Later, we add another interrupt to output debug data through a communication port. This should be a background task of medium priority, something that should get done but shouldn't block the system from handling a button press. However, if the debug task interrupts the main loop, it is doing exactly that.

What is the most important thing for the processor to be doing? That should be the highest priority. If someone had asked whether debug output is more important than button presses, we would have said no. If that is true, why is the processor running the debug interrupt and not the button handler? The simple fix in this case is to disable all interrupts (or all interrupts that are lower in priority than the button handler) when the button interrupt occurs.

As we look at different ways of task management without an operating system, be alert for situations that cause the processor to inadvertently run a task that isn't the highest priority.

State Machines

One way to keep your system organized while you have more than one thing going on is to use a *state machine*. This is a standard software pattern, one that embedded systems use a lot. According to *Design Patterns: Elements of Reusable Object-Oriented Software*, the intent of the state pattern is to "allow an object to alter its behavior when its internal state changes. The object will appear to change its class."

Put more simply, when you call a state machine, it will do whatever it thinks it should do based on its current state. It will not do the same thing each time, but will base the change of behavior on its *context*, which consists of the environment and the state machine's history (internal state). If this all sounds clinical and theoretical, there is an easier way to think about state machines: flowcharts.

Almost any state machine can be represented as a flowchart. (Conversely, a problem you solve with a flowchart is probably destined to be a state machine.) State machines can also be represented as finite state automata (as shown in Figure 6-3), where each state is a circle and a change between states (a state transition) is an arrow.

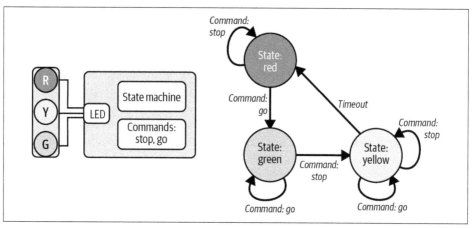

Figure 6-3. Stoplight system

We'll look at each element of this figure in the following section. The arrows in the diagram are as important as the circles. State machines are not only about the states that a system can occupy, but also about the events that the system handles.

State Machine Example: Stoplight Controller

To talk about state machines properly, we need an example that is a bit more complicated than a blinking LED and a button. Figure 6-3 shows a stoplight controller. When the light is red and the controller gets a message to go, it turns the light green. When the controller gets a message to stop, it turns the light yellow for a time and then red. We've implemented this stoplight so it stays green as long as no one needs it to change. Presumably, a command to stop will be generated when a car arrives on the cross street.

One state transition—which is the formal term for what each arrow shows—is a bit subtle. When the light is yellow and the controller receives a message to go, it should not change the light back to green. Yellow lights should change to red, not green, so the message to go just leaves the light in the yellow stage. This subtlety is an example of the gotchas that state machines create for you. You have to be prepared for every event that can happen in every state, including very rare cases—even cases that shouldn't take place but that may happen because of errors.

To work with a state machine, the first thing to do is to figure out the states and the events that can change states. With a system as simple as this, drawing a diagram is the best thing to do. Once you've identified the states (red, yellow, green), look at its connections. The stop and go commands should happen only in the green and red states, respectively. Even so, the commands are asynchronous, coming from outside the system, so each state should be able to handle them, even if they occur improperly. The easiest way of handling improper commands here is to ignore them, putting a loop back to the associated state.

 If an improper event occurs, it may be better to generate an error of some sort. Use your judgment.

State-Centric State Machine

Most people think of a state machine as a big if-else statement, or switch statement:

```
while (1) {
  look for event

  switch (state) {
  case (green light):
    if (event is stop command)
      turn off green light
      turn on yellow light
      set state to yellow light
      start timer
    break;
  case (yellow light):
    if (event is timer expired)
      turn off yellow light
      turn on red light
      set state to red light
    break;
```

```
   case (red light):
     if (event is go command)
       turn off red light
       turn on green light
       set state to green light
     break;
   default (unhandled state)
     error!
   }
}
```

The form of the state machine here is:

```
case (current state):
  if event valid for this state
    handle event
    prepare for new state
    set new state
```

The state machine can change its context (move to a new state). This means that each state needs to know about its sibling states.

State-Centric State Machine with Hidden Transitions

Another way to implement the state machine is to separate the state transition information from the state machine. This is theoretically better than the model in the previous section because it has more encapsulation and fewer dependencies. The previous model forced each state to know how and when to trigger each of the other states that can be reached from it. In the model I'll show in this section, some higher-level system keeps track of which state reaches which other state. I'll call this the "next state" function. It handles every state and puts the system into the next state that it should be in. By creating this function, you can separate the actions taken in each state from the state transitions.

The generic form of this would look like this:

```
case (state):
  make sure current state is actively doing what it needs
  if event valid for this state
    call next state function
```

In the stoplight example, this model would create simpler code for each state, and it would also be similar for almost all states. For instance, the green light state would look like this:

```
case (green light):
  turn on green light (even if it is already on)
  if (event is stop)
    turn off green light
    call next state function
  break;
```

The next state function should be called when a change occurs. The code will be familiar from the previous section because it is a simple switch statement as well:

```
next state function:
    switch (state) {
    case (green light):
      set state to yellow light
      break;
    case (yellow light):
      set state to red light
      break;
    case (red light):
      set state to green light
      break;
```

Now you have one place to look for the state and one for the transitions, but each one is pretty simple. In this example, the state transitions are independent of the event, one clue that this is a good implementation method.

This model is not always the best. For example, if a go command in the yellow state led back to green, the next state function would depend on both the current state and event. The goal of this method is to hide transitions, not to obfuscate your code. Sometimes it is better to leave it all together (as described in "State-Centric State Machine" on page 157).

Event-Centric State Machine

Another way to implement a state machine is to turn it on its side by having the events control the flow. With this approach, each event has an associated set of conditionals:

```
case (event):
  if state transition for this event
    go to new state
```

For example:

```
switch (event)
case (stop):
  if (state is green light)
    turn off green light
    go to next state
  // else do nothing
  break;
```

Most state machines create a comfortable fit between switch statements and states, but in some cases it may be cleaner to associate the state machines with events, as shown here. The functions still might need a switch statement to handle the dependency on the current state:

```
function to handle stop event
  if (state == green light)
    turn off green light
    go to next state
```

Unlike the state-centric options, the event-centric state machine implementation can make it difficult to do housekeeping activities (such as checking for a timeout in the yellow state). You could make housekeeping an event if your system needs regular maintenance, or you could stick with the state-centric implementation shown in the previous section.

State Pattern

An object-oriented way to implement a state machine is to treat each state as an object and create methods in the object to handle each event. Each state object in our example would have these member functions:

Enter
  Called when the state is entered (turns on its light)

Exit
  Called when leaving the state (turns off its light)

EventGo
  Handles the go event as appropriate for the state

EventStop
  Handles the stop event

Housekeeping
  Called periodically to let the state check for changes (such as timeouts)

A higher-level object, the context, keeps track of the states and calls the appropriate function. It must provide a way for the states to indicate state transitions. As before, the states might know about each other and choose appropriately, or the transitions may be hidden, so the state might only indicate a need to go to the next state. Our system is straightforward, so a simple next-state function will be enough. In pseudo-code, the class looks like this:

```
class Context {
  class State Red, Yellow, Green;
  class State Current;

constructor:
  Current = Red;
  Current.Enter();

destructor:
  Current.Exit();
```

```
Go:
  if (Current.Go() indicates a state change)
    NextState();

Stop:
  if (Current.Stop() indicates a state change)
    NextState();

Housekeeping:
  if (Current.Housekeeping() indicates a state change)
    NextState();

NextState:
  Current.Exit();
  if (Current is Red)    Current = Green;
  if (Current is Yellow) Current = Red;
  if (Current is Green)  Current = Yellow;
  Current.Enter();
}
```

Allowing each state to be treated exactly the same frees the system from the switch statement, letting the objects do the work the conditionals used to do.

Table-Driven State Machine

Although flowcharts and state diagrams are handy for conceiving of a state machine, an easier way to document and fully define a state machine is to use a table.

In the example table in Figure 6-4, each state has a row with an action and multiple events. The action column describes what should occur in that state (which particular light should be on). The other columns show the transition that needs to occur when the system is in a state and an event occurs. Often the transition is simply to move to a new state (and perform the new associated action).

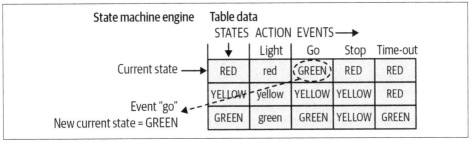

Figure 6-4. The state machine as a data table

When I worked on children's toys, they often offered 30 or more buttons (ABCs, volume, control, etc.). A table like this helped us figure out which events didn't get handled in the flowchart. Even though a button may be invalid for a state, someone somewhere will still inexplicably press it. So tables like these not only aided implementation and documentation, they were critical to designing the game play.

Defining the system as a table here hints toward defining it as a data table in the code. Instead of one large, complex piece of code, you end up with smaller, simpler pieces:

- A data table showing the action that occurs in a state and what state to go to when an event happens
- An engine that reads the data table and does what it says

The best part is that the engine is reusable, so if you are going to implement many complex state machines, this is a great solution.

The stoplight problem is a little too simple to make this method worthwhile for implementation, but it is a straightforward example. Let's start with the information in each table:

```
struct sStateTableEntry {
  tLight light;        // all states have associated lights
  tState goEvent;      // state to enter when go event occurs
  tState stopEvent;    // ... when stop event occurs
  tState timeoutEvent;// ... when timeout occurs
};
```

In addition to the next event for each table, I put in the light associated with the current state so that each state can be handled exactly the same way. (This state machine method really shines when there are lots of states that are all very similar.) Putting the light in the state table means our event handlers do the same thing for each state:

```
// event handler
void HandleEventGo(struct sStateTableEntry *currentState){
  // turn off the light (unless we're just going to turn it back on)
  if (currentState->light != currentState->go.light) {
    LightOff(currentState->light);
  }
  currentState = currentState->go;
  LightOn(currentState->light);
  StartTimer();
}
```

What about the actual table? It needs to start by defining an order in the data table:

```
typedef enum { kRedState = 0, kYellowState = 1, kGreenState = 2 } tState;

struct sStateTableEntry stateTable[] = {
  { kRedLight,    kGreenState,  kRedState,    kRedState},   // Red
  { kYellowLight, kYellowState, kYellowState, kRedState},   // Yellow
  { kGreenLight,  kGreenState,  kYellowState, kGreenState}, // Green
}
```

Typing in this table is a pain, and it is easy to get into trouble with an off-by-one error. However, if your state machine is a spreadsheet table and you can save it as a comma- or tab-separated variable file, a small script can generate the table for you. It feels a bit like cheating to reorganize your state machine as a spreadsheet, but this is a powerful technique when the number of states and events is large.

Making the state machine a table creates a dense view of the information, letting you take in the whole state machine at a glance. This will not only help you see holes (unhandled state/event combinations), it will also let you see that the product handles events consistently.

The table can show more complex interactions as well, detailing what needs to happen. However, as complexity increases, the table loses the ability to simply become data, and it likely needs to return to one of the implementation mechanisms shown earlier, one oriented around control flow statements. For example, if we add some detail and error-finding to the stoplight, we get a more complex picture:

State/events	Command: go	Command: stop	Timeout
Red	Move to green	Do nothing	Invalid (log error), do nothing
Yellow	Do not clear event (defer handling to red)	Do nothing	Move to red
Green	Do nothing	Move to yellow, set timer	Invalid (log error), do nothing

Even when the state machine can't be implemented as a data-table-driven system, representing it as a table provides better documentation than a flowchart.

Choosing a State Machine Implementation

Each option I showed for a state machine offers the same functionality, even though the implementations are different. I prefer table-driven state machines. Not only can I reuse the code that drives the generic state machine engine, I find the encapsulated states make for easier testing.

If you keep the context separate from the state, unit tests can call each state function. If the context is needed in the state, the unit test can pass in a structure of context information and verify any changes to the context after the state-related code has run.

Verifying the functionality of each state with a unit test leads to more robust code. You can do that with any of the implementations, as long as you keep the states encapsulated so test code can call the states, ideally without needing to know the context (or have the context passed into the state as a structure).

When you consider your implementation, be lazy. Choose the option that leads to the least amount of code. If they are all about the same, choose the one with the least amount of *replicated* code. If one implementation lets you reuse a section of code without copying it, that's a better implementation for your system. If that still doesn't help you choose, consider which form of code will be the most easily read by someone else.

State machines are powerful because they let your code act according to its history (state) and the environment (event). However, because they react differently depending on those things, they can be very difficult to maintain, leading to spaghetti code and dependencies between states that are not obvious to the casual observer. On the other hand, there is no better way to implement a reactive system, no way that makes the inherent complexity easier to maintain. Documentation is key, which is why I focused in these sections on the human-readable representation of the state machine before showing a code implementation.

Watchdog

We started the scheduler section mentioning the blink-red state. Its goal is to put the system in a safe mode when a system failure occurs. But how do we know a system failure has occurred?

Our software can monitor how long it has been since the last communication. If it doesn't see a stop or go command in an unreasonably long time, it can respond accordingly. Metaphorically speaking, it acts as a watchdog to prevent catastrophic failure. Actually, the term *watchdog* means something far more specific in the embedded world.

Most processors or reset circuits have a watchdog timer capability that will reset the processor if the processor fails to perform an action (such as toggle an I/O line or write to a particular register). The watchdog system waits for the processor to send a signal that things are going well. If such a signal fails to occur in a reasonable (often configurable) amount of time, the watchdog will cause the processor to reset.

The goal is that when the system fails, it fails in a safe manner (fail-safe). No one wants the system to fail, but we have to be realistic. Software crashes. Even safety-critical software crashes. As we design and develop our systems, we work to avoid crashes. But unless you are omniscient, your software will fail in an unexpected way. Cosmic rays and loose wires happen, and many embedded systems need to be self-reliant. They can't wait for someone to reboot the system when the software hangs. They might not even be monitored by a human. If the system can't recover from certain kinds of errors, it is generally better to restart and put the system in a good state.

Using a watchdog does not free you from handling normal errors; it exists only for restarting an otherwise unrecoverable system. There are ways to use a watchdog that make it more effective. But first, let's look at some suboptimal techniques, based on models earlier in this chapter, that would make the watchdog less effective:

Setting up a timer interrupt that goes off slightly more often than the watchdog would take to expire

If you service the watchdog in the timer interrupt, your system will never reset, even when your system is stuck in an infinite loop. This defeats the purpose of the watchdog. Never do this.

Setting the delay function (`DelayMs`) to service the watchdog, with the idea that the processor isn't doing anything else then

You'll have delay functions scattered around the code, so the watchdog will get serviced often. Even then, if the processor gets stuck in an area of code that happens to have a delay, the system won't reset as it should.

Putting the watchdog servicing in places that take a while for the processor to perform, maybe the five or six longest-running functions

By scattering the watchdog code around, it waters down the power of the watchdog and offers the possibility that your code could crash in one of those areas and hang the system.

The goal of the watchdog is to provide a way to determine whether any part of the system has crashed. Ideally, watchdog servicing is in only one place—a place that the code has to pass through that shows all of its subsystems are running as expected. Generally, this is the main loop. Even if it means that your watchdog needs to have a longer timeout, having it watch the whole system is better than giving it a shorter recovery time while trying to watch only part of the system.

Sadly, for some systems, the watchdog cannot be segregated so neatly. When the signal to the watchdog must be sent in some lower level of code, recognize that the code is dangerous, an area where an unrecoverable error might occur, causing the system to hang. That code will need extra attention to determine whether anything could go wrong (and hopefully prevent it).

Generally, you don't want the watchdog active during board bring-up or while using a debugger. Otherwise, the system will reset after a breakpoint. Having a straightforward way to turn off the watchdog will facilitate debugging. If you have a logging method, be sure to print out a message on boot if the watchdog is on. It is one of those things you don't want to forget to enable as you do production testing. Alternatively, you can toggle an LED when the watchdog is serviced to give your system a heartbeat that is easy to see from the outside, letting the user know that everything is working as expected.

Main Loops

This chapter started with a few important notes about RTOS terms (even though I'm not supposing you have an RTOS on your system, the concepts transfer to bare metal). Then there were a bunch of ways to put together state machines. This is all well and good, but how do we really get started?

We usually start in the main loop. As with state machines, there are many ways to set up a main loop. They all have advantages and disadvantages, so you'll need to figure out what is best for you.

Polling and Waiting

I like Arduino's simple and clear program structure:

```
setup:
  init
loop:
  toggle LED
  delay
```

Behind the scenes, the Arduino development environment puts in a main function that calls the setup function to do initialization. The hidden main function does other board and processor initialization that it needs. Once your setup and the hidden initialization is complete, it starts a forever loop, calling your loop function on each pass (but also possibly calling its own set functions as needed). Figure 6-5 shows how the

---

pieces of the system interact. The development environment hides the details from you, but somewhere, there is a main function.

We don't need someone else to do this for us; we can make `main` ourselves:

```
main:
  init
  while (1)
    toggle LED
    delay
```

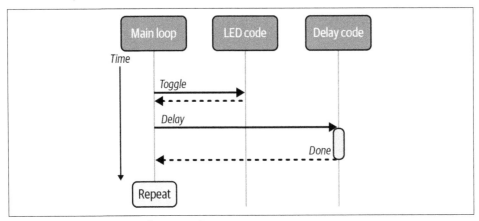

Figure 6-5. Simplest main loop: toggles an LED

This is how main loops begin their lives, as something simple. Of course, this blinking light is extremely boring, so I'm going to need to add something:

```
main:
  init
  while (1)
    read inputs
    write outputs
    toggle LED
    delay
```

Note that the "read inputs" and "write outputs" could be something else in your code: a function to check on your command handler interface; where you update your state machine based on the current time or polled buttons; or the code transforms the inputs you have into the outputs you need. See Figure 6-6 for the sequence of how things happen in this loop.

Everything happens as expected in this loop but there is a big problem: it is blocking. If inputs come in while the system is running the delay, they won't get handled until the next pass of the loop. If the inputs need to be dealt with quickly, this may not work.

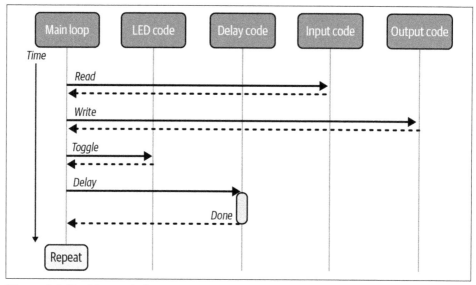

Figure 6-6. Blocking main loop

Timer Interrupt

Blocking the processor with a delay is silly when a timer interrupt could do the work toggling of the LED:

```
timer interrupt: toggle LED
main:
  init
  while (1)
    read inputs
    write outputs
    pet watchdog
```

Toggling an I/O pin takes very little time; it is safe to put it in an interrupt.

One downside is that the LED is no longer connected to reading and writing; it tells us only that the timer interrupt is firing off at regular intervals. However, I added a watchdog to make sure the loop stays running as expected. The sequence diagram for this (Figure 6-7) shows the LED code separated from the other pieces of code. The increased system complexity is balanced by decreased local complexity (main doesn't need to pay attention to the LED).

This method assumes that the read inputs and write outputs are not blocking each other and that they each happen quickly enough not to interfere with the timing of the other.

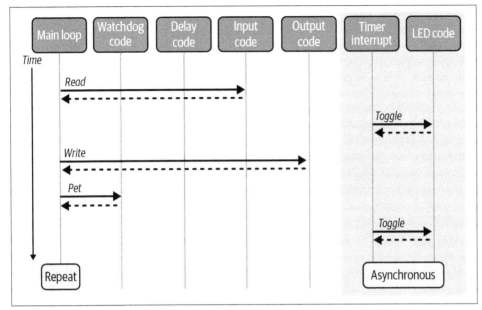

Figure 6-7. Main loop with timer interrupt controlling LED

Interrupts Do Everything

But what if they can't? What if sometimes the input needs to run immediately and can't wait for the output to finish doing its thing?

Assuming there is a way to set an interrupt when the input data is available, we can have an interrupt handle copying the data in. This may be a sensor that sends an interrupt to start sending data or a communication pathway that lets you set up an interrupt when its buffer is half full. On the output side, perhaps there is a communications pathway that takes time but will interrupt to tell you when it is ready for the next message. So what if the interrupts do all the work?

```
timer interrupt: toggle LED
data available interrupt: copy data in
output ready interrupt: copy data out

main:
  init
  set up interrupts
  while (1)
    pet watchdog
    sleep
```

There is a lot of goodness to this. The decoupling of the subsystems is good as it leads to a separation of concerns with every interrupt doing its own thing, not depending on the others. Also, with the interrupts indicating when things happen, the main loop can go to sleep until it's awoken by the interrupts. This behavior is great for power reasons (more about that in Chapter 13).

As the sequence diagram in Figure 6-8 shows, each of these pieces of code is asynchronous, happening whenever it happens, not dependent on each other. Well, mostly not dependent. If an interrupt wakes the processor, the ISR runs, then returns to the main loop directly after the sleep call. In my case, it pets the watchdog and goes back to sleep. The downside of the asynchronous approach is that understanding the flow of execution is much harder (which makes debugging much more difficult).

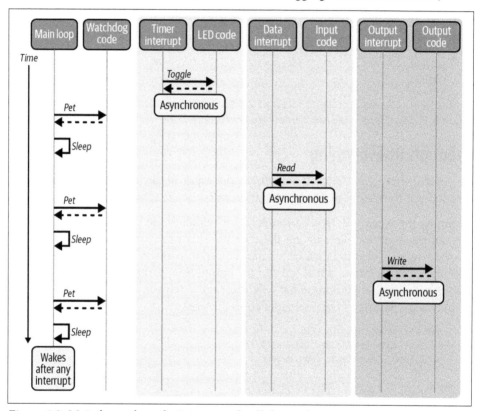

Figure 6-8. Main loop where the interrupts do all the work

Because the interrupts happen when they need to, their response time (system latency) should be fast, as long as another interrupt isn't blocking them from running. Priority and missed interrupts can become issues if interrupts take too long.

Of course, interrupts are supposed to be short. Copying a bunch of data is usually not a short process; in fact, it is the sort of thing we want to avoid doing in an interrupt service routine.

Interrupts Cause Events

Instead, we can set a variable that tells main what to do, keeping our interrupts short, allowing the processor to sleep, and keeping the system responsive to the current needs:

```
timer interrupt: set global led_change variable
data available interrupt: set global data_available
output ready interrupt: set global output_ready

main:
  init
  while (1)
    if led_change: toggle led; led_change = false
    if data_available: copy input; data_available = false
    if output_ready: copy output; output_ready = false
    pet watchdog
    sleep
```

This adds a bunch of global variables to the code, often a good way to create spaghetti code. However, the ordering of events is less uncertain as we can use the global variables to control ordering (only run output_ready after data_available). The interrupts are still asynchronous, but as the logic is in normal execution, we can add a few logging calls which will make debugging much easier.

Plus, the processor can still sleep because the interrupts will wake it up.

Not shown in the pseudocode are two important points I've already mentioned earlier in the book. First, the global variables are volatile, so they don't get removed by the compiler's optimizer (because, according to the compiler's view of the main loop, nothing ever changes about event variables). Second, the global variables are only modified with the interrupts disabled to prevent race conditions.

And if that code with all of its if statements looks like a state machine to you, well, thank you for paying attention.

Figure 6-9 shows the events being created by the interrupts and handled in the main loop. Note that the interrupts are asynchronous, so main will handle whatever event happens next, not in any particular order.

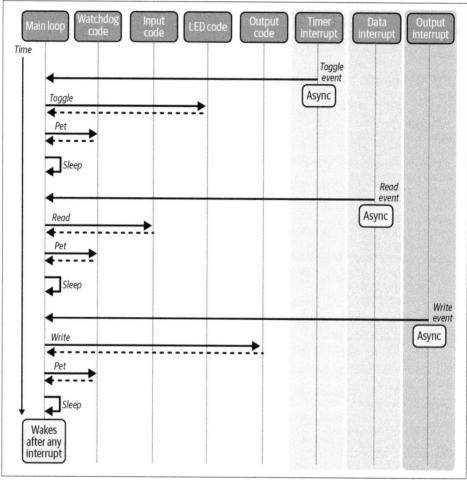

Figure 6-9. Interrupts signal events that are handled in the main loop

Very Small Scheduler

What about the very small scheduler from Chapter 5? How does that look in this form? As noted above, it looks through a list of tasks, calling their associated callback function when it is time for that task to run. It is entirely time-based:

```
system tick interrupt: increment current time

main:
  init
  while (1)
    for each task
      if time to run task
        call task callback function
        set new time to run task
    pet watchdog
```

With this method, each task *runs to completion*. It is a function call so it may be interrupted by an interrupt like the system timer tick (aka *systick*) but not by any other task. It will finish before the next task can run. That also means that if it takes a long time, functions scheduled after it can be delayed and that all tasks might run back-to-back before the watchdog is petted. Though it is rare that all tasks run in one iteration of the scheduler, you must configure your watchdog timer with a long enough time-out to allow for such a possibility.

If this seems totally normal to you, I agree; but an RTOS can be *preemptive*, which means that a more important task can interrupt a less important task to use the processor. The RTOS's scheduler usually looks for the opportunity to do this anytime an RTOS-related function is called.

But the small scheduler runs in main and doesn't do anything fancy. When a task is done, it returns from its function. Then the processor can do other things like go on to the next task that is ready to run.

The processor can also sleep, as long as it can schedule a wake-up interrupt when the next task is ready to run. Most timers allow this sort of thing but not all. If not, the system will have to wake up on each new systick interrupt.

The sequence diagram in Figure 6-10 shows this in action. Note that the tasks are asynchronous with respect to each other (they don't need to go in the order shown in the diagram). Instead, each task depends on how often it needs to run.

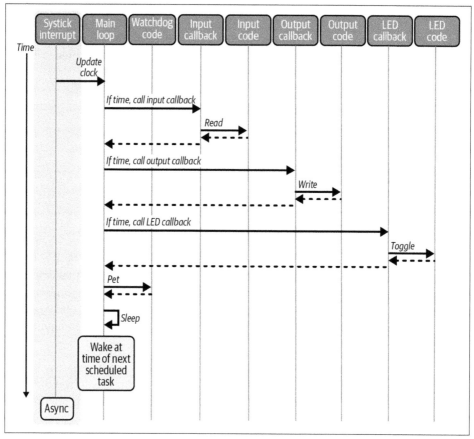

Figure 6-10. Very small scheduler drives all tasks, running them at given times

Not everything has to go through the scheduler; you can have other interrupts. For example, a data available interrupt may change the list of tasks so that the input callback happens immediately (well, the next time the scheduler checks if that task is ready to run).

Additionally, the LED could still be toggled by a separate timer interrupt. There is no hard and fast rule for any of these main loop styles; mash-ups are allowed.

Active Objects

There is one more style of main loop that I'd like to share. If you combine the synchronous (non-interrupt-y) simplicity of the very small scheduler with the lovely separation of concerns when everything is done in interrupts, you get *active objects*. This one needs an RTOS to be effective because it needs truly separate tasks. However, I see it a lot in embedded systems from vendor demo code that uses Bluetooth or a state machine. This is framework code, where you need to add your functions and tasks to an existing system.

The goal is to spend very little time in interrupts, let everything be completely asynchronous, and make each piece of code as separate as possible. That way, your code won't interfere with whatever system you are integrating into.

A key characteristic of active objects is *inversion of control*. Instead of your code controlling the system, the framework is in charge and will call you when it needs you:

```
timer interrupt: send event to timer task
timer task:
  while (1)
    wait for event message
    if message is toggle LED, toggle LED

data available interrupt: send event to data task
data task:
  while (1)
    wait for event message
    if message is data available,
      handle data
      send output ready to output task

output task:
 while (1)
    wait for message
    if message is output ready,
      output data

main:
  init
  while (1)
    pet watchdog
    sleep
```

While more complicated on the surface, each task is completely devoted to what it does. Each task keeps its data private: tasks only communicate via message queues that are filled asynchronously. They try to remain autonomous from each other. The first few times I saw active objects, it seemed like a lot of repetition, having to dig deeply through vendor code to trace how event messages travel through multiple tasks to be handled by the correct ones. However, looking at it from the vendor's perspective, the events are a sort of contract, telling you what is going on without knowing anything about your code.

 Inversion of control is often referred to as the Hollywood Principle: Don't call us, we'll call you.

One good way to identify an active object is to see if the task is organized around a *message pump*. Usually this is implemented by a `wait for message` area followed by a large switch statement that depends on the message event received. Once the event is handled, the task goes back to waiting. The task should not do any blocking calls, the only place it waits is in that one spot (`wait for message`). (Not all code follows this rule, some systems allow delays or other RTOS calls to give up control. But it is good practice to have the message pump be the single blocking point.)

Figure 6-11 shows how separate each component of the system is, minimizing dependencies and only allowing specific methods of communication between tasks.

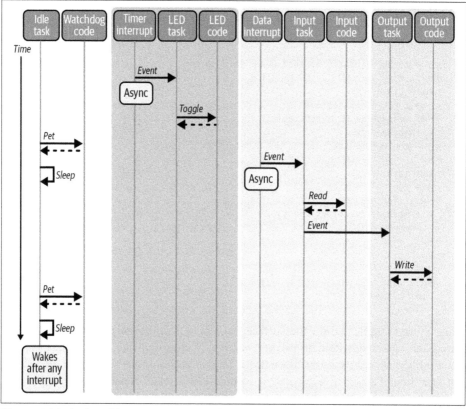

Figure 6-11. Active objects run as true tasks in an operating system, using a message pump to separate dependencies between tasks

Another name for an active object is the actor design pattern. These active objects are usually implemented as event-driven state machines. And if you recall dependency injection from Chapter 4, it shares a lot of the same philosophy as inversion of control. I want to say the terminology doesn't matter; the principles are the important part, but the jargon makes it easier to discuss the principles.

You might think all this technobabble is overwhelming and not that important, but you never know when you might find yourself in a Star Trek episode where the Enterprise must be saved by a carefully designed active object.

Further Reading

Running an embedded system without an operating system (running on bare metal) doesn't mean you can be ignorant of operating system principles. If anything, because you are doing the work yourself, you need to know more about how OSs function so you can re-create the parts you need. There are many good OS books, but my favorite is the classic text book *Operating Systems: Design and Implementation* by Andrew Tannenbaum (Pearson). For a free resource, check out the OSDev Wiki (*https://osdev.org/Main_Page*).

I also recommend finding an old book about programming a small processor, something published in 1980 or before. For example, I have *Programming the 6502*, third edition, by Rodnay Zaks (Sybex). You can find one in a library or used bookstore. This sort of book takes out the modern fluff surrounding processors (the fluff that makes them easier to use) and provides insight into how the processors worked when they were simpler. Also, they make for pretty entertaining reading because the assumed knowledge is much different from current user manuals (mine starts with a section called "What is programming?").

Embedded software engineers sometimes focus more on the hardware details that we need to learn or the algorithms associated with application of the device. Good software techniques aren't new. One of the best introductions to good software practices is a paper from 1988: "Designing Reusable Classes" (*https://oreil.ly/ZA-zZ*) by Ralph Johnson and Brian Foote. It is free online if you want to take a look.

Miro Samek of Quantum Leaps is an enthusiastic advocate for the active object pattern and good software in embedded systems (see the "Resources" section of the Quantum Leaps website (*https://state-machine.com*)). His books and blog postings are filled with excellent information, but his YouTube videos are particularly instructive because he codes the systems as he talks.

Interview Question: Stoplight Control of an Intersection

A small city has decided its intersection is too busy for a stop sign and needs to be upgraded to a light. The city managers asked you to write the code for the light. There are four lights, each with a red, yellow, and green bulb. There are also four car sensors that can tell when a vehicle is stopped at the light. Where do you start? Tell me about your design, and then write some pseudocode. (During this time, I've drawn an intersection like the one shown in Figure 6-12. I tend to draw this intersection on the interviewee's piece of paper if I can.)

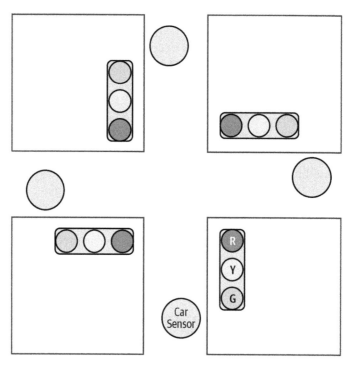

Figure 6-12. Intersection in a small city

This is a problem that lets the interviewee drive the interaction. If they want to talk about design patterns, there are plenty. If they want to skip design and talk about timers or the hardware of the sensing, that works too.

An interviewee should clarify the problem if it isn't clear. In this question, they should ask whether there is a left turn light (no, the intersection is small, and the city doesn't need that yet). Some people also ask about a crosswalk (also not to be handled in the initial development).

Very good interviewees notice that the problem is only half of what it appears to be on the surface. The goal is not to control four stoplights, since two lights are always in sync.

As with all of my interview questions, naming is very important. The reason I draw on their paper is to encourage the interviewee to add their own information to the diagram. Some good names include identifying the intersection by compass directions (north/south and east/west), and some moniker that makes sense for the situation (First and Main) or place on the page (right/left and up/down). Until they have put names on the elements in the drawing, any pseudocode will be gibberish.

Once they start digging into the problem, I like to hear about the state machine (or automata, or flowchart). I want to see diagrams or flowcharts. Some people get stuck on the initial state because we all tend to want to start with "what happens first." However, the initial state is relatively uninteresting in this case (though, if asked, I'll suggest they start with an all-red state).

Once they've laid out the basics, I tend to add a few curveballs (though great interviewees tend to handle these before I ask).

First, what if a sensor is broken? Or what if the city wants to be friendly to bikes (which don't activate the car sensor)? This adds a timer to the state machine so that the intersection doesn't get trapped in any state forever.

Second, the intersection has been getting a lot of accidents with folks running the yellow light. Can they do something to improve the safety of the system? (Hint: Add a short all-red state to allow traffic to clear the intersection before going to the next green.)

Because this interview question is simply a logic problem, I often spring it on other engineers, particularly those who work in quality departments ("How would you write a test plan for this controller?").

CHAPTER 7

Communicating with Peripherals

A peripheral is anything outside your processor core that the processor communicates with. Peripherals come in all shapes and sizes. Because your processor core has direct access to memory inside the processor, it barely counts as a peripheral (though memory can also be outside your chip).

So which is the best way to communicate with peripherals: UART, SPI, I²C, or something else? I get asked this question a lot. So let's talk about why there isn't an answer. I need a whole chapter to explain.

We've investigated what goes on inside your processor during the course of this book. Before you can build a system, we need to consider what goes on in other components. Communicating with the other components is a start to this. I want to show you what to look for when deciding what kind of communication method to use or writing a communications driver.

For the most part, you'll end up using a driver from your processor's hardware abstraction layer (HAL). You'll need to configure it according to the external device's datasheet and your processor's manual. However, that breaks when you meet a new way of communicating, one without an easy driver. So let's look at protocols and methods we'll often use as a way of identifying the important pieces to look for in a new protocol.

Serial Communication

At its broadest definition, serial communication is the process of sending data one bit at a time over a communication pathway (usually a wire, a physical wire).[1] Under this

---

1 This is in contrast to parallel communication where each bit has a dedicated communication pathway.

definition, even Ethernet is a serial form of communication. Let's narrow the definition down a bit and say a serial protocol is something that can be implemented with a universal synchronous/asynchronous receiver/transmitter (USART, pronounced "use-art"). That probably doesn't help you much, does it? Let me define some terms, and then we'll look at the most common serial communication methods.

A UART (pronounced "you-art") implements the default protocol for when you want to hook up a serial cable between your device and your computer.

Even high-end internet routers often have a serial port for configuration or debugging. Not only is it cheap to implement, a serial port is also like a Torx screwdriver: most people don't know what they are looking at.

UART (universal asynchronous received/transmitter) is missing the S in USART so before going on, let me take a step back and talk about terms. The S is for *synchronous*, which means the clock is a separate signal from the data. An *asynchronous* pathway has an implicit clock, usually using start and stop bits to indicate when communication is occurring (thereby decreasing its bandwidth). Because the implicit clock needs to allow for some timing errors, a synchronous bus can operate at a faster speed than an asynchronous bus. Often the generator of the clock also controls the bus, making it an *asymmetric* pathway. Usually only the bus controller can initiate data transfers.

Another important factor when considering serial ports is whether you have two wires to communicate on (transmit and receive) or only one wire (which switches direction depending on whose turn it is to talk). Having two wires is called *full duplex*; sharing a single wire is called *half duplex*. I²C and 1-wire bus are two of the most popular half-duplex protocols. Of course, half-duplex communication is a little more complicated to debug because you can't be sure on your oscilloscope (or logic analyzer) which chip is the source of the bytes.

The timing diagrams from the peripheral's datasheet are often critical for getting a communications driver working. As you bring up a driver for the first time, expect to spend some time setting up an oscilloscope and trying to re-create those diagrams (to verify your driver). Look in Chapter 3 for tips on datasheets and O-scopes.

When encountering a new communication bus, the things to pay attention to include:

- How is the communication clock generated? Is it asynchronous (all parties agree upon it ahead of time) or synchronous (explicitly carried on a wire on the bus)? If it is synchronous, does the clock generator have any other special responsibilities?

- Is the communication symmetric (anyone can talk) or asymmetric (only the bus controller initiates communication)?

- Is it full duplex (enough I/Os so everyone can send data) or half duplex (they take turns sending data over shared I/Os)?

- How many hardware lines does it need?

- Is it point-to-point or is there point-to-multipoint? Is addressing done in the protocol or via chip select?

- What is the maximum throughput of the system? How many data bits can be transferred every second? How much of that is overhead?

- How far can the signals travel?

The goal with these questions is to figure out how long it will take you to implement a driver using the communication bus in question.

 Many processors come with example code, particularly for their communication drivers. Sometimes this code is excellent, but sometimes it is only an example to get it running (but not working robustly). Be sure to review this code if you incorporate it into your project.

Moving on from the higher-level terminology and general questions, let's look at how some popular buses behave. Remember that this is still just an introduction. In the end, you'll need to look at your datasheet to see what the peripheral needs and at your processor manual to see how to provide it.

Figure 7-1 compares the number of lines needed for some of the most popular buses and peripherals.

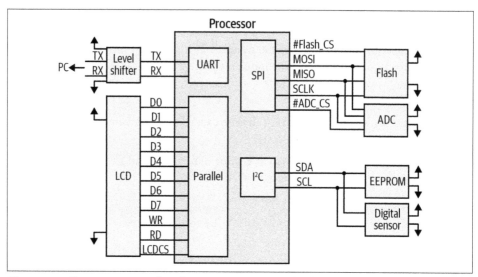

Figure 7-1. Comparing peripheral communication methods

TTL Serial

As we've seen, the word "serial" is overloaded to mean many protocols. Even the most common serial interface (the one between your system and your computer) has several names. I already mentioned UART, which is the part of your processor that implements this interface. However, it sends out TTL-level serial signals. By definition, TTL (transistor-transistor logic) means 0–5 V. However, in practice it means whatever voltage level your processor's digital I/O is at: 0–5 V, 0–3 V, 0–1.8 V, etc.

While there can be other signals (see "RS-232 Serial" on page 185), the most important signals are transmit (TX) and receive (RX). You can interface your embedded system with your computer using those alone. Note that both systems have a TX and an RX, so they need to be swapped to connect each TX to the RX on the other side.

Not swapping TX and RX is the most common hardware issue I've seen. If a component isn't responding over the communication bus, check that the TX and RX (or clock and data) lines are correct.

To connect from your board to your computer, you will need a USB-to-serial cable (sometimes called an FTDI cable, after the company that makes it). Make sure to get a cable that is the correct voltage for your processor for the TTL side.

This form of serial communication resides at the physical and data link layers of the OSI model (more about this soon in "Layered Model of Communication (OSI)" on page 186). There is no built-in addressing scheme, so it can be established only between two parties (symmetric point-to-point communication).

It uses an implicit clock (asynchronous!) so both parties must agree upon the baud rate (bits per second), parity, number of start and stop bits, and flow control. While it is commonly not used at all, flow control can be done in the hardware using some of the other UART lines or in software using the Xon/Xoff protocol. "Further Reading" on page 209 provides resources that explain these conventions.

> To talk to a processor's debug serial port, usually you should choose 8 data bits, no parity, one stop bit, and no flow control. This is often abbreviated as 8N1, no flow.

The baud rates are usually between 2,400 and 115,200 (though they can go as high as 921,600). Certain baud rates are very popular: 9,600; 19,200; and 115,200. Due to the implicit clock, you will need to configure the same baud rate on both devices (i.e., your processor and your computer).

Because of the start and stop bits sent for each data byte, most serial connections have a throughput in bytes about equal to their baud rate divided by 10. If you have a baud rate of 19,200 bits per second, your system is going to be able to send and receive about 1,920 bytes per second. Compare this with standard 100-megabit Ethernet (though 1-gigabit is pretty common too), which gives a throughput of around 11 megabytes per second, depending on the protocol. Serial is slow.

RS-232 Serial

RS-232 is similar to TTL serial with only electrical changes and no software ramifications. A serial port used to mean an RS-232 port with a DB-9 connector. The signals were (+/– 12 V) . Figure 7-2 shows a common use of serial cabling in embedded development. Although RS-232 defines eight signals (and ground), the most important are the transmit and receive lines that come from your processor as TTL signals.

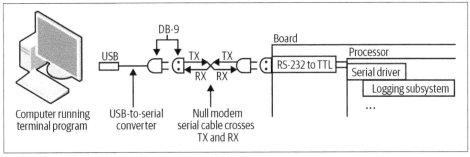

Figure 7-2. Serial connection from the embedded system to a PC

However, if you are hooking up to a cellular data modem or a serial-to-Ethernet converter, you may also need some of the other UART lines to indicate when each device is ready to receive data (specifically RTS/CTS handshaking for hardware flow control). Even though the clock is implicit, you'll need to designate which side is the bus controller, because the signals are not exactly symmetric. In RS-232, the bus controller (usually your computer) is the data terminal equipment (DTE) and the other side is the data communication equipment (DCE). Yes, pretty much every protocol has different names for similar things.

The relatively high voltage of RS-232 (12 V!) means it can travel pretty far before the signals deteriorate—up to 50 feet (15 meters) with a normal serial (or null modem) cable. A special cable (low capacitance) can increase the distance by about a factor of 20.

RS-232 has been around seemingly forever and continues to be widely used. Even though its demise is often heralded as new protocols take its place (Ethernet, USB, etc.), RS-232 keeps coming back because it is easy to implement in software and cheap to implement in hardware.

Layered Model of Communication (OSI)

Communication protocols are often layered so we can talk about the pieces separately. The layers in embedded systems are often limited to:

Electrical
> TTL and RS-232 have different voltages, though the same number of wires

How bits and bytes flow
> Those terms from above: synchronous, symmetric, duplex, and so on

Packets and networks
> How clumps of data get to their destination: more about that in a bit

The standard Open Systems Interconnection (OSI) model is a way to talk about communication protocols as a series of layers (see Table 7-1). Each layer provides some feature to the one above it to build up a communication pathway.

You don't need to memorize this. This model is far more complex than you'll need for most embedded systems, but by having an idea of how a big, complicated communication pathway works, you'll get some ideas about how little ones work.

Table 7-1. OSI model

Layer	Function	Questions for this layer	On a PC's Ethernet
1. Physical	Provides the electrical and physical specification	How many wires connect your processor to a peripheral? At what voltage? At what speed?	Ethernet cable
2. Data link	Describes how bytes flow over the physical wires	Do the bytes have parity checking? How many bits are sent and received in each frame?	Ethernet (802.xx)
3. Network	Gets a variable length of information (packets) from one place to another	How is each system addressed? How does the layer break up (and re-form) big blocks of data into amounts that can go over the communication pathway?	IP
4. Transport	Moves blocks of data in a reliable manner, even if those blocks are larger than the lower levels can handle	How do you count on data being received even when there is a glitch in the wires? How are errors recovered from?	TCP
5. Session	Manages a connection between the local and remote application	How is this data sent from here to there?	Sockets
6. Presentation	Provides structure to the data, possibly encryption	How is the data organized when it is sent?	TLS and SSL
7. Application	Takes user interaction with the software and formulates a communication request	What command should be sent when a button is pressed?	HTTP

SPI

RS-232 and TTL serial work have some deficiencies: about 20% of the bitstream is overhead; both sides have to know the setup (e.g., baud rate and parity); and the RX/TX crossing requirement is a pain because which wire is RX (or TX) depends on your point of view.

Instead we can use SPI, which uses four wires to connect your processor to a SPI peripheral:

MISO (Micro-In Sensor-Out, formerly Master-In Slave-Out[2]) or SDI (Serial Data In)
    Receive for the bus controller, usually your microprocessor.

MOSI (Micro-Out Sensor-In, formerly Master-Out Slave-In) or SDO (Serial Data Out)
    Transmit for the bus controller, usually your microprocessor.

---

2 Terms matter. For controllers: principal, host, primary. For peripherals: agent, worker, subordinate, secondary.

SCK, CLK, or SCLK (Clock)
    Generated by the controller; this is the clock for both sides of communication.

CS (Chip Select) or SS (Sensor Select, formerly Slave Select)
    One line per peripheral. This is generated by the bus controller and is usually active low.

SPI is a synchronous, asymmetric protocol, with the clock provided by the controller. One oddity with SPI is that both controller and peripheral have to send data when the clock is going, always trading data, even when one of them doesn't have anything important to say.

Sometimes the controller will not have a command that it needs to send, but it will need to transmit a byte in order to receive one. The value 0xFF is the traditional byte to transmit when you want to force the peripheral to send data. This is called "clocking out" the data.

With RS-232's implicit clock, both sides of the communication need to have a relatively precise oscillator; otherwise, they may lose synchronization. Since the controller provides the clock, SPI doesn't require either side to have a precision oscillator. The controller probably still has an oscillator of some sort, but it doesn't need to be as precise, so it can be cheaper.

The clock speed can be slow (tens of Hz) or fast (up to 100 MHz). The clock speed is the baud rate, and there isn't any overhead, so a clock of 8 MHz leads to 1 MB/ second, much faster than RS-232 and, at high clock speeds, even comparable to Ethernet. Finally, the clock speed can be whatever your processor can clock and the particular peripheral can receive. There is no need to try to run at precisely 8 MHz; it is acceptable to run at 8.1234 MHz or 7.9876 MHz. The flip side of running a clock so fast is that it doesn't travel very far. SPI signals usually don't leave the board.

The protocol defines a chip select, so multiple peripherals can often share a single SPI bus as long as there is one CS line per peripheral.

 Check your peripheral datasheets; not all peripherals play nicely on a shared bus.

A SPI driver is even easier to implement than an RS-232 driver. The only tricky part is to figure out whether you want the data on the line to be valid when the clock edge rises or falls (clock polarity and phase). Your peripheral datasheet will tell you what it wants, and the processor manual will give you some registers to configure it.

If your datasheet isn't sufficient, look at the Wikipedia page on SPI (*https://en.wikipedia.org/wiki/Serial_Peripheral_Interface*). Many protocols are best described on Wikipedia, often in more detail than terse datasheets.

Bit-Bang Drivers

The SPI interface is so orderly and methodical that it is often implemented as a *bit-bang* interface. A bit-bang driver uses I/O lines directly to do the work of the communication interface instead of a processor's built-in registers. Honestly, you can create a bit-bang driver for any of the serial interfaces, but it consumes far more processing power than a built-in processor interface. However, sometimes your processor doesn't have the hardware interface to implement the communication method you need, so you make your own.

To make your own SPI interface:

1. Start with three unused I/O lines and a built-in timer. The chip select line works the same as it does in a processor-provided interface, so I'm not counting it here.

2. Set up a timer to interrupt at four times the clock speed (so 8 MHz for a 2 MHz communication rate). Each of the four interrupts has a purpose:

   - Toggle the I/O line
   - Write an output bit to MOSI
   - Toggle the I/O line
   - Read an input bit from MISO

3. Every eight bits (or 32 interrupts), start a new byte.

Note, that you need to write a bit and read a bit for each full clock cycle. However, the peripheral datasheet will probably show you that the safe-to-read time is half a clock cycle away from the safe-to-write time, which is why we need the timer to interrupt at four times the intended communication clock frequency.

Overall, you don't have to do all that much for each interrupt, but you have a lot of interrupts, which means tons of context switching.

I²C and TWI

I²C stands for inter-integrated circuit, and is pronounced "eye-squared-see" or "eye-two-see." I²C is sometimes called TWI, for "two-wire interface." Like SPI, the I²C bus has a controller that provides the clock and starts the interaction. However, unlike SPI, the I²C bus can have multiple controllers. A controller can even switch sides, allowing a peripheral to drive the interaction.

I²C is the result of trying to figure out how few wires can be used to connect a whole bunch of things together. It uses two connections: SCL (serial clock line) for the clock and SDA (serial data line) for the data (going both ways on the same wire, making this a half-duplex protocol).

The simplicity of hardware design is paid for in software complexity. Not only that, but because this is a multipoint protocol, allowing multiple peripherals (and multiple controllers), it specifies an address scheme, which moves it beyond OSI layers 1 (physical) and 2 (data link) to layer 3 (network). On the other hand, I²C is fairly widely used, so you should be able to find some example code to help you implement your driver.

I²C drivers (or processor hardware) invariably include a state machine to deal with the complexity of switching the direction of the bus between the controller transmitting and the peripheral transmitting. The controller starts communication by sending a 7-bit address and indicating whether it wants to read from or write to the peripheral. The peripheral with that address then sends an acknowledgment (ACK). Next, the controller sends a command to (or reads from) the peripheral, and the interaction proceeds. When the communication is complete, the controller sends a stop bit.

The number of components attached to the bus is limited by the address space (and by the capacitance of the bus). Many components let you set the last few bits of the address using pull-ups, so you can put several instances of the same part on the bus. Alternatively, some components have slightly different part numbers that result in different I²C addresses.

Common I²C bus speeds are 100 Kb/second (standard mode) and 10 Kb/second (low-speed mode). It is synchronous, so the controller sends the clock, and these frequencies don't need to be precise. Some peripherals implement faster speeds: 400 Kb/s, 1 Mb/s, and even 3.4 Mb/s.[3]

Although some overhead is built into the I²C bus—the bus arbitration and start/stop bits—if you are moving large amounts of data around (e.g., reading from an ADC [analog-to-digital converter] or an EEPROM), the overhead becomes a negligible percentage of the traffic. So standard mode can achieve 12.5 KB/s throughput on the I²C bus.

I²C generally isn't used to communicate to distant peripherals, but it can go a few meters before the cable degrades the signal too much (though you can get transceivers and special cables to increase the distance). As the protocol needs only two wires to go to many peripherals, the cable can be only four wires: SDA, SCL, power, and ground.

---

3 Remember, "b" is for bit and "B" is for byte (almost always), so to convert from Mb to MB, divide by 8.

1-Wire

I²C doesn't actually win the award for having as few serial wires as possible; there is still the aptly named 1-wire bus. It provides low-speed data communication and power over a single wire. (Well, you need ground, too.) It is similar in concept to I²C (controller, arbitration, a software driver with a state machine), but it has an implicit clock of 16.3 Kb/s. Although this is a fairly low data rate, it can be used for longer ranges, up to 10 m (100 m with special cables).

Like I²C, the bus can be used with a wide variety of peripherals, including memory, sensors, ADCs, and DACs. After simple temperature sensors, the most common 1-wire implementations are in authentication chips. These are used to authenticate the origin of pieces of the system that can be replaced. For example, if you are making a printer cartridge (or any form of consumable) and you want to deter competitors from making a drop-in replacement, a 1-wire secure authentication chip will force your consumable to send the correct password to your firmware before it can be used.

And while you can't really only have one wire to communicate to a device, some devices use *parasitic power*, using the communication line as a power source so the cable only needs two wires (data/power and ground).

Parallel

Parallel communication just means having several I/O lines so that you can send multiple bits to and from a peripheral at the same time. By putting 8 or 16 bits on the bus at once, you can communicate very quickly. The data bits of the parallel bus are almost always combined on a single bank of I/O pins. This lets you set all of the bits by writing the data byte to the I/O register. Instead of setting a single bit, as shown in Chapter 4:

```
P1OUT |= BIT2;        // IO1_2 high
```

you can modify several I/O lines at once:

```
P1OUT |= data & 0xFF; // put 8 bits on parallel bus: IO1_0 to IO_7
```

A parallel interface tends to make a chip more expensive. I/O lines take up space in the silicon, and the size of the silicon is proportional to the cost of making the chip (though for many chips, RAM is a larger consumer of silicon than the I/O lines).

Parallel interfaces tend to be reserved for things that have high data throughput requirements: displays and external memory, components we'll talk about soon. A small color LCD with a 320×480 pixel display needs 450 KB per screen (if you update the whole screen, though you won't usually do that).

With an update rate of at least 30 Hz, you'd need to move about 13 MB/s (105.5 Mb/s), which is faster than SPI can manage. However, with an 8-bit-wide parallel bus, the bit rate per line goes down to 13 Mb/s. The data gets spread over the whole bus, so the more lines in parallel, the higher the throughput.

Purely parallel buses tend to be half duplex, with control lines to indicate which direction the data is going (read and write lines) and whether the bus is connected to a chip (chip select line). The control lines also tend to be the clocks for the system, so a write interaction would look like the following:

1. De-assert the write control line.

2. Select the chip.

3. Set the parallel bus to the data intended.

4. Assert the write control line.

5. Go to step 2 until all data has been transferred.

Check the timing of your peripheral datasheet to figure out whether you need some delay between these steps. All in all, implementing a parallel bus is pretty easy, on the order of a SPI driver, although debugging is a bit harder because there are so many lines to look at.

Note that parallel buses can be combined with other protocols (usually SPI) so that you can send more data by having two or four MOSI data pins acting in parallel.

 If you have spare I/O lines available during design, bring them out to a header or test points. You can write error or event codes to the I/O lines to make a parallel bus for debugging (and profiling!). Hook the lines up to a logic analyzer to get a peek into what your system is doing (without the timing changes that a serial output would give you).

Dual and Quad SPI

What do you get if you cross a parallel bus with a SPI bus? Something that transmits data even faster.

Where a normal SPI has MISO and MOSI for communication, a component that supports a dual SPI bus will shift those lines to be both input (or both output) for certain operations, allowing double the amount of data to go through. When the operation is complete, the bus will return to normal full-duplex operation.

With a quad SPI bus there are four pins to send data. Two of the pins will start out as MISO and MOSI, then with certain operations will become a four-wire parallel bus to transfer data four times faster than normal SPI.

USB

All of the serial protocols previously mentioned can be bit-banged if you don't have the hardware (and you have enough processing power). I wouldn't try that with USB, because it is pretty complicated, with more going on electrically. It is an asynchronous system, with an implicit clock and up to 127 devices. Depending on the version, it can be full or half duplex. It is always asymmetric, though usually the terms here are host and device instead of controller and peripheral.

It is also fast (1.5, 12, 480, or 4,000 Mb/s, depending on the version). The cable can be of medium length (five meters) and still maintain signal integrity. USB manages high throughput over a longish cable by having differential signals (which requires twice as many wires, so they can travel farther).

USB provides not only communication, but also power (the amount of power depends on the version of USB). That's why consumers can power up their cell phones or cameras by plugging them into a USB port on their computers.

Like Ethernet, the USB interaction usually is complicated enough to warrant an operating system (or a USB protocol stack that goes far beyond a simple driver). Further, USB applications usually implement all or most of the OSI layers (see the sidebar "Layered Model of Communication (OSI)" on page 186).

Considering Other Protocols

I hope you are seeing the commonality of the different serial protocols. There is no need to memorize what is what. When you get a datasheet for a peripheral, it will tell you what it needs, and your processor will tell you how to implement that (or if it doesn't, Wikipedia will probably give you pseudocode for a bit-bang driver). The goal is to think about what makes a protocol easy or hard to implement. Some takeaways:

- The more layers you need, the more complicated the implementation. Many protocols don't fit neatly in the OSI model, but it is still useful to know the framework for estimation.

- Point-to-point is easier than a network, which requires addresses.

- Half duplex is harder than full duplex because you have to switch the direction of communication.

- Synchronous is easier than asynchronous because you know exactly when you'll get a byte.

- Having a controller on the bus (asymmetric) is generally easier than trying to figure out who gets to talk when no one has control.

- Explicit clocks are easier than implicit.

Say you need to implement a contact interface to a smart card. Smart cards use ISO-7816, which is a half-duplex, point-to-point, asymmetric protocol, where the controller provides the clock (in the 1–5 MHz range). How hard will it be to implement a driver?

Given that information, it looks more complex than SPI but simpler than I²C. Add a little to your planning estimate because the protocol is relatively rare and you probably won't be able to find good example code. Now what if I tell you that it implements four or more of the OSI layers, though somewhat simplified? That should raise your implementation estimation by a factor of three (at least).

How about something more industrial, like RS-485? Designed to travel long distances, it can be full or half duplex. When it is full duplex, it is asynchronous. The clock is implicit (100 kHz–10 MHz), and only the physical and data link layers are specified. Usually there is a bus controller, but that isn't required. With only that information, the difficulty of implementing the protocol sounds like a cross between RS-232 and I²C.

If you can find the commonalities between different protocols, then once you've written something similar, you'll know what to expect when implementing something new.

ASCII Characters

If your test code for a new serial driver sends "Hello" as its first word, you can't expect to see an electronic hand waving on the oscilloscope during debugging. The letters get translated into numbers, usually 8-bit numbers according to the ASCII character encoding scheme.

Letter:	H	e	l	l	o
ASCII:	0x48	0x65	0x6C	0x6C	0x6F

So when you see "Hello" starting on your transmit line, it will start with H, which is 0x48, which looks like 01001000. Because ASCII uses only seven bits (it has 128 characters), the first bit is always 0, which makes it easy to find ASCII characters on an oscilloscope. In Figure 7-3, I've shown how to make it a little easier to know where you are in the data stream by starting the transmission high, to show the falling edge of the data. You might be able to see the start of the signal by triggering on chip select (if your protocol has one).

Or, you can select some letters that will be easier to pick out on the O-scope. I like "UU3." Each U is 0x55, which means every other bit is set so it looks like a clock signal. And 3 is serendipitously 0x33, or binary 00110011, so it looks like a clock at half the speed.

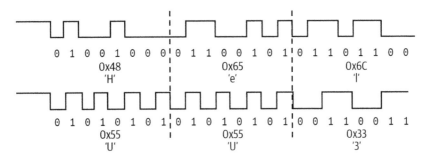

Figure 7-3. Comparing ASCII "Hello" with UU3

Learning the ASCII chart is a lot like learning Morse code. It is very handy if you use it, but if you are just learning it for fun, don't expect long-term retention. On the other hand, if you end up writing about one serial driver a year, you may start remembering the highlights. The ASCII chart is set up in a logical way, so it is easier to remember only the important stuff:

```
'0' -> 0x30
'A' -> 0x41
'a' -> 0x61
```

The numbers and letters increment from those starting points (hence 0x33 for the digit 3). My shorthand doesn't help you to know where the punctuation and the control characters are, but it does summarize the table well enough to talk to another embedded engineer in case you get trapped somewhere with only a single LED for communication.

Although ASCII is the most prevalent encoding scheme in embedded systems, it can't fit characters from other languages into 8-bit words. Unicode uses 16 bits (sometimes more). If your product will be internationalized, figure out whether Unicode is the right choice for you.

Communications in Practice

One of your primary concerns in reading the datasheet for the digital sensor is how to communicate with it. Does your processor have the type of communication method needed by the sensor? That helps with implementation and probably the driver if your processor has a HAL.

Consider an external ADC attached to a processor via SPI. (An ADC is an analog-to-digital converter; more about what this actually does in Chapter 8.) With the ADC's part number, that seems like enough information to get started.

And it is enough to get started. However, to be efficient with your communications, there are a few more things to consider. Looking at an external ADC will let me show you some of the intricacies of dealing with the driver and FIFO. Many digital sensors will have very similar communication patterns. Also, while I'll use SPI in my examples, the other communication methods have similar considerations.

External ADC Example: Data Ready with SPI

You'll need to start with the configuration. First, set up the I/Os as the reference manual says for the SPI subsystem to work. Then, set up the SPI subsystem to work as the ADC demands. Here are the configuration steps:

1. Set I/O pins to have chip select, clock, and MOSI as an output. MISO will be an input.

2. Set I/O pins to belong to the SPI function.

3. Set SPI configuration according to ADC datasheet: serial clock rate, clock polarity (CPOL) and clock phase (CPHA), length of data frame, etc.

   Initially, during board bring-up or prototype testing, you'll probably poll the sensor, asking it for information to make sure everything is connected. However, waiting for SPI communication to finish is inefficient, so you might need an interrupt to take care of sending (and receiving) the SPI bytes.

4. Set SPI interrupt to happen when the transmit buffer is empty.

Even with a SPI interrupt to facilitate communication, the data you get from the ADC will be on demand. You'll need to set up the SPI buffer to send a command to the ADC to start conversion (aka gathering data). Then you'll keep sending ADC commands, asking if it is done yet. When it is done, you finally set up the SPI command to read out the data. It is a lot of back and forth; we'd rather simply get data when the ADC is ready to send it.

But how will we know when the data is ready? An ADC (or other digital sensor) will often have an interrupt line to indicate when data is ready for you to read. Once configured, this I/O line will cause an interrupt on the processor. While it will probably be implemented as a generic I/O interrupt, we'll call it the *data ready interrupt* when talking about sensors.

The data ready interrupt will start the SPI interaction, asking the ADC to send data. In the interrupt (or based on an event flag in main), the code will:

1. Fill a transmit buffer with information to send to the ADC. This may include commands to the ADC, including requesting data and starting the next conversion.

2. On SPI, configure which buffers are used for transmit and receive and how many bytes to send.

3. Enable the SPI transmit-empty interrupt.

That last will cause the TX empty interrupt to occur and the transmit and receive buffers to be sent and filled (respectively). When the number of bytes to send has been sent, the main loop should receive a flag to indicate the transfer is complete (so it can do something with the data). See Figure 7-4 for how the transfer would occur.

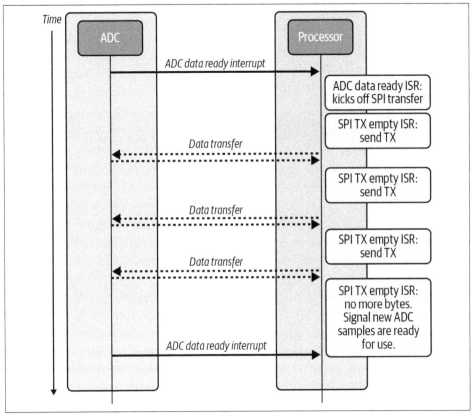

Figure 7-4. Example communication sequence diagram of an ADC data ready interrupt starting SPI communication to receive data

Use a FIFO If Available

The slowest possible way to communicate with a digital sensor is usually with a bit-bang driver. It is an only-in-desperate-times option. The next fastest is to use the processor's communication mechanism, like the integrated SPI or I²C peripheral bus, transferring or receiving a byte on each interrupt.

The system can go faster if the hardware supports a *FIFO* (first in, first out) queue. This provides a small buffer that allows the data to build up a bit before you have to deal with it. The FIFO queue may be part of your processor or it may be part of the digital sensor (or both, but don't use both at the same time).

Using a FIFO is pretty simple. To send data, write to the transmit holding register (THR). Writing to this address sends data to the transmit FIFO. The data will get sent when it reaches the end of the FIFO queue and the transmitter is available. Unlike the circular buffer, there is no dealing with pointers; you write to the THR to fill the FIFO, and the data eventually reaches the pins. While the peripheral is streaming out the data stored in its FIFO, the processor can do other things.

These systems usually have both transmit and receive FIFOs. To get data from the receive FIFO, check to make sure something is available (using a status register), and then read the receive buffer register (RBR) to get the oldest data in the FIFO.

The transmit and receive registers (THR and RBR) can be the same register, changing roles depending on whether you write to it or read from it.

Processor FIFOs use a set of flags to signal the software. The status flags generally include full, empty, half full, and half empty. (If you are thinking that the FIFO has optimist/pessimist issues, usually a receive buffer signals half full and a transmit buffer signals half empty.) These levels can be used to interrupt the processor.

Some processors will let you set specific levels at which to interrupt. For maximum throughput, determine how long it will take your processor to get to the interrupt (its latency) and how much data can be sent in that amount of time. For example, suppose you want to keep a steady stream of data flowing on the SPI bus. If you are running SPI at 10 MHz and it takes you a maximum of 3 microseconds to respond to an interrupt, you need to get an interrupt when the FIFO has 4 bytes remaining (10 MHz clock→1.25 MB/s→0.8 µs/byte, 3 microsecond latency / 0.8 µs/byte→3.75 bytes).

A transmit interrupt usually fills the FIFO with available data. A receive FIFO interrupt drains all of the data, putting it where the software can use it (often in a circular buffer). The goal is to balance the trigger levels so that you maintain a constant stream of data with the fewest interrupts.

Your processor manual (or component datasheet) will describe how to configure your FIFOs in more detail. FIFOs are usually 8 or 16 bytes deep. But what if your FIFO depth wasn't so limited? What if your FIFO was more like your circular buffer, using as much RAM as you need?

Direct Memory Access (DMA) Is Faster

A processor that supports direct memory access (DMA) can transfer far more data than one that implements only a FIFO.

Without DMA, the processor has to read each piece of data and store it to memory. For each byte transferred, there is software overhead when reading the data from the peripheral and storing it to your buffer. DMA bypasses the processor, transferring data without running software.

To use DMA, you give the processor a pointer and a number of bytes to read (or write). When receiving, the processor reads data from the peripheral into the specified memory until it reaches the byte count, at which point it interrupts the software. Similarly, when transmitting, the processor moves data from the buffer to the peripheral, interrupting when the count is complete.

DMA is a lot like having another thread do the data handling for you. It is very convenient while running, though setting it up can be a pain. Look in your processor manual for the DMA registers: transmit pointer register (the buffer to write to on the device), transmit count, receive pointer register, and receive count. If your data comes in chunks instead of a constant stream, you can use a DMA controller with one channel. If your data is a constant stream, you may need to copy the data from the DMA controller to another location so your software has time to work with it.

To avoid the need to copy (which is an inefficient use of your processing cycles and RAM resources), many DMA implementations can alternate between two buffers. This allows the software to use one buffer while the processor transfers peripheral data into (or out of) the other. This two-buffer, back-and-forth movement is called a *ping-pong buffer*.

DMA is used with peripherals that have very high throughput. It is also used in multicore processors to communicate between cores. If you know how many bytes you'll be receiving (or you are transmitting a block of data and not just a dribble), DMA is a great way to reduce processor overhead, making your processor seem faster than it is.

External ADC Example: SPI and DMA

The initialization will start as before, with the I/Os set as inputs and outputs that belong to the SPI functionality on the processor. The next step is to configure the DMA to work with the SPI subsystem:

1. Find the correct DMA channel and communication method (peripheral) address (SPI for this example).

2. Set the transfer direction (peripheral-to-memory for input; memory-to-peripheral for output).

3. Configure when DMA should cause an interrupt (usually when the DMA buffer is empty, half full, or full, depending on input or output).

Once the system is running, you'll need to set up the SPI transfer. For an ADC, it will probably contain information such as:

- Number of bytes you want to send or receive
- Transmit buffer address
- Whether to increment the transfer buffer address or send the same data over and over
- Receive buffer address
- Whether to increment the receive buffer or ignore the incoming data

When the ADC data ready interrupt occurs, the ISR will enable the DMA channel to act. When the DMA complete interrupt occurs, it will signal the running code that the transfer is complete. See Figure 7-5.

When you handle the transfer complete message, you probably want to set up the DMA again with a different receive buffer. Then you have time to process the last received buffer. And if you finish that, you can sleep or do other things while you wait for it all to happen again.

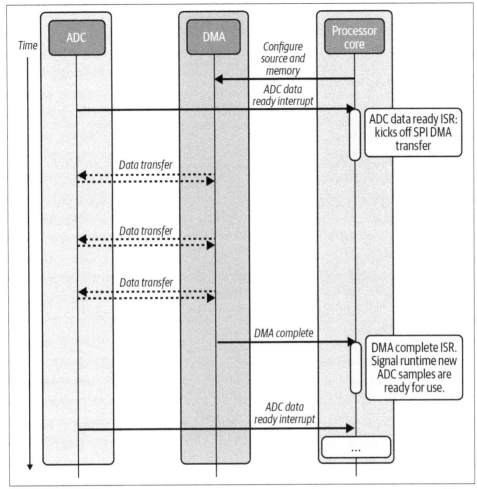

Figure 7-5. Example communication sequence diagram of ADC interrupt starting SPI DMA communication

DMA adds at least one layer of complexity for configuration, but reduces the processor cycles that deal with memory. You'll need to decide if the trade-off is worth the effort.

Comparison of Digital Communication Buffering Schemes

How much do FIFOs and DMA really matter? Well, let's compare how much processor time would be needed to implement a SPI interface running at 1 MHz with 8-bit (single byte) transfers.

The slowest implementation would be a bit-bang SPI driver. The next-fastest implementation would be a hardware-supported interface. When your processor datasheet says something like:

> One Serial Peripheral Interface (SPI) – 8- to 16-bit Programmable Data Length, Four External Peripheral Chip Selects

you have built-in SPI. You can configure it to run at 1 MHz (sometimes not precisely, as this will depend on your processor clock and how you can use dividers, but usually you can get close enough). Then you'll need to configure it to interrupt when a byte has been exchanged, every 8 μs or at 125 kHz (1 MHz/8 bits).

In that interrupt, you'll need to get the byte from the receive register and put it into some sort of buffer. You'll also need to put the next byte in the transmit register. Not only is the interrupt shorter than the bit-bang solution, but there are also many fewer interrupts.

Of course, if your FIFO is 16 bytes deep, you only have to interrupt at 7.8 kHz (125 kHz/16). Well, you could if you interrupt when the FIFO is completely full. But that means your communication will fall behind if your interrupt doesn't start emptying the FIFO in 8 μs (before the next byte comes in).

To give you more latitude, interrupt when the FIFO is half full. That will give you a more frequent interrupt rate of 15.6 kHz, but there will be more time available before communication falls behind (64 μs).

At every interrupt, you need to move the bytes in the receive FIFO into another piece of RAM and move the transmit bytes into that FIFO.

Now for DMA. If your goal is to maximize throughput, divide your RAM into a small piece for local variables and a large piece for a ping-pong buffer. If you have 32 KB of RAM, you could save 2 KB for variables and have two ping-pong buffers that are 15 KB each. That means you'll get an interrupt eight times per second, leaving you with plenty of time to actually do the processing.

Table 7-2 compares the processing difference of the interrupt overhead alone (assuming each interrupt has only 10 cycles of overhead, a very small amount). Instead of making a massive DMA buffer, I gave it a reasonable 512 bytes to work with. Note that to implement a bit-bang solution, you would need a processor that is more than 16,000 times faster than a comparable DMA solution. That's just for the overhead! A bit-bang driver is more complex than the DMA interrupt, which just needs to switch pointers and set a flag for the processing to occur on the already full buffer.

Table 7-2. How much faster is DMA?

Buffering methodology	Bit-bang interface	Hardware peripheral interface	16-byte FIFO (interrupt on half)	DMA with 512-byte buffer
Processor cycles with interrupt context switching each second (10-cycle interrupt overhead)	40 million	1.25 million	156 thousand	2.44 thousand
Times faster than the bit-bang interface	1	32	256	16,384

Circular Buffers

I mentioned that FIFOs are like circular buffers because I hope you've heard of circular buffers before. However, in embedded systems you might need to actually implement one, designed for your specific needs. Let me explain a bit more about what a circular buffer is.

The circular buffer is a key implementation tactic among data-driven systems. Unlike the LIFO stacks mentioned in Chapter 5, circular buffers are FIFO.

A data producer puts data in the circular buffer at some rate. The consumer takes it out of the buffer at the same *average* rate. However, the consumer can take it out in chunks while the producer puts it in in dribbles. This lets the processor do other things while the data accumulates to the size needed for the algorithm. (Or it could go the other way, with the producer putting a large chunk of data into the circular buffer to be read out at a steady rate to feed another part of the system.)

A circular buffer needs to keep track of a chunk of memory, its length, where to put the next element that comes in (write or start), and where to get the next element (read or end). See Figure 7-6. Note that understanding a circular buffer is easier when the read pointer is before the write pointer. This is true for everyone; most of the common circular buffer bugs happen when the read and write pointers cross, even though the software will spend half of its existence like that.

When the buffer is empty, the read pointer is equal to the write pointer. This is easy enough to check. However, the problem is that when the buffer is full, the read pointer is also equal to the write pointer.

One option is to call the buffer full when the write pointer is one away from the read pointer. This is easy to understand and implement, though it wastes an element's worth of memory. Another possible solution is to add a variable to keep track of the length by having an enqueue function increment the length and a dequeue function decrement it. Now you've traded a variable for a position in your circular buffer. Depending on the size of the elements in the buffer, that may be worthwhile.

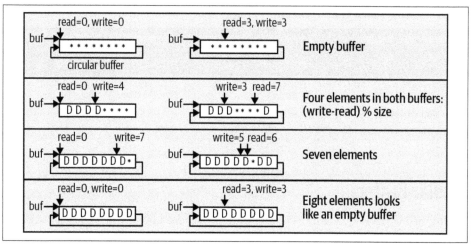

Figure 7-6. Example of pointers in a circular buffer

Usually one user of the circular buffer is an interrupt (either the producer or the consumer) while the other is not. We saw in Chapter 5 that all sorts of interesting things occur when you have interrupt code and non-interrupt code trying to modify the same variable. If you use the blank element to know when your buffer is full, you can isolate the producer's variables from the consumer's, making the circular buffer interrupt safe, as long as the read and write pointers update atomically. (Otherwise, a request for the length of available data will give an invalid response.) However, since the pointers wrap around when they get to the end of the buffer, an atomic operation may be unfeasible.

Most common implementations in embedded systems constrain the circular buffer length to be a power of two to avoid this issue. So let's start with an implementation using a structure like this:

```
struct sCircularBuffer {
    tElement *buf;    // block of memory
    uint16_t size;    // must be a power of two
    uint16_t read;    // holds current read position: 0 to (size-1)
    uint16_t write;   // holds current write position: 0 to (size-1)
};
```

In the initialization function, we'll set the buffer pointer to a block of memory (one that holds a power-of-two number of elements). We will also need to set the size to the length of memory and the read and write offsets to zero. From there, we need to implement only a few other functions. The first is probably the most difficult to follow. It does a wrapped subtraction to determine the length of the data available in the circular buffer:

```
uint16_t CBLengthData(struct sCircularBuffer *cb){
```

```
/*            **********
    |-----|----------|-------|
        read        write
*/

int32_t length = cb->write - cb->read;
if (length >= 0) {return length;}
/*
    bbbbbb            aaaaaaaa
    |-----|----------|-------|
        write        read
*/
return (cb->size - cb->write) +    /* aaaa */
            (cb->read);            /* bbbb */
}
```

Actually, that doesn't use the constraint that says the buffer size has to be a power of two. A more efficient implementation looks like this:

```
uint16_t CBLengthData(struct sCircularBuffer *cb){

    return ((cb->write - cb->read) & (cb->size - 1));
}
```

Even though the read and write variables are unsigned, the length is correct thanks to that bitwise AND; the following sidebar explains why.

Representing Signed Numbers

You know about unsigned binary numbers (take a look at "Binary and Hexadecimal Math" on page 87 for a refresher). "How Many Bits in That Number?" on page 114 showed the highest number you could fit in an 8-bit or 16-bit variable, where signed numbers were always half as much as unsigned numbers because the sign takes up a bit. There are several ways to encode the sign in one bit; consider how we do it in decimal with a sign to the left of the value. One way to do it in binary is to have the sign be the leftmost bit (most significant bit) while the other bits encode the number:

```
snnn nnnn = <1-bit sign> <7-bit number>
0000 0000 = +0
0000 0001 = +1
...
0111 1111 = +127
1000 0000 = -0
1000 0001 = -1
1111 1111 = -127
```

Note that there is both a 0 and –0. Many encodings have that. It is a little odd and a little inefficient.

However, that sign and value encoding isn't how your computer normally stores numbers, because there is a way to make processing faster using a different encoding.

This ingenious method is called *two's complement*. In this representation, the leftmost bit still holds the sign of the number, and a positive number is encoded just as you'd expect. However, a negative is encoded by inverting all the bits and then adding one to the result:

```
snnn nnnn = <1-bit sign> <7-bit number>
0000 0000 = 0
0000 0001 = +1
...
0111 1111 = +127
1000 0000 = -128
1000 0001 = -127
...
1111 1110 = -2
1111 1111 = -1
```

I find the "invert and add one" instructions difficult to remember. However, the neat part of two's complement is that when you add a number and its opposite in sign, the numbers obliterate each other:

```
0000 0001 = 1
1111 1111 = -1
---------------
1 0000 0000 = 0 (and a carry bit)
```

Being able to always add numbers (and not perform a different operation for subtraction) makes this number encoding very powerful.

Remember that –1 is equivalent to the highest unsigned value. If you write code:

```
uint8_t value = -1; // set to highest value this
                    // unsigned type can hold
```

your value will be 255 (0xFF). To figure out other unsigned numbers, subtract normally from –1:

```
-1 = 0xFF = 1111 1111
-2 = 0xFE = 1111 1110
-3 = 0xFD = 1111 1101
-4 = 0xFC = 1111 1100
...
```

Let's see how this encoding works on the modulo math from this chapter. For example, here are the steps to do the wrapped subtraction of cb->write (5), cb->read (6), and cb->size (8):

```
  (cb->write - cb->read) & (cb->size - 1)
= (     5    -    6    ) & (    8   - 1)
= (          -1        ) & (    7     )
= (       1111 1111    ) & (  0000 0111 )
=    0000 0111 = 7
```

> The power-of-two length makes the bitwise AND eliminate the sign information, leaving us with the correct result.

An empty buffer would return a length of zero. A full buffer would have a length of (cb->size-1). Keeping that in mind, writing the enqueue function is pretty simple:

```
enum eError CBWrite(struct sCircularBuffer *cb, tElement data){

    if (CBLengthData(cb) == (cb->size-1)) { return eErrorBufferFull;}
    cb->buf[cb->write] = data;
    cb->write = (cb->write + 1) & (cb->size - 1); // must be atomic
    return eSuccess;
}
```

The modification of the write variable needs to be a single instruction. But setting only the write variable needs to be atomic; the preparation ((write+1) and (size-1)) can be multiple instructions. These variables are declared as uint16_t, so if this code runs on a 16-bit processor, the setting of the write variable will be atomic (but for an 8-bit processor, it won't be; in a 32-bit processor, usually the uint16_t write instruction is a single operation, but not always).

Also note that the circular buffer rejects data that would overflow the buffer. This goes back to the question of how you want your system to fail. Do you want to reject new data, as this code does? Or do you want to drop some old data to make room for the new data? What is your strategy for falling behind? I'll stick with the error for now, but you do have options to consider.

Taking things out of the buffer is similar, but deals with the read offset instead of the write offset:

```
enum eError CBRead(struct sCircularBuffer *cb, tElement *data){

    if (CBLengthData(cb) == 0) { return eErrorBufferEmpty;}
    *data = cb->buf[cb->read];
    cb->read = (cb->read + 1) & ( cb->size - 1);
    return eSuccess;
}
```

If you don't constrain the buffer size to a power of two, you need to use extra checking or modulo arithmetic to wrap the pointers. Modulo arithmetic (like division) is a relatively slow operation, and not the sort of thing you want to do in an interrupt. Chapter 12 talks more about what forms of math are fast and slow on an embedded processor.

Note that the data element is copied out of the buffer to another location. In general, copying memory is not a good use of your embedded system because the act of copying uses up limited processing cycles, and having two copies of the same information uses up limited memory. Why don't you just leave the data where it is?

You can add another pointer to your circular buffer to indicate when data is free for use by the write pointer. However, this is where buffers start to get complicated. This is also where you might want to pull out a paper and pencil or get to a whiteboard. For many circular buffer problems, the solution is far easier to see when you can sketch out the options (see Figure 7-7).

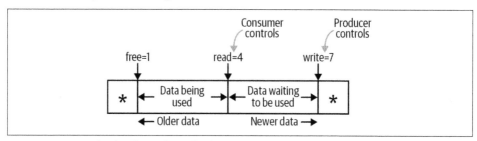

Figure 7-7. Circular buffer with multiple pointers

Once you get it straight in your head, the code will be pretty simple. First, add a free variable to the structure and initialize it to zero. Next, you'll probably need to know the lengths of the different sections of data:

How much is free and ready to be written?
    Wrapped subtraction of write from free

How much data can be read?
    Wrapped subtraction of read from write

How much data is currently checked out for reading?
    Wrapped subtraction of free from read

Handling the free pointer is straightforward. When the code is done with the element it took, simply increment it past the element, so the write pointer can use it again:

```
enum eError CBFree(struct sCircularBuffer *cb){

    if (CBLengthReadData(cb) == 0) { return eErrorBufferEmpty;}
    cb->free = (cb->free + 1) & (cb->size-1);
    return eSuccess;
}
```

Note that the element wasn't passed in to this function, because you always free elements in order. Also, this looks an awful lot like both the CBRead and CBWrite functions; they all follow the same principles.

You may want to do more than read parts of the buffer. Many data processing steps lend themselves to in-place modification. Once you get the hang of handling multiple pointers into the circular buffer, you may want to keep using them to avoid copies. Such streamlining will make your system faster.

Figure 7-8 shows how the processing might work. The analog data is sampled by the ADC. The digital data is written to a circular buffer at a constant rate. The data may be obtained from the buffer at a different rate because the processing is done in chunks (you do something to several samples at once) or because the processor does something else while the data queues up. The processing module reads and modifies the data. It could put the data in another circular buffer for output to the DAC or return it to the same circular buffer (or modify it in place). Once the DAC outputs the processed data, the circular buffer element is free to be used again.

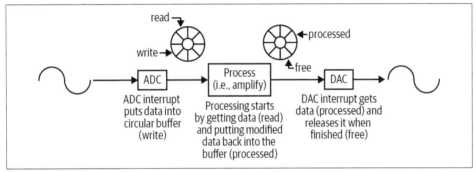

Figure 7-8. ADC to DAC data-driven system with multiple pointers into a single circular buffer

To implement a system like this, you'd need to add one more pointer to the system, called processed. As the pointers move independently of one another, adding another is fairly straightforward. The code is nearly the same as we added for CBRead or CBWrite. Don't forget to add a new length function, too.

Further Reading

For an example implementation of FIFO versus DMA, look for James Lynch's write-up on Atmel's AT91SAM7 serial communications (*http://www.sparkfun.com/data sheets/DevTools/SAM7/at91sam7%20serial%20communications.pdf*).

Embedded Artistry has an excellent and lengthy blog post about circular buffers (*https://oreil.ly/3u7-0*) that includes a GitHub repository of working code.

When coming across any new serial interface, I tend to hit Wikipedia first. There are so many variants of different protocols, and the datasheet for a device may be filled with acronyms and complex timing diagrams. Wikipedia gives me an overview that puts it all in perspective.

Interview Question: Choosing a Processor

How would you go about choosing a processor for our next-generation platform?

This question is multifaceted, starting out with a basic check of the interviewee's listening skills. Do they know what we build? Are they interested enough in the company to spend some time doing research? Have they been awake while I blathered on about the current system?

From there, it moves into checking their design skills and experience level. I want the candidate to know which questions to ask (what are the bottlenecks on the current platform, and how have we identified them?). They should have specific questions about the types of processing and the bandwidth requirements of the system to help them understand the problem better.

Most companies don't want to go backward in their feature set, so it is relatively safe to start with the assumption of more processing power, more RAM, and more code space than the previous design. However, I want the candidate to check these assumptions. Ideally, as we talk about these, the candidate should describe ways to unburden the processor (peripherals often take up an unreasonable amount of processor overhead).

A good candidate will also consider the underlying goals of a new platform (i.e., why are we looking for a new platform?). A candidate with a product view is often a better fit than someone whose scope is more limited. To that end, I hope they ask about the goals for volume and cost. An excellent candidate will also ask whether the requirements are expected to change significantly over the development cycle, helping them determine whether they want a general-purpose processor or can choose something very specific.

I hope the candidate discusses the advantages of using a popular part (one that is widely supported with compilers, debuggers, toolchains, and even RTOSs). It is also good to hear them consider lead times and end-of-life expectations (hint: don't start a new platform on a dying chip). Good candidates also mention the goal of having a new processor be in the middle of a family of processors, allowing for future platforms (and possible cost reductions using less fully featured parts).

Processor selection is difficult because many factors enter into a decision. I don't expect someone to come in for a day's worth of interviews and produce a suggestion for a new processor. Most people don't keep the processor lines from the various microprocessor vendors in their head. If they immediately suggest something concrete, I take it as an indication of what they've been working on. At that point, I tend to ask why they think that is a good path for our particular product. The goal is to get them to tell me *how* they would choose, not the actual choice. In interviewing, the methods people use to confront problems are far more interesting than the solutions they generate.

CHAPTER 8

Putting Together a System

During the course of this book, we've investigated what goes on inside your processor. Now, before you can build a system, we need to consider what goes on in other components of your system. Communicating with the other components is a start to this. The next step is to get a feel for common peripherals, data handling methods, and design patterns for adapting your system to different needs.

Ultimately, the information you need for using peripherals is in their datasheets, but there are enough commonalities that you can get a feel for what to look for.

However, putting together a system goes beyond connecting each piece; you have to start looking at the system as a collection of parts working together. The last part of this chapter gives some tips on data handling and putting together algorithms.

Key Matrices

You've already seen buttons with a simple I/O interface in Chapter 4. However, if you have a bunch of buttons (maybe a keyboard), you don't need one I/O line per button. You can create a matrix of input lines to get a lot more out of your I/O than you expect. There are two ways to implement a *key matrix*: a *row/column scan* is useful when you need the peripheral to be cheap, whereas *Charlieplexing* (aka *tri-state multiplexing*) is more expensive but minimizes the number of I/O lines needed.

With a row/column scan, you can implement an M × N matrix with M + N lines. So if you want to implement a 12-digit number pad, you could do a 3 × 4 matrix and use 7 lines (far fewer than the 12 lines it would take to do direct I/O). Of course, matrix input requires more complicated software.

In the electronics, each button is connected to one row and one column (and not an input pin to ground, as would be the direct I/O interface). On initialization, configure all of the row connections as outputs and set them to be high. Then, configure all of the column connections as inputs with internal pull-up resistors.

Note that matrixing the buttons means that they need to be polled. Although you can set up a timer interrupt to do that, you can't use a processor interrupt to tell you when an input has changed. The software needs to keep cycling through the rows.

As you are scanning (reading) for button presses, set a row low, read the column's inputs, set the row high, and move on to the next row. A button that is pressed will be low when you read its column. You will need to map the row/column value to the button's actual meaning. Figure 8-1 shows a snippet of a schematic with the row/column scan. Each circle is a button.

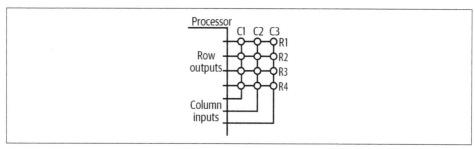

Figure 8-1. Row/column-scan-style key matrix

The software scanning requirement is also true of Charlieplexing. Named after the originating engineer (Charles Allen) and immortalized in an application note, Charlieplexing requires more electronics (diodes) than the row/column matrix method. Instead of using N pins to receive N inputs in direct drive, or M + N pins to receive M × N inputs in a row/column matrix, Charlieplexing lets you use N pins to get $(N^2 - N)$ inputs.

For the 12 buttons in a number pad, you can use a mere four I/O lines and 12 diodes (maybe fewer if you don't care about detecting multiple buttons pressed simultaneously). Although the software is more complicated than the row/column matrix, it is just a matter of taking it step by step, usually as a state machine. Start with all of the associated pins as inputs. For each pin, set that one pin to be an output and high, read the other pins (as inputs). Then set that output to be low, and read the other pins again. Then set the pin to be an input. After each pin has had a turn to be the output, you can look up (or calculate) what button was pressed.

While Wikipedia has related code, the repository for this book links to some websites that show both types of key matrices as animations, along with proper schematics for each.

Both of these methods may give strange and incorrect results when multiple buttons are pressed simultaneously.

Row/column matrix and Charlieplexing can be used on outputs (LEDs) as well as inputs (buttons). The methodology is the same in each case, so once you wrap your head around matrices, you'll find plenty of places to implement them.

Segmented Displays

We've already spent a lot of time on individual LEDs in Chapter 4, even making them dim using PWM control. A seven-segment display is probably the next most basic display that you'll see. Most seven-segment displays are ordered as shown in Figure 8-2.

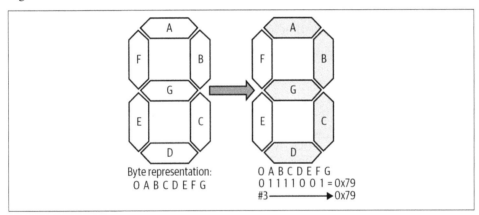

Figure 8-2. Seven-segment display with canonical segment ordering (clockwise ABCDEF, then G across the center)

Each LED in the segment can be represented as a bit in a byte (the extra one bit is sometimes used for the decimal-place segment found on some displays). The segments are accessed in order, usually from most significant to least significant bit: abc defg (or sometimes gfedcba). So if you want to put a 3 on the display, you need to turn on the LEDs at abcdg and turn off the LEDs at fe. In hex, using abcdefg, you'll want to write 0x79 to the display to represent the number 3.

The actual implementation here is not that important. The critical idea is the decoupling between human-readable data on the display and the representation in the code. Get used to having to map between the display's context and other parts of the software.

Taking a step back, do you remember solar-powered calculators? The LCD display with eight digits (each one a seven-segment display)? The ones that were amazing technology in the 1960s but were handed out for free by the 1980s? They also had at least 17 buttons. They could total up to 81 different settings (17 (buttons) + 8 (places) × 7 (segments in each character) + 8 (decimal points)), but the processors that ran inside those calculators didn't have 81 I/O lines.

As noted in "Key Matrices" on page 211, you can matrix the button inputs: 17 buttons can use 9 lines (4 × 5), and you can get three more buttons for "free." The same method can be used to matrix the display outputs.

Using row/column scanning, for eight characters on the screen with decimals (64 segments), we can use an 8 × 8 matrix, so only 16 I/O lines are needed.

With buttons, the response time depends on the number of rows because you cut the time spent looking at each column into that many slices. With outputs, the time slice determines how long each segment can be on. So, if you use an 8 × 8 LED array, the LEDs will be on only 1/8 of the time. Most LEDs are so bright that this doesn't matter. With LCDs (such as those found in our solar calculator), the limited amount of on-time can make segments look washed out and difficult to see, particularly when the power is low.

LCD segments don't run with a constant "on" setting like LEDs do. Although LCDs can be driven through a matrix, it is more difficult because they need a changing AC signal. Usually you'll use an LCD controller, but if you want to try matrixing it (or just want to understand it better), check out STMicroelectronics Application Note AN1447 (*http://www.st.com/stonline/books/pdf/docs/8187.pdf*).

The 8 × 8 matrix is very convenient because it lines up well with our character mapping. We can either power all of one character at one time, or power all of the a-segments, then all of the b-segments, and so on. Either method works. As long as you refresh the display fast enough (get through all of the segments faster than 30 Hz), the user will never know.

If you update too slowly, the display will flicker. I find 30 Hz to be a good rate. To test your system, look past it, as motion is more noticeable in your peripheral vision.

Pixel Displays

Unfortunately, seven segments per character isn't enough to represent much. You can choose a 14-segment display to get decent looking letters for English applications (or a 16-segment display to incorporate Latin letters and Arabic digits). At some point, you might as well use a dot matrix display and build your digits, characters, and graphics out of dots. Well, dots sound so plebeian. Let's call them "picture elements." Naw, that takes too long, let's call them *pixels*.

Now the mapping between the number 3 and what appears on your display may be even further apart than 3 and 0x79. Each thing you want to put on the screen needs a *bitmap* to describe what bits are on and what bits are off. Anything that goes on the screen is a *glyph*, whether it comes from a bitmap or is generated by the code (such as a graph).

All of your bitmaps together are called your graphic *assets*. Graphic assets are usually split into fonts and other graphics (pictures, logos, etc.). A *font* is a set of glyphs representing a set of characters (typically the ASCII character set). As before, the goal of designing a display subsystem is to keep images of the data loosely coupled to the data itself. This allows you much greater flexibility to change screens, give your system a new look, and reuse your display subsystem in a different product.

Display Assets

Figure 8-3 shows one way to set up graphic assets. First, there is a table of data, usually with a header file that tells you where the logo is or perhaps the offset to the animations. It is important to version the file (and the asset list) because if they change without your software knowing it, you could display garbage to the screen.

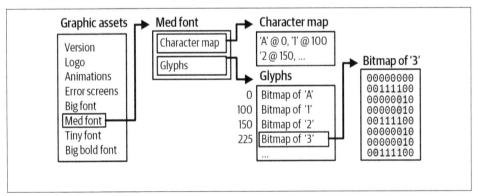

Figure 8-3. Graphic subsystem organization

To put the number 3 up on the screen, first you need to know what representation of 3 to display: is the bitmap going to be small or fill the whole screen? Is it going to be bold or italicized? Each of these options will lead to a different font set in your assets. Once you know the font, you'll need to map from the character to the bitmap, usually by searching through the character map to get an offset into the bitmap glyphs.

Bitmaps can be stored in monochrome (1 bit per pixel), as shown in Figure 8-3. Look at all the wasted data, though, that can be compressed. Compressing it may speed up retrieval from wherever the asset is stored (often off-chip flash). However, uncompressing the data becomes one more thing for the processor to do, which may slow down the display of new glyphs.

One form of compression that might not slow down the processor at all is *run-length encoding* (RLE). Sections of data that are the same are stored as a single data value and a count, rather than each pixel being replicated. This is great when you have a lot of the same color on the screen. For example, you might get a stream of white pixels (W) and black pixels (B) that look like WWWWBBWWW. This would encode to W4B2W3. If the data is stored as one bit per pixel (so the whole image is only black and white), that would give you no savings. However, if the image is one byte per pixel (or two or three bytes per pixel), RLE provides significant compression without much processor overhead.

Display subsystems end up pushing a lot of data from one place to another. A monochrome bitmap is fairly small. In Figure 8-3, the number 3 glyph will be 8 pixels wide and 8 pixels high, so it can be represented in 8 bytes. However, it will probably look terrible with those blocky edges. To make it look better, you'll want to add *antialiasing*, which softens the edges by putting grayscale pixels in. Figure 8-4 shows a little bit of smoothing on the number 3 bitmap. It uses five levels, so it would need three bits per pixel.

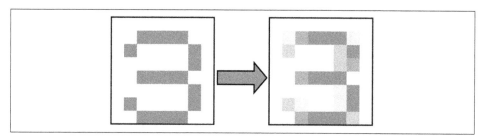

Figure 8-4. Antialiasing of a character: using more data per pixel to make it grayscale instead of black and white

With antialiasing, the bitmap is no longer monochrome. You could use 2, 4, or even 8 bits per pixel to describe the antialiasing. An 8-bit-per-pixel encoding means the number 3 glyph takes up 64 bytes—still a really small amount, but you're on a slippery slope. Before, your whole A–Z, a–z, 0–9 monochrome font could fit into 500 bytes, but now it is almost 4 KB, and that is for 8-pixel-high letters. Once you have a 2.4-inch LCD display (24-bit color, 240 × 320 pixels), each screen can take up to 225 KB.

Coding a display subsystem often means optimizing your code so the parts handling this data throughput don't cause problems with the screen. Most LCDs automatically *refresh*, which means the display hardware redraws the data on the screen. The LCD refreshes the screen with the same image over and over again until your data changes. *Tearing* is when the data changes part way through a refresh, showing half of the new image and half of the old image. To completely eliminate tearing, you need to synchronize the image update with the screen refresh and get all of the pixels to their intended value before the next refresh (it can be difficult to transfer all the data in such a short time).

Note that how you pack the assets into the storage mechanism is important. In addition to compression concerns, you need to store them in a way that makes sense for the space available, the interface between the graphic assets storage (usually flash) and your processor, and the interface between the LCD and the processor. Another issue might intrude as well: what if your display has to go into the product enclosure upside-down due to electro-mechanical requirements? It may require more frontend processing to put the assets in a different orientation, but it is better than having the processor turn them upside down and backward each time the asset is read.

 Being an embedded systems specialist does not excuse you from writing programs to pack data assets. Since you'll be the one using the information, you'll find your life is much easier if you control how the graphics are stored. More on that in "External Flash Memory" on page 220.

Finally, once you have the bitmap ready to send to the screen, you'll need to know where to put it. Figure 8-5 shows the number 3 glyph on the screen.

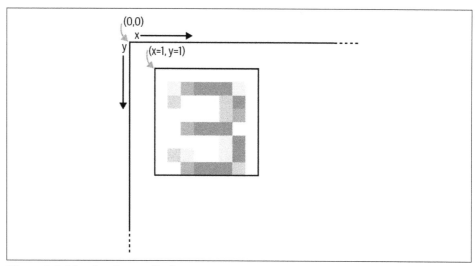

Figure 8-5. Number 3 on a display

To sum up the steps:

1. Determine what is going on the screen and where.
2. Look in the assets to find the correct font.
3. Find the character in the font.
4. Read the bitmap, possibly uncompressing it.
5. Copy the bitmap in the correct location in the display buffer.
6. Send the buffer to the display, ideally right after the last refresh.

To put up a logo or other fixed graphic, combine steps 2 and 3 into one: looking up the image glyph.

Changeable Data? Flyweight and Factory Patterns

This method to store character and image glyphs, retrieving them as needed to put on the screen matches a design pattern: the *flyweight pattern*. Well, the way I described it mashes it together with a *factory pattern*, so it is more correctly called a *flyweight factory pattern*. Let me untangle the two so you can see them separately and be able to use the concepts outside the LCD.

The typical example of the flyweight pattern is a document with many characters. Each character is an object describing the character's size and encapsulating a bitmap. In a non-embedded world, there is some temptation to instantiate each character object on its own. Eventually, when there are enough characters, this leads to sluggish behavior. In an embedded device, we wouldn't have that problem, as there is never enough RAM to let us get into trouble this way. The solution is to point to a single instance of the character object (which for us is in flash memory).

That is the pattern: when you have lots of things used repeatedly, create a pool of instances (one for each object) and point to the pool instead of instantiating each object directly. Each of the shared objects is called a flyweight (like the lightest weight in boxing, not like the weight used to increase inertia in flywheels). Each flyweight must be relatively interchangeable with the others, though they may describe their state (e.g., a character may describe its width because that differs unpredictably between characters).

The factory pattern is a bit more complicated, centering on the factory method. Remember the Unix driver model from Chapter 2? Almost all drivers implement the same interface (`open`, `close`, `read`, `write`, `ioctl`). If you are writing a program to use a driver, you open it as though it were a file (`/dev/tty0`). The driver gets instantiated and returned to you as a generic handler on the surface, but underneath it represents a serial port. The factory method (open) knows how to create a specific widget (subclass) that is of a generic type (class). All of the specific widgets implement the same interface (the class interface).

If you found the previous paragraph a bit daunting, Figure 8-6 may help. It shows the classic factory pattern diagram, with the Unix driver model example underneath, followed by the LCD graphics example. The factory pattern often is implemented in a very object-oriented way, with specific subclasses being instantiations of a class. The creator class (the code that calls the factory method) controls the whole thing.

 Figure 8-6 is in UML (Unified Modeling Language), a useful visual language for describing software, particularly object-oriented software. It can be simple (like this) or far more complex, going so far as to become an interpretable language.

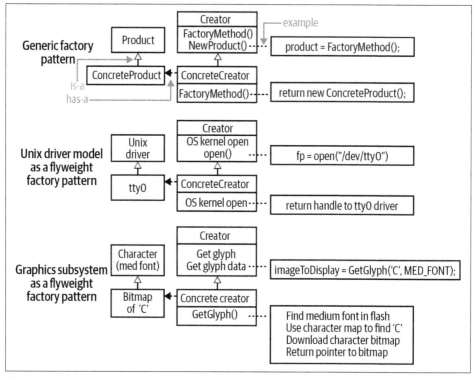

Figure 8-6. Factory pattern and flyweight factory pattern examples

The factory pattern is all around you, decoupling instances from a generic ideal. It is a fairly physical pattern, so its name makes sense. Imagine you have a real live factory. It is flexible enough to make any one of several relatively similar products (the product class). The factory contains a machine (the creator). Today, you configure the machine to make sprockets (a concrete product) by putting a template (factory method) into the machine. When you push the "on" button, the factory will generate sprockets. Tomorrow, you may switch out the template to make gadgets (a different concrete product) ensured by a different template (factory method).

When we do this in graphics software and with flyweights, pressing the "on" button is more like the software requesting a glyph. With a flyweight factory pattern, the factory part manages the flyweights, making sure they are shared properly and decoupling characters from the way they are displayed on the screen.

External Flash Memory

We've already looked a bit at memory and how it is classified into volatile memory (lost when the system turns off) and nonvolatile memory (retained through power cycles). RAM is the most predominant form of volatile memory.

Nonvolatile memory comes in two primary flavors: EEPROM and flash. EEPROMs are generally smaller, and their bytes can be written individually. They are straightforward enough that the datasheet will likely be enough to make your development go smoothly.

 The volatile keyword in C/C++ refers to something different from the idea of volatile memory. This keyword tells the compiler, "this variable may change outside the code that is currently running," whereas volatile memory loses its contents when power is lost.

Flash is made up of sectors (or pages) that must be erased all at one time (the larger the flash, the larger the sector). Once a sector is erased, flash can be written one byte at a time. This requirement adds a lot of complexity.

However, flash is incredibly useful, in part because it can be very large. You'll probably want to store display assets there. Flash is also useful for that little bit of data that changes occasionally, like the reason the system reset. It can also act as a data storage location if the system takes data over a long period, but uploads to some other source less frequently. You can even have a file system. (We won't talk about updating firmware until Chapter 9 but flash will come up there too.)

Flash is almost always controlled via SPI because it is the fastest of the common protocols. Even SD cards can be accessed via SPI.

Display Assets

Initially you can compile your display asset in code, including a small font. There are online tools and Python scripts that will turn your image into C code, an array of constant variables that represent which pixels will be lit on the screen (or what color those pixels will be).

However, you may have enough on-board processor flash to handle a small display doing a few simple things. Once you hear the words "animation" or "internationalization," plan on a SPI flash to store the font and image information.

While Figure 8-3 shows a good architecture for the display assets, the implementation has a few sticking points. First, how large will the display assets need to be? This is a matter of the display size, but also the glyphs and fonts you need.

Do you need all the letters, numbers, and symbols? There are 94 for English—more if you want to support other languages (another 94 for French, Italian, German, and Spanish). You'll need one set for each size (pixel height and width) of each font. Are they single bit-depth or are they antialiased to look better?

Consider one font with 94 characters, 8 × 6 size, and 8 bits of grayscale color:

- font space = characters × pixel height × pixel width × bit depth for color
- font space = 94 × 8 × 6 × 8 = 36,096 bits = 4,512 bytes

However, even with antialiasing, that font is only going to be good for very small text. With a medium-sized screen, we might have 30 × 40 characters. With 94 characters and 16 bits of color, that is 220 KB. Fonts can take up a lot of space; they may take up more space than your code.

Thus, display assets are often put on external SPI flash, loaded in the processor as needed, then transferred to the display interface. Surprisingly, the first step is one of the most difficult:

1. Calculate how much space you'll need for the display assets:
   a. How many fonts? What sizes? How many bits per pixel?
   b. How many other glyphs/icons/images? What sizes? Color or monochrome?
   c. Total these up and try to leave at least 25% extra for growth.
2. Determine how data will be accessed:
   a. How long does it take for the communication bus to send one data bit?
   b. How long does it take for the display to receive one data bit?
   c. Using the maximum of the previous two, how long will it take to update the whole screen? (number of display pixels × maximum time/bit)
   d. If you have an animation or quickly changing area (think spinning "thinking" circle), how long will it take to update that part of the screen? (number of pixels × maximum time/bit)
3. Obtain the asset files (the actual images of each letter and glyph you'll put on the screen). Ideally these will come with some sort of device mock-up so you know how to group the data and where to put icons on the screen. You'll need to make this data available to your program. I usually code up a Python script to:
   a. Map the filename of the image to an identifier in the code.
   b. Map the identifier in the code to the location in flash (likely from the start of the area allocated to display assets).
   c. Add any other metadata about where the glyph should go on the screen (if there is a default). Adding the width and height into the metadata can be very helpful.
   d. Pack the image data into a binary file with the assets in the order above.

At this point, you'll probably have a header file with a list of identifiers that the code uses to indicate what should be on the screen. That list of identifiers will likely lead to their offset location in the packed binary (and any characteristics that make sense for the application, though you can put that in the binary too). You will also have a binary of the assets, all smushed together.

Next, program this into your display flash, another step that sounds easy, that should be easy, but will likely cause you to write more code. Usually I end up with a debug/ manufacturing command line to take data from a serial port and put it in the SPI flash. In manufacturing, there may be a special flash programmer that bypasses your processor.

At this point, you may be ready to get back to the satisfying work of coding up the display. However, I strongly recommend taking a few minutes to make your asset packing script a little nicer. It is one of those things I often think will be temporary but turns out to be reused many times.

Emulated EEPROMs and KV Stores

I hope your flash isn't full of display assets, as there are a few other uses for it. I mentioned EEPROMs previously as a nonvolatile memory that is smaller and more straightforward than flash. Usually with an EEPROM, you set up a list of addresses and what data you'll put in each.

Address	Data	Size
0	Serial number	4 bytes
4	Last time unit was booted	4 bytes
8	Cause of last reboot	1 byte
9	Number of boots since initial	3 bytes
12	...	

Every time your system resets, you can update the boot status information. It won't change the unit serial number ("Of course!" you say, but keep reading and ignore the scary music).

From one perspective, this is a tiny database, where you look up data based on the address. Somewhere in your code is a header that maps the EEPROM address to the data you want to access so you can say something like:

```
uint32_t sn = readEeprom(constSerialNumberAddr, constSerialNumberSize);
```

or

```
writeEeprom(constLastBootTimeAddr, constLastBootTimeSize, (void*) & currentTime);
```

However, EEPROMs are expensive, small, and slow compared to flash memory.

On the other hand, flash must be erased before being written. And you can only erase in blocks, which are usually several kilobytes. Also, flash can wear out if you erase or write the same place over and over again (so can EEPROMs, though they usually have a higher number of cycles).

The solution is a *key-value store* (*KV store* or *emulated EEPROM*). You choose a key for a piece of data (usually a number) and then look up the data for that key: a tiny database.

However, instead of a fixed address in flash, the data is part of a list that the processor sifts through to find the matching key. So when you write new data for a key, the previous data is found and invalidated, then new data is added to the end of the list.

KV stores take time to access for reading or writing and contain state machines to figure out where they are in the find-erase-write cycle. Additionally, because they keep lists of data (including invalidated data), KV stores take up a lot more room than the data alone might: you'll need at least two flash blocks, so that the data can be stored in one, while the other one is being erased.

I don't recommend writing your own KV store because many processor and RTOS vendors provide the code for you. To find it, search for both terms: KV store is the software engineering perspective and emulated EEPROM is the hardware engineering perspective. Either will lead you to code that does the same thing.

Little File Systems

Putting a file system on the flash suffers from the same problem as the KV store: you have to erase flash in blocks and not write the same addresses frequently. Some flash has a life-span of around ten thousand erase/write cycles. If you updated data at a particular address at once a second, the flash would last for less than twenty minutes (10,000 writes / 60s/min = 16.7 min).

Flash doesn't catch on fire when it fails. Instead, the bits get sticky. After writing 0x55 ("U") to an address, it may be read back as 0x57 ("W"). When using flash extensively, the code needs to look for sticky bits and mark the section as bad so it is not used in the future.

Flash file systems need to be power-loss resilient so random failures during an update cycle don't cause file loss. They also need to handle wear leveling, using all of the blocks allocated to them equally, and they need to identify bad blocks and work around them. Oh, and they need to fit into our system, not taking up too much memory or processor cycles.

One of the big advantages of an RTOS is that it can likely provide a flash file system for you. There are many other bare-metal file systems (my favorite is `littlefs` one of the many open source filesystems).[1]

Data Storage

Another common use for SPI flash is to store data collected by the device. This is especially useful for systems that generate a constant stream of data that is read out in a big burst. Consider Bluetooth-connected pedometers or earthquake sensors: while the sensors are regularly getting data, they only transmit when they are connected.

You could use a file system for storing data, but often that causes too much overhead, with more flash accesses than necessary and unpredictable erase cycles. I've already mentioned that flash requires whole sectors to be erased. I probably should have mentioned that erasing the flash takes seemingly forever: sometimes tens of milliseconds!

Sadly, tens of milliseconds in this context is a lot. Let's say you are recording data at 20 kHz, 20,000 samples per second. The time between samples is inversely proportional to the frequency:

$$time\ between\ samples = \frac{1}{sampling\ frequency} = \frac{1}{20\ kHz} = 0.05\ ms$$

If the part has a maximum erase time of 25 ms, then the device may collect 500 samples while waiting for the flash to finish erasing and be available for writing new samples. Thus, the code will need enough RAM allocated to the sampling subsystem to store 500 samples (of whatever size your samples are).

 As with the display update questions above, these numbers are necessary to make sure the processor and flash can do what you need them to do. While I'll talk more about throughput calculators toward the end of this chapter, please start getting comfortable with the idea there will be some math involved. Spreadsheets are your friend. (And the GitHub repository (*https://github.com/eleciawhite/ making-embedded-systems*) for this book has samples.)

---

1 littlefs is nice because it explains the many trade-offs it makes. It can be found in GitHub (*https://github.com/ littlefs-project/littlefs*).

In addition to working out how the speed of the flash will affect RAM sizes, you also need to determine how much space to allocate to the datastore. Here are some questions to help you along:

- What are the sample rate and sample size?

- Do you sample continuously or in bursts? If in bursts, how long is the longest burst?

- How often should the data be collected? What is the maximum time between transfers?

- Do you erase after transfer or keep data for possible re-reading in the future until the flash fills up?

- What should happen to the data if it is never collected? Do you want to write over it with fresh data or keep the old?

You may need other items related to the particular application (What time did the sample occur? Did an algorithm identify this as interesting? What was the location for the sample? and so on). Data that describes your data is called *metadata*. It is easy to forget this as you work on the data storage calculations. Plan on some metadata overhead to go along with your data (10% is a good starting number if you aren't sure).

Timestamp Woes

Timestamps are the most common form of metadata. There is a balance to having a good timestamp that doesn't take up too much space and has enough accuracy and resolution. While it is extremely tempting to use a 32-bit counter describing the number of milliseconds since the last boot, you will find that 2^{32} milliseconds is only 49 days. A simple tick counter is not enough.

A *real-time clock* (RTC) may be required. An RTC implies the need for a battery or battery-like capacitor. The current time will be lost when the battery dies. Oh, and you need to set the time initially as well as when the battery dies. For data collection, I recommend always using UTC because you really don't want to deal with time zones and Daylight Saving Time.

The accuracy of the RTC depends on the accuracy of the clock it uses as input. As the temperature gets colder, the clock will run slower. RTCs are generally accurate but they aren't perfect.

Trying to synchronize between different devices leads to all kinds of headaches. Your server should probably be in charge, able to make corrections to the device, but if that isn't good enough, you may need a GPS to get a more accurate time source (then you also need a view of the sky). Many GPS modules output a pulse-per-second (PPS) signal that can be used to correct the RTC.

In summary: while it's vastly tempting to sort out the timestamps later, it is a part of design that should not be neglected because it has ramifications through the whole system. Alternatively, never work on time.

Once you've identified the pain of erase times and scoped out the necessary size, the next piece of unwelcome news is that the power to the system will definitely go out at the worst possible moment. One evil edge case is when data transfer is complete, but the system reset before it could mark the flash as ready for erase. Can the receiver handle duplicate data?

Having the power fail while erasing can lead to corruption in the data. This can be difficult to determine, but one way to solve the problem is to have a modification list in a different part of flash. In the modification list sector of flash, program the address block that is about to be erased. Then do the erase. Then add to the modification list that the erase completed. On boot, go through the list, scanning for any starting marks that don't have corresponding erase-completed marks. At some point, this list will fill up and need to be erased itself, so allocate two sectors to this modification list.

Power can fail while writing to flash as well. You could use the same modification list, but if you write small amounts of flash, writing to the mod list, then putting in the data, then writing to the mod list again becomes quite cumbersome. Instead, I recommend putting in checksums to verify that a block of data has been written completely. How often you should do this depends on your application: how much data can you lose when the power goes out? If you need every sample to count, then use smaller blocks. If a power cycle means data won't be ready for a few seconds anyway, then a larger block is probably fine.

Another consideration for the data store is retrieving the data. When connection happens, how long does it take to read out the buffered data? Are you still acquiring new data at the same time? Flash reads are fast, so it probably won't cause a problem, but you'll need to check the numbers to be sure. (More about this in "Calculating Needs: Speeds and Feeds" on page 236.)

But for all this talk about storing data, what kind of data is it? That is where sensors come in.

Analog Signals

A button could be called a type of sensor. The methods used to talk to buttons are similar to those used with sensors, and the choices are similar (e.g., interrupts versus polling). However, buttons are either pressed down or not, whereas sensors can provide all sorts of data—high, low, 1.45, 10,342.81, 12, 43, or out of range. What you read depends on your sensor.

Your system may have its own input sensors while serving as a sensor to another system.

A microphone, like your ears, picks up audio in analog form. You can use an ADC (occasionally called an A2D) to move from real-world analog to software-friendly digital. Your software can do any number of things with the digital data: watch for events in the analog stream, filter it, or change it back into analog with a DAC (aka D2A). In analog form, the signal can be played through a speaker. Figure 8-7 shows a simple system.

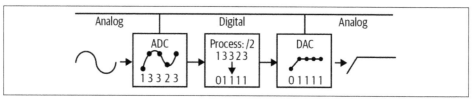

Figure 8-7. Analog-to-digital-to-analog system

The *signal* is the underlying thing you are listening to, whether it is currently digital or analog. *Noise* is what makes it hard for your software to see the signal properly. A goal of the system is to make sure there is plenty of signal compared to the noise, giving you a high *SNR* (signal-to-noise ratio).

Digital signal processing is a software technique for changing data from analog to digital, and often doing something to make sense of the data. Sometimes the data gets transformed to look like something different. Often this change converts the data to a combination of sine waves because these are easy to compute with. The sine waves are frequencies (think of radio station frequencies or musical pitches). So this conversion is called *conversion to the frequency domain*.

In Figure 8-7, the signal is reduced by dividing each integer sample by two. The resulting analog sound should be quieter (attenuated), but integer division isn't a good idea with such small numbers, so the signal morphs more than it should. (Receiving a higher signal input at the ADC or sampling more bits in the ADC would reduce this problem with integer math.)

This is a relatively silly example because you could get a better attenuation effect without digitizing the input. More often, the data goes through multiple stages of processing. Some of these might include filtering (to reduce noise or enhance a particular signal characteristic), companding (attenuating loud sections and/or boosting quiet ones), and convolution (finding one signal hidden inside another).

ADCs and DACs are characterized by their sample frequencies (how fast they work) and number of bits. An 8-bit ADC has 256 levels in its digital signal; a 16-bit ADC has 65,536 levels. What you need depends on your application, but those two numbers can drive how your whole software system is organized by constraining the speed of your processor and the amount of RAM you need. How fast your system can process data is called its *throughput* or *bandwidth*.

Some processors are built with signal processing in mind (digital signal processors, aka DSPs). They have special processor instructions that work with the signal much faster than a general-purpose processor does.

Of all of the embedded systems areas, signal processing is my favorite. However, it is a complete book unto itself. Well, two books, because you need to understand the math (Fourier is fun) and how to apply that to real-world problems (fast Fourier transforms!).

I don't want you to think you are ready to go off and make a great analog system with this tiny section. For instance, I haven't talked about sampling and the *Nyquist* frequency. Either you already know about it, or you need far more than this brief orientation. I recommend my favorite signal processing books in "Further Reading" on page 239.

I started this section with a microphone, but analog sensors come in all sorts of types: motion sensors (accelerometers, gyroscopes, magnetometers), weather sensors (wind, humidity, temperature), vision sensors (cameras, infrared detectors…), the list goes on and on. You may have only five senses, but your system can have many more.

 I once heard an electrical engineer say, "All sensors are temperature sensors, but some are better than others." That's true. Sensors respond to ambient temperature even when they are supposed to be measuring something else. Expect to have to calibrate your system for temperature and give a sigh of relief if you don't need to.

Digital Sensors

If I have made you a little nervous with analog sensors and the arcane world of signal processing, I do apologize. You'll like digital sensors a lot more. A digital sensor will do the analog-to-digital conversion for you, ideally giving you exactly the data you need. As with analog sensors, the range of digital sensors is staggering. Although digital sensors are usually a bit more expensive than their analog counterparts, the price is often worth it because they produce meaningful samples, offload a lot of work from the processor, and are less susceptible to external noise (see "EMI: Electromagnetic Interference" on page 230). Digital sensors may also include integrated filters and temperature compensation.

EMI: Electromagnetic Interference

As signals travel along wires, they pick up noise from all the things around that have clocks. Wait a minute, you say—my system has a clock? Probably more than one, actually.

So you can't expect your analog system to be free of noise. The wires that the analog signal travels along are like antennas picking up static from everything around them. Your electrical engineer can shield the signal and reduce its susceptibility to noise (usually by putting a shiny metal box connected to ground, called a Faraday cage, around the signal). But you still might have to worry about noise.

 Although digital signals emit more noise to the environment, they are more immune to outside sources of noise.

Sometimes, before you can fix the issue, you need to find the culprit causing the noise. That can be difficult. If it is not external to your system, it could be any of your communication paths, any of your peripherals, or your processor itself. Even worse, it may be some combination of these interfering in tandem, giving you hard-to-reproduce errors. Radiating noise internally is not the only problem.

Sometimes, after bring-up but before the end of your project, your electrical engineer will take your system off for electromagnetic compatibility (EMC) testing. Different countries have different regulations (and certification processes) necessary to use products in the country. In the US, if your system has a clock that is over 9 kHz, it needs to go through EMC testing to ensure that it doesn't radiate signals that will interfere with communication (to comply with FCC part 15).

This test will put the unit into an anechoic chamber and monitor it at many radio frequencies to see whether it emits any noise above the tolerated level. As you prepare the software used in hardware bring-up, you may need to put together an EMC test version that will transmit data through all communication pathways as fast as possible, to generate chatter and verify that nothing much radiates from your device.

The same EMC test lab usually can blast your unit with different frequencies to see whether it is susceptible to noise in any particular range.

Your primary concern in reading the datasheet for the digital sensor is how to communicate with it. Does your processor have the type of communication method needed by the sensor? After that, the questions center on throughput: can your software keep up with the amount of data the sensor is going to send? What is it going to do with the data? How long will it take? How will it know when data is ready?

Data Handling

So far, we've seen the data generators and the data consumers. And we've seen how to send and receive data. However, there are some pieces missing between these two. Understanding how to move the data around in your software is critical to making a great system. Let's start with the big picture of handling the data at a system level, and then work down into the mechanics.

In Chapter 5, we looked at systems that were event-driven: things happened because sensors were activated, causing events that in turn caused changes to the state of the system. However, not all embedded systems can (or should) be set up as event loops and state machines.

There is a class of problems where the goal is to get data, process it, do something with the results, and repeat. In such *data-driven systems*, there are no events, just an ever-increasing mountain of data for your software to process. Ideally, the system can wade through the data just a tiny bit faster than it is generated. Some examples of data-driven systems include:

- An airplane's black box, which continuously records audio and telemetry.
- A gunshot location sensor that listens to its environment. Upon identifying an impulsive sound, it generates an event to send to a host.
- A reconnaissance satellite that records image data, compresses it, and (when in range of a link point) sends it to Earth.
- An MP3 player that reads data from its audio store, decompresses it, and sends bits out of a DAC to generate a signal that sounds like music to your ears.
- An auto-following system that reads position and adjusts vehicle velocity.

A data-driven system can be understood by looking at the flow of data. The rate of the data and how quickly it needs to be processed are the primary features of the system.

Reboots and errors can cause the system to fall behind. This is one type of system where failing gracefully is important. If the system has an error that causes it to fall behind, should it skip some of the data and catch up? Or should it do some sort of reduced processing until the system returns to normal? What are the consequences of missing data?

Happily, implementing a data-driven system is pretty straightforward because the processing of the data is repetitive. Consider the analog-to-digital system described in Figure 8-7, where digital data comes from the ADC, gets attenuated, and goes out the DAC. The system can usually be divided into a producer of data (the ADC) and a consumer of data (the DAC). These must remain in Zen-like balance. As long as the processor can keep up with the ADC by running the algorithm and sending the data to the DAC, the system can run forever.

Most systems have some elements of both an event-driven system and a data-driven system. As you consider your system, try to figure out what aspects belong to each. This will unravel some of the complexity of your software by allowing you to implement them separately.

Changing Algorithms: Strategy

Sometimes the path of your code needs to change based on the environment. If you are thinking that we saw a way to change what the code is doing based on commands from the host in the command pattern in Chapter 3, you are correct. The command pattern is used to make short-term command/response changes. The *strategy pattern* is used to make longer-term changes, usually to data processing. According to the official definition from *Design Patterns: Elements of Reusable Object-Oriented Software*, the strategy pattern is used to "define a family of algorithms, encapsulate each one, and make them interchangeable. Strategy lets the algorithm vary independently from the clients that use it."

Consider the data-driven system in Figure 8-7, where analog data is digitized by an ADC, attenuated by the processor, and then sent back to analog via the DAC. What if you weren't sure you wanted to attenuate the signal? What if you wanted to invert it? Or amplify the signal? Or add another signal to it?

You could use a state machine, but it would be a little clunky. Once on every processing pass, the code would have to check which algorithm to use based on the state variable.

Another way to implement this is to have a pointer to a function (or object) that processes data. You'll need to define the function interface so every data-processing function takes the same arguments and returns the same data type. But if you can do that, you can change the pointer on command, thereby changing how your whole system works (or possibly how a small part of your system modifies the data).

 Some embedded systems are too constrained to be able to change the algorithm on the fly. However, you probably still want to use the strategy pattern concepts to switch algorithms during development. The strategy pattern helps you separate data from code and enforces a relatively strict interface to different algorithms.

A related pattern is the *template pattern*. A template provides a skeleton of an algorithm but allows the steps to change (without changing the algorithm's structure). Usually these aren't function pointers; the steps are part of the organization of the algorithm. In our data-driven system, we could make a template that looked like the following:

```
class Template {
private:
  struct sCircularBuffer *cb;

public:
  enum eErrorCode sample();
  enum eErrorCode processData();
  enum eErrorCode output();
}
```

Even though each of these functions has the same prototype, they aren't interchangeable, unlike the strategy pattern. Instead, they provide an outline of how the system works. An instance of this template for the system described would have the ADC sampling the data, the data being amplified, and the DAC outputting the result. The instantiation of a template may override certain (or all) parts of the default implementation. For instance, if the default implementation sets up the order "ADC-process-DAC," a test version of the class may override the sample function to read data from a file while leaving the other two functions in place.

You can, of course, combine patterns. Here is a strategy pattern inside the template's skeleton:

```
class Template {
private:
  struct sCircularBuffer *cb;
public:
  enum eErrorCode sample();
  enum eErrorCode (*processData)();
  enum eErrorCode output();
}
```

Object-oriented software has the concept of *inheritance*, where an instance *is-a* concrete version of an object. Template patterns are like that (the template is a series of these steps). An alternative approach is *composition*, where the software *has-a* concrete version of an object. Strategy patterns are more like that (they offer a function to call). Composition is more flexible than inheritance because it is easier to switch what things have than what they are. On the other hand, building (composing) a system at runtime might not be a good use of limited resources. Balance the trade-offs for your system.

Algorithm Stages: Pipelines and Filters

Sometimes processing the data takes multiple steps. A *pipeline* is a design pattern where the output of each processing step is the input to the next step. Usually, the analogy is an assembly line with partially assembled items that move from station to station or a load of laundry: something where there are multiple stages, each one needing to complete before the process goes on. These steps are called *filters* (though they may not be the same thing as signal processing filters!). They may also be called stages or processing elements.

As shown in Figure 8-8, say we have a system that collects data, maybe a heart rate monitor:

1. Data comes into the system from an ADC as samples.
2. The samples are processed to remove noise.
3. Then they go through a low-pass filter to remove different noise.
4. An algorithm piece selects the two channels of data to keep.
5. The reduced and filtered data is stored in the data store.
6. The reduced and filtered data is downsampled.
7. The downsampled data is put on a display as a rolling window rolling graph.

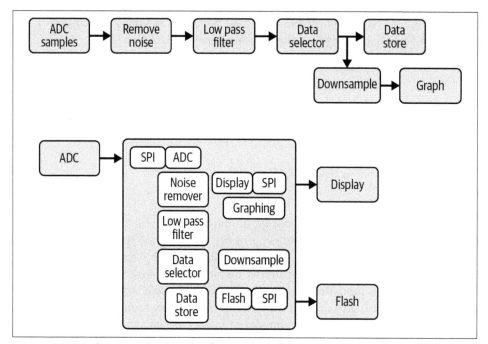

Figure 8-8. Pipeline view (top) and software block diagram (bottom) of an example heart rate monitor

The noise removal and low-pass filter are part of the pipeline. These happen with every sample from the ADC: a sample goes in, a modified sample comes out in a constant stream of data. It is important to note that the samples are processed in the order they are received. For that to happen, with some filters the samples need to be buffered so that as you put in a sample, you get out an older sample. Buffering leads to data latency (which is a lot like system latency but for data). As shown in Figure 8-9, this latency accumulates with each filter.

As the modified data is ready to go to the data store, it may be broken into chunks to limit flash accesses. Instead of writing one sample at a time, it will write many.

 You can also think of pipelines as message queues where the filter stages process each message, writing the results to another message queue.

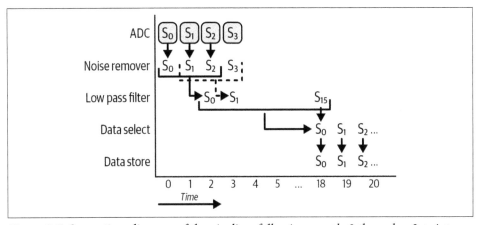

Figure 8-9. Space-time diagram of the pipeline: following sample 0 through a 3-point noise filter and a 16-point low-pass filter to the data selector and data store, latency accumulates with each buffered pipeline element

While storage could be considered part of the pipeline, it is an endpoint, a consumer, not a filter. The data may go on to other filters:

- Find the maximum and minimum of the filtered data
- If max-min is large enough to be interesting, then process the lowpass filtered data with convolution to find the start of the interesting event
- Report the event time and interesting characteristics (such as min and max)

These filters are different from the previous ones because they work on *windowed* data: you don't want the all-time min and max, the goal is to find the characteristics in a shorter period of time. For example, you may not expect to see a heart rate faster than 250 beats per minute and choose the window accordingly. The windows are often overlapped in case the event of interest is on the border between two windows.

If you were to go look for the *pipeline* design pattern or the *pipes and filters* design pattern, you might see that it is marked as something that is primarily useful if you have multiple processors that can handle the filter stages in parallel. The different filters are a good way to break the processing up so it can be shared.

I promise the pipeline pattern is very useful in an embedded context. Like state machines, most systems have aspects that can be considered pipelines. The pipeline pattern is a good way to think about how data moves through the system: at what speeds, whether constant throughput or windowed chunks, and with data of different sizes. If you think about data streams this way, you can break up the filters to test them individually, making them more readable and possibly reusable.

Calculating Needs: Speeds and Feeds

It is easy to get lost in the low-level details of a system: trying to get I²C sensor samples into a circular buffer, then outputting them to SPI flash, before calculating a graph and sending it to a display. Each piece requires a dedicated piece of software.

However, as you do more system design, there are system-level issues to consider. I've been sprinkling in breadcrumbs throughout this chapter; now it's time to put them together.

The goal is to determine the specifications of your parts given the product features (or update the product features given the parts available). Like pipelines, it is a matter of connecting the outputs of one piece of the system to the inputs of the next.

I often use a spreadsheet to figure out if all of the pieces of my system can be linked together.

Data Bandwidth

Going back to the heart monitor in Figure 8-8, the ADC provides data. But what kind of data?

- What is the sample rate? How many samples per second? Usually this is in hertz (Hz).
- How many channels of data are in the sample?
- How big is each sample? Usually this is in bits.

Say we have a SPI four-channel 16-bit ADC sampling at 44.1 kHz. How much data is the system dealing with each second?

$bandwidth = sampleRate \times channels \times size\ of\ sample = 44,100 \times 4 \times 16 = 352,800$ *bytes per second*

When you look at the SPI clock, you will need to receive that much data. Is your SPI clock fast enough to transfer that much data? (Assume for now that DMA is working so the transfer overhead is minimal.)

transfer clock (minimum) = bandwidth (in bits) = 352,800 × 8 = 2.8 MHz

Is it still fast enough if the SPI bus is shared with other peripherals? Even if the other peripheral is the display? Or flash? All of these things add up, so you'll need to determine how much of your total SPI bandwidth is used by each device. Calculate the normal (nominal) number and the worst-possible number to make sure you have margin.

So far we are talking about a continuous sample. You may also have bursts of samples, such as recording an interesting event for 4 seconds. That would give you a total recording snippet size of:

snippet size = bandwidth × length = 352,800 × 4 = 1.3 MB

How does this work if your processor has only 512 KBs of RAM? Do you need off-chip RAM for temporary storage? (Is it SPI? Does it need to go into the clock speed calculation?)

Can you write to the flash fast enough to store the data? If the goal is recording (with or without bursts), you'll need to go back to the flash datasheet to see if it can keep up. Putting the data throughput in terms of bytes/second will help you total up shared buses and compare different resources.

And then, how do you get the data off the device? (More on that in Chapter 10.) Do you have to keep sampling while also reading the data out?

Figure 8-10 shows some of the speeds and feed information for this system. The calculations for each step are in the Speeds and Feeds Calculator in the GitHub repository for this book (*https://github.com/eleciawhite/making-embedded-systems*).

For each bus and each peripheral, you'll need to estimate how much of the possible throughput is used. Some buses will be simple; for an underutilized I²C with a few simple sensors, you probably won't even need to grab a calculator. Then for each processing element, you will need a buffer to hold the samples needed for processing. But embedded systems are purpose-built applications; they are often cost-sensitive, so extra RAM and faster SPI devices may not be on your BOM unless you can prove they are necessary.

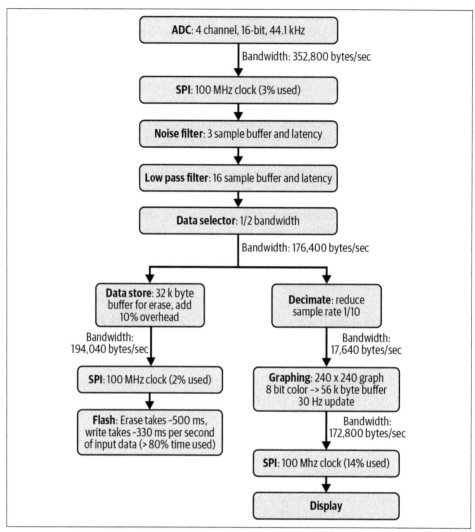

Figure 8-10. Looking at the system as a series of elements with inputs, outputs, buffers, and necessary bandwidths to maintain

Memory Throughput and Buffering

Most microprocessors have both volatile (RAM) and nonvolatile (flash) memory on the chip. This is handy, but for many applications it isn't enough. External RAM is often used to buffer data, stage screens for display, or temporarily hold data. Display assets, file systems, long-term data storage, and firmware updates are often put into external flash.

Memory often ends up being a shared resource, used by different parts of the system. As you may recall from Chapter 2, shared resources add complexity to the system and to the code. Mutexes will be required. Beyond that, flash may be busy as it erases or accesses large display assets. This is an area where a priority inversion can cause the system to lock up as several tasks wait for the flash system to complete commands.

While internal memory also takes time to access, it is not usually an issue unless you are trying to wring every cycle out of the processor or writing to internal flash (often for firmware updates). External memory might be a bottleneck if there are too many different subsystems trying to access different parts of the flash. As noted in "External Flash Memory" on page 220, erasing takes more time than writing, which takes longer than reading. So an inopportune erase of the KV store may cause delays in data storage writes or display asset retrieval.

As you look at the types of memory you have available, you'll need to estimate how much of each you'll be using to determine if you have enough space for the intended purpose.

When you look at memory, here are some questions to ask:

- How large is it? Don't be fooled by memory sizes given in megabits (Mb) instead of megabytes (MB)!
- How long does it take to read and write the memory? This may depend on communication bandwidth as well as the memory characteristics.
- How much do you need to erase at a time? How long does an erase operation take?
- How many times can it be rewritten? Flashes can be erased and rewritten only a limited number of times.

While we often think about protocols connecting external peripherals to the processor, during system design, those connections are more about how each element flows, which means looking at bandwidth and buffers. The memory type and speed your device has available constrains the application.

Further Reading

This chapter covered many things, so I have lots of places for you to look if you want to dig deeper into a particular area. As mentioned elsewhere in this book, Erich Gamma et al. *Design Patterns: Elements of Reusable Object-Oriented Software* and Eric Freemen et al. *Head First Design Patterns*, are great references for understanding design patterns.

Signal processing and motor control have a lot in common in their underlying math (Laplace and Fourier transforms). If you haven't had those in school (or cannot dredge up the memories), you might consider taking a class. It isn't the sort of thing to learn from a book. But if you are going to anyway, the seminal textbook is *Signals and Systems* by Alan V. Oppenheim et al. (Prentice-Hall).

Or, you can skip to practical applications with a really fantastic book, *The Scientist and Engineer's Guide to Digital Signal Processing* by Steven W. Smith (California Technical Publishing). It is also available online for free (*https://dspguide.com*).

If you really want to understand pipelines, take a look at GStreamer (*https://oreil.ly/ptOqg*), an open source tool for audio and video processing. It is amazingly powerful and horrifically complicated.

The GitHub repository (*https://github.com/eleciawhite/making-embedded-systems*) that goes along with this book has a spreadsheet that shows the calculations for "Calculating Needs: Speeds and Feeds" on page 236.

Interview Question: Designing a System

What are some considerations you take into account when designing a sensor system?

Sometimes the goal of an interview question is to make sure the interviewee will ask questions. Sure, they could answer with statements: power, connectivity, operating environment, criticality, accuracy, cost, and so on. Of course, I'd like them to mention pipelines and bandwidths.

However, what I really want to see is when they stop answering my question and start asking their own. There is something amazing when someone stops reacting and starts getting curious. You can't force that, especially in a tense interview situation. But you can invite it with interview questions like this one.

The questions they ask will shine a light on how they think about systems. Their initial questions will show their experiences.

I have to admit that my response to this question would be a flood of questions:

- Is the design for a distributed network of homogeneous sensing devices? Or is this a single device?

- If it communicates with another system, is it a continuous flow of information or bursty? What should it do if it can't communicate? What if it can't communicate for a long time?

- What is the level of precision and accuracy needed for the sensors? For the output?

- Is the signal being monitored for anomalies? Is the data being stored?

- What kind of processing is likely to be needed? What processing power is available? How much manipulation does the signal need? Is data being processed locally or remotely? How much latency is allowable at each stage?

- What sensors are specified and why were they chosen? What are their failure mechanisms?

- Is sensing happening at a fixed interval, on demand, or in reaction to something?

- What kind of environment does it need to work in? Are there requirements related to size? How will it be installed?

- What kind of power will it use? Does it have to run on a battery?

- Is operation critical to something? What are the stakes (ramifications) if it fails? How are low battery or other faults supposed to be handled?

- What is the budget and what are the cost goals?

- Who are the users?

Detailed initial questions are likely to be reflections of what not to do from a previous project. You can always dig in with a query as to why a point is important. Hopefully, you'll hear about a project they still think about.

More importantly, the questions will show that they will ask questions. I'm not going to claim that there are no dumb questions. But questions show that the person is thinking about something, not passively taking in information or responding by rote. Questions are an indication that they are engaged. Even seemingly dumb questions show that. And often, they aren't as dumb as they sound, simply asked from a different frame of reference.

(Thanks to members of the Embedded.fm Slack for sharing their thoughts on this question!)

CHAPTER 9

Getting into Trouble

I've already talked about the importance of testing as you go and unit tests. However, sometimes there are bugs. And if you knew what was wrong, you'd have fixed it by now. Unless you are reading this book while sitting on a beach (as is recommended), you are probably looking for concrete advice about your current issue. If I were sitting next to you, my mental checklist would look like this:

- Is it powered? Are you sure?
- Are you sure that the device is running the code you think it is?
- Can you test only that part of the system?
- Did you check the errata for the chip? Did you check the part number for the chip?
- If it's intermittent, is it a timing error? Stack overflow?
- Is it related to uninitialized variables? Does making variables global make it better or worse?
- Can you turn optimizations off and see if it still happens?
- Have you looked at the map file? (More about that in Chapter 11.)
- In case of emergency (and random nonsensical error): could it be a ground loop problem?

You'd be surprised how often a problem is found in the first few steps. These questions come from the experience of being wrong, of failing and trying again, of finding the problem only to wish I'd looked there first.

Make your own checklist. Learn your own common issues. While I'll go through many items on my list in more detail, let your list grow with your experience.

For the most part, I don't want to talk about the errors that can be found through compiler warnings, code reviews, unit tests, and stepping through with the debugger. I want to talk about getting into real trouble with optimization, impossible bugs, hard faults, and memory. However, before we get there, I need a quick word about the compiler.

Fighting with the Compiler Optimizations

My worst bugs seem to be typos, things I can't see because my eyes don't register the problem. Thus, I love compiler warnings, especially the one that indicates I've written an assignment in a conditional expression:

```
if (i = OH_NO_THIS_IS_WRONG) {}
```

Instead of:

```
if (i == YES_I_MEANT_TO_DO_THIS) {}
```

Having the compiler or linter tell you about these issues is a gift. Use them. Enable all the compiler warnings you can, then fix all the warnings. This is the first step in debugging your code.

I know that vendor code doesn't always compile warning-free. I don't think you should change it unless you must (usually for certification reasons). Because updating to a new version of vendor code is a pain after you've made modifications, I suggest marking your modifications with a comment so you can easily port the changes:

```
// START_MY_COMPANY_MODIFICATION
…
// END_MY_COMPANY_MODIFICATION
```

Another option is to keep an unmodified copy of the vendor code with your code as source control patch files.

One issue with difficult bugs and the compiler is caused by compiler optimizations. The compiler reorganizes the code to make it faster. And many variables are put into registers and eliminated early.

Suddenly, you can no longer walk through code because the debugger bounces around, reflecting the optimized order of operations, instead of going from line to line. And when you check the value of a variable, your debugger tells you it doesn't exist.

Worse, sometimes your code starts doing weird (wrong) things when you turn optimizations on. This is almost never the compiler's fault. Stop blaming the compiler. Truly, it is your code. I'm sorry.

Occasionally, it is the fault of the language. Where languages have undefined behaviors, compilers are free to implement them however they see fit, which means different compilers do different things. This is most commonly exposed when compiler authors are trying to do the cleverest optimizations possible.

Optimizations are supposed to change the timing: they make the system faster. Unfortunately, if your code depends on a little delay or the precise order of operations, it will break when you set optimizations on.

More likely the problems will arise with variables.

Optimizers remove code they don't think is useful. If you don't use a variable, it will remove the variable, even if it is a global such as a flag set in an interrupt and watched for in a loop. Without optimizations on, the compiler will allow this inefficiency of two functions reading or writing a variable that never seems to be used. But once you ask the compiler to be smart, it notices that the loop is silly, nothing happens. So it doesn't need to run the loop or keep the flag variable (even though you and I know that the interrupt modifies the variable outside the scope of the main loop):

```
#include <stdio.h>

int global = 0; // without volatile here, the while loop below may
                // be optimized out

void isr(void) {
  global = 1;
}

int main(void)
{
    global = 0;
    while (1) {
        if (global == 1)
        {
            printf("Interrupt occurred!");
        }
    }
}
```

When you turn on optimizations, the (supposedly) unused parts of your code are removed.

Finally, optimizations change the way your variables are handled, often bringing to light issues with initialization and memory overruns. Without optimizations, your variables likely live in RAM and are casually strewn about. Once they are packed into tighter quarters, their values are more likely overwritten with an off-by-one error or the byte alignment suddenly matters.

Uninitialized global and static variables are set to zero upon initialization of your code. A function's local variables are not! Uninitialized function variables contain random values!

So, if a piece of code starts acting badly with optimization on:

- Make sure variables used in your interrupt and non-interrupt space are marked volatile.
- Move variables to temporarily be global (thereby initializing them all to zero).
- Temporarily add space at the end of arrays to check for off-by-one-errors.
- Slow down the system (with temporary periodic delays or with a timer that interrupts and wastes a little time).

If any of these make the code work, you have a way to start digging into what is wrong.

When you start optimizing heavily, you can get into trouble that is far more ineffable. Whether it is random crashes or random behavior, no one likes the Heisenbugs that disappear when you recompile with one debug `printf` commented out or when the weather is sunny.

Impossible Bugs

There should never be an impossible bug. And code should always compile and work the first time. "Should" is a stupid word.

The key to impossible bugs is to make them possible, to stop thinking about how they can't possibly happen and dig into how they are happening. There are two methods to doing this.

The first method is to focus on reproducing the bug. The second method is to focus on explaining the bug. You should use both, switching between them as you get stuck on one path.

Reproduce the Bug

For the first path, it seems obvious that the first step is reproducing the bug, but it is the critical step. It doesn't matter if you have to hop on one foot and cluck like a chicken, you have to make it happen again. And again. Steps that shouldn't matter need to be recorded if that's how the bug gets reproduced. Once you have that, go on to the other steps:

1. Reproduce the bug.
2. Reproduce the bug with the minimal amount of code.

3. Go back to the last working version: does it still work? Can you find when the bug was introduced?

4. Reproduce the bug on command (or on boot) so you don't have to do ten steps to reproduce it. Reduce the steps to reproduce the bug as much as possible.

5. After making exploratory tweaks, are you sure you are running the code you think you are?

6. Is this really the minimum amount of code needed to reproduce the bug?

When you've got a minimal code set, you may be able to post the issue on a vendor website, or use a debugger to explore the root cause, or get help from another person.

More likely, before you've gotten to step 6, you've gotten stuck. So you need to switch strategies.

Explain the Bug

When someone asks me for help with a bug, the first thing I do is ask them to explain what they were trying to do. I'm no longer surprised when they wander off halfway through their monologue.

Explaining the bug helps you understand it better and see the disconnect between what you intend to do and what is happening. It is a more thinky type of action than reproducing the bug. Here are the steps:

1. Describe the bug's symptoms.

2. Explain how the bug could possibly do what it does. List all possible causes (without using ground loops [but cosmic rays are OK]).

3. Explain the bug and what you've tried to a duck.[1] If you realize you forgot to try something, note it down.

4. Take notes on what changes have what effects. (You will not remember after the third tweak or fourth test attempt.)

5. Figure out what changed from the last known good code.

6. Get a code review.

Describing the issue seems so easy, but saying "it doesn't work" isn't enough. What doesn't work? How is it different than expected? Is it a single version of code? On a single board? Be detailed.

---

1 I've always kept a stuffed animal on my desk. I loan it out to others who need a friendly ear. I was startled to discover this is an official debugging technique called *rubber duck debugging*. I like my fluffy dinosaur better, but to each their own.

The second step assumes the bug exists (this is harder than it sounds) then suggests using inductive reasoning to find the cause. It is backward from most debugging: instead of finding the cause for the issue, you try to find all possible causes. You can even go a step further: if you were trying to make this happen, how would you do it?

Explaining the bug only gets you so far. You can develop lots of theories and ideas, but then you need to take some data, which means going back to reproduce the bug. You can't fix what you can't measure.

Creating Chaos and Hard Faults

Hard faults are interrupts caused by the processor identifying a (potentially) cata-strophic issue related to the execution of the code. These are usually nonmaskable interrupts (NMIs; you can't disable them). So how do you create hard faults?

Oh, you thought I was going to tell you how to avoid hard faults? Naw, the best way to understand why the processor is sending you love letters (exceptions) is to see what they look like when you aren't also frantically trying to fix your code.

As painful as hard faults are to debug, be glad they exist. At least something is trying to tell you what went wrong.

I'm going to show you some hard faults, how they happen, and what the processor can tell you. This list isn't all-inclusive, and some may not be faults that your system can issue.

If you run the terrible example code, you can learn how your system responds when your code does terrible things.

Dividing by Zero

Obviously, dividing by zero is wrong. If anyone successfully does that, I have it on good authority the action will create a singularity that causes a black hole that devours the galaxy (maybe the universe; how would I know?).

```
int divide_by_zero(void)
{
    int a = 1;
    int c = 0;
    int b = a/c;
    return b; // forces compiler to actually run this
}
```

So what happens if you call this code? On a Linux machine, you get an abnormally terminated process (SIGSEGV or SIGFPE or SIG*something*).

On a Cortex-M, you get a result of zero if your configuration and control register (SCB->CCR) doesn't cause a fault on a divide-by-zero. Alternatively, if your CCR is set to let you know about these errors, you get the DIVBYZERO bit set in the *usage fault* status register which causes a hard fault, a nonmaskable interrupt that likely stops your processor in its tracks. It may cause a reset or wait for a watchdog timer to cause a reset.

Unless you dig into the code a bit, your hard fault handlers likely go to a placeholder interrupt handler, the one causing a reset or an infinite loop.

Of course, it is easy to see what the divide-by-zero example code does. It isn't so easy when it is buried in thousands of lines of complex signal processing code. The goal of the processor fault handlers (which look just like interrupt handlers in that they are in the vector table) is usually to narrow down where the processor was when the issue happened. The stack can be used to figure out where the processor was before the fault occurred. More about that soon, in "Creating a Core Dump" on page 256.

Talking to Things That Aren't There

We all know you can't access a NULL pointer. Of course not. But why?

Well, a NULL pointer is a pointer that is set to zero. That zero is an address in memory. It may be the start of your processor's flash memory. Or it may be nothing at all: an address with no associated memory.

We set pointers to NULL so that we know that the pointer isn't to be used. Take a look at this terrible code:

```
int* global_ptr_to_null = NULL;
int* global_ptr_uninitialized;

void write_to_null(void) {
  int* ptr_to_null = NULL;
  int* ptr_uninitialized;

  *global_ptr_to_null  = 10;      /* tries to write to address zero */
  *global_ptr_uninitialized = 10; /* tries to write to address zero */
  *ptr_to_null  = 10;             /* tries to write to address zero */
  *ptr_uninitialized = 10;        /* tries to write ?? somewhere ?? */
   // … rest of function
```

The global_ptr_uninitialized is an uninitialized global. Global variables are sneaky; they are automatically (implicitly) set to zero, same as those set explicitly to NULL.

Writing to zero when it is flash or has no actual memory associated with the address may lead to a hard fault, probably a data access or bus fault, depending on your processor, hard fault configuration register(s), and memory configuration.

This doesn't apply only to NULL. Writing to any address that has no actual memory associated with it can cause a fault if the processor is configured to identify them.

The last one in the code, `ptr_uninitialized`, is particularly troublesome. It may equal anything, including a valid memory address. This one is worse than a hard fault. Unless you get lucky and the address doesn't matter or isn't valid, writing to this pointer may work…sometimes. Where this pointer points depends on what is currently on the stack, which is a lot like saying "it depends on randomness."

Watchpoints: Data Breakpoints

A *watchpoint* is a form of breakpoint that stops on access to an address in memory instead of stopping when the program counter reaches its goal.

When implemented in hardware (by your processor), watchpoints are great. The debugger will stop when the code modifies the memory location.

If watchpoints aren't supported by your processor (or you use too many), then the data breakpoint becomes a software watchpoint where your debugger checks to see if you are accessing the memory on every clock cycle. This is very slow and debugging gets quite difficult.

How many watchpoints you have and how well they work depends on the microprocessor. But if you have them, they are exceedingly handy for finding stack overflows and memory errors.

Running Undefined Instructions

Next up in this showcase of things you should only run for fun, never unintentionally, we have bad code. This is not the normal level of bad code, but instead code the processor cannot run:

```
void (*fun_ptr)(void);    // global defaults to zero
void call_null_pointer_function(void)
{
  fun_ptr(); /* will execute code at address zero */
}

int illegal_instruction_execution(void) {
  int instruction = 0xE0000000;
  int (*bad_instruction)(void) = (int(*)())(&instruction);
  return bad_instruction();
}
```

The `call_null_pointer_function` code executes the code at address zero. For systems with memory that starts at address zero, the first item is usually the address to the reset handler. Will that address itself be valid code? Or will you get a hard fault indicating a bad instruction?

The `illegal_instruction_execution` function executes `0xE0000000` as an instruction. That isn't a valid instruction on my current processor, so I always get a bad instruction hard fault. This action is obvious here; of course you wouldn't do this in your code.

This usually occurs because a function pointer has gone awry. If you are running code from RAM (for updating flash or because it is faster), memory problems can overwrite the running code, leading to illegal instructions and other forms of chaos.

Incorrect Memory Access (Unaligned Access)

Let's say you have a 32-bit processor and you want to write to only one byte…Wait, how does that work? How do you access one byte if your processor has 32-bit (4-byte) registers?

It depends on the processor. Many processors have instructions to let them access smaller pieces of memory. For those that don't, the compiler will truncate a 32-bit value to fit into an 8-bit value:

```
uint8_t unaligned_access_ok(void)
{
    uint32_t bigVariable = 0xAABBCCDD;
    uint32_t  *ptr = &bigVariable;


    uint8_t  smallVariable = *ptr;
    return smallVariable;
}
```

However, if you are doing more complex things with pointers, such as trying to access a 32-bit value in the middle of an array or in the middle of a packed structure, then it isn't a matter of compile time variable type matching. Here is some terrible code that tries to take four bytes out of the middle of a six-byte array:

```
uint32_t unaligned_access_bad(void)
{
    uint8_t buffer[6] = {0xAA, 0xBB, 0xCC, 0xDD, 0xEE, 0xFF};
    uint8_t i = 1;
    uint32_t val_BB_to_EE = *((uint32_t *)( &buffer[i] ));
    return val_BB_to_EE;
}
```

This code may work: your processor may do the extra work of byte access for the byte buffer, even though that is much slower than word (32-bit) access. Or this code may cause a hard fault, with the processor complaining about misaligned memory or a bus error. Or, possibly, your compiler knows enough about your processor to generate the extra code (making it easier for you at the cost of wasted processor cycles).

If you see memory alignment errors, you are looking for a situation where the code is accessing a larger variable out of a byte array. This may be a stream of data or a fixed array of constants.

Returning a Pointer to Stack Memory

What is wrong with this terrible code?

```
int* dont_return_stack_memory(void) {
    int stack_memory[100];
    return stack_memory;
}
```

In the sidebar "Stacks (and Heaps)" on page 129, I had a diagram showing how the stack consists of the memory used by each function. As new functions are called, local variables and a stack frame are added to the stack. See Figure 9-1.

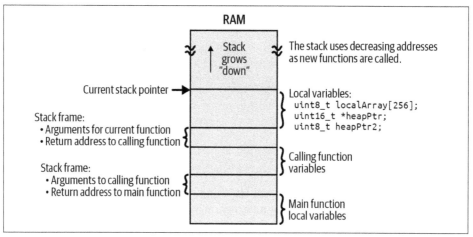

Figure 9-1. The stack is an ephemeral list of function calls and local variables

However, when the function returns, all of that memory is gone. It will be overwritten with the information for the next function called. The memory on the stack is ephemeral: there when the function is running, but it goes away when the function returns. You can't count on a variable being initialized to anything; it is equal to whatever was there from a previous call.

The problem with the above code is that the `stack_memory` variable only exists in the function. Returning the stack memory to the calling function is like handing it a grenade. Another function call will overwrite the data. Worse, if you pass around this pointer, writing to the memory is likely to cause a stack frame to be lost. The stack frame is a map back to the previous function called. If you lose it, the processor will behave randomly, probably ending in some sort of hard fault, though only after causing a fair amount of chaos.

However, this is not a stack error:

```c
int* dont_return_malloc_and_freed_memory(void) {
    int memory = malloc(100);
    free(memory);
    return memory;
}
```

I mean, it isn't good. But no one monitors the heap. When another piece of code allocates the memory, there will be two different users of the same memory location. Bugs like this don't get special handling as there are no hard faults for this, which can be catastrophic as changes to that memory may be unintended.

Stack Overflows and Buffer Overflows

Have you ever wondered how stack overflow errors can lead to device hacking? Here is some terrible code that shows how a simple name-entry form can lead to taking over the whole system:

```c
void unbounded_fill_from_input(char* name)
{
    int i = 0;
    char ch;
    ch = getchar();
    while (ch != '\n') { // wait for new line
        name[i] = ch; i++;
        ch = getchar();
    }
    name[i] = NULL; // NULL terminate string
}

void overflow_the_stack(void)
{
    char name[MAX_NAME_LENGTH];
    printf("Hello! Tell me your name: ");
    unbounded_fill_from_input(name);
    printf("Hello %s", name);
}
```

Even if the name variable size MAX_NAME_LENGTH is set to something long, it doesn't matter; the person who enters a name longer than MAX_NAME_LENGTH overflows the name buffer. Then what happens?

Looking at Figure 9-1, if localArray writes outside its boundaries (overflows), it may write into the value of the heapPtr and heapPtr2. Then, they point to something random. You won't be able to free their memory, and trying to write to those bogus addresses may cause a hard fault as you try to access memory that doesn't exist on the processor.

In our current code example, name is on the stack because it is a local variable. Then unbounded_fill_from_input is called, so the stack frame is after the name buffer. In addition to local variables, the stack frame tells the processor where to return to. A knowing hacker could put a different RAM address in where the stack frame has a return address. When the function ends, the processor goes to the new hacker-provided return address, which likely points to runnable code in RAM (entered instead of their name).

 There are *stack-smashing protection* (SSP) options built into many compilers. They create *guards* (aka *canaries*) on the stack when a function is called. When exiting the function, if the guard is modified, they call a failure function instead of returning normally.

Unbounded entry and other user-entry issues can cause stack overflows in addition to buffer overflows. Often user input is parsed with recursive functions. Stack overflows occur when too many functions are called: too many variables, plus stack frames, end up filling the space that the linker allocated for the stack. The effect is similar to buffer overflows, including the part where a hacker can cause the stack pointer to move to code they want to run instead of what you intended.

However, as with buffer overflows, the most common cause is usually something simpler: an error in design or implementation. Stack overflows are often seen in systems with RTOSs with constrained RAM, where each task gets its own stack but the developer neglected to realize how deep the call stack would need to be.

Debugging Hard Faults

It has all gone horribly wrong. What now?

If you know *where* things went wrong, figuring out how it happened is much easier. Happily hard faults will *help* you determine where they happened. This is processor specific, so consult your manual. I'll give the general outline and then the code for the Arm Cortex-M processors. The steps you want are:

1. Find the information sent to you from the processor about what went wrong.
2. Find the stack and look to see where you were (and a bit about what you were doing).
3. Store this data into a special place in RAM so when you reboot, you can log it.

Processor Registers: What Went Wrong?

Once you've hit a hard fault interrupt, you know your system is in some sort of bad and possibly delicate state. The first step is to preserve this state so we can determine what went wrong later.

This is one of the few areas that is still almost always done with assembly. Fortunately, it is usually in the C/C++ file, but expect to see a hard fault handler that starts with something like this:[2]

```
__asm volatile(
    "tst lr, #4 \n"      // test bits in lr to determine which stack
                         // pointer to use
    "ite eq \n"          // conditional coming up next
    "mrseq r0, msp \n"   // if the bit was set, use msp stack register
    "mrsne r0, psp \n"   // else the bit was not set, use psp stack
                         // register
    "b fault_handler_c \n" // call the C function
)
```

Well, that's pretty awful, made worse by the fact the Cortex-M processor has two stack pointers: the main stack pointer (msp) and the process stack pointer (psp), which can be used by an RTOS to run tasks. Anyway, what happens here is that the stack pointer is passed into the fault_handler_c function. The goal of those assembly instructions was to get us into C code where things won't look so bad.

The next step is to determine what fault(s) happened. The Cortex-M has several fault status registers that cover memory faults, bus faults, and usage faults (like divide-by-zero). While digging through your documentation to decode what each of these do seems like a bothersome amount of work, the processor is desperately trying to tell you what went wrong. You have to look.

Let's start with a very simple handler in C:

```
void fault_handler_c (unsigned long *hardfault_args){
    __asm("BKPT #0\n"); // Break into the debugger
    while(1) { ; }      // Spin until the watchdog resets
}
```

This will cause a breakpoint if the debugger is attached (though that breakpoint line may differ in syntax on your processor/compiler combo). If a debugger is not attached, this code will spin in a while loop. When the hard fault happens and the debugger stops, you can manually look at the processor registers that describe the

---

2 If your hard fault handler is blank, see Interrupt Blog's "How to Debug a HardFault on an ARM Cortex-M MCU" (*https://oreil.ly/WJxT4*). Not only is it a fantastic resource, it has good hard fault handler code. If you aren't on a Cortex-M processor, search online for a hard fault handler. While I'm going through the steps here, implementing them yourself is time consuming.

faults. If you are lucky, then your debugger will show you a stack trace that takes you back to where the problem started.

Once you know what went wrong and where it went wrong, everything is golden. Usually. Sometimes. Maybe. Well, at least it is a good start as to where the end of the problem is. You can start pulling on this thread to find the start of the problem.

However, seldom do we get to debug so easily. Problems that happen on your desk are much easier to figure out than problems that happen in the field (or anywhere that is not your desk with the debugger attached).

Creating a Core Dump

You need the code to write a memo to yourself to indicate what went wrong. (We'll call this memo a *core dump*.) This means recording the fault registers and the stack information. Unfortunately, with the processor already in a bad state, writing the core dump to flash or sending it via some communication method may lead to more troubles.

The solution is to do the following:

- Write the core dump to RAM.
- Upon reboot, check that piece of RAM for information.
- Clear that RAM so we know it is not valid.

This is actually a bit odd. Upon power on, the RAM will be in an invalid state (we don't know if it is all zeros, all ones, or some combination). So our core dump will need something to indicate it is valid.

Also, upon reset, after C Startup, all of our global variables will be either zeroed out or set to their initialization values. So this core dump cannot go into a global variable. It can't go on the stack, because the stack may have been corrupted as part of the hard fault (and how will the rebooted processor know where the old stack pointer was?). It can't go on the heap for the same reason.

Thus, this cannot go in RAM. Wait, no, really, we are going to put it in RAM, but not in any of those sections.

Instead, we're going to do something devious. We're going to steal some RAM from the processor as a whole, give it a name, then link to the name (or address) in the C code. While this RAM will be part of your processor's normal RAM, it won't be part of your *program's* normal RAM because we are going to change how your program sees your memory layout.

It starts with the linker file. Linker files are one of those arcane topics in embedded systems that no one tends to talk about. I'm going to start with an intro to linker scripts, but expect more about them in the future.

Intro to Linker Scripts

Although you may have seen a linker script as you got your code working, chances are it was a file that came with your compiler or vendor SDK and you haven't needed to open it. After your source code gets compiled and assembled, the object files (and libraries) are combined by the linker into an executable file. The resulting code has four main sections:

bss segment
> Contains uninitialized global variables. This will go in RAM. The odd name is due to historical reasons that don't concern us here.

Data segment
> Contains global variables that are initialized. This will go in RAM. The data segment may include bss as a subsegment. It may also include the heap and stack.

Text segment
> Contains code and constant data. This may be put in read-only memory or in RAM.

Vector segment
> A special part of the text segment that contains the exception vector table to handle interrupts.

The linker reads a text script to determine the memory layout of the output. To move the code or place buffers at certain addresses, you'll need to modify the linker script. Don't write one from scratch. When you build your executable, it already has a linker script, usually ending in *.ld*. Find the existing one and modify that. (Or look for an example specifically for your processor and start with that one.)

For example, if our system has flash for storing and running code and some internal RAM, the memory map might look like the following table:

Address	Size	Memory type	Segments that can be placed here
0x000000	0x10000	Read-only memory (flash)	Text, vector
0x010000	0x08000	Internal processor RAM	Text, vector, data, and bss

A simple linker script representing that memory map would look like the following:

```
SECTIONS
{
    /* Memory location is in Flash; place next commands at this location */
    . = 0x000000;
```

```
  Code : {
    *(.vectors) /* Put interrupt table at very first location in memory */
    *(.text)
  }
   /* Now put everything in RAM */
  . = 0x08000;
  Data : { *(.data) *(.bss)}
}
```

The script is very order-dependent. The line . = 0x000000 indicates that the cursor (where the next section will be placed) is at 0x000000. The next lines say to put .vectors and .text in a section called Code.

A more complex linker file would define the size and addresses of the memory so that the linker could give an error if the segments don't fit in their allotted spaces. Also note that the type of memory (readable, writable, or executable) is specified to enable more error-checking:

```
MEMORY
{
  /* Define each memory region */
  Flash (rx)  : ORIGIN = 0x000000, LENGTH = 0x10000  /* 64k */
  Ram   (rwx) : ORIGIN = 0x010000, LENGTH = 0x08000  /* 32k */
}
SECTIONS
{
  Code : {
    *(.vectors)
    *(.text)
    } > Flash
  Data : { *(.data) *(.bss) } > Ram
}
```

Linker scripts can get very complicated. Don't get bogged down in the details; focus on the addresses and how they match the table. Look up the language, start out by making small changes, and look in the program's output map file to see the effects. (Reading a map file is discussed in Chapter 11.) As with many scripting languages, it is pretty easy to build up a linker script that is so complicated no one can decipher it. Be careful. If you have a gnarly linker script to start with, look in "Further Reading" on page 262.

To create the core dump, first we need to steal some RAM and link it to a name (_coredumpBuffer):

```
MEMORY
{
  /* Define each memory region */
  Flash   (rx)  : ORIGIN = 0x000000, LENGTH = 0x10000  /* 64k */
  Ram     (rwx) : ORIGIN = 0x010000, LENGTH = 0x07F00  /* most of 32k */
  DumpRAM (rwx) : ORIGIN = 0x017F00, LENGTH = 0xFF     /* 255 bytes */
```

```
  }
SECTIONS
{
  Code : {
    *(.vectors)
    *(.text)
   } > Flash
  Data : { *(.data) *(.bss) } > Ram
  Coredump (NOLOAD) : {
    _coredumpBuffer = .;
  } > DumpRAM
}
```

As for using the `_coredumpBuffer` variable in your code, it depends very much on your compiler. Here is one way I've seen it handled. The `_coredumpBuffer` variable comes from the linker script, and the program just creates an ad hoc struct called `sCoreDump` to access the data at that point:

```
extern unsigned long _coredumpBuffer;
struct sCoreDump *gCoreDump = (struct sCoreDump *) &_coredumpBuffer;
```

At this point, `_coredumpBuffer` will be available to the code as a piece of RAM that isn't initialized by the normal C Startup code. It is a chunk of RAM cut off from normal use. (Which means if you allocate too much of it, you may have problems later, but that is for Chapter 11 to consider.)

Using the Core Dump

What do you put in the core dump? On the one hand, everything you can fit. On the other hand, do as little as possible with the processor in a delicate state.

Start with a known value to indicate a valid core dump (let's call this the *core dump key*; it doesn't matter what it is as long as it is not all zeros or ones).

Next, put in the fault cause. After debugging manually, you should have found the manual that describes the possible exceptions. Next, record where you were when things went bad. That may mean parsing the stack trace, something that should be easy but is often complicated by virtue of its being in a fault. The goal really is to find a list of return addresses (often in the `lr` link register). Ideally, this will include the stack pointer and parameters passed into each function. Realistically, this can be a pain to trace through, depending on your compiler and processor. There may be special compiler features to make unwinding the stack simpler.

Finally, if there is space, add any information that might be important to your system; the last input voltage ADC reading is one of my favorites, because I've needed to debug low-battery issues, thinking they were code catastrophes.

```
#define COREDUMP_KEY 0x0BADC04E

struct sCoreDump {
    uint32_t key;   // must equal COREDUMP_KEY for this to be valid
    uint32_t cause;
    uint32_t r0;
    uint32_t r1;
    uint32_t r2;
    uint32_t r3;
    uint32_t returnAddress;
    uint32_t stackPointer;
    int32_t  lastBattReading;
};
```

Once all of the data is packed into your secret stash of RAM, reset the processor. Then, after initialization, look for a valid core dump key. If it exists, record it for posterity (to flash, to serial print, to the internet). Finally, erase the core dump so the next reset doesn't improperly indicate the problem again.

 When you commit your code for release to manufacturing, you will need to keep a copy of the binaries. I strongly recommend committing the *.map* file with your binaries as you can use that to decode the stack information in released code. More about map files in Chapter 11.

Merely Very Difficult Bugs

Many people are concerned about memory bugs. Rightly so. There are many ways to make pointers fail. It is hard to gain confidence in this area. I like to believe embedded software is easier because we have real memory cells. Every single thing you address leads to an actual set of transistors on the silicon.

However, pointers are pointers. They take practice. Since you are at least one step removed from reality, they are more difficult to debug. I find that drawings help—and making sure what I intend to do is what I wrote the code to do.

Most of my memory bugs come from one of these sources:

- Buffer overflows and off-by-one errors leading to writing to memory that isn't mine
- Stack corruption from returning memory from a function
- Stack overflows, usually from recursion or calling too many functions
- Uninitialized variables

I have a bag of tricks I use to debug memory issues. The first is to make variables static or global to see if it is a stack issue (or an uninitialized variable issue). Note: if the problem goes away when this happens, the problem is not solved, it is hidden; you still have to fix it.

Second, you can add extra buffers between buffers (*red zones*). Fill these with known values (such as `0xdeadbeef` or `0xA5A5A5A5`). After running for a while, look in the red zone buffers to see if the data has been modified, indicating one of the buffers went outside its boundaries.

You can do similar things with stacks: fill them with known data at boot and then look for how much of the stack is used after running for a significant amount of time. The highest point the stack reaches (on the edge of where the red zone data has not been modified) is called the *high-water mark* and represents maximal stack usage.

If you are experiencing odd issues, try making your stack(s) larger to see if it takes longer for the problem to occur. Alternatively, does making the stack smaller cause the issue to happen sooner? Reproducing the bug is an important part of moving from impossible bug to merely very difficult.

Finally, replace heap (`malloc` and `new`) buffers with fixed buffers. Not only can this avoid using freed memory, it alleviates issues with trying to allocate too much memory (or trying to allocate a large block when the heap is fragmented).

Consequences of Being Clever

If hard faults are love letters from the processor asking for help, compiler warnings are mundane traffic signs. It is easy to miss a no-turn-here sign or knowingly go through a yellow light. Most of the time, the consequences for ignoring warnings are nothing, no big deal.

However, many of the hard faults discussed in this chapter could have been found by enabling all compiler warnings and fixing each one.

Spend time removing the seemingly trivial compiler warnings so you can see the incredibly important ones:

```
hardfaults.c:51: 'ptr_uninitialized' is used uninitialized in this function
hardfaults.c:78: function returns address of local variable
```

So once you've reproduced the bug and explained the bug and tried everything you can think of, maybe go back to cleaning up the warnings you've let build up. Or even better, don't let them accumulate in the first place.

Finally, you aren't a robot. When you reach the end of your concentration, enter the pit of despair where things will never work and it is all your fault, or generally run out of things to try next, take a break. Go for a walk. Get a snack. Talk to someone about something else. Get some sleep. Your subconscious needs time and space to process without you handing it more information about the problem.

Further Reading

In "Ending the Embedded Software Dark Ages: Let's Start with Processor Fault Debugging!" (*https://oreil.ly/7rV7x*), Phillip Johnston at Embedded Artistry goes through the whole process of debugging, from manually walking through the hard fault to creating good handlers to making a mini-core dump for later use.

That article links to Interrupt Blog's "How to Debug a HardFault on an ARM Cortex-M MCU" (*https://oreil.ly/SEZNj*), which is the most tactical hands-on resource.

There's more detail about the stacks and heap in "Smashing the Stack for Fun and Profit" (*https://oreil.ly/MesK4*).

Miguel Young de la Sota's post "Everything You Never Wanted to Know About Linker Script" (*https://oreil.ly/buHw9*) is an excellent post about linker files. Another great resource is Thea Flowers's post, "The Most Thoroughly Commented Linker Script (Probably)" (*https://oreil.ly/LwKVW*).

Interview Question: Taking a Breather

What should I ask you about?

Sometimes interviews go horribly wrong. Sometimes it is because the candidate isn't qualified, but sometimes the candidate is perfectly qualified but they are unduly stressed or having a terrible day. Interviewing is exhausting. The stakes are high and the possibility for failure is also abominably high.

When it becomes clear that the interview has gone awry, I ask the candidate what I should ask about. I want to let them talk about something they know, something they want to share. Some candidates come alive, showing they have the interest and expertise in the position (but not as much in the interviewing process).

When folks ask me about strategies from the interviewee side, I often suggest taking a portfolio project to the interview. This essentially puts a big "ask me about this!" sign over the hardware they brought. It lets the candidate control part of the interview and pushes part of the conversation toward topics the candidate understands and can talk about.

Whether because they brought a project or I've decided to take a breather in the interview, it is often a confidence booster for the candidate to talk about their project. Use this short interlude between planned questions to remember that almost no one knows everything they need for the job they are interviewing for. However, it is possible they have skills that are important and useful, maybe even ones that are more important than what you thought you needed.

CHAPTER 10

Building Connected Devices

Whether you have IoT devices, ubiquitous sensors, distributed systems, or edge computing, your device is going to connect to a wider world. It may be a closed system or the whole internet. Either way, suddenly there are many new problems and features.

While your connection mechanism is important to the design of your system, once you are connected, you'll need to consider getting data to and from the devices, updating the code remotely, and monitoring the whole system's health. Oh, and of course, don't forget security.

Connecting Remotely

From your processor's point of view, a cloud server or a host computer is just another object to talk to, the same as any other peripheral. Sure, the host might meddle with your device, such as changing your processor's code or instructing it to move the motor to a different location. But all of those things are just digital communications.

In fact, anything that your processor has been sending bytes to over a digital interface has its own processor. The motor you're controlling over SPI and the humidity sensor you're reading over I²C each have their own processor. To those processors, your processor is a host computer.

Just as each of your peripherals has a documented interface, your system's interface to its host should be reasonably well documented (even if you control both sides). Putting a documented interface in place will let the two systems change independently (as long as the interface remains fixed). As for implementation, the command interpreter in Chapter 3 is a good place to start.

As more of our everyday objects enter the networked world, we build up detailed pictures of the environment. Whether it is a fridge that sends a shopping list to your phone when you've entered a grocery store or a scattering of small sensors monitoring a forest for fires, we are building distributed sensor networks. Increasing the intelligence of the sensors makes each one better able to deal with irregularities in its particular location, making the whole network more robust. The information can return to a host for integration and processing (e.g., forest fire sensors) or be generated with each piece contributing its knowledge in a hostless system (e.g., groceries).

The strength of the sensor network is that each element works together to construct information that is greater as a whole. However, that is also its weakness; if the system cannot communicate, it is much less useful. Further, if enough sensors go offline, the system can become degraded to such a degree as to be useless.

There are many ways to implement the connection. The easiest to understand is connecting the device directly to the cloud as shown at the top of Figure 10-1.

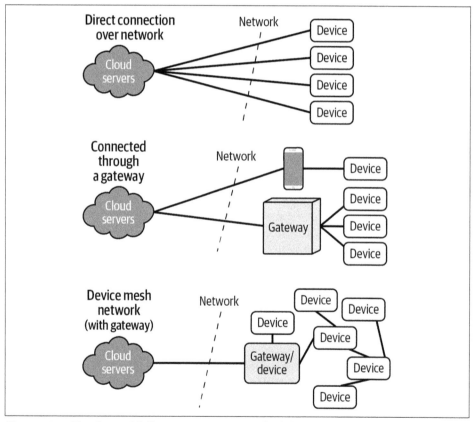

Figure 10-1. Topology of different connection methodologies, including direct connection, gateway device, and mesh networks.

Directly: Ethernet and WiFi

Because it is so complex, using Ethernet usually implies an operating system. Since this book doesn't make any assumptions about you having an embedded OS, I'm not going to spend many words on this. However, as systems become more intelligent, Ethernet becomes more important. Due to the standard infrastructure around Ethernet, it is easily integrated into a large system. While Ethernet is the data link layer, it implies that there will be a network layer and a transport layer as well, so your software will interface to a networking protocol, usually TCP or UDP (User Datagram Protocol). (TCP provides a reliable communication path so your data always gets there, but it is more complicated than UDP.)

Robust communication isn't that important when you are communicating with an LCD controller that shares board space with your processor. However, if your device is in the middle of an ocean, monitoring for tsunamis, you may want something more reliable than serial communication.

If you are using a wireless network, you definitely want something reasonably reliable. Radio networks are hard. I mean, they are *really* hard. Murphy (of Murphy's Law) loves radio networks.

 One of the most difficult parts of dealing with a radio network is its dependence on the environment. I know of one device that worked when it was installed in November but gradually stopped working as spring came: tree leaves absorb 2.4 GHz radio waves.

There are amazing and fascinating applications of networked systems. However, when faced with the cost of a good radio, most companies flinch. At that point, someone will say, "Let's just implement our own. The components aren't that expensive." I know you want to agree, as your product is amazing and the radio cost is a big hurdle to make it truly compelling in the market. I've been there, thinking, "How hard could it be?" Take how hard you think it could possibly be and multiply that by at least one order of magnitude.

Don't reinvent the wireless radio wheel, as expensive as it seems. Spend the time making your system work. Once that's done, you can cost-reduce the product to implement your own Ethernet controller or wireless network. A precertified radio module is a good shortcut.

In the meantime, you'll need to learn a bit about networking: packets, routers, gateways, IP addresses, data forwarding, and network topology diagrams. That is a whole book on its own; see "Further Reading" on page 282 for suggestions.

Through a Gateway

A networked sensor may not connect directly to the cloud, opting instead to go through a gateway, some intermediate device that aggregates and filters the data. For my purposes, I'm going to call this a smartphone. (Probably by the time this book comes out, smartphones will be passé and you'll be on to supersmartphones, which I hope you call supes.)

A smartphone is usually more general-purpose than the embedded devices we build. While the smartphone may connect to a camera or pedometer via BLE (Bluetooth Low Energy), those devices don't need to know about each other. Instead the smartphone has an application specific to the device, acting as an intermediary between the cloud services and the device.

 When developing with a gateway, don't forget the software that runs on the gateway! Whether it is a phone app or a small Linux system, that software is the glue that holds the whole system together. If it is weak, the system will fall apart.

The gateway usually handles some of the communication difficulties, such as making sure data is transferred correctly and helping the device through updating code (more about that soon). However, this means you need to define the way your device communicates with the gateway. Even within a well-structured system like BLE GATTs, there will still be a need to figure out what bits and pieces of data need to go to the cloud. Some data needs to go to the users of your system, but there will always be data you need for the health of the device (more about that in "Managing Large Systems" on page 280).

As with network administration for direct connection, you will need to learn the connection method in detail. While we all want to simply use these protocols, they aren't that simple, and there is a good chance you'll need to dig in deeper to optimize the speed and power for your system.

 Chapter 6 talked about active objects as a way of setting up the main loop of a device. Manufacturers of BLE chips often use this design pattern to integrate your application with their code.

Via a Mesh

In a mesh network, the nodes (your devices) try to build a network. If you thought that learning how to do direct networking configuration was a pain, imagine how hard it is for your devices when they don't even know the overall network topology.

Some popular mesh protocols include Zigbee, Thread, BLE, and Matter. Some mesh networks configure on initial boot or inability to connect from some timeout. Other meshes reconfigure regularly (necessary if the nodes are moving around).

Some meshes have coordinator nodes that have more visibility and responsibility in shaping the network. This allows some nodes to conserve power as they aren't needed for network traffic. However, it limits the network. There are many of these balancing issues with advantages and disadvantages for each option.

The main issues in a mesh network are:

- How do you create a fairly efficient communication path from each node to the cloud?
- How do you identify and recover nodes that get lost and are unable to connect to their neighbors?
- Should the system configure once (or occasionally) to have a stable path, or configure often to keep up with changes?
- Is every device always on and participating in routing, or can they conserve power by sleeping?
- How do you avoid data traveling in loops around the mesh?

All of the mesh network implementations try to solve these problems. As you create a system, you will probably want to know how much data can be passed, how quickly the data from a node can get to a cloud server, and how far apart the nodes can be. Unfortunately, those numbers will change depending on the network configuration. The answers are not a matter of simple calculation. While meshes can be extraordinarily flexible, their complexity makes their use a special case.

We Still Use Modems

Sometimes we need to reach farther than those weak little network technologies above can manage. When we need to reach into the depths, risking the possibility that our pointless human transmissions might awaken eldritch horrors lurking in antediluvian caves and tunnels beneath the ocean, we fall back on what might seem like older and more arcane systems: cell phone networks, satellites, audio-based modems, and the occasional interdimensional rift opened via rituals and incantations.

For that, we turn to a short text language dating back to 1981 called AT commands. These are a series of commands that control the modems themselves, describing how to connect to another modem, ideally one hooked up to something that gets to the internet. While there are other, more modern, modem configuration and communication methods, the AT commands will likely outlive the existence of computers as we know them.

However, from your device's point of view, the connection to a modem is probably straightforward: a serial connection where you read and write data, just as you would on a command line to a debug port. Then the data magically appears where you needed it to go, often tunneled through a layer of Ethernet, but still looking like the serial command line.

That magic comes with costs:

Financial
> Cell and satellite modems are quite expensive to run, with limited transmit and receive data bandwidth.

Power
> While remote systems often have limited power, most modems are still power hogs so that they can get back to civilization. The modem is usually powered off unless the device is communicating or there is a scheduled window to listen for transmissions from the home office.

Configuration
> While a command line seems like a good idea, determining which modem belongs to which device can be a challenge. As systems scale to the thousands, the organization must scale beyond the Excel spreadsheet on a shared drive.

Modems remain an excellent option for devices that need to always be available, even when WiFi coverage is unlikely, such as traffic light cameras, open-ocean sensors, and smartphones.

Robust Communication

Once you can connect to the cloud, how are you sending the data? I know, I asked this question before, and the answer was: directly, through a gateway, with a mesh topology (or network), or with a modem. But this question of "how" keeps going because now I'm asking about the application layer communication protocol.

When you communicate with an ADC via SPI or I²C, there is a structured way of talking to it: commands you send (often called registers) and data you can read, sometimes with a FIFO. In that sense, what is the interface your device presents to other systems?

The term I'm looking for is *data serialization*. Is the data going to be encoded as something humans can read? Maybe in a JSON or XML file that is passed back and forth via HTTP? Or is it going to be a packed C structure in binary format? Will you create a protocol that conforms to a format like type-length-value (TLV) or develop one more specific to your application?

The good news is you can do anything you want. That is also the bad news.

Version!

Your protocol should identify the protocol version. This can be a specific command, or you can embed the version into each command. Someday, in the future, the cloud and devices will be on different versions of the code and will need to negotiate what version of the protocol they can both speak.

Checksums, CRCs, Hashes

No matter your throughput, you need to know that the data you received is the data that was transmitted.

The simplest form of checksum is just to sum all of the bytes in question, ignoring any overflow. If your buffer is {10, 20, 40, 60, 80, 90}, your checksum should be 300. If you are using only an 8-bit checksum, that becomes 44 (300 mod 256). There are many other combinations that could sum to the same value (e.g., {44} or {11, 11, 11, 11, 0, 0}), but those aren't likely to happen by chance (statistics says there is a 1 in 256 possibility if all of the bytes are random). Even this paltry 8-bit checksum is likely to save you if a byte or two gets corrupted, as long as two bytes don't get corrupted in ways that cancel each other out.

If you have lots of data, 1 in 256 aren't very good odds. You could sum everything as 16-bit words, which gives you a much lower probability of good checksums with bad data. Note that you need to sum the data as 16-bit words, not just keep the overflow from an 8-bit sum.

The types of errors you get depend on the memory or communication pathway. A simple checksum will always catch a single bit change, but it cannot detect when two bytes in the stream are swapped. And errors can cancel each other out in the checksum if multiple bytes are modified. In many communication methods, the errors tend to be bursty, so that many bytes will get corrupted at once.

So when people say "checksum" they often mean "CRC value." *CRC* stands for *cyclic redundancy check*, which you don't need to remember. CRCs give you more protection than a checksum against multiple-byte and swapped-byte errors. The math behind the CRC is designed to find transmission errors. However, CRCs require more computational power than the simple sum. If there isn't a CRC engine in your processor itself, there are many versions available online; see "Further Reading" on page 282 for pointers to code.

Remember, the main goal of a checksum is to detect that an error has occurred. A more complex scheme might be able to tell you where the error occurred or even correct small errors.

Like CRCs, *hash* functions take in a chunk of data and produce something smaller which represents that chunk of data. The result is sometimes called a digest (or a hash). The math behind a hash function is designed to distinguish between different chunks of data. It is more like a unique identifier than an error detector. (Though if your unique identifier hashes don't match after transmission, then there was an error.)

Encryption and Authentication

Checksums and CRCs are not preventions against hacking. That is, they don't protect against intentional modification of data. There are two main forms of protection against that.

Encryption ensures that no one can read (or modify) your data without having the correct keys and method of decryption.

Some processors come with cryptographic hardware acceleration. Check your processor manual before implementing it in software.

Authentication lets you know that your software is talking to something you know. Printer manufacturers want to make sure the printer cartridges come from a known source (partly because the wrong ink could ruin a printer and partly because consumables are profitable). The authentication may be an encrypted hash acting as a digital signature.

When a consumable is cloned, the authentication information is copied to make a hacked consumable look good to your software. A common precaution against this is to use a database to indicate that your system has seen the same serial number more frequently than it should expect.

Authentication and encryption are difficult. It isn't the same as a complex algorithm where once you understand, you can test your implementation and then be done. Authentication and encryption are things you can never finish successfully. Sure, you might implement the algorithm correctly, but that doesn't mean the data is safe. The more valuable your consumable or data is, the more likely someone will take the time to reverse engineer your encryption or authentication method. A determined hacker will eventually succeed, though sometimes only by a brute-force attack (it is probably easier to get into the manufacturing building and access the source code than figure out a 128-bit AES key).

You can't be in charge of locking all the doors; the best you can hope for is that your code is robust enough to fend off the casual attacker and create enough headaches that they leave your product alone. You probably don't have a lot of processing power for your system. Trying to implement AES or some other well-understood encryption when you are running an 8-bit processor at a few MHz may lead you to throw up your hands and put out a welcome mat for the hackers.

However, not all encryption methods have symmetric processing burdens. Some algorithms make it easier to decrypt than encrypt (or the other way). Let the cloud server do the hard math. Alternatively, you can run encryption only on the critical data, leaving the rest in clear text (or with a reduced encryption level). It may make your code more complex, but if the choice is between good encryption for the important part or mediocre encryption for all, I know which I'd take.

Even if you have to use an encryption algorithm that isn't good enough to stand up to a government agency, use a well-understood algorithm. Though you may have a tricky mind, your 8-bit encryption solution will not be better than a well-understood algorithm. Use one of the most common algorithms: RSA, DES, or AES. You may have to use a smaller key for an embedded system, but then you can estimate the time it takes to crack the key and give your management a reasonable effort level, something you may not be able to do if you design your own algorithm. (Which is a bad idea.)

Risk Analysis

As you design your system, put on your malevolent hacking hat. What would you do to attack the system? Assume the hackers know the algorithm but not the keys.[1] The next section describes ways to protect your code from being read via JTAG. Given that, is the easiest way to obtain the keys the relatively difficult matter of putting the chip under an electron microscope to read out the code? Or can intruders read it from your email because another developer sent it to you in clear text, or log in to your source code repository with the guest account? Your authentication and encryption algorithms are only as good as the weakest link.

Risk assessment is about figuring out what can go wrong and how much it will cost to reduce the risk. It is also about considering how much it might cost to leave the security flaw(s)—not only in embarrassment and irritated customers, but also in legal fees and class action lawsuits.

Mild paranoia aside, protecting your system is hard. Your management team will need to determine how much time (and money) they are willing to spend on developing protocols to keep your data (or consumables) safe. It is a business decision as well

---

1 In cryptography, this is called *Kerckhoffs's principle*: a cryptosystem should be secure even if everything about the system, except the key, is public knowledge.

as a technical decision. It is also a long-term decision; staying ahead of the hackers is an ongoing concern, not a one-time algorithm choice.

In the short term, there are many top ten security checklists for designing systems and for coding. Use them; security is a field that is always changing. Getting different perspectives as you work is important.

As developers, we're under pressure to deliver projects under time constraints. Hackers don't have that problem. It feels like they will always win. We do what we can to make it better, which means we make today better than yesterday. That's all.

Figure 10-2 shows some good points to remember about designing for security, privacy, and robustness.

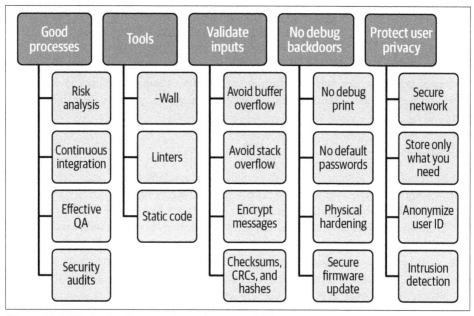

Figure 10-2. Designing for security, privacy, and robustness is an ongoing process.

Updating Code

Whether you call it over-the-air update (OTA), firmware update (FWUP), device firmware update (DFU), or downloading the code, the goal is to take your newly built image and put it on a remote system. This seems like it should be straightforward, essentially a remote copy operation. Sadly, this is the opposite of straightforward (curvy-roundabout?). There are good reasons for the complexity: there are many features and corner cases that can cause catastrophic issues. Each piece of complexity addresses the problems someone else encountered.

Let's start with the idea that you have a connected device with code space and some form of additional flash. Figure 10-3 shows what you want to have happen and then the first few steps of complexity.

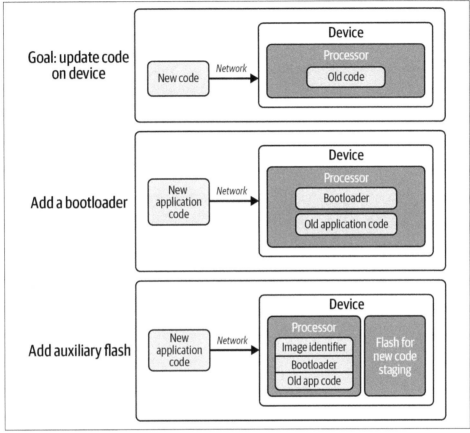

Figure 10-3. In the increasing complexity needed for updating firmware, there are a few stages pushing toward a bootloader solution.

To start with, it is a simple copy. However, the device is running (in order to handle the communications), and you can't overwrite a running program. You'll need to break the code into two pieces: the bootloader, in charge of doing the update, and the application code, which is all the good stuff.

In this second example in Figure 10-3, the bootloader needs to handle communication, which is often quite a lot of code, something the application always needs to do.

To solve that problem, in the third example, the old app can get the new code and put it in another piece of memory. Then the bootloader can update the code without interacting with the outside world, allowing the bootloader to be simpler.

In systems like these, as shown in Figure 10-4, upon boot, the bootloader will:

1. Check to see if there is code in the auxiliary flash.
2. Check the flash code's version against the processor's current code version.
3. If they are the same, call the current code and run normally.
4. If the flash's code is newer, copy over the flash code to the processor's memory.
5. Reboot (after which the system will end up at step 3 and run normally).

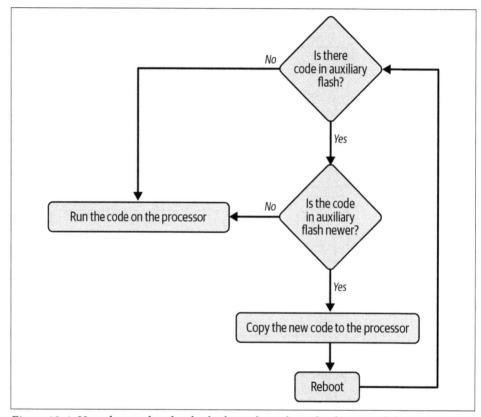

Figure 10-4. Upon boot, a bootloader looks at the code in the device and the code available to the device to determine what to run. In your HAL documentation, this flowchart may get more complicated as additional checks are added.

There are several good things about this last bootloader pattern. First, in the initial example where the bootloader communicated over the network, it was possible to lose the connection or power, causing the device to be partially updated. Second, the bootloader can do additional checking of the new code, verifying the new code is good and was signed by a trusted source. Third, the bootloader can check the flash's code for validity and update it if the code has been corrupted. Finally, the bootloader can decrypt the new code as it programs it to the processor.

 Don't wait until the end of the project to start developing the firmware update process. The more testing you can get on this critical feature the better. If your firmware update process has a bug, you may not be able to fix it in the field, resulting in costly recalls and replacements.

Firmware Update Security

Adding security into the mix tends to make updating code exponentially more complex. In general, winning against a sea of hackers is impossible, but you can make casual attacks more difficult. The first step is to identify what you are protecting: a secret algorithm in the code? The ability to create or verify consumables? The integrity of the hardware? What you choose to implement depends on your priorities.

You might get a little bit of help from your processor. Many chips offer *code-read protection*. Once it is turned on, on-chip memory becomes unreadable. The processor can still execute the code, but a debugger (or a loader) cannot read the code space.

Oftentimes, the code-read protection will limit the processor's ability to erase sector by sector. Instead, you have to erase all of it before updating code. (Some levels of protection won't even let you write new code at all.)

Once you've done that, the weak point is in the way new code is handled. Ideally, the new code is seen only by trusted associates who will be updating the code (and the code will travel only over secure networks). However, we can't usually ensure that, so we must add security to the updating process.

There are two components to firmware update security:

- Secure the device so only intended code can run on the hardware
- Secure the code so no one can look inside

The first part is usually done with a hash and a signature. Like a checksum, the hash is used to verify the code integrity, to make sure the image we sent is the image the device received. The signature shows that the new code came from a trusted source. Code is often encrypted so it cannot be read, disassembled, and used by other people.

Where before we had only the new code, now our firmware bundle becomes like that shown in Figure 10-5. The bootloader uses the public key to verify the signature and calculate the hash. If those are good and the version is newer than the current application, it will decrypt and program the new code.

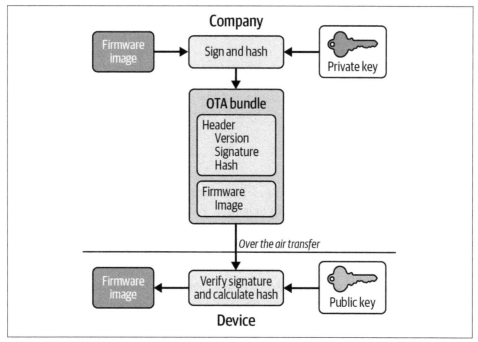

Figure 10-5. Working with a secure bootloader means creating a firmware bundle that is signed and encrypted.

Cryptography has come a long way, and the chip vendors, compiler vendors, HAL vendors, and the RTOSs have made it possible to have decent security on an embedded device. Use these features instead of making your own.

In systems like these, upon boot, the bootloader will:

1. Check to see if there is code in the auxiliary flash.

2. Check the flash code's version against the processor's current code version. If they are the same, call the current code and run normally.

3. Check the flash code's hash and signature using the private key. If it does not match, erase the flash code and reboot.

4. If the flash's code is newer, decrypt the flash code in sections, programming each section.

5. Reboot (after which the system will end up at step 2 and run normally).

Sometimes the bootloader will also check the hash and signature of the current code. This prevents problems with the microprocessor flash becoming corrupted. It can program the defective code with good code from the flash. Of course, if the processor's code and the flash's updated code are both bad, the unit will likely be in an infinite reboot cycle.

High Security: Per-Unit Keys

For the best security, each device should have its own key. This way, if one key gets loose or the device is cracked, the other devices remain secure.

However, this means you have to program that key during manufacturing, and then have to keep track of that serial number–key pair for the life of the product. You'll also need to write a script to create each over-the-air firmware bundle individually when you are ready to update the units. Your server will need to make sure each bundle gets to the right unit.

Oh, and don't forget to keep all of those keys protected, possibly for millions of units. Per-unit encryption is a matter of managing data. It is a significant amount of extra work.

The way you handle your keys depends on how much of a target your system is. You have to assess the risks to determine how much of your development budget will be spent on defending your device against bad actors.

Multiple Pieces of Code

Often there are multiple pieces of code, even apart from your application and bootloader. There may be an operating system (or other binary library from a vendor). You may have a multi-core processor that requires two firmware images.

Each of these may need to be updated separately. As you can imagine, this increases the complexity significantly. In Figure 10-6, I have a processor's program flash on the left showing what it is running. On the right, is the device's auxiliary flash that has recently received an update over the air.

Upon reboot, the bootloader will identify the new code, verify it, load it into the program flash, and run it.

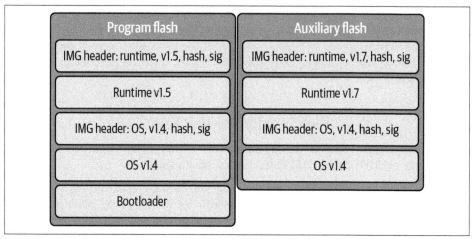

Figure 10-6. An example of a processor's program flash running an application, an OS, and a bootloader. In the auxiliary flash there is a new runtime that will be loaded upon the next boot (if it is valid).

Fallback Lifeboat

Changing the code on your device carries some inherent risks: the device could lose power during programming, the source firmware might be corrupted as it goes into the auxiliary flash, cosmic rays could rain down, and so on. As you grow to a million devices, your chances of a failing firmware update increase.

There is a way to mitigate the possibility of creating a brick out of your hardware. As shown in Figure 10-7, you can keep old images around in case you need them.

In the auxiliary flash are version 1.0 of the runtime and OS images. These were programmed in the factory and are stored in case updating firmware goes horribly wrong. This is essentially a lifeboat, something to fall back to in case of icebergs. Factory reset is often a last resort that comes with clearing any settings kept on the device. The user will be mad about their lost data, but at least the device isn't a brick.

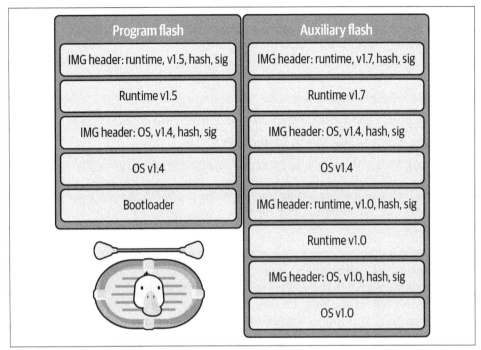

Figure 10-7. The auxiliary flash stores other versions of the runtime and OS to allow the device to do a factory reset.

Staged Rollout

Updating the firmware on your desk unit is generally no big deal, a programmer can usually fix the issue if the update goes poorly. Updating the firmware for everyone on your team may be slightly more difficult. As they update with their own programmers, they'll ask questions and probably choose the wrong bundle, not knowing which version they are on or which they are going to.

Next, you update firmware for the whole company, getting some non-engineering beta testers. At this point, the process has to be push-button or invisible so the users don't complain. If something catastrophic happens, folks will be annoyed but understanding. After all, they are part of building the thing. If it is truly necessary, all of the units can be collected and updated with good firmware.

That stops being possible when you update to the public. Remote units may not be accessible at all (satellites, deep sea equipment, and so on). Consumer units may number in the millions. Breaking these with a bad firmware update will be unrecoverable.

What you need to do is plan for a *staged rollout*: send it to groups of customers in small numbers to find bugs that you can't find locally. Some problems I've encountered that weren't obvious at my desk:

- Normal (for customers) power fluctuations triggering a flood of alerts
- Global time zones with different daylight saving schemes
- GPS readings parsed incorrectly, as they weren't anywhere near my desk
- Haywire ADC readings due to Boston's salt fog
- Excessive battery drain on one particular manufacturing run of the hardware

Even as management and marketing want all of the promised features to be delivered and the bugs fixed, moving too fast on firmware updates can create problems that aren't solvable.

Sadly, a staged rollout may not be something you have control over (due to cost or a different team being responsible). Once your firmware is released (whatever that means for your company), there is probably a server that provides the new firmware to your devices (either pushing the firmware to them or the devices polling for the update). In general, it is more complex for the server to keep track of which (groups of) users should get the new update.

However, this is necessary for making sure the new firmware doesn't crash more often or deplete its battery more quickly. Of course, adding new features might deplete batteries, but in a good, users-are-using-the-new-feature way, while adding more diagnostics could cause the batteries to die in a bad way. The statistics alone don't have enough information; you'll need to combine them with knowledge of what was in the firmware update.

Oh, but you do need those statistics. Let's stop talking about updates and move on to monitoring large numbers of units.

Managing Large Systems

Scaling up from a few units to a few hundred is exciting. Scaling up beyond that requires a lot more infrastructure.

When you hit a million devices, one-in-a-million problems shows up. Reproducing those is very difficult. It might be the Bluetooth stack of a particular Android version. It might be someone whose magnetometer reading makes no sense because they are actually at the South Pole. It might be a minor solder ball from a particular day in manufacturing.

Identifying the frequency of the problems can be more important than identifying the cause.

Monitoring actual product business data is separate from the device health information. While I can't really speak to your business data—other than to say checksum, encrypt, and privacy—the device health should have a few important features:

- Boot cause: when the device reboots, why did it reboot? If it was a hard fault, there should be some tracking (see "Debugging Hard Faults" on page 254). If it was a user reboot or battery depletion, indicate those with different codes.

  — Frequent user reboots may indicate a hang or other user frustration.

  — An increase in battery-related reboots may indicate a change in firmware has caused an increase in battery drain.

- Voltage over time can help you determine issues with battery drain before it becomes a reboot issue, but the battery life also depends on usage patterns. You may need to also keep track of active time versus sleep time to make battery level monitoring useful.

- Heartbeats are small packets sent to the server to let it know that the device still exists, that it is still operating. The size and frequency depends on the application. More heartbeats give up-to-date information, but they require more power. Heartbeats may include other information (sometimes temporarily for debugging, sometimes permanently) such as firmware version and other diagnostics.

Scaling to talk to many devices means working with a cloud service to provide a dashboard or way to access the data to use it in debugging. It is odd because this doesn't look like firmware programming, but you still have to be involved to keep track of which units checked in, which units crashed, which units rebooted and why, and which units are running old firmware.

Finally, crashes or errors logged become a matter of statistics. You can't chase hundreds of crashes a day. You try to reproduce the most common ones and the worst ones. Over time, you may see patterns (like devices that crash every Tuesday at midnight in their time zone). Finding these patterns likely requires digging through a database or CSV file, possibly with a Python script or some fancy spreadsheet work. Hopefully, it gives you a path to determine the most productive way to spend your engineering time.

 There are services that can handle the server side of monitoring and analytics for you; look for *device operations* and *fleet management*.

Manufacturing

The first units are probably built by hand by someone you know. Eventually, the device goes to a manufacturer. Well, usually it goes to a *contract manufacturer* (CM) that does assembly and packaging for a number of different companies.

The CM may need you to write software to test the firmware before shipment. The goal is always to know whether a board or system passes or fails. The CM doesn't tend to want wishy-washy numbers, hoping instead for a big green or red light. Manufacturers don't debug for you; their goal is to keep their manufacturing line moving.

The CM will need to know how to program the devices, ideally in multiples, not singletons. It will also need to *provision* the device, which is to say put on the secure keys and enable it to connect to your cloud service. As the CM is not part of your company, you may end up doing the final provisioning at your company instead of handing over your secrets. That tends to cost more, but as previously noted, security is expensive.

Note that provisioning is different from *onboarding*, which is what customers do when they get the device to link it to their account.

 Often part of manufacturing is to test the device with the radio on. If there are many devices, this can cause interference. While you can make a reasonable Faraday cage from tinfoil and a shoebox, planning to update firmware via Bluetooth may not be viable in such a noisy environment.

Further Reading

Network administration is its own field. The online book *An Introduction to Computer Networks* (*https://intronetworks.cs.luc.edu*) by Peter L. Dordal is an excellent resource on how to understand networks. For those of us needing only to become knowledgeable users, the introduction to the book, "An Overview of Networks" (*https://oreil.ly/8lGsr*), is excellent. The Networking Fundamentals (*https://oreil.ly/eZocP*) YouTube playlist by Practical Networking (*https://oreil.ly/XDkUa*) is also an in-depth resource.

For more about different ways to put together messages, take a look at Memfault's "Event Serialization" (*https://oreil.ly/7QxvM*).

For an introduction to CRCs, along with some code, look for Michael Barr's CRC implementation code (*https://oreil.ly/0APFK*).

For more about how contract manufacturing works and what you need from the firmware to make it work efficiently, check out Alan Cohen's *Prototype to Product: A Practical Guide for Getting to Market*.

Interview Question: Getting a Goat Safely Across a River

A man is taking home a goat, his partially tamed wolf, and a cabbage. They reach a river, but the bridge is washed out. The boat, conveniently tied on his side of the shore, is very small and can hold only the man and one passenger at a time. If the goat and the wolf are left alone, the wolf will eat the goat. If the goat and the cabbage are left alone, the goat will eat the cabbage. The wolf, however, will not eat the cabbage. How can they cross the river safely? (See Figure 10-8.)

Figure 10-8. Taking everyone home safely.

Although this style of question is pretty common, I am strongly opposed to interview questions that involve goats crossing water, so I wouldn't ask this one. Basically, if it is necessary for me to herd goats, I don't particularly want the job.

However, loading code is a lot like this problem. There are dangers and resource limitations at multiple points. You have to know what to look for and then use some little mental twist you learned along the way to make the leap to the solution. I generally prefer to see how people think instead of whether they are in the club that already knows the answer. Since I don't know what I'd look for in a candidate's response, I'll just provide the solution.

In this case, the trick is to note that the goat is the dangerous one and must be kept away from the others. If you frame the problem that way, the solution falls out a little easier.

The man starts on side A with the wolf, goat, and cabbage. He crosses to side B with the goat, then returns to side A. He takes the wolf (or the cabbage, it doesn't matter) to side B. Now, he has to take the goat back to side A, leaving it there while he ferries the cabbage (or wolf) back to side B. The man crosses back to A, gets the goat, crosses back to B, and moves the parade along.

The trick behind the problem is that he can take extra trips to get the job done, as long as the job is done properly. Updating firmware is a lot like that.

CHAPTER 11

Doing More with Less

Engineering requires technical skills and a deep understanding of the relevant technology. Writing good embedded software goes a step further, also requiring a devious mind with an affinity for puzzles.

Implementing the requirements on a system that has everything you need is a matter of turning the metaphorical crank to get the answer. Some solutions are more elegant than others, but most will work well enough to get the product shipped. It all gets more interesting when you have a system that seems as if it can't possibly contain everything you need. You could compromise on the features, but where is the fun in that?

For me, the great part of embedded systems implementation is the thrill of finding just the right tweak that liberates a few more processor cycles, being excited about freeing eight bytes of RAM, digging through the map file to find a whole section that you can reclaim for the use of your code, and realizing you can get your product that coveted green award if you can just squeak out a few more milliseconds of deep sleep.

The downside to all of this is that you'll probably make the system more fragile. For instance, when you free the RAM by having two otherwise decoupled subsystems share it, those subsystems become linked. Maintainers of the system become confused and frustrated by hidden linkages. The code is no longer modular, and subsystems cannot be reused. Flexibility is lost.

This chapter looks at ways to get more out of your system. We'll need to start by characterizing the resources we have and those we need. Some of the resource optimization techniques allow you to trade one resource for another. Identifying the plentiful resources is almost as important as determining where the scarce ones disappear to.

One of the most important resources is development effort. Your time is valuable. You will need to balance the value of a solution versus the time it takes to implement it. For example, moving to a larger, faster chip in the family is a cost to all units, which could be a win if you are building only a few; trading memory and processor cycles may require you to restructure some code; and going line by line to optimize assembly code is going to take serious effort (and skill).

Need More Code Space

Implementing an application on a system without enough code space is like trying to write a term paper in a booklet that is too small. Even though you plan ahead and try to figure out how much space should be allocated to each point, in the end you will have to write in tiny print on that last page and wind up using the margins. This section will help you cope with the code space situation.

Reading a Map File (Part 1)

I get a sinking feeling when the linker gives an error message during a build. The compiler provides all sorts of friendly advice and critiques my typing. But the linker usually doesn't talk back unless it is something important.

On the other hand, the linker provides a wealth of information if you know where to look. "Intro to Linker Scripts" describes the linker input. The output map file is easier to read, though still foreign to most developers.

 You may need to configure your linker to output the map file. Look in the directory where your executable is located for a *.map* file. If it isn't there, check the compiler or linker manual.

Map files are toolchain-specific. The examples in this section come from a GNU-based toolchain for the NXP LPC13xx. Most map files have the same information, though it may be in a different order or have different formatting. You'll need to make some educated guesses as you look through yours. If you aren't sure that your map file is giving you the information you are looking for, try this: make a copy, change the code, rebuild, and then diff the resulting map file with the original.

The GNU linker for the LPC13xx starts off with a list of the library modules that are included and which module is responsible for the inclusion. In this example, *libcr_c.a* is included in your build because your code module *aes256.c* calls memcpy(). Note that only part of the *libcr_c.a* library is included (specifically *memcpy.o*):

```
Archive member included because of file (symbol)
../lib/gcc/arm-none-eabi/4.3.3/../../../arm-none-eabi/lib/thumb2/libcr_c.a
                    (memcpy.o)./src/aes256.o (memcpy)
```

If you find that a library is large, this section helps you figure out which part of your code is calling functions in that library. You can then decide whether the code module needs to make that call or if there is a way around it.

Next in the map file is a list of global variables and their sizes:

```
Allocating common symbols
Common symbol       size            file
gNewFirmwareVersion
                    0x6             ./src/firmwareVersion.o
```

Limiting the scope of the variables using the static keyword will cause them to be later in the map file (sometimes the linker won't list them at all), so if a common symbol such as the one just shown isn't in your file, you've done a good job of getting rid of global variables. If you have a lot of data here, review "Object-Oriented Programming in C" on page 31 to remember the difference between global variables and file variables.

Next is a list of sections, addresses, and sizes of code that is not referenced by anything. This section, titled "Discarded input sections" in the LPC13xx map file, shows which functions and variables are cluttering your code but not taking up any code space. Often the unused code remains in the codebase when it is part of a library, some vendor code you don't want to modify, or test code that is used only in special circumstances.

A reflection of the linker script is shown in a memory map:

```
Memory Configuration
Name       Origin      Length      Attributes
Flash      0x00000000  0x00008000  xr
RAM        0x10000000  0x00002000  xrw
*default*  0x00000000  0xffffffff
```

This can be useful as you test out your linker-modification skills. Also, some map files give you the amount of each resource used, which is very helpful for determining how close you are to running out of resources.

The next section of the map is a tedious list of all the files included in your project. Skip over that.

Eventually you get to a section that lists each function, the address where it is located, its size, and the file it came from. These are in the order they occur in the compiled image, generally grouped together by file (module). The function listings start with the first section in the linker file (you may want to pull up the linker input *.ld* file as you go through the map file so you know what to expect). The line at the top gives the section (.text, which contains all the code), the address, and the size of the section:

```
.text           0x00000000      0x7ccd
```

Other than experience and expectation, there is nothing to indicate that this line is more important than the others. In the "Memory Configuration" snippet shown earlier, the total flash size is `0x8000` (removing the preceding 0s in the length from before). Here we see that the code is taking up nearly all of that.

Next, the listing breaks down the contents of the code section:

```
.text.Initialize
                0x0000037c      0x7c ./src/main.o
                0x0000037c           Initialize
    .text.main  0x000003f8      0xb4 ./src/main.o
                0x000003f8           main
```

In the map output, most functions have two lines like this, giving slightly redundant information, though this is often configurable via command-line options to your linker:

```
.section.functionName   address     size        file
                        address                 functionName
```

This part of the map file shows you the size of every function. The first step to reducing the footprint is to find out which pieces are particularly large. Many of the largest pieces will be libraries, especially if you are using floating-point, C's standard I/O (`scanf`/`printf`), or C++'s `iostream`. Even operators, such as division, end up calling functions:

```
.text.__aeabi_ldiv0
    0x00006c6c  0x4   ../lib/gcc/arm-none-eabi/thumb2\libcr_eabihelpers.a(rtlib.o)
    0x00006c6c        __aeabi_ldiv0
.text.__bhs_ldivmod
    0x00006ec0  0x20c ../lib/gcc/arm-none-eabi/thumb2\libcr_eabihelpers.a(rtlib.o)
    0x00006ec0        __bhs_ldivmod
```

The `aeabi_ldiv0` function is a wrapper because it is only four bytes, just enough to jump to another function. However, `bhs_ldivmod` is a real function. Doing signed long divides is costing the program `0x20c` bytes, more than twice the size of the main function.

Some map files don't break out the function sizes in the same way. Instead they list the address of each function in the image, and you need to calculate the differences to get the size.

Functions are not the only things that take up code space. Later in the example map file is the section for read-only data:

```
*(.rodata*)
 .rodata.str1.1
                0x000070cc      0x36 ./src/main.o
 .rodata        0x0000715c      0x10 ./src/aes256.o
 .rodata.str1.1
                0x0000716c      0x35 ./src/aes256.o
```

Here, main has 0x36 bytes of str1.1, not something I'd name a variable. Actually, this is the automatic name that this compiler gives to string variables. So wherever there are constant strings (such as "Hello world"), the compiler collects them into one area that goes into the read-only data section. In addition to the 0x35 bytes of string data in *aes256.o*, the previous snippet also shows unspecified data in the file (0x10 in length). In the source file's test function, a variable is declared with static initializers:

```
uint8_t buf[16] = {0xe5, 0xaa, 0x6d, 0xcb, 0x29, 0xb2, 0x71,
        0xae, 0x0e, 0xbc, 0xfa, 0x7a, 0xb2, 0x2b, 0x57, 0x59};
```

Because this is inside a function, it isn't visible by name to other files. Therefore the map file doesn't show the variable name, but it lists the constants because they take up space in the executable image.

All constants take up space, whether they are declared in #define declarations or with the keyword const. Global constants are often visible in the map file, but constants declared with #define end up in the code, so they aren't called out in a similar way. You can see the variables declared with const in the map file under .rodata:

```
 .rodata        0x00007ab8      0x6A ./src/displayMap.o
                0x00007b8a           kBackgroundInfo
                0x00007bf4           kBorderInfo
```

There may be some sections that say fill. These indicate that the data between files got misaligned, generally because a file used a constant that was smaller than the native format of the processor. For example, a character string that is five characters long will consume 1.25 words on a 32-bit processor, causing the linker to fill three bytes (usually with zeros). This is wasted space but difficult to recover. Unless you really need every byte, it is better to focus on the larger users of memory.

The rest of the map file is filled with juicy RAM details (we'll get to those later) and debug information (generally not useful, though your debugger unit will probably use the information).

If the map file doesn't present the data in a way that is useful to you, write a script to parse it yourself! Read the map file, and create an output table where the height of the cell is proportional to the size of the function. This is pretty easy to do in Python, especially if you use HTML as the output.

Process of Elimination

Now that you know what is taking up your code space, you can start to reduce the size. Start with your tools. In addition to the different optimization levels you normally see to make your code go faster (e.g., the -O3 compiler option), there are special optimization flags to make your code smaller (for instance, in GCC, -Os tries to optimize for code size instead of speed of execution). This may be enough to solve your code size issues.

 If you get a different runtime outcome when you turn on optimizations, check that all of your variables are initialized and that volatile variables are marked as such. Occasionally a compiler will disallow rare but legal features, so if you've eliminated the obvious, check your compiler manual.

If compiler optimizations aren't enough, as you look for memory, it is useful to keep score so you know which changes lead to the best improvements. Not only does this give you a feel for the types of improvements, but it will also help you express trade-offs to your colleagues (e.g., "Yes, that code is uglier now, but it saves 2 KB in code space").

As shown in Table 11-1, create a spreadsheet, starting with the baseline numbers. For every change, fill in a row so you can see the relative value of the changes. If your linker output gives you the numbers in hex, you might want to let the spreadsheet translate to decimal (or the other way around).

Table 11-1. Optimization scorecard example

Action	Text (code)	Data	Total	Total (hex)	Freed	Total freed
Baseline	31949	324	32273	7E11		
Commented-out test code	26629	324	26953	6949	5320	(Reverted change)
Reimplemented abs()	29845	324	30169	75D9	2104	2104
Calculated const table at init time	29885	244	30129	75B1	40	2144
= comment from you	= size of .text section	= size of .data section	= total image size	= hex of total image size	= bytes freed with this change	= total bytes freed since start

The table documents how you tried multiple actions, including commenting out a large block of test code. As described in Chapter 3, it is often good to be able to run code tests in the field. However, these take up precious space. Although feature reduction is undesirable, when looking at code space reduction, the relative importance of features should be kept in mind.

"Reduced size of code by 40%" is a super line on your resume. Hard numbers are great, but be prepared to explain how you did it and the trade-offs you considered. (And the explanation shouldn't consist solely of "turned on compiler optimizations"!)

Libraries

As you go through the memory map, look at the largest consumers first. You may find that some unexpected libraries are included. Trace through the functions to see where the calls to these libraries are coming from.

While some (monolithic) libraries are included if any function is used, other libraries are granular, loading only the required functions. Even the standard libraries can be monolithic so that using the built-in string copy function leads to a large footprint. Your map file will show you these space hogs.

Many times you can write a function to replace the library. Other times you'll need to figure out how to work around a limitation. Here are some common examples to get the ideas flowing:

- Replace floating-point numbers with fixed-point representations (see Chapter 12).
- Replace `printf` with a few functions that don't take variable arguments (e.g., `Log`, `LogWithNum`).
- Replace `strcpy` with your own implementation to exclude the strings library.
- Replace the `abs` function with a macro to remove floating-point math library dependencies.

Note that there is no magic in standard libraries. The ones that come with your development environment may not be the most efficient for your device. There is no law saying you have to use the standard library that is buried in your tools directory. There are other options if you look for them.

Embedded Artistry has a C standard library (LibC, available in GitHub) (*https://github.com/embeddedartistry/libc*) specifically for embedded systems usage. It has a reduced set of functionality appropriate for very constrained environments. It is designed for portability and quick bring-up. Its documentation is also excellent and the code is a good read. The related blog posts (*https://embedde dartistry.com/blog/tag/libc/*) are also useful.

That said, don't write your own libraries if you don't have to. Standard and off-the-shelf libraries are often better specified and tested than the one you can write yourself in the time allotted. Use the time and effort other folks have put in.

Functions Versus Macros: Which Are Smaller?

Keeping your code modular is critical to readability. However, each function comes with a price, increasing code space, RAM, and processor time. The code space cost is easy to quantify.

For example, I needed a small implementation of the algorithm to find the minimum of three variables (Example 11-1).

Example 11-1. Minimum-of-three algorithm

```
if a < b,
  if a < c, return a
  else, return c
else,
  if b < c, return b
  else, return c
```

I put together some code to try out the different implementation options. First, I wrote out the code in the main function and compiled it to get my baseline code size in bytes (given the other cruft automatically compiled in, this was almost 3 KB). I changed the implementation to be a macro:

```
#define min3(x, y, z) (((x)<(y))?(((x)<(z))?(x):(z)):(((y)<(z))?(y):(z)))
```

 Don't remember the ternary conditional operation? It is a shorthand version of an if statement:

```
test ? value if test is true : value if test is false
```

Not only does this make your code more dense, but there are also times when it nudges the compiler into more optimal code.

Then I modified my code to run the macro a few times to get different code space sizes. I changed the macro to a function and ran the same tests. It was a bit odd: the compiled code size was the same, regardless of whether I used an inline function, a regular local function, or an external function.

The inline keyword should have made the function behave as the macro did, replicating the code into each location. However, inline is only a suggestion to the compiler, not a requirement. How the compiler takes the suggestion is very compiler-specific. There is often a compiler-specific pragma to disallow inline (e.g., __attribute__((noinline)) in GCC).

After I recorded the size, I turned optimizations on and reran the tests, recording the difference in bytes from the baseline for each implementation (see Table 11-2). All along I had all my variables marked as volatile, so the compiler couldn't remove code that appeared to have no side effects (e.g., the interim function or macro calls).

Table 11-2. Optimization scorecard showing the difference from the baseline for macros versus functions

Implementation	1 call	2 calls	3 calls
Macro	0	76	152
Function (local or external)	20	60	96
Macro with space optimization	−40	8	56
Function with space optimization	−40	−20	0

The key thing to note from the table is where the crossover points are (two calls without optimizations, one call with). A macro uses the same amount of space as copying the line of code into your function (essentially the preprocessor does a search and replace). Once you've called the min3 macro a few times, it would take less code space to turn it into a function. Although the function call generally makes for smaller code, we'll have to return to the issue when we look at functions in RAM and processor cycle optimization.

Macros do have the advantage (of sorts) that they don't do type checking; the same macro could be used for integers, unsigned integers, or floating-point numbers. If you need to perform an operation on many different types, you'll need to compare the space consumed by multiple functions against the equivalent macro.

Finally, a smaller snippet of code might never have a crossover point, so a macro may always be better. (Even the innocuous minimum-of-two-variables function has a crossover point of three calls, so a smaller snippet of code could be very small indeed.) Crossover points depend on many factors, including processor architecture, compiler implementation, and memory layout. You may need to do some experimentation on your system to determine the code space trade-off between macros and functions.

Constants and Strings

Going through the map file, you may find that your debug strings take up a lot of your code space. This is a really tough dilemma because those debug strings provide valuable information and useful comments.

If you've implemented a logging API (described in "Creating Interfaces" on page 27), you already have the ability to turn the debugging on and off per subsystem at runtime. To get rid of the debugging strings, you'll need to go a step further and remove the functions at compile time.

You can still get some flexibility (and some documentation) using this common idiom that lets you turn off the logging in a particular subsystem (the motor subsystem in this example):

```
#define MOTOR_LOG 1 // set this to zero to turn off debugging
#if MOTOR_LOG
#define Log(level, str)              Log(eMotorLog, (level), (str))
#define LogWithNum(level, str, num) LogWithNum(eMotorLog, (level), (str), (num))
#else
#define Log(level, str)
#define LogWithNum(level, str)
#endif
```

When you change the value of MOTOR_LOG to 0 in the #define, all strings get compiled out (even though the code looks the same). This is part of *motor.c*, on the principle that you want to touch only the code you are working on. However, some systems use the more global *log.h* to allow (and disallow) logging in each subsystem. Either way, it can be a little frustrating if you forget and try to turn debugging on during runtime, so you'll need to find the balance between runtime flexibility and code space.

 Adding a significant amount of complexity might give you even more compression. If you really need to know what is going on, consider a macro system that replaces strings with constants and uses a separate script to build a dictionary of all the strings from the code. The output looks useless, but a postprocessing script makes it readable, and you've potentially saved a ton of code space.

As for other constants, why are they there? Do you really need them? Are there ways to calculate the data at runtime? Or compress it? Can you move the information to another storage mechanism (an external device such as a flash or EEPROM)? The options depend on your system, but now that you know where the space is going, you can dig into the problem.

Need More RAM

Unlike the angst produced when your linker says you are out of code space, a RAM resource error from the linker should give you a sense of relief at having dodged a bullet. The alternative symptom for a RAM shortage is a system that crashes randomly.

Some of the same techniques for finding more code space work for RAM as well. However, it's more difficult to find out where the RAM is disappearing to. You can make it easier on yourself with some design choices.

Remove malloc

To really understand where your RAM goes, eliminate dynamic memory allocation.

Because some local variables are hard to see thanks to compiler optimization and register use, you can make the variables global. Then you can use the memory map output of your linker to determine where the RAM is used. Dynamic allocation is always invisible in the map file.

> If your system uses a language with garbage collection, you might not have the luxury of knowing where your RAM is going. For embedded systems written in such languages, dealing with RAM constraints becomes much more difficult.

If I haven't convinced you that transparency is a good enough reason to get rid of dynamic allocation, there are some other reasons. If you have an operating system, malloc makes an application nondeterministic. Even without an OS, malloc makes the same function run differently depending on the current state of the heap. Say you have a heap that is 30 bytes in size (this is a little small, but it makes my example easier), and in a particular function you allocate a 10-byte buffer and a 5-byte buffer. Then you free the 10-byte buffer so you can allocate a 20-byte buffer. What is wrong with this picture? More than you might expect:

Wasted RAM
    The heap requires RAM to keep a data structure describing the memory that's in use. Every dynamic allocation has some amount of metadata overhead.

Lost processor cycles
    Keeping track of the heap is not free. Searching the heap data structure for available memory is usually a binary search, which is pretty fast, but it is still a search.

Fragmentation
    As shown in Figure 11-1, after you've allocated the 10-byte and 5-byte buffers, the first half of the heap is used. After you free the 10-byte buffer, there are 25

bytes available. However, there isn't a contiguous block for the 20-byte buffer so `malloc` will fail to allocate a buffer, returning NULL. By mixing buffer sizes, the heap gets fragmented. With a heap that is much larger than the variables (and few or no small allocations), this is less of a problem. However, in an embedded system, you probably won't have the luxury of a large heap.

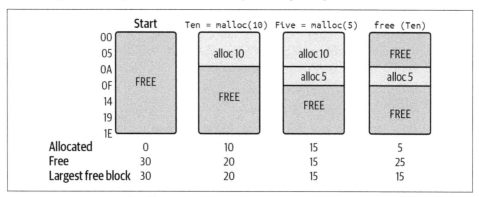

Figure 11-1. An example of heap fragmentation

If you have a buffer that can be recycled after it is used, there are options besides using the built-in dynamic allocation system. If you need two buffers—say, one for an interrupt to write to and one for the normal code to read from—use a ping-pong buffer as described in "Direct Memory Access (DMA) Is Faster" on page 199. If you have a queue of data, implement a circular buffer (see "Circular Buffers" on page 203). If all of your buffers are the same size, consider a chunk allocator (there are many examples on the web and in Wikipedia). However, avoid reinventing the wheel. If your memory system is so complex that you end up rebuilding `malloc`, use the built-in version. Its benefits will probably outweigh the costs on your system.

Reading a Map File (Part 2)

Going back to the map file, we may find some RAM information in the `.data` and `.bss` sections. These sections are not always obvious, and you may need to search for them; they often look like the text section filled with functions. For each section there is a summary that shows the total amount used:

```
.data      0x10000000      0x144
...
.bss       0x10000000      0x1b7c
```

In some map files, the `.data` section is called `.cinit`. Most linkers are pretty standard, but if you see things you don't recognize, you may need to break out the linker manual or search online.

Looking back at the overview memory map (the memory configuration in "Need More Code Space" on page 286), this program is taking up quite a lot of its 0x2000 bytes of RAM.

Note that this total doesn't include the heap or the stack; see "Stacks (and Heaps)" on page 129. There is no heap in this program, so all remaining RAM is allocated to the stack. Often allocation for the heap and the stack is done in the linker file (or as an argument passed into the linker). Without malloc, the heap can be allocated to zero (or only as large as your libraries require). Long function call chains can make for a large stack, particularly when the intermediate calls have many local variables.

To determine the size of your stack, in a debug build, fill a larger-than-expected stack with a canary pattern (such as 0xDEADCODE). Then exercise as much of the system as possible. Finally, check how much of the stack is undisturbed to see how much you can eliminate. The stack allocation should be a bit larger than the amount you calculate (I'd say 25% larger). Stack overflow bugs are very difficult to solve, and a bit of buffering will save you from needing to do so. (If you have an operating system, each thread may have its own stack and heap.)

 Recursion is seldom used in embedded systems, because the stack may be exhausted before the solution is obtained.

Returning to the map file, the .data section contains constants for your initialized variables, and .bss contains all of your uninitialized global and static variables. The .data section variables also require code space for their initial values, which is captured in the .rodata section. The .bss section variables are RAM only. The layout is similar to the one for functions:

```
.section       address    size     file
               address             global variable name
               address             global variable name
```

If your variables are local to your file (or static variables in a function), only the size and filename are shown:

```
.bss           0x10001bb4       0x14 ./SharedSrc/i2c.o
```

As with functions, the goal here is to look for the larger variables, as those are where the best savings can be had. (Reducing a 12-byte array by 50% is not as exciting as doing the same for a 200-byte array.)

Registers and Local Variables

Unlike global variables, it is more difficult to estimate the RAM consumed by local variables (those within functions). Registers are the memory pieces of a CPU. Some processors can't perform actions on RAM directly. Instead, they have to load the value from RAM into a register, perform the action on the register, and then store the information back to RAM. That's a lot of instructions for a line of code that says:

```
i++;
```

Not every processor needs to go through such gymnastics, but registers are faster for any processor to use. The reason local variables are difficult to count when tallying up RAM usages is that many local variables spend their whole existence as registers.

C has a keyword called register that is supposed to give a hint to the compiler about which variables you think should go in registers. The keyword is generally ignored, if it is implemented at all.

Function parameters

A function's input arguments are often in registers instead of on the stack (RAM). You can encourage the compiler to do this if your function has only a few parameters. A good rule of thumb is fewer than four parameters per function. If you have a 32-bit processor, that would be four 32-bit variables, not a dozen pieces of data crammed into four structures.

In fact, if you have an N-bit processor, try to stick to N-bit variables. Larger variables generally are not candidates for precious registers. (Smaller variables often add processor steps because the compiler tries to access only the part you find interesting.)

To use registers, you usually want to pass arguments by value. If you pass by reference (or by pointer), you are sending the address of the data. The address may be in a register, but the data will need to be accessed in RAM. For example:

```
int variable= 10;
function(&variable);  /* this takes more RAM than passing by value
                         because variable has to be in RAM to have
                         an address */
```

There is an exception to the pointer guidelines if you pass a structure to a function. If you pass a structure by value, you are likely to have two copies of it in RAM: the original and the stack version of the copy. Pass pointers to structures to eliminate duplication.

Minimize scope

You are probably familiar with namespace (where a variable is valid according to the programming language). A variable may be global, in which case its namespace scope is the whole program. Or it may be declared in a file, a function, or even a designated area of a function (e.g., inside a loop). However, there is another form of scope: where the variable is used by the code. You might define 10 variables in your function in such a way that their namespace is the whole function, but if you use each one in a limited area, its scope is that area, not the whole function.

For the most efficient register use, each function should use only a small number of variables at any time. When optimization is on, your compiler will move around the code to limit the scope of the variables and free up registers. However, you can help it figure out what is going on. For a simple (and somewhat lame) example, take this code snippet that needs to make each array value equal to its place in the array. It does some processing and then needs the array to be reinitialized to its original values before going on:

```
for (i=0;  i < MAX_ARRAY_LENGTH; i++) { array[i] = i; }
… /* do stuff to array, need to set it up again */
/* i still equals max array so subtract one and run through
   the loop again*/
for (i--; i >= 0; i--) { array[i] = i; }
```

The programmer thought that avoiding the need to reinitialize i would save a few cycles. However, as the code is written, its value has to be remembered across other processing steps, even though it doesn't really matter. The variable's scope is increased without cause. We can rewrite the code to enable the compiler to forget about i when it isn't in use (and the compiler can reuse a register for a different variable):

```
for (i=0;  i < MAX_ARRAY_LENGTH; i++) { array[i] = i; }
… /* do stuff to array, need to set it up again */
for (i=0;  i < MAX_ARRAY_LENGTH; i++) { array[i] = i; }
```

For this example, the solution is a no-brainer (and has cleaner code). However, when you look at your code, can you see places to decrease the scope of the variables? Maybe do all the processing on one variable before shifting to another?

Don't worry about the total number of variables you have in a function. If you limit the scope of each variable and within each scope limit the total number of variables in play, the compiler can figure out the rest. It doesn't always pay to reuse variables, particularly when your compiler can't recognize an old variable used in a new scope.

Look at the assembly

How do you know if you've been successful in your attempts to mind meld with the compiler? Look at the assembly code. No, wait! Stop running away!

I'm not suggesting you learn assembly language for this. Well, maybe read it a little. I definitely am not suggesting you write in assembly language (that is in "Coding in assembly language" on page 318). However, you can learn a lot about your compiler (and your code) by looking at the list file (.*lst*) or walking through the assembly in your debugger. Make sure you can see the higher-level language at the same time as the assembly. Your code acts as sort of a comment for the assembly code so you know what it is trying to do. (You may need to add a compiler option to retain the list files; look on the web or in your compiler manual.)

> The first few times you look at assembly and walk through it, make sure optimization was off during compilation. The tricky things that occur during optimization are not a good introduction to learning how to read assembly code.

As you look at the code in a new light, note that when the compiler optimizes for speed, it will put the most often used variables into registers so that it doesn't have to load and store them for each access. If you can set your compiler to optimize for RAM usage, it will instead put the largest number of variables in registers, possibly leaving an often-used variable in RAM if its scope is large.

Function Chains

We saw in "Stacks (and Heaps)" on page 129 that each function call increases the size of the stack. Say we have three functions: main calls first, and first calls second. At that point, our stack looks like the left part of Figure 11-2.

Only a few registers are available on the processor, so everything else goes on the stack. You don't get extra registers for making function calls; there is a static number through the whole system. So, if you have a chain of functions, the local variables and parameters from earlier functions will have to go on the stack to make way for the latest calls. Even when a parameter or a local variable starts out as a register, if it has a large enough scope, it may end up on the stack when you call another function.

As shown in the right side of Figure 11-2, if you can tweak your design to have a flatter function structure, your stack can be smaller (and each stack frame will be smaller as you increase the register usage).

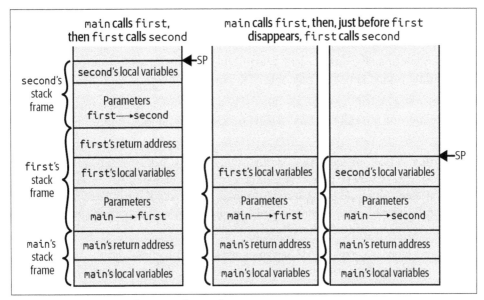

Figure 11-2. Function chains in the stack

One exception to the rule that functions calling functions incur RAM costs is a technique called *tail recursion*. It isn't really recursion (remember that recursion is bad in an environment with limited RAM!). In tail recursion, you call the next function as the last statement of the current one (for instance, call `second` at the very end of `first`). This lets you retain encapsulation for your modules *and* keep the stack small. The compiler will remove `first`'s local variables and parameters from the stack, allowing the `second` function to return directly to `main` (without passing through `first`). Even though `first` called `second`, the stack looks like the right side of Figure 11-2.

Also, whereas an earlier section discussed the trade-offs of macros in terms of code size, macros play a different role in RAM reduction. Macros take up no stack frame at all, so they are good for decreasing the RAM footprint (especially for little functions such as the one in Example 11-1). A little more code space might lead to less RAM (and faster execution).

Pros and Cons of Globals: RAM Versus Stack

Global variables have a bad reputation. They've been party to all sorts of spaghetti code, they continually conspire with inexplicable outside forces to control the flow of code, and they don't know the meaning of the word reentrant.[1]

Coders that use global variables are often accused of being lazy. But laziness and convenience are not the only reasons for using global variables. They do have a good side.

But a little more about their bad side first. Global variables always take RAM. They are almost always slower to access than a local (register) variable. So if you have a global variable that could be replaced by a local one, make it local. Even if it ends up on the stack instead of in a register, once the program execution goes out of scope, that RAM is free for use elsewhere.

When can a global save on RAM? Say you have a function chain and need a particular variable in several functions (or worse, you need the data only at the end of your function chain). If you pass the data in via a parameter to each function in the chain, with intermediate processing, the compiler may be unable to keep the data in a register all the way through the chain. Because it is a parameter to each function, the data will go on the stack multiple times. A global variable is stored outside the stack and short-circuits the process.

Clever Memory Overlays

Does your system have a few large buffers? Some of the particularly bulky ones I've found on some of my systems include display buffers, communications buffers, and sensor input buffers. Once you've identified the large buffers in the system, ask yourself whether they all need to be used at the same time.

For example, maybe your display buffer is used to build up the image and then sits idle until the next time you need to update the display, at which point you build it up again. Or the sensor input buffer isn't needed while you're waiting for an interesting event. Once you notice the event, you need the whole buffer to queue up the data, but until then, only a small area of it is needed. Or maybe you have a large communications buffer for when you are receiving new code to load, but in general you need only a little of it. Does any of that sound familiar?

If your system uses dynamic memory allocation, these subsystems might allocate and free their memory to avoid tying up the RAM resources. However, if you've banned dynamic memory allocation (and if a chunk allocator is overkill), your system might

---

1 A subroutine is reentrant if it can be interrupted in the middle and then safely called again before its previous invocation has been completed. (More in "Reentrant Functions" on page 134.)

---

benefit from RAM overlays. This is where two (or more) subsystems share some or all of their allocated memory, but only one gets to use it at a time. By overloading the resource, you effectively get a lot more RAM. Figure 11-3 shows a 4 KB RAM buffer available on a processor. Without the overlay, the buffers overflow the available space and the system won't compile. With the overlay, the buffers fit. However, the subsystems depend on each other in a way that is not obvious to the casual observer (since you've smashed encapsulation to bits).

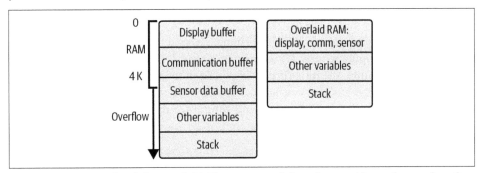

Figure 11-3. Example of sharing RAM between modules where, without the overlay, the buffers overflow the available 4 k RAM

There are several ways to implement memory overlays. The simplest is to treat the buffer as private to one module and allow access to it through a single function, as described with the modified singleton pattern in "Creating Interfaces" on page 27. Another method is to implement a union of several arrays, possibly with an owner tag to indicate the current user of the memory.

Alternatively, to make the subsystems less entwined, you can modify the linker script to overlay the RAM buffers on each other. This eliminates any direct interaction between the two subsystems, but requires that any future developer understand that the two subsystems cannot run at the same time (without catastrophic results).

Need More Speed

Of all the places to spend your valuable development time, the worst can be sunk in trying to squeeze out a few more cycles from the processor. Try to avoid that position by starting with the design of the system, maybe building in some overhead when selecting a processor. However, there are times when you have to make the code go faster to respond to a real-time event, to add another feature, or to reduce power consumption (see Chapter 13).

Before delving into serious system tuning, start by profiling your application to make sure you focus on the important parts. Profiling is not as simple as reading the map file, but it is still unwise to optimize the wrong thing (e.g., cutting half of your initialization time, which runs only once at system boot, instead of focusing on the problem in your main loop).

Profiling

To know where to spend your time optimizing the code, you need to know where the cycles are going. Many compilers (and operating systems) have some built-in analysis tools, including profilers. If you have those, learn them. If you don't, you may want to build your own rudimentary profiler to give you some insight.

In physics, the Heisenberg uncertainty principle says that electron momentum and position cannot simultaneously be known to an arbitrary precision. In profiling, there is also uncertainty: the more precisely you need to know how long each piece of code takes to run, the less you can know about the whole of the execution. That is, your profiler will change the behavior (and timing) of the code. Understanding the impact your profiler has on your code is an important part of profiling.

Profiling usually starts off trying to answer questions about where the processor time is spent. By digging down into a particular function, you can apply the same method to determine which part of that function is longest (and so on). Each of the four profilers discussed here has a slightly different focus to help you get a broad and deep view of your system.

Similar to the code space and RAM score cards, use your profiler to track which modifications were most effective.

I/O lines and an O-scope

If you have a few open I/O lines going to test points, they can show you where to start on the path to profiling your code. As you enter a function of interest, set an output line to be high. When you leave, set it low. Watch these lines on an oscilloscope to see how long each function takes.

For example, we have a system that waits for data to be ready, reads the data, transforms it, and displays the result to an LCD:

```
Interrupt sets data ready variable when data is available to be read

Main loop:
  Loop, waiting for data ready to be set
  Read the data in the buffer
  Transform data into information
  Write the information to the LCD
```

If we had four I/O lines, setting and clearing one for each stage, the result might look like Figure 11-4. Each I/O switches exactly as its predecessor completes (often you don't need to instrument everything; you can look at the gaps). In the beginning, it looks like everything is good; the bulk of the time is spent waiting for the data to be ready and writing information to the LCD. Eventually, the data to be ready goes to zero, but the other tasks take up the same amount of time.

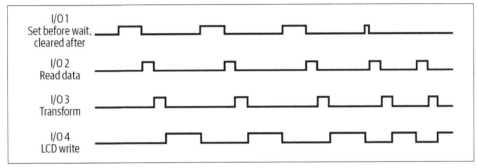

Figure 11-4. Profiling using I/O lines on an oscilloscope

Two things in the graph are important. First, as time goes on, the data is always ready as soon as the LCD write is finished. Let's assume the data is ready at a fixed interval (e.g., sampled from an ADC). The narrowing data-wait time means that you will start to miss data because the system can't keep up. Second, the system time is dominated by the LCD write, which is the activity on the bottom. If you can fix what is taking so long in there, the system might be able to keep up with the input.

The great part about I/O line profiling is being able to set and clear an output line in an interrupt. It will slow down your system to add the I/O changes to interrupt service routines, but only by a tiny bit. The profiling information you gain about the system is often worth the temporary slowdown.

Timer profiler 1 (function timer)

For a system with few interrupts, another way to implement a profiler is to time how long a section of code takes to run. In "System Tick" on page 143, I talked about how to build a system clock to measure how long things will take. We built the TimeNow function to return the number of milliseconds since the processor started. Using that as a simple timer profiler might look like the following:

```
struct sProfile {
  uint32_t count;
  tTime    sum;
  tTime    start;
  tTime    end;
} ;
void main(){
```

```
    struct sProfile profile;
    ...

  profile.count = 0;
  profile.sum = 0;
  while (1) {
    profile.start = TimeNow();
    ImportantFunction();
    profile.end = TimeNow();
    profile.sum += profile.end - profile.start;
    profile.count++;
    if (profile.count == PROFILE_COUNT_PRINT) {
      LogWithNum(eProfiler, eDebug, "Important Function profile: ", profile.sum);
      profile.count = 0;
      profile.sum = 0;
     }
    ... // continue with other main loop functions
  }
}
```

The function profiled (ImportantFunction) should be longer than the timer tick—at a minimum, twice as long, and preferably at least 10 times as long. It is also critical that the profiling function (TimeNow) takes a negligible amount of processing compared to the profiled function.

Note that the summation and logging are outside the scope of the profiler. Try to sample only the things you care about and not all of the accoutrements of profiling. If you aren't sure that you've eliminated the profiler overhead, try commenting out the function of interest so that you are profiling only the start and end time acquisition. The result should consistently be zero if the profiler is working properly.

 If you have a few functions of interest and are trying to decide where to spend your development time, you might use three or four profiler variables to monitor different areas of code.

Finally, using many samples will average out any minor differences (for example, if you have a short, intermittent interrupt). By sampling multiple times, you also get a small increase in precision as the integers get larger. For example, with one sample, the function may take 10 ms. But with a thousand samples, the sum may give you 10,435 ms, indicating an average of 10.4 ms.

Figure 11-5 shows how this function timer profiler measures one area of interest at a time.

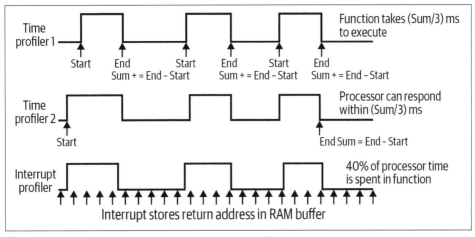

Figure 11-5. Comparing timer and interrupt profilers

Timer profiler 2 (response timer)

If you want to profile a function that is much shorter than your timer tick, you can use a shorter timer tick in your profiler or change the way you sample. The following example, for instance, profiles the whole main loop because the profiler timer doesn't stop until the counter has reached its goal, as shown in the middle of Figure 11-5. This may yield valuable information if you are trying to react to an event within a certain amount of time:

```
profile.count = 0;
profile.start = TimeNow();
while (1) {
  ImportantFunction();
  profile.count++;
  if (profile.count == PROFILE_COUNT_PRINT) {
    profile.end = TimeNow();
    profile.sum = profile.end - profile.start;
    LogWithNum(eProfiler, eDebug, "Important Function profile: ", profile.sum);
    profile.count = 0;
    profile.start = TimeNow();
    }
  ... // other main loop functions are also part of the profile
}
```

This timer profiler has a larger impact on the results because it increments the counter and compares it to a constant inside the profiled area. If your loop is very quick, these activities may be non-negligible. As before, you can check this assumption by commenting out everything in the main loop except the profiler. By taking this measurement, the baseline of the profiler can be subtracted out of your final analysis.

As shown in Figure 11-5, this profiler gives you a longer view of the system timing. Both of the timer profiling methods break up the flow of code. They tend to be temporary pieces of code that you remove after gathering the information you want. Instrumenting the code in this fashion is straightforward, so reproducing the code as needed is usually better than leaving it in to slow down the code and/or confuse future generations.

Sampling profiler

If you have an interrupt-driven system, profiling can be more difficult. However, if you can allocate a block of RAM to it, you can implement a sampling profiler with a timer-based interrupt.

First, create a timer interrupt that is asynchronous to everything else in the system. For example, if you have 10 Hz and 15 Hz interrupts, make sure your new timer is not 1, 2, 3, or 5 Hz. Instead, make it something like 1.7 Hz so it is not evenly divisible into any of your other time-based interrupts. This ensures that your results are not biased by periodic functions. Figure 11-5 illustrates the relative timing of two functions and your custom timer (the little arrows at the bottom).

Now, on every profiler timer interrupt, save the return pointer to the block of RAM (you'll need to know the stack frame format of your processor and possibly some assembly to do this). The return pointer tells you what code was running when the timer interrupted. Once the RAM buffer is full, stop the timer and output the list of addresses. Armed with a list of return addresses, figure out where these are in the image using the map file. A scripting language will significantly help you parse the map file and count up the number of times the profiler sampled from each function. You can thus figure out what percentage of the processor time each function is taking.

This method works best when your processor allows nested interrupts, and the profiler timer is the only one allowed to interrupt other interrupts. If you have other nonmaskable interrupts, you won't be able to see those in the results.

This sampling profiler doesn't slow down any particular function, but it does place a tiny drain on the whole system. (Outputting the list of addresses may be a larger drain, depending on your implementation.) This sort of profiler is readily left in the code, with the timer (and output function) turned off when they are unneeded.

Optimizing for Processor Cycles

Armed with the knowledge of what is slowing down your system, you can now explore the options available to you. Definitely start by turning on optimizations in your compiler. The less tweaking you need to do, the better your code will be.

Next, try to get most of your variables into registers. Even if you have a long function call chain and variables end up going on the stack while another function is called, if they can at least be registers in a smaller scope, the code will be faster.

Having done those basics, consider the techniques in the following sections.

Memory timing

Wait states are a bane to efficient use of the processor resources. Many types of memory cannot be accessed as fast as the processor runs. To get information from such memory, the processor has to wait some number of processor cycles to offset the timing difference. Memory has a number of *wait states*. For example, if your code runs from a four wait state flash, every time it needs a new instruction, the processor has to wait for four clock cycles.

I should point out that four wait state memory doesn't (always) mean your code runs four times slower than in one wait state memory. Processors can pipeline instructions to reduce the impact of slow memory—in other words, look up the next instructions while executing the current one. If the number of pipeline stages is greater than the number of wait states, the memory will slow execution only when the pipeline stalls (which tends to happen at branches, such as if statements, and function calls because the processor can't just assume that it will execute the next instruction in memory).

By knowing how many wait states each type of memory has, you have options for speeding up execution by moving code to faster memory. For example, you may want to copy a critical function to zero wait state RAM if that is faster than your normal program flash. If you need the function occasionally, you can overlay the memory with another buffer. When the function is needed, copy it out of code space into RAM (though you'll need to do some profiling to make sure the overhead of copying it is balanced by its amazing speed in RAM). Many compilers support a keyword (ramfunc), pragma, or macro that lets you indicate that the function should be stored in code space but loaded into RAM on boot (by the startup code that runs before main). Often you'll need to modify your linker file to put the section into RAM. Check your seldom-used compiler manual for this, not your handy processor manual.

Variable size

When you are working on an 8-bit processor, it is easy to understand that using a larger variable will incur a higher cost in terms of processor cycles. Although it might not seem as logical, using a smaller variable on a larger processor may have some unwanted overhead as well. For best results, local variables should match the size of the registers.

When the compiler needs to reduce the size of a local variable from a native 32-bit variable to an 8-bit char or a 16-bit short, it has to extend the sign, which means every manipulation takes two instructions (or one extra instruction to zero extend unsigned variables). Thinking about this tedious level of optimization all the time is a job for your compiler. However, you can give it better hints if you generally implement variables using native types.

Along the same lines, try to use the same type of variables for the bulk of your processing. Type conversions are a waste of processor time. Converting between signed and unsigned also should be avoided as much as possible.

 Signed ints are upgraded to unsigned ints when the two are compared. So a small negative-signed variable is likely to be considered a numerically larger value when unwisely compared with an unsigned variable. Stick with unsigned variables unless you really need negative numbers.

One last look at function chains

Functions make your code run more slowly because the processor switches context by pushing data on the stack (and usually having to refill the pipeline). Of course, functions make your code maintainable (and usually make it more correct), so don't eliminate them entirely. However, the drive toward encapsulation can have cost as well as benefit.

For example, take an LCD display driver. LCD drivers are often optimized because the data needs to be on the screen before the screen refreshes. If there is no other form of control and only part of the data is available in the LCD's buffer, the screen may tear (show part of the old image and part of the new) until the next refresh cycle. Our example driver is for an LCD that is 240 × 320 pixels, and each pixel is 16-bit (meaning it has 2^{16} colors). When putting an image on the screen (or part of the screen), the driver reads from a buffer of RAM and puts it on a GPIO-controlled parallel bus that is 8 bits wide. The code starts out looking like this:

```
// in Lcd.c
void LcdWriteBuffer(uint16_t* buffer, uint16_t bufLength){

  int i = 0;
  while (bufLength) {
    LcdWriteBus(buffer[i] & 0xFF);        // write lower byte
    LcdWriteBus((buffer[i] >> 8) & 0xFF); // write upper byte
    i++;
    bufLength--;
  }
}
void LcdWriteBus(uint8_t data){

  IoClear(LCD_SELECT_N);          // select the chip
  IoWriteBusByte(LCD_BUS, data);  // write to the I/O lines
  IoSet(LCD_SELECT_N)             // deselect the chip
```

```
}

// in Io.c
IoWriteBusByte(uint32_t io, uint8_t data){

  // ioBus was configured during initialization
  ioBus[io] = data;
}
```

That is a lot of code, and when it's lined up like that you may see some chances for optimization. When the code is scattered in multiple files, it can be harder to see.

When you find a spot that seems worth optimizing, look at its call chain as a whole.

Selecting and deselecting the LCD for every write is silly. The LcdWriteBus function has to do it because it doesn't know what else is going on around it. However, the LcdWriteBuffer function knows it is sending a large amount of data. Although the LcdWriteBus function is probably used by other parts of the code, the LcdWrite Buffer code won't call it, instead implementing its own version:

```
//in lcd.c
void LcdWriteBuffer(uint16_t* buffer, uint16_t bufLength){

  int i;
  IoClear(LCD_SELECT_N);                        // select the chip
  while (bufLength) {
    IoWriteBusByte(LCD_BUS, buffer[i]);         // write lower byte
    IoWriteBusByte(LCD_BUS, (buffer[i] >> 8)); // write upper byte
    i++;
    buffLength--;
  }
  IoSet(LCD_SELECT_N)                           // deselect the chip
}
```

So you've eliminated one link in the function chain. The function will run faster, and there is no way the compiler could have done that optimization for you. All you had to do was copy code from one function to another, not sell your soul or anything. However, if there was a bug in LcdWriteBus, now it is likely to be in LcdWriteBuffer. Maybe you should add a comment in each function cross-referencing the other, so a maintainer will know to change both locations.

The slope gets much more slippery from here. The next function in the chain is IoWriteBusByte. It is only one line of C code, but underneath, it does some indirect addressing to write to the I/O register. It does that every time the function is called, even though the byte is written to the same LCD I/O lines each time.

It seems like an easy change. However, the I/O function is in the I/O module, not the LCD module. If you change this, your code becomes faster but less portable, as it won't have any abstraction between the LCD and the hardware. Is it worth it? Are you looking at a situation where you need a few more cycles or one where you absolutely need a lot more cycles?

The cost of making a dramatic improvement is often high. Even if the change is fast to make now, future development time will need to be invested as the system becomes less flexible and more information-intensive. The next person is not going to recognize the trade-offs, so they will stumble over the code and ask why you made it so ugly.

There is another option. By making `IoWriteBusByte` a macro, you can preserve the modular boundaries and still eliminate the stack manipulation. The macro will take up a little more code space (especially if `IoWriteBusByte` is used in many other functions). Worse, you are still spending processor cycles with the pointer access. However, before we think about breaking encapsulation further, let's think through some other options.

Consider the instructions

If you were the processor, what would go on with the instructions that appear in the two `IoWriteBusByte` calls that read `buffer[i]` twice and then increment `i`? Though the machine code is processor-dependent, we can estimate the steps for each line of code:

```
IoWriteBusByte(LCD_BUS, buffer[i] & 0xFF); // write lower byte
  (Variable i would already be in a register, already initialized)
  Copy the buffer pointer from the stack into a register
  Add the buffer pointer to i
  Read the contents of memory at that address
  Perform bitwise AND with contents
  Put i on stack
  Call IoWriteBusByte, passing data
  Pop i off the stack

 IoWriteBusByte(LCD_BUS, (buffer[i] >> 8) & 0xFF); // write upper byte
  Copy the buffer pointer from the stack in a register
  Add the buffer pointer to i
  Read the contents of memory at that address
  Perform shift with contents
  Perform bitwise AND with result
  Put i on stack
  Call IoWriteBusByte, passing data
  Pop i off the stack

i++;
  Increment register i
```

I broke the process down into pretty granular steps. Although some assembly languages could combine some of my instructions, most of them would need a few more. The goal is to think like a microprocessor. And if you do this, even if you are wrong sometimes, you will write better and more easily optimized code. Thinking along those lines, it would be more efficient if we didn't have to add the index to the buffer pointer:

```
IoWriteBusByte(LCD_BUS, *buffer & 0xFF); // write lower byte
  (Variable buffer would already be in a register, already initialized)
  Copy the buffer pointer from the stack in a register
  Add the buffer pointer to i
  Read the contents of memory at that address
  Perform bitwise AND with contents
  Put buffer on stack
  Call IoWriteBusByte, passing data
  Pop buffer off the stack


IoWriteBusByte(LCD_BUS, (*buffer >> 8) & 0xFF); // write upper byte
  Copy the buffer pointer from the stack in a register
  Add the buffer pointer to i
  Read the contents of memory at that address
  Perform shift with contents
  Perform bitwise AND with result
  Put buffer on stack
  Call IoWriteBusByte, passing data
  Pop buffer off the stack
buffer++;
  Increment register buffer
i++;
  Increment register i
```

This doesn't really change anything important; it only gives a hint to the compiler about what choices it could make to go faster. (And some compilers are intelligent enough to have parsed the code to get to the same point.)

The immediate lesson is to use pointer arithmetic (`buffer++`) instead of arrays and indexes where possible. Pointer arithmetic uses a little less RAM and gives the compiler a clearer path toward optimization. The larger lesson is to understand how your code is translated into machine language, and to make it easy for a compiler to take a faster route. (Compiler Explorer is a great resource for this, see "Further Reading" on page 320 for more information.)

Reduce math in loops

What next? Ideally, we'd like to do less math during a loop. The shift and bitwise-AND are relatively cheap, but if you do them on every pass, they add up. It wouldn't be necessary if the buffer were a byte buffer instead of a word buffer:

```
void LcdWriteBuffer(uint16_t* buffer, uint16_t bufLength)
{
  uint8_t *byteBuffer = (uint8_t *) buffer;
  // buffer is now a buffer of bytes.
  // This works only if your endian-ness matches what the
  // hardware expects
  bufLength = bufLength*2;

  IoClear(LCD_SELECT_N);          // select the chip
  while (bufLength) {
    IoWriteBusByte(LCD_BUS, *byteBuffer);
    bufLength--; byteBuffer++;
  }
  IoSet(LCD_SELECT_N)             // deselect the chip
}
```

The code now relies on a feature of the processor (endian-ness) that will not be portable. However, the change will speed up the code—probably. Remember that memory size matters. This change would improve the speed of an 8-bit chip significantly. For a 32-bit chip? Well, it shouldn't slow it down much, because we were already doing the bit manipulation previously shown. At least now we are letting the compiler do the best optimization it can. The potential improvement depends on your architecture.

Usually, making the loop smaller is a good idea, as is making it do exactly the same set of operations each time. Keep if statements out of loops, as they mess with your pipelining and slow it all down.

However, there is a conditional statement (while) in the previous loop. At this point, it may be taking a nontrivial number of cycles. If you were to walk through the assembly code, you might see that the loop is writing the byte, decrementing and incrementing some registers, and checking to make sure one register is not zero.

Checking against zero is cheaper than checking against a constant (much cheaper than checking against a variable). Make your loop indexes count down. It saves only an instruction or two, but it is good practice.

Making a PB&J

There is a neat experiment you can run if you have some 5–9-year-olds handy. Ask them to pretend that they have a robot (you) and want to make a peanut butter and jelly sandwich (PB&J). The 'bot is very dumb, so they have to give it complete and detailed instructions.

The robot already knows how to grasp and lift objects (bread, peanut butter, jelly, bread, and spreaders). But it doesn't know how to put it all together to make a sandwich. What are the steps, and how do they go together? As the child writes (or says) the steps, the robot often creates a mess instead of a sandwich as it interprets each command literally.

Breaking down the process of making a PB&J is a fun way to get kids to understand a little bit about the process of writing software. Plus, you get to say "does not compute" like a Dalek until they manage a sandwich.

(Thanks to Walter and Emma Stockwell for letting me experiment upon their sons, Alasdair and Toby.)

Loop unrolling

By now, when you look at the assembly for the loop in this function, the check against zero may be one of about 10 instructions. The decrement of bufLength is another. You are spending 20% of your time dealing with loop overhead.

The compiler can't get rid of that, but you know more about the situation. You have more context about what your code is trying to do. For example, you know that there are an even number of bytes (because you made it that way). There is no need to check the loop on every pass, only on every other pass:

```
void LcdWriteBuffer(uint16_t* buffer, uint16_t bufLength){

    // Use a buffer of bytes. This works only if your endian-ness
    // is correct.
    uint8_t *byteBuffer = (uint8_t *) buffer;
    bufLength = bufLength*2;


    IoClear(LCD_SELECT_N);          // select the chip
    while (bufLength) {
      IoWriteBusByte(LCD_BUS, *byteBuffer);
      byteBuffer++;
      IoWriteBusByte(LCD_BUS, *byteBuffer);
      byteBuffer++;
      bufLength--;
    }
    IoSet(LCD_SELECT_N)             // deselect the chip
}
```

Now, if this loop previously took 10 instructions to write a 16-bit pixel, now it will run in 8. We've eliminated an increment to bufLength and a check against zero for a 20% improvement (yay us!). This process of loop unrolling reduces the number of iterations by duplicating code inside a loop. Improvements that large are not usually so cheap. Now we look back to IoWriteBusByte as the largest consumer of cycles in the loop, even as a macro. We'll stop here because, as noted earlier, it accesses variables in another file, so it is a more egregious modification with respect to maintaining modularity.

Why don't I care about removing the bufLength multiplication at the top of the function? For the same reason I never mentioned breaking modularity to reduce IoClear and IoSet. Reducing the code outside the loop is much, much less important because it runs only once (or once per function call).

When you are optimizing, focus on the loops and the repeated actions.

When I introduced the LCD function, I mentioned the screen was 240 × 320 pixels. Could you have a single function write out a whole screen's worth of data without any conditionals? Of course. And it would be faster than having conditionals. However, you'll be sad when you've lost count after pasting the 12,243rd instance of:

```
IoWriteBusByte(LCD_BUS, *byteBuffer); byteBuffer++;
```

Worse, when you compile, you may find that all those repeated instructions come with a cost: code space.

Explaining Optimization to a Business Major

Ultimately, optimization is an economics problem. You start out with a portfolio of assets associated with your system. The major ones are the RAM, processor cycles, and code space. You may also have some auxiliary assets in power consumption and peripheral support on your processor. Your most liquid asset is development time, so think of that as money. Once you invest (or allocate) these assets to parts of the system, you lose the opportunity to use them in other subsystems.

If the set of investments you initially selected does not deliver the expected returns, you might partially recoup the spent resources, but to do so you will need to sink more development time into the project. As you go further along the development path, switching the allocations becomes more and more costly (and less and less possible). Making the right call at the start of the design process can mean the difference between buying at the bottom of the market and losing your shirt.

In order to make strategic trades that are truly beneficial, you need to understand your resources in terms of the assets and debts. Unfortunately, the system portfolio is not yet a slick, prepared prospectus that comes in the mail. An accurate, precise understanding of it takes a lot of time (aka money). Estimation can suffice for certain areas; others require in-depth investigation (profiling).

Your system's assets are somewhat fungible. For instance, you can trade RAM for processor cycles or code space (you will need some development time to facilitate the transaction). Sometimes you don't have to trade anything, and spending more development time will reduce your debt load. However, the total amount of any resource is fixed, and a resource can become so scarce that any amount of development time (and assets) will fail to produce any more of it.

As you consider different optimization strategies, consider as well the high opportunity cost that comes with investing your assets. Buying futures is almost always cheaper than buying stock. Similarly, selecting resources at the design phase is cheaper than waiting until the last minute and realizing you are seriously in debt with no easy way to recover.

(Thanks to Jane Muschenetz for helping with the business side of this analogy!)

Lookup tables

Nothing is ever free in optimization. Even turning on the compiler optimizations takes development time because the debugger no longer works as it did. When you step through line by line, the debugger won't show you most of the variables (the ones the compiler removed), and it jumps around (because the compiler rearranged the assembly instructions).

Loop unrolling trades code space for speed. Using a macro instead of a function also trades code space for speed. These trades go either way, so if you need more code space, you may want to roll up any loops and eliminate macros.

There is another trade-off between cycles and code space (or RAM) that goes beyond macros: lookup tables. These store the values needed for operations on a particular parameter. When the running code needs the information, instead of performing calculations, it finds the result in the table, often with a simple index.

For a simple example, if you need to transform the 128 ASCII characters into their Unicode equivalents, you can put them in a table to look up the result. Lookup tables go far beyond this, though. Many complex algorithms (e.g., encryption's AES) have two implementations: a fast, large one that uses lookup tables and a slow, small one that computes the values it needs. (Generating lookup tables to reduce math overhead is covered in gory detail in Chapter 12.)

Lookup tables can be code-based (where the values are calculated at or before compilation) or RAM-based. The latter are useful if your RAM access is fast (fewer wait states), or you have plenty of RAM but not enough code space (calculate the table on initialization). They can also be useful if your lookup values need to change when circumstances change (e.g., a networking router's lookup tables change when a different protocol is needed).

The compiler may create a lookup table when you use a switch statement in place of an if-else. Looking at your assembly code will tell you whether it has (and whether it is a savings to you).

Coding in assembly language

Looking at your assembly code is an important part of optimizing. Even if you don't start out knowing the meaning of the instructions in your assembly language, following along in the debugger for critical functions will help you figure out what the processor is really doing. Once you understand that, you may be able to tweak your high-level language code to help the compiler do something more efficiently.

That said, your time is valuable. *Don't program in assembly language.* Really, it isn't a good idea. The resulting code is usually a mess and almost always easier to redo from scratch than it is to maintain, even by the original programmer. That isn't to say it is easy to rewrite, just that it can be impossible to read. Maintenance of assembly code tends to be in the form of major refactoring (aka rewriting it all and fixing the old bugs, but indubitably writing new ones).

However, if you have a function that really, really needs to be superfast and the compiler is clearly not doing all it can, well, programming in assembly can be kind of fun, in a furtive playing-Tetris-at-work sort of way.

Start off with the high-level code. Understand the assembly generated by the compiler. Next, turn on optimizations and really understand the new assembly generated by the compiler. You are smarter than the compiler, and you have more system knowledge. But the compiler almost certainly knows the assembly language better than you do. Let it show you what it thinks is important before you start tweaking the assembly that the compiler generates.

That is the big secret: don't start with a blank slate. Start with the assembly your compiler gives you and go from there. Paste the equivalent high-level code into the assembly code as comments so that your future self can remember the goal of each section.

Summary

I can't provide a comprehensive list of optimization techniques. They depend on your processor and your compiler. Even more importantly, they depend on your requirements and your available resources. I can say that if you've gotten to the end of the project and are looking for cheap ways to reduce your code by 40%, you have seriously misjudged the capacity of your hardware resources. But I've made that mistake, too.

Optimization starts with a good design, preferably one with a little extra overhead just in case the future features turn out to be larger, slower, and more RAM-intensive than you'd planned. Even at the end of the project, you need a few spare resources to fix bugs and respond to hardware changes.

 In medical and safety-related products, that margin needs to be larger. Recompiling the code is a paperwork-intensive process, even for a minor one-line change. If you end up changing 50 lines because you need one more byte of RAM or just a few more processor cycles to implement the change, the paperwork and testing grows exponentially.

Although there is some fun to be had in reducing the resources as far as possible, you'll get diminishing returns. The first 10% of improvement shouldn't be too difficult, but the next 10% will probably take twice as long (and so on). Start with a goal, and don't optimize much beyond there.

There are trade-offs in optimization. You can share resources between subsystems, but every time you do that, your product becomes a little less robust and a little more fragile for the next person to modify. There is something incredibly embarrassing about handing a project off to another team and explaining that they should never change subsystem X, because it will change the very precise timing of subsystem Y.

A better way of utilizing development time is to look for ways to optimize using well-understood algorithms. Keep reading books (and blogs) for ways to solve common (and not-so-common) problems. A proven algorithm is well worth the time invested. Instead of inventing the wheel all over again, you can refine someone else's.

One last point: many times, the tuning of the system is left to the end of the development cycle, even after the first testing has completed. I've heard that this is done on the theory that the features should work before they get tuned. The process of keeping the system within its resources should be planned for and maintained during system development. Introducing complex changes right before you ship a product will lead to an unstable system. Balance the risk of making a premature optimization (e.g., reading all of your assembly list code looking for ways the compiler could have reduced a single instruction) against the benefit of making an optimization early so it can be tested thoroughly and have an impact on other design considerations.

Further Reading

Have you ever done something that pleases you whenever you look at it? Well, I gave a talk about memory maps (*https://embedded.fm/blog/mapfiles*) that makes me happy. The talk and the graphics I created make me laugh. I'd love to share it with you.

Although I have attempted to give you some tools to take care of the largest problems, there are almost always ways to squeak out a little bit more. For more optimization techniques, look at your processor vendor's application notes and your compiler manual. Atmel has a particularly good application note for one of their 8-bit processors: *AVR035: Efficient C Coding for AVR* (*https://oreil.ly/R-uM1*).

Another great resource showing how to wring the most out of your limited resources is the Stanford Graphics Bithacks site (*https://oreil.ly/__M8F*). It shows how different algorithms can be implemented with different resources.

Small Memory Software (*https://oreil.ly/z4yqW*) by Charles Wier and James Noble describes design patterns that are specific to systems with memory constraints. Many of the patterns are tactical (using bitmasks in a structure, having client functions handle the memory in interfaces, implementing memory pools, and so on). While showing its age with discussions of operating systems from long ago, the tips on reducing memory usage are still relevant. The book is free and online.

To compare how these different implementations work (or different versions of your own implementation), take a look at Compiler Explorer (*https://godbolt.org*), also known as Godbolt, as it is named after its creator Matt Godbolt. This web tool lets you compile functions and see the assembly output. Many compilers and languages are supported. The assembly is documented and interspersed with the code. The goal is to let you see how your coding choices affect your assembly. It is a growing tool with ever-expanding features.

Interview Question: Reverse Bits in a Byte

Start by reversing the bits in a byte using limited memory. Once you've finished, modify the code to be as fast as possible (but without the memory limitation).

In an interview setting, I don't mind if the interviewee starts out slowly with a simple solution. Optimization should take a backseat to correctness:

```
uint8_t SwapBitsInByte(uint8_t input) {
  uint8_t output=0;
  for (uint8_t i = 0; i < 8; i++) { // for every bit in the byte
    if (input & (1 << i)) { // need to set the bit in the output
      output |= 1 << (7-i);
    }
  }
  return output;
}
```

Generally, I don't look for syntax during interviews (that is what compilers are for). However, in this problem, parentheses are important, because the bit-shift operator has lower precedence than addition or subtraction. If the interviewee has missed this, I'd ask about operator precedence. Not everyone has that memorized, though it can cause havoc in your code if you get it wrong (might as well use parentheses everywhere, just to be safe).

Ideally, the programmer should check their own code, running through it with a couple of values to make sure that following the instructions works. Like mental unit tests, I like to see the interviewee do this as they write the code (or even before).

When I look at the solution, naming is important, for both function names and variable names. Comments are nice as long as they are useful ("// set the bit in the output" might be useful on an `if` statement, but it probably isn't on the line that actually sets the bit).

Using variables to implement the problem is a good start to the solution, although there is a straightforward way to do it with one variable (by unrolling the loop). If the candidate mentions that both variables (and the input parameter) are likely to be in registers, I can point out that the use of an extra register probably meant some other variable got pushed onto the stack. Despite the correction, the interviewee gets a lot of points for the observation.

As for the second part of the problem, I don't know many people who have successfully worked out the problem in an interview situation. It is one of those tricks that you just need to know: use a lookup table. If you can allocate 256 bytes (in RAM memory or in code space, whichever is faster), to quickly find the reverse of a byte, all you need to do is use the value of the byte as a lookup into the array of bytes:

```
uint8_t SwapBitInByte(uint8_t input) {
    const uint8_t lookup_table[256] = {0x00, 0x80, 0x40, 0xC0... 0x7F, 0xFF};
```

```
        return lookup_table[input];
    }
```

This technique is often used in embedded situations when the system has more code space than time. I hope that by this point the interviewee has mentioned that they'd look up the algorithm to make sure they had a reasonably optimal solution for the design constraints.

There is a more optimal solution to the first part of the question. Instead of reversing the bits one after another using a temporary variable, the code can reverse the bits pairwise, then reverse the pairs, then reverse the nibbles, all without a temporary variable (and I suspect one fewer register can be used):

```
    uint8_t SwapBitInByte(uint8_t val) {
        val = ( ( val & 0x55 ) << 1 ) | ( ( val & 0xAA ) >> 1 );
        val = ( ( val & 0x33 ) << 2 ) | ( ( val & 0xCC ) >> 2 );
        val = ( ( val & 0x0F ) << 4 ) | ( ( val & 0xF0 ) >> 4 );
        return val;
    }
```

I would not expect an interview candidate to come up with this on their feet. I had to adapt it from *Hacker's Delight* by Henry S. Warren (Addison-Wesley). On the other hand, now I'm tempted to make future interviewees explain what the code does (and how to make it faster, hoping they will come up with a lookup table).

CHAPTER 12

Math

When we looked at trading resources in the last chapter, you had to choose between RAM, code space, and processing cycles. Trading these resources goes only so far. Sometimes you need to make your code go faster. Not knowing what you'll need for your system, I can still guess that you'll need to implement some math (because that is where processors excel).

The less your system does, the fewer resources it needs to do it. Sometimes we confuse accuracy, which is important, with precision, which can go too far. If you can quantify the range of data you expect and your error budget, there are some useful methods to reduce unnecessary precision for all sorts of algorithms, thereby saving RAM and processing cycles.

Accuracy Versus Precision

Accuracy is a measure of how correct you are. *Precision* is how many digits you show in your answer. Both have degrees to them; one answer can be more accurate and/or more precise than another. A really accurate answer knows its limitations. For example, what is the mass of an electron?

Mass of an electron	Is it accurate?	Is it precise?
12.12345124 kg	No	Stupidly so
10^{-30} kg	Far more so than 12 kg, and accurate enough for most conversations	No
9.109×10^{-31} kg	Even more so	Yes
$9.1090000001 \times 10^{-31}$ kg	Same accuracy as the previous answer	Uselessly so
$(9.1092 +/- 0.0002) \times 10^{-31}$ kg	Yes, best answer yet	Yes

Precision can be noise. If the extra bits of precision don't mean anything, they can needlessly complicate your system, use precious RAM, and waste processor cycles. As you implement complex algorithms and perform mathematics on your data, you need to determine just how much precision is required to maintain sufficient accuracy for your product.

Identifying Fast and Slow Operations

Optimizing your system to do its mathematical operations quickly requires you to understand a bit more about your compiler and processor. Once you understand which operations occur quickly (and which ones take up one line of code but compile to use two libraries and an absurd amount of processing), you'll have a basis for optimizing your system.

So, addition and subtraction are fast. Shifting bits is usually fast. Division is very slow. Anything with floating-point is dead slow, unless you have a floating-point unit (FPU).

What about multiplication? On a DSP, it is fast: multiply and add form a single instruction (MAC, for multiply-accumulate). On a non-DSP (e.g., an Arm or your PC), multiplication falls between addition and division, but closer to addition.

 For many processors, division isn't built into the hardware, unlike the other arithmetic operators. On those processors, the divide operator calls a library function—usually a pretty large one, as you can tell by looking in your map file.

Just because an operation can be described in one line of code doesn't mean it takes a short time to run on the processor. Chapter 7 mentioned that modulo math was useful for circular buffers. It is also useful if you want to do something on every nth pass of a loop:

```
for (i=0; i<100; i++) {
  if ((i%10) == 0) {
    printf("%d percent done.", i);
  }
}
```

However, that %10 is actually a hidden division, a relatively costly instruction (though nowhere near the processing cost of printf—but that is another story). If you make the interval a power of two, you can replace the modulo math with a cheap (single-instruction) bitwise logic operation (take a look at "Representing Signed Numbers" on page 205 for the reason why):

```
for (i=0; i<100; i++) {
  if (!(i & 0x07)) { // this will print out every 8th pass
    printf("%d percent done.", i);
  }
}
```

In general, shifting bits takes a single processor cycle when the number of bits to shift is a constant. It is a cheap way to do division and multiplication if you can keep your constants to a power of two so that an integer shift can replace the arithmetic operation. (We discuss this one later in a lot more detail in "Fake Floating-Point Numbers" on page 345.)

Using constants is faster than using variables. But they need to be real constants (#define in the C language), not constant variables (const), which most compilers load into registers instead of putting the number in the assembly file. Now you know why embedded system programmers are still addicted to ugly #define statements.

There are a ton of these rules, and you'll learn them with time. Once you get a feel for the details of your processor and compiler, much of it is common sense, considering what your system really needs and how to implement it. Let's take a look at a common system example to see how different choices can change an algorithm.

Taking an Average

For many signals, you'll need to calculate the average (aka mean) and standard deviation. Sometimes that is your output. Sometimes it is just a sanity check to make sure your signal hasn't gotten overly corrupted by noise.

With a rolling N-point average, you calculate the average of the last N points. You don't even need to add them all up and divide each time; you can add the new point and subtract the oldest (like a FIFO):

```
newAverage = lastAverage + (newSample/length) - (oldestSample/length);
```

However, you have to perform division at every step. And if you are averaging over a large number of small-valued samples, this division may truncate the result and give you an inaccurate average (take a look at the sidebar "The Downside of Integer Math" on page 328).

The other downside to a rolling average is that you need to keep the sample buffer intact until the oldest sample leaves the average. If the average is calculated over a large number of samples, this could be a big RAM buffer.

Instead of jumping into optimization, take a step back and consider the needs of the system. Do you *need* a new average value at every time step? Or can you use the same value for a period of time? If the latter, you might be able to implement a block average instead of a rolling average. In a block average, you accumulate a number of samples until you need the average, then restart the calculation:

```
struct sAve {
  int32_t blockSum;
  uint16_t numSamples;
};
void ClearAverage(struct sAve *ave) {
  ave->blockSum = 0;
  ave->numSamples = 0;
}
void AddSampleToAverage(struct sAve *ave, int16_t newSample) {
  ave->blockSum += newSample;
  ave->numSamples++;
}
int16_t GetAverage(struct sAve *ave) {
  int16_t average = ave->blockSum/ave->numSamples;
  ClearAverage(ave);
  return average;
}
```

Figure 12-1 shows a set of samples with the rolling average (over five samples) and the block average (also over five samples). Note that each time the block average changes, it is the same as the rolling average result at that point. The rolling average changes faster, so it is a more accurate representation of the data during the other four time steps. If you need the average only at every fifth (or hundredth) time step, the block average is just as accurate as the rolling average, but at a much lower cost in terms of RAM and processor cycles.

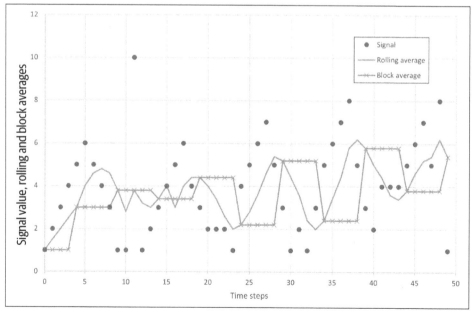

Figure 12-1. While a rolling average tracks each sample, the block average stays constant for several samples.

Different Averages: Cumulative and Median

There is a way to do a rolling average that doesn't require a RAM buffer and constantly recalculating the sum: a cumulative average treats all past values as equal to
the mean. Each new value is calculated with:

```
int16_t UpdatedCumulativeAverage(int16_t prevAve, int16_t newSample,
                                 int16_t numSamples)
{
  int32_t sum = (numSamples-1) * prevAve;
  sum += newSample;
  return (sum/numSamples);
}
```

While not exactly the arithmetic mean, it is usually very close, as shown in
Figure 12-2. It tends to be slightly less responsive to sudden changes in signal, moving more slowly than the rolling average.

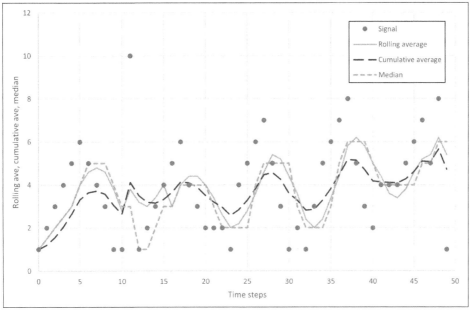

*Figure 12-2. The rolling average represents the 5-point arithmetic mean of the signal. The
cumulative average is much simpler to calculate. The median takes more computation to
calculate but is resistant to glitches.*

Another averaging method is the *median*, where the goal is to take the midpoint
value. This removes outliers and temporary glitches in the data (like that value 10 in
sample data in Figure 12-2). However, this requires ordering the data and selecting
the middle, something that requires more RAM (keeping all the data around) and
more processing (sorting is far more expensive than adding and subtracting). On the

other hand, if you have an ADC that glitches every once in a while due to radio inter-ference, median filters are great, just keep them small, in the 3 or 5 point range.

The Downside of Integer Math

What is 4/4? 1. Excellent. What is 5/4? Um, according to the processor, that is still 1. As are 6/4 and 7/4. Integer division truncates the number, like running the `floor()` function on a floating-point number. It can lead to serious trouble.

For example, what if you optimized the rolling average to avoid an unnecessary division:

```
newAverage = lastAverage + ((newSample- oldestSample)/length);
```

If your samples are all about the same, your average will be horribly incorrect.

Figure 12-3 shows three different forms of the rolling average. First is the floating-point version, which tracks the signal reasonably well (though it is slightly delayed, of course). Next is the sample implementation, but with integer truncation, as the oldest and newest samples are divided individually by the length. It tracks reasonably well, but you can see some inaccuracies. Finally comes the implementation I just showed with truncation. It saves a costly division step, but the result is junk.

You want to save resources but not generate junk.

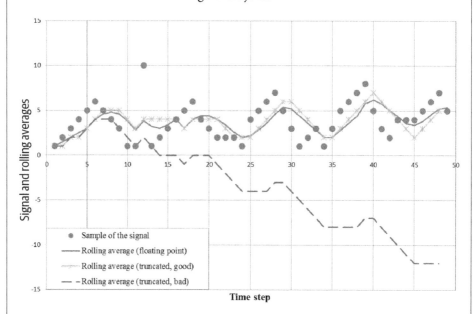

Figure 12-3. Truncation failure in rolling average.

The solution is easy to state: large values should be divided by much smaller ones; they shouldn't be similar in magnitude.

Implementing this solution is more difficult than stating it. If you know that you are going to have the problem, you can choose to increase the magnitude of your numerator (that is, multiply every sample by some fixed constant). To take the average, multiplying by any constant greater than the number of samples in the average will suffice. That would be fine in our case. The resulting average will be off by that amount, so if you need to retrieve the actual value, you will need to divide by the multiplication factor later. If you're just comparing values, you never need to divide, because their relative values are correct.

You can choose any constant, as long as you don't multiply the samples to the point where they are too big to fit in their variables. While division can cause underflow, multiplication can cause overflow, which also results in odd behavior. That means you need to know the range you are expecting to receive. Using your knowledge of your system to optimize it is very useful, but it can lead to a brittle system where seemingly minor changes (e.g., the input range changing by 10%) lead to errors.

Thus, the downside to integer math is that you need to know and depend upon a range of input values so that you can make sure your accuracy is not degraded by the lack of precision.

Using an Existing Algorithm

Now that you have a bit of a feel for what is fast (addition, shifting, and maybe multiplication), I'm going to share the most important thing to do when you need to implement an algorithm using minimal resources: look it up. If it is a standard algorithm, search online or pull out a numerical recipes book. If someone has already put in the time and effort of explaining how to reduce the processing cycles or the RAM usage, use their work. Make sure you pay attention to copyrights, but most instructional materials exist so someone will use them. There is a lot to be found online about optimizing some algorithms, but some of the trusted resources described in "Further Reading" on page 352 are worth having on your bookshelf when you need them.

There are probably several ways to implement an algorithm, but only one or two will save the resources you need to preserve. For example, let's look at *standard deviation*.

The standard deviation (σ) is how far the samples in a set vary from the average of the same set. The standard deviation is calculated using each sample in the group (x_i), the mean or average of the group (x_{mean}), and the number of samples in the set (N), as shown in the equations in Equation 12-1 (though it is unintuitive, the two equations shown are equivalent).

Equation 12-1. Two equivalent equations for calculation of standard deviation

$$\sigma = \sqrt{\frac{1}{N}\sum_{i=1}^{N}\left(x_i - x_{mean}\right)^2}$$

$$\sigma = \sqrt{\frac{1}{N}\sum_{i=1}^{N}\left(x_i^2\right) - x_{mean}^2}$$

How do you make this friendly for your embedded system? Well, take the square root piece first. The simple answer is to not perform the square root. Although it changes the value of the result, it doesn't change the information it gives you about how much the samples vary. Since many people do this, the un-square-rooted standard deviation is called the *variance*.[1]

(Think of how many processing cycles we've already saved by redefining the goal!)

We can start by implementing the variance pretty much as it is in the equation:

```
floatGetVariance(int16_t* samples, uint16_t numSamples, int16_t mean) {
  uint32_t sumSquares = 0;
  int32_t tmp;
  uint32_t i;

  for (i = 0; i < numSamples; i++) {
    tmp = samples[i] - mean;
    sumSquares += tmp*tmp;
  }
  return ((float) sumSquares / numSamples);
}
```

Note that the mean was passed into the function. It has already been calculated for this block. Another piece of code has already looked at each of the samples, so this function is a second pass through the data. In addition to the inefficiency of running through the loop twice, you have to keep all of the data around in a buffer, which is probably a waste of RAM.

However, like the block average, you can calculate variance as you go along, which is shown more clearly by the second equation in Equation 12-1. Note that the block average happens for free in this variance calculation:

---

1 If you aren't familiar with the definition of variance (or any mathematical operation), look it up. Wikipedia (*https://en.wikipedia.org/wiki/Variance*) is a great place to start. There is also a page (Algorithms for calculating variance (*https://en.wikipedia.org/wiki/Algorithms_for_calculating_variance*)) covering different implementation techniques, including those described here.

```
struct sVar {
  int32_t sum;
  uint64_t sumSquares;
  uint16_t numSamples;
};
void AddSampleToVariance (struct sVar *var, int16_t newSample) {
  var->sum += newSample;
  var->sumSquares += newSample*newSample;
  var->numSamples++;
}
float GetVariance(struct sVar *var, float *average) {
  float variance;
  *average = (float) var->sum / var->numSamples;
  variance = (var->sumSquares - (var->sum * (*average)))
                       / (var->numSamples-1);
  return variance;
}
```

There is one problem with this implementation: the variable sumSquares can get
quite large (even sum can get pretty large when you have many samples). Instead of
the signed 16-bit samples in the code, let's say the function used signed 8-bit samples.
If you have two samples, each with a value of 127, your sumSquares would be
32,258—almost 15 bits. By the time you had five samples at the maximum value,
you'd need 17 bits to hold sumSquares, which means moving up to a 32-bit variable.
If you are using 16-bit values, the sumSquares needs to be a 64-bit variable. Using
large variables takes RAM and processing cycles.

That wouldn't happen in the two-pass implementation because the subtraction of
mean from each sample keeps the sum of squares reasonably small. However, there is
a way to do it without using a large intermediate variable and without taking two
passes at the data:

```
struct sVar {
  int16_t mean;
  int32_t M2;
  uint16_t numSamples;
};
void AddSampleToVariance(struct sVar *var, int16_t newSample) {
  int16_t delta = newSample - var->mean;
  var->numSamples++;
  var->mean += delta/var->numSamples;
  var->M2 += delta * (newSample - var->mean); // uses the new mean
}
uint16_t GetVariance(struct sVar *var, int16_t *average) {
  uint16_t variance = var->M2/var->numSamples;
  *average = var->mean; // running average already calculated
  // get ready for the next block
  var->numSamples =0; var->mean = 0; var->M2 = 0;
  return variance;
}
```

I don't think I would have come up with that on my own, especially when I was focused on building a way to see how much the samples in my system varied from the mean. Even Donald E. Knuth credits an article by another author (B. P. Welford).

Let's look at the code in more detail. To store the intermediate variable for the variance, you only need a variable that is double the size of your sample (so if your sample is 8 bits, M2 can be 16 bits). This method lets you use a variable that is the same size as your data to store the mean (as opposed to the earlier `sum` variable, which depended on the number of samples). However, the code is less legible, and if you change the order of the lines in `AddSampleToVariance`, it will break. It also does a division operation on every pass; and worse, the division to calculate `mean` can cause problems because `delta` is likely to be small—so small that integer truncation may lead to means of zero.

Yes, everything has consequences. Sometimes trying to save processor cycles is like trying to hold on tightly to a balloon; the more you grip it, the more some other area will poke out between your fingers. If you stick to a well-understood algorithm, there is a good chance that the failure analysis will be done for you already.

If you really need to know the standard deviation (instead of the variance), there are many methods of approximating the square root. More than 10 are listed on the "Methods of Computing Square Roots" Wikipedia page (*https://en.wikipedia.org/wiki/Methods_of_computing_square_roots*). Choose one or two, and then use your profiling tools to compare them with your compiler's math library.

Designing and Modifying Algorithms

Sometimes your algorithm goes beyond simple math and yet isn't something you find as a recipe in a book. There are many tips for implementing different processor-intensive operations. If you learn some of the building blocks, you can optimize for yourself. As with cooking, the more recipes you know, the more likely your modifications will succeed.

Factor Polynomials

Say you have something that can be implemented as:

```
y = A*x + B*x + C*x;
```

That is three multiplications and two additions. If you factor your polynomial, you can do it in two additions and one multiplication:

```
y = (A + B + C)*x;
```

Much better. Let's take a nonlinear example and use factoring to simplify the processing load. It is a matter of turning the polynomial inside out:

```
A*x³+B*x²+Cx   ==>   ((Ax+B)x+C)x
```

On the left, if you had cubed x and multiplied it by A, and so on, you would have done nine multiplications and two additions. If you go the other way, the same answer arrives in three multiplications and two additions. How you frame a polynomial is very important to minimizing processing cycles.[2]

Taylor Series

Polynomials are important because they constitute one way to model complex steps in your algorithm. A *Taylor series* represents a function as a sum of infinite terms. It works for most functions, including trigonometric (sine, cosine, tangent, arcsine, etc.), more difficult polynomials (x^{-1}), square root, and logarithms. As more terms in the infinite series are added, the result becomes more precise (and more accurate). And you can turn that around: you don't need infinitely many terms to generate an accurate enough answer for your function.

Creating a Taylor series for a generic polynomial is a fair bit of math, beyond the scope of this book (much more than the slight trickery of Horner's scheme). However, you can look algorithms up easily. For example, the sine function can be replaced with its Taylor series expansion (see Equation 12-2).

Equation 12-2. Sine function in Taylor series, rearranged via Horner's scheme

$$\sin(x) \approx x - \frac{x^3}{3!} + \frac{x^5}{5!} - \frac{x^7}{7!} + \cdots$$

$$\sin(x) \approx x = Ax^3 + Bx^5 - Cx^7, \text{where } A = \frac{1}{3!}, B = \frac{1}{5!}, C = \frac{1}{7!}$$

$$\sin(x) \approx x\left(1 - x^2\left(A + x^2\left(B - Cx^2\right)\right)\right)$$

$$\sin(x) \approx x\left(1 - x^2\left(\frac{1}{3!} + x^2\left(\frac{1}{5!} - \frac{1}{7!}x^2\right)\right)\right)$$

All angles in this section are represented in radians. Remember that π radians = 180°.

For the Taylor series with four terms, the error for the argument values between π and $-\pi$ is small (0.000003). If this error is still too large, you can add the next term in

---

2 This method is called *Horner's scheme* and was developed by mathematician William George Horner.

the Taylor series for more accuracy ($+x^9/9!$). Or if you can deal with a larger margin of error (particularly at the edges of $+/-\pi$), you can use fewer terms.

 Physicists often stop at the first term, approximating $\sin(x)=x$. The closer x is to 0, the better this works.

As before, to really optimize, you need to understand your input and the acceptable error of your system. If your input is in the range of -0.2π to 0.2π and you need an accuracy of 10%, you can use the physicists' approximation. Or if you need an error of less than 1%, you can use two terms of the Taylor expansion. A Taylor series lets you balance the processing power with the accuracy required by your application (see Figure 12-4).

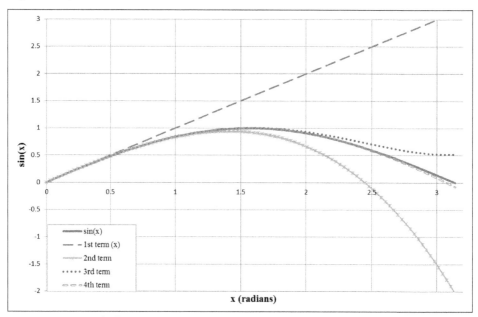

Figure 12-4. Graph showing accuracy of different numbers of terms for the sine Taylor series.

Because they use just multiplications and additions, Taylor series are relatively light in processor intensity. Putting in constants and using Horner's method, we can implement four terms of sine (in floating-point) as:

```
xSq = x*x;
sinX = x * (1 - xSq * (INVERSE_THREE_FACTORIAL + xSq *
        (INVERSE_FIVE_FACTORIAL - INVERSE_SEVEN_FACTORIAL * xSq)));
```

```
// or taking it apart and writing multiple steps, starting with
// the end and moving toward the front:
tmp = - INVERSE_SEVEN_FACTORIAL * xSq;
tmp = xSq * (INVERSE_FIVE_FACTORIAL + tmp);
tmp = xSq * (-INVERSE_THREE_FACTORIAL + tmp);
sinX = x * (1 - tmp);
```

Why does this have to be floating-point? Because INVERSE_THREE_FACT and the other constants need to be between zero and one. However, there are ways to avoid this problem.

Dividing by a Constant

Division is a relatively costly arithmetic step. But when you divide by a constant, there are ways of cheating. Using sine's Taylor series for an example, let's say you need to divide by 3!. That is $3 \times 2 \times 1 = 6$. Well, that won't be too difficult:

```
uint16_t DivideThreeFactorial(uint16_t input) {
  const uint16_t denominator = 6;
  return input/denominator;
}
```

For now, let's not worry about x being between $+/-\pi$. Instead we'll take a larger number to play with. If the input is 245, the result will be 40 in integer math (245 / 6 = 40.833 in floating-point). I'm not yet concerned about the truncation here, just about the division operation. Is there a way to make it faster?

A shift is much faster. Sadly, six is not a power of two. However, there are other ways of formulating the number 1/6, such as 2/12, etc. What we want is a multiplier/power-of-two that is equivalent to 1/6 (0.166667), at least within some small amount of error. Then we can multiply the numerator by the input and shift the result to finish the division. We'll trade division for a multiplication and shift. Table 12-1 shows some multipliers with their power-of-two divisors and resultant errors.

Table 12-1. Approximating 1/6 with a power-of-two divisor

Multiplier	Divisor	Equivalent shift	Result	% Error
1	6	None	0.166666667	0
3	16	4	0.1875	12.5
5	32	5	0.15625	6.2
11	64	6	0.171875	3.1
21	128	7	0.164063	1.5
43	256	8	0.167969	0.78
85	512	9	0.166016	0.39
171	1,024	10	0.166992	0.19

Multiplier	Divisor	Equivalent shift	Result	% Error
341	2,048	11	0.166504	0.09
683	4,096	12	0.166748	0.04

Note that the errors in the table are halved for every additional shift. So if you implement a function to divide by 3!, it could look like this:

```
#define DIVIDE_THREE_FACT_MULT 171
#define DIVIDE_THREE_FACT_SHIFT 10

int16_t DivideThreeFactorial(int16_t input) {
  int32_t tmp = input* DIVIDE_THREE_FACT_MULT;
  return (tmp >> DIVIDE_THREE_FACT_SHIFT);
}
```

The input and output are 16 bits, but a 32-bit variable is necessary to hold the multiplication result. Even using a larger temporary variable, this function is cheaper than division. Probably.

 If you don't do the final shift, the result can be more precise than the truncated division. You'll need to remember that the value is multiplied by 1,024 when you use it.

However, there is a big downside to this implementation: you need to know the divisor ahead of time to construct the function. Although this method is useful any time you need to divide by a constant, it isn't generic enough to get rid of all division.

Scaling the Input

The sine function takes an input from −π to π and outputs a value from -1 to 1. That is all pretty difficult to do if you are avoiding floating-point numbers. However, you can multiply everything by a constant to get more granularity than an integer implements. For example, if you want to get rid of floating-point numbers in the sine function, you can change the input to the range $+/-(1,024*\pi)$ and compensate for getting an output that is too great by a factor of 1,024.

For mathematical operations where $f(Ax) = Af(x)$, optimization is as simple as using the scaled input. Even for functions that are $f(Ax) = f(A)f(x)$, removing the scalar is straightforward: divide by $f(A)$. However, the sine function doesn't fit this criteria; there is no easy way to remove a scalar.

Instead, we'll need to make sure that each term of the Taylor expansion is multiplied by 1,024 once and only once. That means any time x is multiplied by x, we need to divide by 1,024 so that our scale factor doesn't get squared along with the input value:

```
xSq = (x*x) >> 10;   // right-shift by 10 is equal to divide by 1,024
tmp = - DivideSevenFactorial(xSq);
tmp = (xSq * (INVERSE_FIVE_FACTORIAL + tmp)) >> 10;
tmp = (xSq * (-INVERSE_THREE_FACTORIAL + tmp)) >> 10;
sinX = x - ((x * tmp)>>10);
```

The great news here is that with the scaling, the division at some of the steps becomes easier. Everything must be multiplied, including the constants. Instead of multiplying by 1/3! (essentially dividing by 6), we are multiplying by 1,024/3!, which is approximately 171. Since 5! is 120, there is more error when rounding 1,024/120 to 8 (8.533). The last term (7! = 5,040) is still large, so it requires some actual division, though still dividing by a constant. Because it is a small constant, there is some error associated with it, as shown in Figure 12-5.

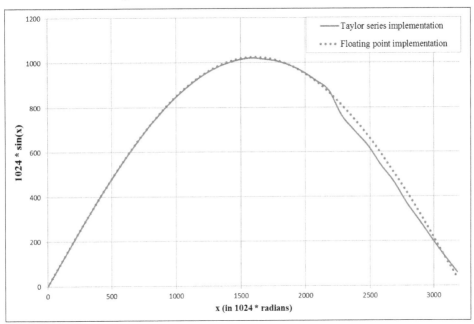

Figure 12-5. Errors in scaling the input with a Taylor series (0 to π).

There are ways to alleviate these errors (such as scaling by a larger number). As you are implementing your changes, you will need to understand where error comes into the system. As with profiling, the bulk of your time should be spent on the sources of the largest error, not optimizing a minor contributor.

These ideas of scaling and division by shifting are common in fixed-point math. They are going to help us create a method to avoid floating-point numbers entirely. Before we go there, let's look at a very popular way to save processor cycles.

Lookup Tables

As mentioned in Chapter 11 (and expounded on in the interview question), lookup tables are blazingly fast and just require a bit of code space.

However, to use a lookup table, you need to know the range of the input and the acceptable error. In Taylor expansions, these considerations drive the number of terms you calculate. In lookup tables, they determine the number of entries in your table.

Implicit input

Each entry in the lookup table requires two pieces of information: the input (x) and the output (y). However, not all lookup tables require both to be in the table. With implicit input lookup tables, the position in the array indicates the input value. For example, here is a sine lookup table with an input in milliradians ($-\pi/1,000$ to $+\pi/1,000$) and an output also scaled by 1,000. (Lookup tables reduce the need for shifts and therefore power-of-two operations, often leading to more human-readable scaling.)

```
const int16_t sinLookup[] = {
  -58,   // x =  -3200
  -335,  // x =  -2800
  -676,  // x =  -2400
  -910,  // x =  -2000
  -1000, // x =  -1600
  -933,  // x =  -1200
  -718,  // x =  -800
  -390,  // x =  -400
   0,    // x =  0
   389,  // x =  400
   717,  // x =  800
   932,  // x =  1200
   999,  // x =  1600
   909,  // x =  2000
   675,  // x =  2400
   334,  // x =  2800
  -59    // x =  3200
};
```

Where the Taylor expansion covered all possible inputs (even though I showed only 0 to π), this table covers only the range $-\pi$ to π. If you put in 2π for the Taylor expansion, it will work. That is not true for lookup tables; you have to know the range of your input.

To use the table, you'll need to calculate the index that matches your input. To do that, subtract the lowest value in the table and divide by the step size of the table:

```
uint8_t index = (x - (-3200))/400;
y = sinLookup[index];
```

Wait a minute, why are we killing ourselves optimizing a sine function if we are just going to do a division now? Right. The step size of the table not only changes the precision of your table, it can also change your processing requirements. The non-power-of-two step size was a bad choice. If we'd chosen 512, the table would be only a little bit smaller (less precise), but the processing would have been shorter:

```
uint8_t index = (x - (-3145))>>9; // use #defs, not magic numbers!
y = sinLookup[index];
```

Given only 13 entries, the table is not very precise, but will the results be accurate? Figure 12-6 shows points and where they'll land in this calculation. By default, the lookup results are offset (the triangles in the figure). The table would be more accurate if the lookup value covered the center of the range, as shown with the Xs. Either way, we get a stair-step approximation, but we can center the stairs on the goal output to reduce the error.

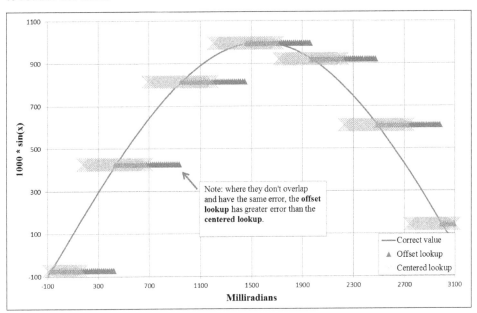

Figure 12-6. Comparing sine offset lookup table output with half-step centered lookup table output.

The table itself doesn't need to change to make this happen, just the indexing. In effect, we need to add half a step when calculating the index:

```
uint8_t index = (x - (-3145 - 256))>>9;
y = sinLookup[index];
```

This idea of adding a half step to center the result is prevalent in almost every well-implemented lookup table.

Once you change the valid range, I'd recommend making the comments describe the range as well as the value:

```
#define BASE_SIN_LOOKUP (-3124 - 256)
#define SHIFT_SIN_LOOKUP 9
const int16_t sinLookup[] = {
   3,    // x @ -3145, for range -3401  to  -2888
 -487,   // x @ -2633, for range -2889  to  -2376
 -853,   // x @ -2121, for range -2377  to  -1864
-1000,   // x @ -1609, for range -1865  to  -1352
 -890,   // x @ -1097, for range -1353  to  -840
 -553,   // x @ -585,  for range -841   to  -328
 -73,    // x @ -73,   for range -329   to  182
 425,    // x @ 493,   for range 183    to  695
 813,    // x @ 951,   for range 695    to  1207
 994,    // x @ 1463,  for range 1207   to  1719
 919,    // x @ 1975,  for range 1719   to  2231
 608,    // x @ 2487,  for range 2231   to  2743
 142,    // x @ 2999,  for range 2743   to  3255
};
```

Note that this new table has a step size of 512 and 13 entries. The values look like Figure 12-7. This table covers the expected input (−π to +π) and a little more besides. However, if there is a possibility of getting data outside the table's range, add code to verify the inputs. After all, if your input is 2π, your index will be 19, outside the range of the table. However, accessing sinLookup[19] may work in C/C++ but give you a completely incorrect result (or it may just crash the system).

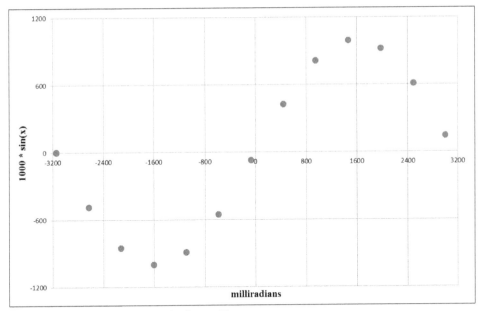

Figure 12-7. Points in the sine lookup table.

Linear interpolation

In the lookup table, even with the center biasing, there are times when your result should be more accurate than a single number covering a range of inputs. In that case, linear interpolation may be the way to go.

> You can use other interpolation methods. Consider the trade-offs between the increased computational requirements of a polynomial fit against the code space of putting in a larger table.

As shown in Figure 12-8, linear interpolation isn't hard; it's just a bit of algebra you might not have used for a while. You'll need two values from the lookup table: the one below the input you have and the one above. In the figure, the goal is to find the output for a particular value of x, so the two closest points are used. Since the input and output values are linked, for interpolation, I find it simpler to treat them as points instead of individual values:

```
struct sPoint {
    int16_t x;
    int16_t y
};
```

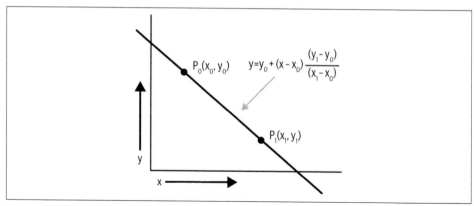

Figure 12-8. Linear interpolation.

The linear interpolation code is simple math; just be sure to keep the bits from over-flowing during the multiplication:

```
// This linear interpolation code does:
// y = p0.y + ((x-p0.x)*(p1.y-p0.y))/(p1.x-p0.x);
// but in a bit-safe way.
int16_t Interpolate(struct sPoint p0, struct sPoint p1, int16_t x) {
    int16_t y;
    int32_t tmp; // start and end with int16s,
                 // but can need a larger intermediate
    tmp = (x - p0.x);
    tmp *= (p1.y - p0.y);
    tmp /= (p1.x - p0.x);
    y = p0.y + tmp; // now safe to go back to 16 bits
    return (y);
}
```

This method works even when the input is not between the two points. If you end up with an input that is just outside your table, you can use the last two points in the table to interpolate past the end (though possibly with a degradation of accuracy).

Note that a division is used in linear interpolation. You are trading some processor cycles to get more accuracy with a smaller table size (code space). You can avoid division by making the size of the x-steps in the lookup table a power of two (as I did with the last sine lookup table). The divisor is then a power of two, so the divide can become a shift.

While the table lookup depends on the table itself, interpolation is a step away from that. When you optimize away the division, your interpolation function depends on the table data. If you have multiple tables, you'll need multiple interpolation functions (or a parameter to describe the shift value). Be careful, as it will make your code less readable, and linking data and code will make it more brittle. If you need the processing cycles, it may be the best way to conserve them. But it makes for awfully tangled code.

Explicit input in the table

For some functions, you can create a smaller or more accurate table by allowing variable step sizes, interpolating between them. The sine function is very linear toward the center, as seen in Figure 12-7. We could easily take out the three centermost points and let linear interpolation handle it (which is why sin(x) = x for small x is so popular). Even the outermost edges could have a sample removed; it is those tricky curves that need more points.

Sometimes a lookup table has a variable step size to decrease errors in certain areas. Linear interpolation can be used between the areas, as shown in Figure 12-9.

An explicit input lookup table is often used if you have to build the table from the environment, such as when calibrating a sensor for temperature effects. The x value would be the temperature read via a thermistor (aka temperature sensor), and the y value would be the offset from the expected value.

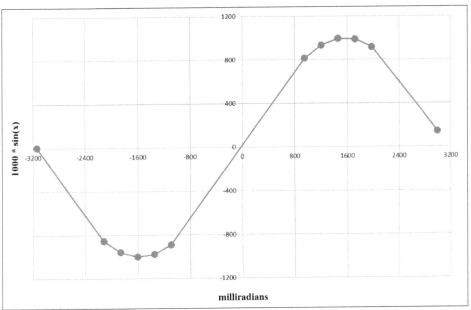

Figure 12-9. Using linear interpolation between points on an explicit lookup table.

The lookup table is now nearly double in size because we have to put in the start of the covered range as well as the value. It takes up more code space, but we gain accuracy in the areas we need it most:

```
struct sPoint sinLookup[] ={
  { -3145 , 3 },
  { -2121 , -853 },
  { -1865 , -958 },
  { -1609 , -1000 },
  { -1353 , -977 },
  { -1097 , -890 },
  { 951 , 813 },
  { 1207 , 934 },
  { 1463 , 994 },
  { 1719 , 989 },
  { 1975 , 919 },
  { 2999 , 142 }
};
```

Unfortunately, using an explicit table means you need to search through the entries to find the correct input range. As long as the table is in order, the search is straightforward. The goal is to find the index into the table with the closest *x* value without going above the best value:

```
int SearchLookupTable(int32_t target, struct sPoint const *table, int tableSize)
{
  int i;
  int bestIndex = 0;

  for (i=0; i<tableSize; i++) {
    if (target > table[i].x) {
      bestIndex = i;
    } else {
      return bestIndex;
    }
  }
  return bestIndex;
}
```
You can pair this with interpolation:
```
  index = SearchLookupTable (x, sinLookup, sizeof(sinLookup));
  if (index+1 < sizeof(sinLookup)) {
    y = interpolate(x, sinLookup[index], sinLookup [index + 1]);
  } else {
    y = interpolate(x, sinLookup[index-1], sinLookup [index]);
  }
```

Unlike the implicit input, this method allows the input to exceed the range of the table. It will interpolate linearly using the first two points (if the input is less than the first entry in the table) or the last two points (if the input is greater than the last lookup point).

Fake Floating-Point Numbers

Linear interpolation doesn't always work on nonlinear curves. Even with a lookup table, if the curve is very twisty or the area of interest is very large, you may need to implement the math necessary to generate a solution.

For example, many sensors require some sort of compensation from parameters determined in manufacturing, such as temperature compensation. A temperature compensation equation might look like:

```
y = Ax² + Bx + C
```

The variable x is an input from a 10-bit ADC; A, B, and C are compensation parameters set in manufacturing as part of a calibration process; and y is the compensated sensor value. The compensation parameters are based on the sensor, so the minimum and maximum values come from the tolerances specified in the datasheet. Figure 12-10 shows some possible solutions given different compensation parameters. Even though these look relatively linear, trying to use linear interpolation may lead to too large of an error.

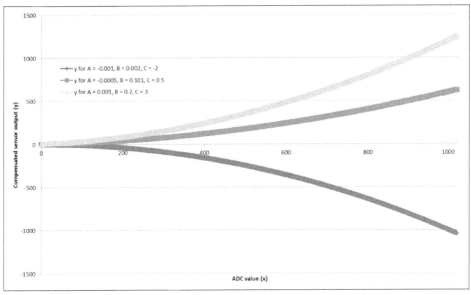

Figure 12-10. Temperature compensation on ADC input.

However, the compensation parameters are floating-point numbers. Floating-point math is very expensive on processors without hardware floating-point support (which are the most common ones in embedded applications). Compared to integer math, floating-point math is dead slow. Each operation calls a library function—a very large library. Even if the floating-point math you need is very simple, the size may be significant. For example, I looked at the map as I added two numbers together. For a compiler optimized for space, modifying an integer add to use floating point took 532 bytes of code space (to add the library functions __aeabi_fadd and __aeabi_fsub, though, I used only the add function).

 Standard input and output functions (such as printf and iostream) often include floating-point handling. Even when you don't use floating-point numbers in your code, if you use these library functions, your code will still include the floating-point math libraries. Check your map file!

Unless you have a really good reason to do otherwise (or your processor has an FPU to do the math), avoid floating-point numbers like the plague. If you can't avoid them, you can fake them. I've been creeping up on a method of doing that (divide by a constant using shifts and scaling the input). In this section, though, we'll go through it step by step, ending with a return to the temperature compensation example.

Rational Numbers

To get the idea, remember back to grade school, when there weren't floating-point numbers in your life. Even before we could write 0.25, we knew what a quarter of a pie was and that it could be written as one over four (1/4). Any rational number can be written as a fractional number (a ratio of a numerator over a denominator). Even irrational numbers can be approximated using a large denominator to reduce error. (For example, π is often approximated with 22/7.)

If we stopped there, we wouldn't get a big improvement (divides are slow). But we've already gotten around divides by shifting by a power of two. I didn't give it a name before, but this technique is called *binary scaling* and forms the basis for our fake floating-point numbers. We'll start with a 32-bit numerator and an 8-bit exponent. The exponent is the number of bits to shift to the left (for positive values) or to the right (for negative values).

We'll start off by defining a structure to hold the values:

```
struct sFakeFloat {
  int32_t num;  // numerator
  int8_t shift; // right-shift values (use negative for left-shift)
}
```

The number held in this structure is represented by:

```
floatingPointValue = num / 2^shift   // (In terms of math)
floatingPointValue = num >> shift;   // in the actual code
```

And now for a few examples. Let's start by going back to a quarter of a pie. The numerator is one, and the denominator is already a power of two:

```
struct sFakeFloat oneFourth = {1, 2}; // 1/4 = 1/2²
```

A negative shift value changes the direction of the shift. We could rewrite 4 using this notation as well:

```
struct sFakeFloat four = {1, -2};
floatingPointValue = four.num >> four.shift ==> 1/(2^(-2)) ==> 1 * 2² ==> 4
```

Fake floating point can also be used to work with numbers larger than you can store in a 32-bit value (or whatever the size of the numerator). The result will be less precise than a larger variable would be. For example, say we want to store ten billion and one (10,000,000,001). We can make the value fit into a signed 32-bit integer by dividing by 8:

```
struct sFakeFloat notQuiteTenBillionOne = { 1250000000, -3 };
```

By doing the division, we've lost the last digit, so the resulting value is only ten billion. But this is within one ten billionth of being correct, and that's good enough for many applications.

Precision

In the structure shown in the previous section, suppose we used a 24-bit numerator and an 8-bit shift for the denominator. Although that would keep everything in a convenient 32-bit variable, it might decrease precision. We've already seen how we can lose digits for big numbers, but the same can happen with more normal-sized numbers as well.

For example, the number 12.345 could be represented as 49/4 with an error of 0.095. With a larger denominator shift value, more precision can be obtained. However, a too-large denominator will cause the numerator to overflow. See Table 12-2 for some of your options.

Table 12-2. Representing the number 12.345 using binary scaling

Numerator	# of bits needed in numerator	Denominator shift values	Equivalent floating-point number	Error
12	4	0	12	0.345
25	5	1	12.5	0.155
99	7	3	12.375	0.030
395	9	5	12.34375	0.00125
12,641	14	10	12.34472656	0.000273
12,944,671	24	20	12.34500027	2.67E−07
414,229,463	29	25	12.345	1.19E−09
1,656,917,852	31	27	12.345	1.19E−09

So as you increase the shift in the denominator, you can decrease the error, but you'll also need to increase the number of bits in the numerator. This brings us back to two questions: how much error can your system tolerate for this mathematical operation? And how large can you expect numbers to get with the multiplications and additions in your algorithm?

I'm going to show you how these fake floating-point numbers work. But you shouldn't implement these yourself. Look for "fixed-point" or "Q numbers" in your math library.

Addition (and Subtraction)

Let's look at addition for a pair of fake floating-point variables. Thinking back to grade school days and fractional math, you need to make their denominators the same before trying to combine numbers. In this case, it means making the shift values the same, generally by left-shifting the smaller number before doing the addition.

The best way to explain this is to walk through an example. Here we'll use a byte for the floating-point numerator. This can be useful when not a lot of range is needed. Looking back at Table 12-2 for 12.345, using 7 bits gave us an error of 0.030, or less than 1%. (Also, using an 8-bit numerator means you and I can imagine what happens at each stage, seeing overflows without trying to keep huge numbers in our heads.)

```
struct sFakeFloat {
  int8_t num;
  int8_t shift;
};
```

This example is going to show addition using only positive numbers, but the method is mostly the same for subtraction and for negative numbers. First, we need to set up our floating-point numbers with some values:

```
struct sFakeFloat a = { 99, 3 };  // 12.375, not quite 12.345
struct sFakeFloat b = {111, 5 };  // 3.46875, not quite 3.456
struct sFakeFloat result;
```

Next, find the least common denominator so we can add them together. Finding the least common denominator when all denominators are powers of two is very easy. In the following, if `b.shift` is greater than `a.shift`, you'll get the left-shift you want. And if `a.shift` is greater than `b.shift`, conveniently enough, you'll get a negative left-shift that turns into the right-shift you want. (The `shift` field is essentially a logarithm.)

```
int16_t tmp = a.num;
tmp = tmp << (b.shift - a.shift);
```

A larger temporary variable must be used, or the result may overflow and get truncated. Note that the numerator is not the only part that can overflow. The denominator (`b.shift` - `a.shift`) must be less than 8 bits (so an overflow may occur if one or both of them are negative). To avoid overflow, in addition to shifting the variable with the smaller denominator up, you may also need to shift the variable with the large denominator down (dividing by two and losing precision).

The sum of the numerators is kept in the temporary variable until we make sure it is small enough to fit into our result variable:

```
tmp = tmp + b.num;
```

At this point, the shift value is the larger of the two (`b.shift` = 5), and the temporary variable is 507, too large for an 8-bit variable. Until this temporary variable can safely fit back into the variable size we have, we'll need to make the numerator smaller (by dividing by two):

```
result.shift = b.shift;
while (tmp > INT8_MAX || tmp < -INT8_MAX) {
    tmp = tmp >> 1;
    result.shift--;
}
result.num = tmp;      // 15.84375, close to ideal of 15.831
```

Finally, we have a result that describes the addition of two floating-point numbers.

The result's numerator is 126, and the shift is 3, for a floating-point equivalent of 15.75. The goal was 15.84 but this is as close as we can get with this fake floating-point precision.

Multiplication (and Division)

Multiplication is a little simpler than addition because you don't have to make the denominators match. In fractional math, you just multiply the top and the bottom separately to get the answer (for instance, $2/3 \times 5/4 = 10/12$).

When you multiply two fake floating-point numbers, multiply the numerators safely, then multiply the denominators (sort of).

We again start by putting the numerator of one number in a larger temporary variable so we don't get an overflow. Unlike addition, where we needed to check the size, we can be certain that the result of two 32-bit variables will be no more than 64 bits. Then multiply the temporary variable by the numerator of the second.

The shift value is not exactly the denominator; it is the exponent of the denominator:

```
denominator = 2^shift;
```

A shift value is a logarithm (for instance, a bit position of 5 represents 2^5, or 32). So instead of multiplying the shift values, we only need to add them together. If the resulting numerator is greater than the number of bits we have available, shift to the right until it fits.

For this multiplication example, we'll return to int32_t to hold the numerator:

```
struct sFakeFloat {
  int32_t num;
  int8_t shift;
};
struct sFakeFloat a = { 1656917852, 27 }; // 12.345
struct sFakeFloat b = { 128, 8};    // 0.5
struct sFakeFloat result;
```

For this example, we'll give the variables precise values so we can check the process at each stage. (Although one half could be trivially implemented as {1, 1}).

The temporary variable noted must be at least as many bits as both numerators combined. Since we are using 32-bit numerators, the temporary variable has to be 64 bits. If we were using 16 bits in the numerator, we'd need at least 32 bits to hold the multiplication. Note that a 64-bit integer might not be native to your processor, so using it will incur some overhead, but not nearly as much as there would be if you used variables of type float or double:

```
int64_t tmp;
tmp = a.num;
tmp = tmp * b.num;
```

The multiplication is done in two steps to upgrade the variables into the larger-sized variables. If you'd just multiplied the numerators together, the result would have been an int32_t before it got upgraded and stored in an int64_t. You need to upgrade, then multiply:

```
result.shift = a.shift + b.shift;
while (tmp > INT32_MAX || tmp < -INT32_MAX) {
  tmp = tmp >> 1;
  result.shift--;
}
results.num = tmp;
```

As with addition, as long as the results of the numerator multiplication don't fit in the results numerator, we need to decrease the shift to avoid overflow. For the values in our example, the loop decreases the shift eight times.

We can also make sure that the shift values don't overflow the shift variable:

```
tmp = a.shift + b.shift;
ASSERT(tmp < INT8_MAX);
result.shift = tmp;
```

The result of the operation is 6.1725 {1656917852, 28}.

Division is a bit more complicated, but works along the same lines as multiplication. It divides the numerators and subtracts the shifts instead of adding them.

The algorithms we've used for both addition and multiplication can sometimes cause errors by not being precise enough. So you'll need to limit the size of your variables or return those errors to a calling function. Recognizing the limitations of the binary scaling algorithms I've shown is one of your responsibilities.

The results will be best if you have plenty of prior knowledge about the numbers you'll be working with, so you can handle overflows and verify the stability of your system. You could make a very generic library to handle every possible case, but you run the risk of reimplementing floating-point numbers with all the overhead. As you look at your algorithm, you'll need to know the range (min and max) of the variables and the precision you need for dealing with them at each point in time.

Machine Learning

Machine learning (ML) is becoming more prevalent in all areas of computing. Machine learning is a giant field, applying statistical methods to all kinds of problems such as classification, detections, and control systems. Data science and algorithm development are far beyond the scope of this book (see "Further Reading" on page 352 for some suggestions). The kinds of problems that can be solved with machine learning on small devices are vastly different from those on internet connected devices or larger devices.

Developing a machine learning system can generally be broken into several phases:

- Data collection (and cleaning)
- Feature identification
- Algorithm design
- Training
- Inference

Embedded devices are most often involved with the inference stage, where new data comes into a system and is put through the trained black box to get to an answer related to all of the past data and training. Training is usually more processor intensive. (Some training can happen on devices, but usually it is slow or much smaller in scope.)

During system development, the machine learning pieces are often developed by another team and, forgive me, these teams often do not have a concept of resource constraints. They live in the world of big data and server racks with giant GPUs. The idea of only 32 k of RAM available is laughable to them.

Usually, as an embedded systems developer, you'll be given the algorithm and the necessary training output to make it work. You'll implement the algorithm on the device, optimizing as necessary (and using existing tools and libraries as much as possible!).

It is critical that you can test the output of the optimized code versus the original algorithm. The different tools and optimizations may make changes. Some of the most popular techniques (neural networks) are exceedingly temperamental with what seem to be minor changes (which may indicate the algorithm is mistuned, but that's a separate discussion). You will also need to be able to test whenever the algorithm is retrained, so make testing straightforward.

For networked devices, even the inference may be moved off the device into the cloud. The device then takes in data and summarizes it into features. These get sent to the cloud, where they are processed through a larger algorithm.

Finally, machine learning algorithms are often resource intensive, which makes them difficult to use in resource constrained environments. Traditional algorithms often perform quite well and are significantly easier to debug and deal with corner cases.

Look Up the Answer!

The most important part of optimizing your processor is to look to other sources for the answer whenever possible. Optimizing algorithms can be lots of fun, but if you need to get to an answer, look for existing libraries. On Arm Cortex-M parts, use the CMSIS DSP Software Library which has a huge set of functions for vector math, trigonometry, motor control, and statistics.

There is also a CMSIS library for neural networks and other machine learning functions. If you are looking for other machine learning tools, check out TinyML which is optimized for microprocessors.

Further Reading

Someday I'd like to sit down and read Donald Knuth's *Art of Computer Programming* front to back. The scholastically inclined part of me is slightly stunned I haven't done it already. The more pragmatic (um, lazy) part convinces me to just look up what I need, when I need it, and not get too distracted by all of the interesting, shiny objects around in the book. Regardless of whether you've read the book, it should be on your shelf: Donald E. Knuth, *The Art of Computer Programming, Volume 2, Seminumerical Algorithms* (Addison-Wesley).

Alternatively, you may want to use a numerical recipe book for more implementation-specific information; I recommend William H. Press et al.,

Numerical Recipes: The Art of Scientific Computing, third edition (Cambridge University Press). Similar books come in language-specific forms (C, C++, Java, etc.).

The best introduction to machine learning for me was *Hands-On Machine Learning with Scikit-Learn and TensorFlow* by Aurélien Géron (O'Reilly). TensorFlow is a lot different than programming a device in C but the author does an excellent job of looking beyond neural networks into other types of machine learning. I had already been studying ML before I started TensorFlow, so if Géron's book looks too academic, I have heard good things about *Deep Learning with Python* by François Chollet (Manning).

For device-based machine learning, check out *TinyML* by Pete Warden and Daniel Situnayake (O'Reilly). There is a lot of work in this area, so be sure to find the latest edition and look at the newest tutorials online.

At the deeply embedded scope there is Henry Warren's *Hacker's Delight* (Addison-Wesley Professional). This is an interesting book to flip through, almost a grimoire of slightly scary optimization techniques. Compiler designers tend to need to know these things. You want people to be able to read and reuse your code, so don't go too overboard in optimization at this level.

Interview Question: Handling Very Large Numbers

Write a program to add the numbers from 1 to 10 in the language of your choice. As the interviewee completes each piece, a new question is asked: what do you need to do to make it generic so it adds 1 to N? What sorts of optimizations can you provide? What limitations are inherent in the implementation? How would you change it for the input to be arbitrary length? (Thanks to Rob Calhoun for this question!)

As the interviewee starts with the first question, do they create a function that takes a parameter to stop the addition (1 to N)? That is better than hard coding it immediately to go from 1 to 10. From there, I look at the size of both input and output variables. Using integers or long variables is OK, but can they explain the limitations it places on the code? Do they use unsigned or signed variables, and can they explain why unsigned variables are preferable?

If they don't know the formula for the sum from 1 to N is equal to $N \times (N + 1) / 2$, I help them through it, typically by writing out 1, 2, 3, 4, 5, 6 and pairing up $1 + 6$, $2 + 5$, $3 + 4$. The interviewee loses no points for not knowing this formula, as long as they're awake and figure it out. Points are lost for interrupting and insisting upon an incorrect formula, even in the face of counterexamples (it happens more often than you'd think).

Next, we go back to the size of the variables. What is the size of $N \times (N + 1) / 2$ compared with N? If N is a 16-bit integer, how big does the output need to be? What if N is 64 bits? I prod to ensure they know that $(2^{16})^2$ is $2^{(16 \times 2)}$.

Finally, we get to the really interesting part of the question, where I get to ask how they'd change it if it needed to work for inputs up to 2^{64}. Now what can they use as an output? If they pick double-precision floats, well, we discuss the limitations of floats. There is no wrong answer here, but I keep building up: what if we need to use even larger numbers? I limit the question to a few hundred or a few thousand digits, always constraining it to not be more than a million hexadecimal digits.

Now how can the interviewee modify their function? I walk them through constructing the data structure used for the input buffer and the output buffer (and they should know by this point how big to make the output buffer: twice the input) and the function prototype.

I look for thread safety and failure to keep track of the size of the byte string, discussing as necessary. Finally, I get them to do as much of the implementation as they can for computing $(N \times N - 1) / 2$ for arbitrary-length integers, reading from the input array, and writing to the output array. If they're having some trouble, I suggest using an 8-bit machine because it is more straightforward to draw out.

Depending on the skill the interviewee shows, this question can move in different directions, drilling down to show strengths and weaknesses. It could easily take the whole interview slot to work through only part of it.

Reducing Power Consumption

Whether you are building a device that fits in your pocket or trying to save the world by reducing your company's carbon footprint, decreasing a system's power consumption can take an order of magnitude more time than implementing the product features. Choosing all the right hardware components is a huge part of making a system power-efficient. But because the processor is likely to be one of the largest consumers of power in the system, software can play a big role in saving electricity.

The pressures to decrease power usage and cost are what lead us to select processors that don't have enough resources to comfortably deliver the product features. Since you are a relatively expensive resource, using your time to save on the cost of the processor is sensible only if you are building enough units to amortize your time.

 How expensive are you? Take your annual salary and divide by a thousand. That is about what each hour of your time costs your company, counting salary, benefits, office space, and all the little things that add up. So if you are making an example salary of $1,000 per year, each hour is worth about $1. If you can buy a $3.50 tool to save four hours, it is usually worth it. Of course, there is a difference between capital outlay (cash) and sunk cost (your salary), so although this is a good rule of thumb, your boss might not let you buy the scooter to get from your desk to the break room, even after you describe the cost benefit of saving 30 seconds every day.

On the other hand, a processor with the minimum amount of cycles, RAM, and code space consumes less power than one with plenty of resources. As suggested in Chapter 11, you may want to optimize to "as low as possible," but that will take an infinitely long time. Start with a quantifiable system goal. Let your electrical engineering team do its part when choosing the components. Then use the points in this chapter to reduce the power further.

Understanding Power Consumption

All electrical circuits can be modeled as resistors, though this is akin to saying all differential equations can be modeled linearly. It is true, but depending on the circumstances, you might expect to see a lot of errors. However, it is a good starting point. Power is measured in watts and is proportional to the square of the current used in the system:

```
P = I² * R
power = (current)² * resistance
Watts (W) = (Amps (A))² * Ohms (Ω)
```

Because your system is modeled as a resistor, if you focus on decreasing your current, you decrease your power consumption. Another way to look at power is as the product of voltage and current:

```
P = V * I
power = voltage * current
Watts (W) = Volts (V) * Amps (A)
```

This is why your processor core may run at 1.8 V even though other parts of your system run at 3 or 5 V. Because the core takes a lot of current, the lower voltage means less power consumption. The two ways of looking at power are equivalent, according to the golden rule of electrical engineering, *Ohm's law*:

```
V = I * R
voltage = current * resistance
Volts (V)  = Amps (A)  * Ohms (Ω)
```

There is a lot more that Ohm's law can do for you, so if this overview has given you a buzz of interest, check out "Further Reading" on page 370 for some electrical engineering reading.

One more useful equation is for energy:

```
W = P * T
work or energy = power * time
Joules (J) = Watts (W) * seconds
```

Finally, we have an equation with time. Basically, it says that if you are designing an energy-efficient system, you can minimize the power it uses or the amount of time it is powered on.

If we want to reduce energy (work), then we need to reduce power or time powered on (or both). If we want to reduce power, we have to reduce current or change our system so it has less resistance (P = I² * R). If we want to reduce power, we need to reduce voltage or current (P = V * I).

To summarize, to reduce how much energy the device uses, we have to reduce voltage, resistance, current, and time. These are not all independent (Ohm's Law tells us that), but let's treat them as though they are for now and try to reduce each:

Reducing voltage
Is generally a matter of choosing lower voltage parts, such as processors and peripherals that work at 1.8 V.

Reducing resistance
Is also about component selection, identifying parts such as new MEMS sensors instead of older mechanical ones.

Reducing current
Is related to the previous two but there are software techniques that are useful here: things like GPIO settings and features you might find in your processor manual (or an application note).

Reducing time
Can be done by turning off as much of the system as possible.

Measuring Power Consumption

It's very hard to optimize what you can't measure. You have to know how to measure power, and low-power things can be difficult to measure; the lower the consumption, the more difficult it is.

One of the easiest ways to measure current is with a power supply. The more expensive ones will give you a simple reading. However, it is not that straightforward.

To start with, you'll need to disconnect your programmer/debugger as well as the serial port to the command line. Essentially you can't have anything connected to the system under test. For example, JTAG programmers may provide power to the processor but that power comes from your computer, not the power supply. While a serial port doesn't provide power, your computer is powered differently than the system under test, and the different grounds may change the measurement.

Thus, step one is to disconnect everything. There should be only one power and one ground going to the system.

For a low-power system, there is a good chance that the sleep states (more on this soon) will read lower than a normal power supply can measure.

Chapter 3 suggested that you get your own digital multimeter (DMM). If you get a good one, you can measure current directly, as shown in part b) of Figure 13-1. Most cheap DMMs will let you measure in the range of milliamps (mA). A small embedded system consisting of a low-power processor and a few peripheral chips will draw tens to hundreds of milliamps. So the DMM is an easy way to measure the current of a running system. However, if you are trying to look at power consumption in sleep mode, you may need to measure lower amounts of current. A good DMM may let you look at hundreds of microamps (µA), but you may need even finer granularity than that.

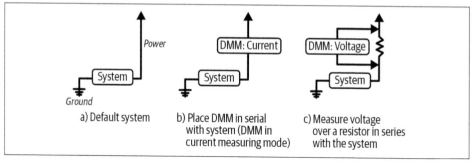

Figure 13-1. Two methods of measuring current

To read power levels with my DMM, I need to move the test probes to another location on the DMM. (I often forget this step.) Next, I have to have an idea of how much current I'm going to read: µA, mA, 10A. If I get the range too high, so my system draws less current, the DMM will read zero. However, if I get it wrong the other way, so my system draws more current than then DMM is set for, I may break my multimeter (or I'll need to replace a fuse).

 There are a lot of ways to do this wrong, so read your multimeter manual. Or watch some YouTube videos.

Using a resistor in series and burden voltage

A safer way to measure current is to put a small resistor in series with the system, as shown in part c) of Figure 13-1. Switch your DMM to voltage mode, something it is better at measuring. You may need to tweak the value of the resistor to get the voltage in the range that your DMM can read. Then apply Ohm's law:

```
current = voltage / resistance
```

Table 13-1 shows some possible combinations to give you the idea. Depending on the current you expect to read, you may have to tweak the resistor value.

Table 13-1. Measuring current in a system using different resistors

Expected current	Resistor in circuit	Voltage measured on DMM	Notes
12 mA	1 Ω	0.012 V	Easily measured on most DMMs
23 μA	1 Ω	0.000023 V	Impossible to read on most DMMs
34 μA	10 Ω	0.00034 V	A very good DMM might be able to read this
45 μA	100 Ω	0.0045 V	Once again, within reach of most DMMs, but the resistor is getting too large

The reason the resistor-in-series method works is because the first part of the circuit (the system I'm testing) and the second part of the circuit (the resistor) must have to use the same amount of current.[1] So I get the system's current by looking at the resistor's current.

This method used to work a lot better before all the processors got so darn power efficient. Now, the resistor's resistance may be a significant percentage of your system's resistance. The resistor needs to be large enough to read the tiny sleep currents, but still small enough that it doesn't become a large consumer of power itself and interfere with the measurement.

When that happens, instead of using the resistor as a measurement tool, the resistor is causing a significant chunk of what you are measuring. The resistor is burdening the system with its own drama. This gives you the wrong idea about your system's performance.

This whole resistor measurement process is exactly what my multimeter was doing, which is why I had to tell it what to measure. Essentially, I was indicating which resistor to use by moving the probes. A digital power supply or $30 voltmeter will give you a satisfactory measurement as long as you are drawing milliamps or tens of microamps.

Since it consumes power on its own, you may choose to have the resistor available only on development boards, with a zero-ohm resistor (also known as a "wire") on the production boards.

 Resistors are associated with a given accuracy. After you measure current consumption, power off your system and measure the true resistance value of the resistor with your DMM.

---

1 This is Kirchhoff's current law.

Sadly, multimeters only measure current right this second, a measure of static consumption. If we have sleep states or are looking for a current change, we really want something like an oscilloscope so we can see little blips as power level changes.

Changing current and orders of magnitude problem

When your device is running, it may consume lots of power. Then when your device goes to sleep, it may drastically reduce the power draw so the battery can last a long time. Trying to measure both of these is difficult. They may be orders of magnitude different, which means they need drastically different resistor values. And remember, using the wrong resistor value (or DMM slot) may end up causing a blown fuse or a broken tool.

There are power profiler tools to help with this, specialized tools that measure current over different ranges. They can be expensive, but they handle burden voltage and the order of magnitude problem for you.

Designing for Lower Power Consumption

While measuring power consumption is critical to getting the most out of your system, several of the ways to reduce power consumption involve choosing the correct components. During the design phase, you have to determine what your power budget is and whether it works for the application.

For battery applications, estimate how much space the battery occupies physically and whether it fits your budget. These two factors can help you choose what kind of battery works for your system.

Batteries have a voltage rating and a capacity. An alkaline AA battery has a nominal voltage of 1.5 V and a capacity of about 3,000 mAh (milliamp hours). Thus capacity isn't rated in power, but in current supplied over time.

If your system takes 30 mA (and 1.5 V) when it is on, then with an AA battery it should last about 4 days (3,000 mAh/30 mA = 100 hours). If your system takes 300 mA, it should last about 10 hours.

However, if your system consumes 3,000 mA, the AA battery won't last an hour, because just as with calling your system a resistor, this rule of thumb goes only so far. Your battery will have a datasheet that explains its capacity, chemistry, peak current draw, and other characteristics.

The capacity will determine how long the device works between charges (or battery changes). However, to calculate that, you will need to identify the pieces of the system most likely to consume power. Going back to Chapter 2 and the hardware block diagram, list the major components. Choose some specific parts and start estimating how much current they consume. This is additive: if you have a screen consuming 12 mA and a processor that uses 0.6 mA at full speed, then the current consumption of both of these is 12.6 mA (assuming they run at the same voltage).

As you create a spreadsheet of components and their current consumption, you will find that parts change current consumption based on their operating status: a screen that is off may consume 0 mA, a processor that is asleep may be more in the 80 μA range. Your device will likely have its own higher level states: "on" and "asleep" are the simplest states to identify. If you have a network sensor, the radio may consume enough power to warrant a separate "high power" system state (especially while transmitting). A robotic system may also need states about how far and fast it can travel.

Note that these are not generally the states in your software flowchart. These device states are usually much less granular, more like the operating modes visible to the user.

These different device states become columns in your spreadsheet, letting you calculate the current consumption of each. From there, determine the amount of time spent per state to find the average consumption. Alternatively, use the amount of current you have available to determine how much time you can spend in any given state.

In summary, when designing for low power consumption applications, you need to answer these questions:

- What is the battery cost budget? How big can it be?
- How long between charges or battery changes?
- What are the major power consuming components?
- What are the states of the system? What is the power draw in each state?
- How much time can you spend in each state given the battery goals? If this is insufficient, recheck the answers to the other questions.

Turn Off the Light When You Leave the Room

The easiest way to reduce power consumption is to turn off components that are not needed. The downside is that those components won't be ready when you need them, and bringing them back will add both some power usage and some latency in responding to events. You'll need to investigate the trade-offs; I tend to use a spreadsheet to help me weigh the power savings.

The following sections detail some of the ways to turn off or reduce the power drain of components.

Turn Off Peripherals

As you review your schematic and your design, consider what your processor has access to and how to design your system to turn off peripherals that are not needed. For example, if you have external RAM, you may be able to move the data to a local location and then power down the RAM instead of leaving it powered on for extended periods of time.

A chip external to the processor will consume no current if it does not have power. If the processor doesn't have access to the power lines, holding the peripheral in reset should nearly eliminate the current consumption (check the peripheral datasheet!). This isn't as optimal as turning off the power, but better than leaving the peripheral running.

Many chips need time to return to functioning after reset, so there is some overhead in powering them down. The goal is to turn off the component for a reasonable amount of time. ADCs are some of the peripherals with longer reset times, but they are often big power consumers, so it is often worth taking the time to balance the power consumption versus the power-on time.

Turn Off Unused I/O Devices

If you have spare I/O devices, you can save a little bit of current by configuring them to be inputs with internal pull-downs. If your chip doesn't have internal pull-downs, try tri-stating it (no pull-up and no pull-downs, just floating) or setting it to be a low output. If that doesn't work for you, an input with pull-ups still has reasonably small amounts of leakage current.

Don't remember pull-ups as anything other than gym torture? See Chapter 3 for more information on both pull-ups and pull-downs.

As for those I/Os connected to the component you've powered off, the preferred order is the same (input with pull-downs, output low, input with pull-ups). Configuring one I/O in this manner isn't likely to save a lot, but if you have a whole bunch of them, the small savings can add up. On the other hand, if some I/Os on your system have an external pull-up or pull-down, set the internal one to match (or eliminate the external ones as redundant). Fighting external resistors wastes power.

If you have a peripheral that is powered off (or in reset), be careful how you connect other processor I/Os to it. Don't leave the lines pulled-up or set high. Chips often have internal protection diodes that could use the high signal to back-power and damage the chip.

Turn Off Processor Subsystems

In addition to setting I/O devices to be low power, often you can turn off whole subsystems of the processor that you don't need (are you using that second SPI port?). Your processor manual will tell you whether this is a supported feature of the processor. Sometimes you can turn off all functionality (best); sometimes you can only turn off the clock to the peripheral (still pretty good).

Slow Down to Conserve Energy

Lowering your clock frequency saves power. This is true for all of the clocks you can control, but especially the processor clock. However, a slower processor clock gives you fewer processor cycles to run in. That is why we spent so much time on optimizing code in Chapter 11, even though optimizing for processor speed tends to decrease the quality (robustness, readability, and debuggability) of your code. Often the most straightforward way to decrease power consumption of your system by 10% is to decrease the clock by about 10%. In other words, the power consumption of the chip is proportional to the frequency it runs at.

If the processor has to be on all the time (for example, to monitor its environment), being able to slow down may be crucial to achieving low power. Some embedded operating systems will do frequency scaling for you, consuming power efficiently when possible and still having the speed available when you need it. You can do this without an operating system. Instead of scaling over the whole range, you might want to create slow, medium, and fast modes and change the performance level based on events. However, as with running a race, there is a balance between slowing the processor down and keeping it on for a longer time (being a tortoise) or sprinting for a shorter period of time and then sleeping (being a hare).

Dealing with Multiple Clock Sources of Different Accuracies

Many power-efficient systems have a slow clock that can drive the processor in low power modes, often generated via a 32 kHz oscillator.[2] This slow clock is used to keep a part of the system alive while in low-power state, often to drive a real-time clock (RTC) so the system knows the current time even when it has been powered "off."

---

2 Actually, it is usually a 32.768 kHz oscillator, so you can count to 1 second with a 15-bit counter.

Such systems also have a crystal-generated fast clock with higher power consumption, higher accuracy, and less temperature-related error. You can use the high-accuracy clock to correct the errors in the low-accuracy one (aka time base compensation or disciplining the timing source). The goal is to determine the difference between the low-accuracy clock's actual values and expected values.

Say your fast clock is 50 MHz for this example. To determine the compensation, set the slow clock as an input to a capture timer. Next, set up a one-second timer interrupt using the more accurate fast clock. The slow clock should have given you 32,768 ticks on the capture counter when the one-second timer expired. However, it probably gave you a value that is a few off from that (depending on ambient temperature and the manufacturing process used on the 32 kHz clock). You can use this offset to move between the 32 kHz cycles that occurred while the system was asleep and 50 MHz clock cycles (or between 32 kHz cycles and real time). For example, say that when you did the compensation, you got 32,760 captured ticks per one-second period (which should be equivalent to 50 M crystal clock cycles). Now the processor can expect 32,760 cycles per second from the 32 kHz clock.

The final outcome is no better than the most accurate clock you have. In fact, it is likely to be worse because you can't tell whether the compensation should have been fractional (32,760.5). (Remember *jitter* from Chapter 5? It applies here.) Also, as temperature changes, the compensation varies, so you'll need to redo the compensation periodically (how frequently depends on the timing accuracy your product requires). The precision clock might not be the fast one. Systems that use GPS for location and timing have access to the PPS signal. This is a very accurate (and precise) clock, but it is too slow to drive a system. However, it can be used to correct your clocks in much the same manner as described previously:

1. Interrupt on the PPS signal.

2. Take a measure of how many system ticks (processor or timer) passed since the last PPS interrupt.

3. Adjust the system timing accordingly.

(Thanks to Matthew Hughes for recommending the addition of clock compensation!)

Putting the Processor to Sleep

Even at a slow clock speed, the processor is consuming power. Slowing down will help, but what if your code spends a lot of time waiting for things to happen?

Many processors designed for low-power systems can go into an energy-conserving sleep when they aren't needed. They use interrupts to tell the processor when to wake up.

On your computer, *sleep* is a standby mode where processing is not running but the memory is still powered. This lets the operating system wake up quickly, exactly where it had left off. Alternatively, in *hibernation*, the contents of RAM are written to the disk (or other nonvolatile memory). It takes longer to wake up from hibernation, but the system uses much less power while in that state (maybe almost no power, depending on the make of your computer).

Most embedded processors offer a similar range of sleep possibilities, with some processors having lots of granularity and others opting to have only one low-power mode. In decreasing levels of power consumption, some sleep modes you might find in your processor manual include:

Slow down
> Going beyond frequency scaling, some processors allow you to slow the clock down to hundreds of hertz.

Idle or sleep
> This turns off the processor core but keeps enabled timers, peripherals, and RAM alive. Any interrupt can return the processor to normal running.

Deep sleep or light hibernation
> In addition to the processor core being disabled, some (possibly all) on-chip peripherals can be configured to turn off. Be careful not to turn off the subsystem that generates the interrupt that will wake up the processor.

Deep hibernation or power down
> The processor chooses which on-chip peripherals to turn off (usually almost all of them). RAM is usually left in an unstable state, but the processor registers are retained, so the system doesn't need initialization on boot. Usually only a wakeup pin or a small subset of interrupts can restart the processor.

Power off
> The processor does not retain any memory and starts from a completely clean state.

Deeper sleep modes place the processor into a lower-power state but take longer to wake from, increasing system latency. You'll need to spend some time with the user manual to determine how to achieve the lowest power level possible that will meet your product's needs.

The wake-up interrupts could be buttons, timers, other chips (e.g., ADC conversion complete), or traffic on a communications bus. It depends on your processor (and your sleep level).

Once you've determined that your processor can sleep, how do you design a system to make the best use of it? We'll explore that next.

Interrupt-Based Code Flow Model

Understanding the interrupt-based code flow model is critical for power-sensitive applications. "Main Loops" on page 166 described how to set up your code to maximize sleep using interrupts and events.

Instead of idling, the microprocessor spends time sleeping, waking up only when an interrupt occurs, then handling the interrupt and going back to sleep. The goal is to maximize the amount of time the processor is asleep, thereby maximizing power efficiency. See Figure 13-2 for a flowchart describing the interrupt-based code flow model.

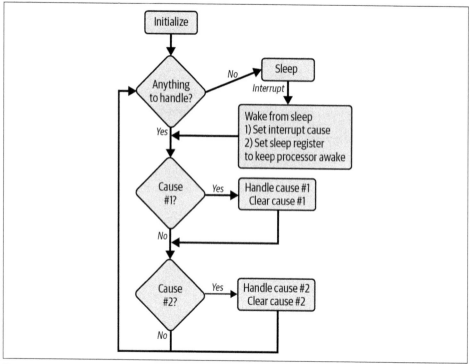

Figure 13-2. Interrupt-based code flowchart

The interrupt may be generated from a peripheral to indicate it needs processor attention (like an ADC finishing with its data, needing the processor to read the result and start another conversion). In other systems, the interrupt may be generated by a button the user presses or a sensor rising above a threshold. The interrupts may also be generated internally, for example, by a timer.

When an interrupt occurs, the processor wakes up and calls the appropriate ISR. The ISR sets a flag to indicate the cause for the wake-up and modifies the sleep register to keep the processor awake. When the ISR returns, because the *sleep register* is set to awake, the main loop runs. The main loop checks each possible flag and, when it finds a flag set, runs the appropriate handler (also clearing the flag). When the main loop completes and all of the flags have been cleared, the processor returns to sleep mode. Figure 13-2 illustrates the general idea with two handlers to check.

Let's say you have a processor that can sleep. To experiment, start with a timer interrupt. These are common in the interrupt flow model because the timer lets you wake up to do any necessary housekeeping. Run the processor without sleep, and set up an interrupt to run so it toggles an output line or LED. The frequency doesn't matter, though a slow interrupt is better. I'd recommend about twice per second (2 Hz). Measure the current of the system as described in "Measuring Power Consumption" on page 357.

Now set your processor to sleep between interrupts. From the outside, the processor behaves the same. However, when you measure the system current, it should be smaller. How much smaller depends on many aspects of your system. For instance, I tried this procedure with the Texas Instruments (TI) MSP430 Launchpad development kit using the G2231 processor. When it was in a while loop, waiting for the next timer interrupt, the system consumed 9 mW (3 mA at 3 V). When I let it enter a low-power mode instead of idling in the while loop, the results were dramatically different. I used the third level of sleep (the processor has four). However, even with a handy 100 Ω resistor, I couldn't measure any voltage drop over the resistor with my cheapo DMM. When I was consuming 3 mA with the 100 Ω resistor, I got about 300 mV of drop. Lower current implies lower voltage, of course. But my DMM wasn't sensitive enough to make the measurement in the low-power state.

The datasheet informed me that the current should be about 0.9 μA (2.7 μW) in this state, which would require additional special tools for me to measure (and/or a much larger resistor, probably 100 kΩ). The timer interrupt to toggle the LED must have spent some time at 3 mA, but the processor woke up, set the timer flag, toggled the LED in the main loop, and went back to sleep before it could make a blip on my meter. Remember, *energy efficiency* is about time as well as current.

The processor on TI's Launchpad kit is designed to be super low power when it is sleeping, so the results might not be so dramatic on another device.

A Closer Look at the Main Loop

Handling the interrupts in the main loop allows you to keep the interrupt service routines short, because all they do is set a couple of flags and exit. Long interrupts tend to decrease system responsiveness. Plus, going through the main loop can aid in debugging, as the system revolves around sleeping and the flags set by the most recent interrupts. (If you can output the cause variable on every pass, you'll get a good view of what the system is doing.) Note that additional interrupts may happen while executing the handlers for the interrupt that caused the processor to wake up.

By putting the flags in the bits of a variable (or two), it becomes simple to check that all interrupts have been processed:

```
volatile uint16_t gInterruptCause = 0; // Bitmasked flags that describe
                                        // which interrupt has occurred

void main(){
    uint16_t cause;
    Initialize();
    while (1) { // atomic interrupt-safe read of gInterruptCause
        InterruptsOff();
        cause = gInterruptCause;
        InterruptsOn();

        while (cause) {
            // each handler will clear the relevant bit in
            // gInterruptCause
            if (cause & 0x01) { HandleSlowTimer();}
            if (cause & 0x02) { HandleADCConversion();}
            // while awake, make sure the watchdog stays happy
            FeedWatchdog();
            InterruptsOff();
            cause = gInterruptCause;
            InterruptsOn();
        }
        // need to read the cause register again without allowing
        // any new interrupts:
        InterruptsOff();
        if (gInterruptCause == 0) {
            InterruptsOn();
            // an interrupt will cause a wake-up and
            // run the while loop
            GoToSleep();
        }
        InterruptsOn();
    }
} // end main
```

The interrupts themselves just need to set the flag and modify the sleep register to keep the CPU awake after they return. The handlers will perform the necessary actions and clear the appropriate bits in the cause register (gInterruptCause) in an interrupt-safe manner.

Remember that working with interrupts can be tricky due to race conditions. See Chapter 5 for more tips on interrupts.

If you have multiple power modes and need to decide which to enter when your main loop has finished, you may need to examine a lot of states scattered through your system. For example, if a peripheral is busy and can't be shut down, or if a communication bus remains active, you may not be able to achieve the lower states of sleep until they have finished. One option is to have a power management module with a table of registered function pointers. Each module that might preclude some sleep level registers a callback. When considering the next sleep state, all functions in the table get called and can veto certain sleep levels.

Processor Watchdog

In "Watchdog" on page 164, I talked about the importance of having a watchdog and how you shouldn't use a timer interrupt to service the watchdog. Now that your system is entirely interrupt-based, how are you going to make sure the watchdog remains content?

In the lightest levels of sleep, your processor will probably let the watchdog continue to run. The processor may let you configure whether you want the watchdog to run while the processor is asleep (consuming some power during sleep and forcing the processor to wake up to service it) or want to have the watchdog sleep when the processor does (losing a fail-safe mechanism for your system). Recognizing the trade-off will help you make the right decision for your system.

If you leave the watchdog on, you may need to set a timer to wake the processor up before the watchdog expires. This goes against the grain of my earlier advice. However, here the watchdog is not only verifying that the system is running properly, but also verifying that the system is waking up from sleep properly.

 For processors with internal watchdogs, you may not need to worry: deep sleep automatically disables the watchdog.

Avoid Frequent Wake-Ups

Since each wake-up requires some overhead from the chip (and the deeper the sleep, the more overhead is required), avoid frequent wake-ups. If you have a low-priority task that doesn't have a hard real-time requirement, piggyback it on another task. This spreads the overhead of waking up the processor over several tasks.

Although a timer to do housekeeping can be valuable, it may be better to check whether enough time has passed to do the low-priority tasks and reset the timer so you can skip a wake-up.

Chained Processors

It is pretty common to have a small, very efficient processor monitor the important signals, waking up a larger processor when needed. In this case the larger processor requires more power to wake up (and possibly more time if it is running an operating system). So the small processor does the housekeeping: checking for buttons pressed, looking for lower power conditions that indicate the system should shut down, or waking the large processor due to a preset alarm.

In such systems, both processors spend as much time asleep as possible, but the system is designed so that the interrupts get triaged in the small processor, which can opt to handle them itself or wake up its larger partner.

Further Reading

As noted in Chapter 3, for a gentle introduction to electronics, I recommend *Make: Electronics*. This step-by-step introduction to putting a system together (and soldering) is an easy read.

For a more serious look at electrical engineering, *The Art of Electronics* by Paul Horowitz and Winfield Hill (Cambridge University Press) is the seminal book, along the lines of Knuth's *The Art of Computer Programming*, discussed in Chapter 12.

If you are somewhere in between those two and looking for a more intuitive grasp of analog components, try *There Are No Electrons: Electronics for Earthlings* by Kenn Amdahl (Clearwater Publishing). This fun book gets away from the plumbing model of electronics and gives you a different story about how resistors and capacitors work.

The GitHub repository (*https://github.com/eleciawhite/making-embedded-systems*) for this book contains a *Power_consumption_Wordy_ring.xlx* worksheet showing the calculation process from the engineering perspective (building it up from components and readings to determine features) and from the design perspective (identifying use goals and determining features based on those and component information).

Interview Question: Is the Fridge Light On?

In two minutes, how many different ways can you figure out how to tell whether the light in a fridge is going off when you shut the door? Please don't damage the fridge. (Thanks to Jen Costillo for this question.)

This question is all about the quantity and creativity of solutions offered. This is not a question with a lot of depth (though I will ask a follow-up if I want more depth). Lots of people come up with the common solutions, some of which are:

- Take a video recording
- Wireless (and presumably battery-powered) light sensor
- Solar panel charger (check the charge of a battery after a period of time, with and without the door open)
- Disable the cooling assembly so the fridge uses only a small amount of power, then check the difference in current with the door open and closed
- With the door open, press the door-closing button to see what happens

Interviewees get credit for the number of solutions, uniqueness of them, what implicit assumptions they make, and how they apply the scientific method to solve the problem. I like to see them note the trade-offs in terms of time and cost, but I'd rather they spend the time generating different answers.

There seem to be three types of responses when faced with this question. First (and worst) are the interviewees who come up with only one of these and can't figure something else out, even with prompting. Second (and most common) are the interviewees who come up with a solution and tweak one thing at a time until they get to another solution. They generally rack up enough solutions and often surprise me with a few really creative ones. The last set of responses can only be classified as mildly insane. These are the most fun, and as long as they manage to get a few of the more sensible answers, these are the best people to work with.

One person suggested a statistical method: First, you get 100 units. Leave the door open on 50 of them and the door closed on 50. Determine the mean time between failure (MTBF) for the lightbulbs in the open units. Now open all the closed doors and wait for those to fail. If they fail about the same time as the initially opened ones, then the light was off with the door closed.

This isn't necessarily sensible or easily accomplished in a reasonable amount of time for testing the lights in fridges, but there are times when this sort of method will work very well. It gets bonus points for extra creativity.

Motors and Movement

The first time I made a motor move under my software's control was the moment I fell in love with embedded systems. It is more than blinking lights and sensing the environment. There is something magical about having my code *change* the world.

Since then, I've caused many small fires trying to recapture that rush. If your hardware is good and your software pays attention, perhaps you can learn from my findings instead of recreating them.

Creating Movement

Actuators are what your software uses to make a mechanical impact on its environment. The simplest actuator is a *solenoid*, which is kind of like a button in reverse. It is an electromagnet that will move a piece of metal: if you set it high, the solenoid is in one position; if you set it low, the solenoid is in another. These are useful for locking things or turning valves on and off.

Haptics are usually piezo buzzers or vibration motors that are used as part of a user interface (like your phone in vibrate mode). While these are often on/off as well, sometimes you can drive them with different frequencies to create musical tones as well as vibration. (Piezos can also be used as speakers, but that's a bit more complicated.)

However, moving things is a lot more fun if you use a motor that can do more than on/off or buzz a tune.

Whether you are making a bipedal robot or moving a widget along a conveyor belt, motors are where the systems really get to play in the real world. While motors are nifty and you should definitely try them out, good motor control requires its own book. I'll list some things to look for, but I can't give you anything more than a brief orientation to motors.

Just as you can buy an easier implementation using a digital sensor, some motor assemblies include a motor controller chip that will implement a control algorithm compatible with the style of motor. The controller will provide a simple API to your processor as well as increase the precision and life of the motor.

There are many types of motors, and your choice will be affected by such characteristics as the life-span of the device, torque (turning power), energy efficiency, and power consumption.

A *stepper motor* is a popular choice, though it can be relatively expensive. A stepper motor can be positioned precisely and will stay there (high holding torque). These are the simplest motors to use because you can run them in an open loop, without any feedback mechanism. Because they have a number of magnets to turn the motor shaft, stepper motors require multiple I/O lines. Each I/O line gets energized to cause the shaft to step forward to the next position (this can cause a bit of a jerk). When you want the motor to go smoothly in one direction, you need to make the I/O lines dance in a complicated pattern dictated by its datasheet (this dance is called *commutation*).

At the opposite end of the motor spectrum is a *brushed DC motor*. This is very cheap and usually requires only one I/O line (two if you want it to be able to go backward). The speed of the motor depends on the voltage applied. You can use PWM to give you more control than the binary choice between "off" and "running full speed." Motors usually don't like to be jerked on and off in a digital manner, so using PWM (and some relatively simple drive circuitry) to give a smoother velocity profile will increase your motor's life-span (we saw PWM control in Chapter 4). A difficulty with DC motors can be stopping them at the precise position you want; they often require a feedback control system to achieve this.

The torque of a brushed DC motor depends on the current. But your processor probably sources only enough current to drive a very wimpy DC motor, and current surges can damage your I/O lines. So these I/O lines will go through some additional circuitry to get more oomph.

A *brushless motor* usually has a longer life-span because it doesn't have the jerkiness of the stepper or any parts (brushes) that touch. As with a stepper motor, it needs a few I/O lines working together to achieve rotation. As with a brushed DC motor, controlling the speed is easier than controlling the position. Brushless motors are power efficient, quiet, and usually priced between stepper and brushed DC motors with similar characteristics. Finally, brushless motors can be DC motors or can use alternating current. *Linear motors* are similar to brushless motors but they go in a straight line instead of around in circles. They are also similar to solenoids but with more granular control.

 The voice coil in a speaker is an example of a brushless DC linear motor. If you have a spare speaker lying around, try connecting a battery across the terminals and watch it work at DC. (Note: depending on the speaker and the battery, you may damage the speaker, so start small.)

There is one more very important motor type: *servo motors* are stepper or DC motors that contain a controller to serve as a built-in feedback mechanism. Essentially, servo motors aren't motors but small systems that contain a motor. You can buy servo motors, but you may be building one as part of your system.

Position Encoding

The second most important thing to understand about your motor system is this: how will you know when it gets to wherever it is going? With a stepper motor, you can count the steps from where you are to where you want to be. However, how do you know where you are starting from?

If your position feedback method gives you an absolute position, you can just read that. However, many systems use a cheaper position sensor that will give you only a relative position, so you need to know where the start of the measuring stick is located.

Most motors (stepper or not) have a *home* sensor that indicates the absolute position in one particular location along the motor's travel. Usually home is at an extreme (e.g., all the way to the left or at the bottom), although sometimes home is the center of travel instead of one edge. Finding home is a matter of moving the motor slowly in that direction until the home position is sensed (sometimes with an optical sensor or contact switch). If the home is at one extreme, it serves as the zero position of the system, and other positions are counted from there. Once your motor is in its home position, you can use relative positioning to start moving to a location.

In a stepper motor, the relative position is calculated based on motor steps. For any other type of motor, you'll need another type of sensor called an *encoder*. It will often be an optical encoder that uses a series of alternating areas (black/white, reflective/matte, opaque/transparent) that lets your software treat the signal as a digital input.

A linear encoder measures the position of the motor along a straight line and is usually incremental, so the software must keep track of where it is in reference to a home position.

A rotary encoder measures the angle of the motor shaft. These can get complex as you increase position precision. Rotary encoders usually have multiple circles of alternating patterns. For example, three circles will need three sensors, which go to three GPIOs. In your code, you'll get three bits of data to let you know which of the eight (2^3) positions your motor is in, measuring off eighths of a circle, which is not a lot of accuracy. But if your motor moves 1 mm per full turn, it may be enough.

Figure 14-1 shows a simple motor system with some PWM control lines going to a motor. As the motor rotates, the encoder rotates with it (the dashed lines indicate the mechanical black box that includes gears and whatnot). An optical sensor sees the black and white areas on the encoder. The sensor connects to a counter on the processor and measures the relative position.

Initially, the motor goes through its homing procedure, where it moves in one direction until it sees the desired edge on the home sensor. Once there, the software can begin to count changes in position using the encoder. Your processor probably has a feature that will do this sort of counting; check the "Counter/Timer" section of your user manual.

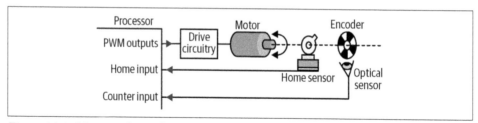

Figure 14-1. Motor and encoder system.

Driving a Simple DC Motor with PWM

For DC motors, speed is proportional to the voltage you supply. They are usually controlled by PWMs as shown in Figure 14-1. The higher the duty cycle of the PWM, the higher the average voltage, and the faster the motor turns.

However, the processor GPIO driving the PWM is not *ever* directly connected to the motor. Motors require much more current than your processor I/O lines can supply.

Instead, the GPIO's PWM output goes through a transistor[1] which switches the voltage on and off from a higher current power source. The simplest way to think about these is that they are automatic doors: when your code uses an I/O pin to press on the FET, it opens a pathway between the motor and power source. If you don't do this, your processor's pin (or the whole processor) will likely fail, possibly letting out the magic smoke.

If you want the motor to turn the other way, you need to make the voltage negative. This usually involves an *H-bridge*, a circuit or part of a motor driver chip that allows the voltage to go positive or negative, allowing a motor to go forward or backward.

Where voltage controls the speed of the motor, current controls the *torque* (the force of the rotation). Starting from a dead stop is hard on a DC motor; it wants to stay as it is. So it requires quite a bit of current to get into motion (DC motors are couch potatoes). So whether you are accelerating or working against an opposing force, generating torque requires a lot of current.

As described in Chapter 13, current is additive in the system. If you have a processor that consumes 3 mA when running and a motor that consumes 2 A, your system will need at least 2.003 A. In low-power systems with motors, the motors are usually the largest consumer of power.

Motors draw (sink) a lot of current: they need it to move. Most systems separate the supplies for the microprocessor and motor to avoid problems. Note that when motors start moving, they are working against inertia, which means there may be a sudden rush of current. This *inrush* current can cause lots of problems, including reducing the system voltage (which can cause the processor to reset). A battery-powered system is especially vulnerable to this as the available current at low battery levels may not be the same as it is at full charge.

Batteries in series give you more voltage; batteries in parallel give you more current.

So how much current do you need? Read the motor datasheet if you have it. For simple DC motors, you can use the tools you learned about in "Measuring Power Consumption" on page 357: essentially, measure the motor's current draw with your

---

1 These transistors are chips external to your processor. Broadly speaking, they can be bipolar junction transistors (BJT) or field-effect transistors (FET). Each of these transistor categories has multiple subtypes, such as the insulated-gate bipolar transistor (IGBT) or the metal-oxide-semiconductor field-effect-transistor (MOSFET). These terms mean important things to some people, but it is OK for you and I to forget them.

power supply. This may not give you a precise value for inrush current, but it can give you an idea of the magnitude of current to expect.

 One way to find a motor's max current is to make it stall (force it to stop moving), though this is bad for the motor, so don't do it often.

Jerk, Snap, Crackle, Pop

To start with, we need some equations of motion:

```
distance = velocity * time
velocity = acceleration * time
```

Turning these around:

```
velocity = distance / time
acceleration  = velocity / time
```

Then we can say smart-sounding things like velocity is the derivative of displacement (distance) and acceleration is the derivative of velocity. Which just means that velocity is how distance changes with respect to time; acceleration is how velocity changes (with respect to time).

Torque is different; it is related to rotation and force, where force is the same as Newton's law:

```
force = mass * acceleration
```

I think of torque as oomph: the ability of a motor to spin against resistance. That resistance may be me holding the motor in place or a gear that is jammed. A low-torque motor will just sit there (getting hot, maybe making sounds); a high-torque motor will spin out of my hands or crush the jammed gear.

Since torque is related to both mass and acceleration, higher torque motors can also change their speed more rapidly as well as move larger masses.

Anyway, I don't want to talk about torque. I want to mention that the derivative of acceleration is *jerk*. This is aptly named: motors with rapid changes in acceleration cause jerky movements. It also causes vibration and additional wear and tear on your motors. Reduce jerk by smoothly changing acceleration.

The derivative of jerk is *snap*. The derivative of snap is *crackle*. The derivative of crackle is *pop*. You don't need to know this to work on motors (or if you do, you've gone beyond my motor experience). But isn't it awesome?

Motor Control

In *feed-forward control* (aka *open-loop control*), you use how the motor is expected to work to tell it to go places. For example, for stepper motors, you can tell them to take 100 steps and they do. Their steps are of a known size, so you have a good reason to believe you know where you are.

In *feedback control* (aka *closed-loop control*), you use a sensor to measure what the motor is doing, changing the commands (or voltage) to the motor based on what you measure. However, this is not as simple as telling it to go until you get to a position and then telling it to stop. By then, the motor has overshot the position. You could tell it to go back, but then you will overshoot again. Unless you are trying to rock a baby, you don't want to keep going back and forth like that.

PID Control

The most common way to handle this problem is to use *PID control*. PID stands for *proportional, integral, and derivative*. Each term handles a part of the problem, and together they can tell you how much power to send to the motor (usually in terms of PWM level). The procedure starts with an error measurement that is simply the difference in position between where the motor currently is (the *process value*, or PV) and where you want it to be (the *set point*, or SP).

The proportional term is easy to understand. It is just a constant multiplied by that position error:

```
error = goalPosition - currentPosition;
PID.proportionalTerm = PID.proportionalConstant * error;
```

So when the motor is far from the goal, your software gives it a lot of juice; whereas when you are close to the goal, it powers down. Sometimes this is all you need. However, starting the motor full-on when you are far away from the target will cause it to jerk, which is bad for it. Further, you may still overshoot the target, leading to oscillations around the goal position. Or, if your error is small, the proportional term will never give the motor enough power to actually move, so you end up stuck in not quite the right position (a steady state error).

The integral term helps these problems by adding up the error over time:

```
PID.integralSum += error;
PID.integralTerm = PID.integralConstant * PID.integralSum;
```

Not only is the integral term proportional to the amount of error (as the proportional term is), it also takes into account how long there has been error. After the motor has been commanded to move, the error has been around for only a short time. But after a few cycles of the PID control loop, if the motor hasn't gotten close to its destination, the integral term lends oomph, accelerating toward the goal. However, it is kind of like momentum. Once the integral term gets going, it tends to cause an overshoot, one even worse than the proportional term would alone. Although the controller will find its way back to the goal position—sans oscillation or constant error, thanks to the integral term—it would be better not to overshoot the target. This is where the derivative term comes in:

```
PID.derivativeTerm = PID.derivativeConstant * (error - previousError);
```

This makes the controller decrease the output if the error is decreasing. This adds some friction to balance the proportional and integral terms, usually counteracting the PI terms as the error term gets smaller.

The output of the PID controller is the addition of these three terms. This output then goes to the motor driver code, which turns it into a PWM duty cycle. Figure 14-2 shows a reasonably well-tuned interaction between the terms and their output as the system is commanded to go to a set point (position). Note that the output of the system feeds back into the controller, so this is a feedback system. As such, it can be unstable. Too much proportional control can make the motor oscillate (or ring). Too much integral control, and the motor may smash itself to bits as it overshoots the position.

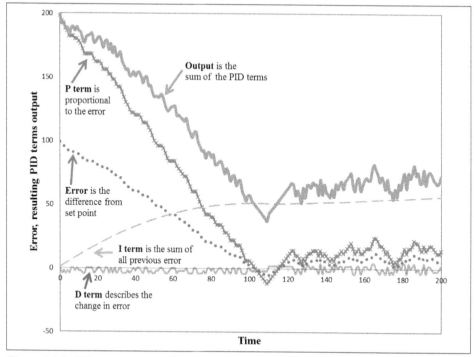

Figure 14-2. PID response to a change in set point, such as a motor being commanded to a new position. The output signal goes to the motor driver (which divides by 2 and outputs it as a PWM duty cycle).

Error signals are often noisy. If they are too noisy, the derivative term can lead to random results. Feedback systems that get out of control can do dangerous things.

Consider including limit switches in your design. Like the home sensor, limit switches can identify absolute positions, though they are usually put in positions where the motor is likely to fail or become uncontrollable.

However, there are many, many engineering problems where a PID controller provides a good solution. I've used PIDs with motors, heaters, and modeling spring systems. This control method is widely used and well understood; consider it an engineering design pattern. And you can see from the earlier code snippets that implementing one in software is simple.

However, those constants? The ones that describe how much weight each PID term brings to the output? Figuring those out is a painful process called *tuning*. The field does provide some easy guidelines: start with proportional control until you get it working pretty well, then add derivative control to smooth out overshoot, then (if necessary) add integral control to avoid smaller errors. But three weeks after the project was supposed to end, you may still be cursing the person who gave you this advice, telling you to just tweak the parameters until the motor works.

There are also some mathematical tools to help you with tuning (e.g., the Ziegler-Nichols method). Despite the mathematical tedium and having to estimate some inputs (the real world doesn't match the mathematical ideal), I recommend using these in addition to trial and error. But these methods often require a formal and deep understanding of the problem.

Note that the PID concept is pretty standard, but implementations vary. For example, because the derivative term is sensitive to noise in the error signal, many implementations will use an average of error over several samples. This hardens the derivative term against noise-induced insanity, but makes it less responsive to the system. There are many dozens of these little tweaks to ensure better performance and deal with system-specific issues.

At this point, I have given you enough information to be dangerous, but not enough to do a good job. "Further Reading" on page 387 suggests some sources to help you implement and tune a PID controller (and some other control methodologies).

Motion Profiles

How do you want your motor to move? Forget all that PID stuff, think about you being in a tiny car, driving that motor. Do you have a heavy foot on the gas and brake? Accelerate hard until you get halfway there, and then decelerate hard?

This type of motion is called a *triangular motion profile*. See Figure 14-3. You'll get there as fast as possible, but is that good for the motor? Or the passengers?

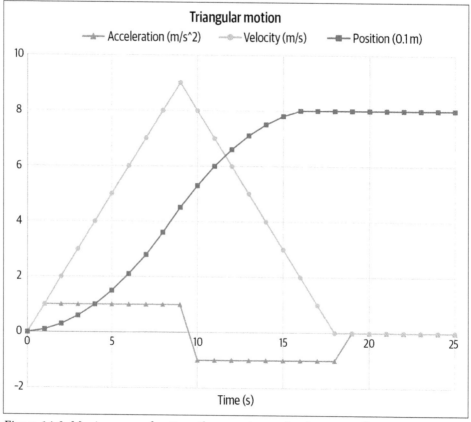

Figure 14-3. Maximum acceleration, then maximum deceleration will get you there fastest, but is tough on your parts.

So another option is to consider something a little gentler: trapezoidal motion. In Figure 14-4, you can see it takes longer to get to the same point, but the motor doesn't have to jerk from full positive acceleration to full negative. (Remember, jerk is the derivative of acceleration: it looks like jerkiness or vibration on the motor.)

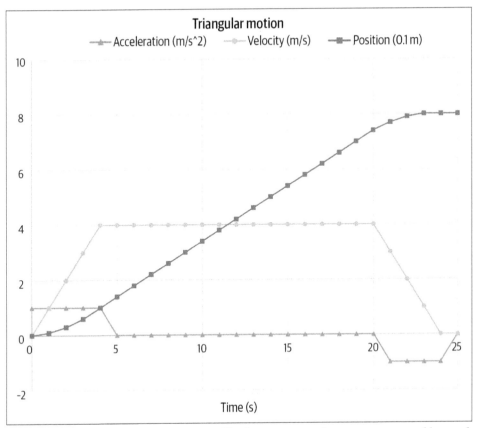

Figure 14-4. In a trapezoidal motion profile, the system accelerates to a reasonable speed and gets to the goal position a little later.

Note that because speed is related to input voltage, it is often easier to control than position, even with position feedback. When writing motion profile code, you often need to consider the goal position in terms of speed (voltage) and time. This is why the triangular and trapezoidal motion profiles describe the shape of the velocity curve, not the position.

Many processor vendors will offer a motor control library tuned to your processor's features. Look in their application notes. These libraries will probably do the math for you so you can have point-to-point position moves instead of worrying about velocity and acceleration.

An even better profile would smooth out the acceleration even more, reducing the jerk until it no longer matters. This is usually called an S-curve as shown in Figure 14-5.

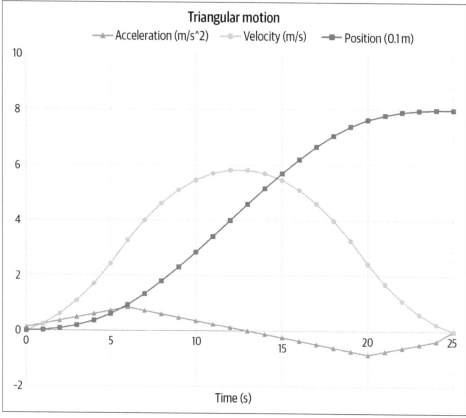

Figure 14-5. An S-curve motion profile reduces jerkiness, leading to far smoother motion.

An S-curve motion profile will take longer than a triangular profile but can be faster than a trapezoidal profile, depending on the maximum speed goal of the motor.

Ten Things I Hate About Motors

I love motors. They do so much: a motor can close a door or make a robot move. A motor can pump liquids into DNA scanners or provide a boost in an electric bike. The applications are endless and fascinating.

But there are things I hate about motors:

Servos aren't even a type of motor (except when they are hobby servos).

Unlike DC, brushless DC, or stepper motors, a servo is simply any kind of motor system with a position feedback. There is no standardization. The exceptions to this are hobby servos (or RC servos) which have two power wires and one control wire. They use a potentiometer for simple feedback control on the motor.

Motors can cause the processor to reset.

If motor power is connected to the processor power, then motor moves may cause the processor voltage to sag, causing brownouts. These may lead to resets or odd behavior involving hard faults.

The power source for the processor needs to be isolated from the motor supply with lots of decoupling between them. (Decoupling usually means lots of capacitors.) You must also use a MOSFET or other transistor circuit to keep the GPIOs on the processor safe from the current that the motor sinks and the transients starting a motor can cause.

Motors are not power efficient.

Where a system with two hundred 5 mA LEDs may require about 1 A of power, that's probably what a single small motor needs. As you work with motors, your power budget is probably mostly consumed by the motors.

Motors and their driver chips get hot.

All that power has to go somewhere and not all of it makes it into motion. A lot of the power goes to the driver chips (they can get so hot that they desolder themselves, though that usually indicates a problem in the circuit design). Imperfect commutation can cause a lot of problems, but so can jams and stalls.

Motors break things.

Depending on the gearing you have, your motor may be too fast or too powerful, so that when you accidentally send a command you shouldn't have (whoops, didn't check for a negative PWM?), suddenly, parts are flying across the room. Motors don't have emergency stops for human safety (until we develop them).

Motors can draw excessive current when starting up. Or holding position. Or when they find a dust mote to play with.

DC motors use a lot of current when starting and when stalled. Stepper motors use a lot of current standing still (holding position).

The usual heuristic is that the supply needs to source and sink three times the maximum current needed for a normal full load. Many power supplies do not sink current at all.

For example, connect a DC motor directly to a linear voltage regulator. The motor turns on OK, but when turned off, the regulator can't absorb current coming back from the load. That's why there is a snubber diode to conduct the reverse current to a safe place, away from the regulator. Without the snubber, the reverse current will cause a voltage spike. (An H-bridge is the fancy way to solve this problem.)

DC motors with "noisy brushes" turn themselves on and off many times a second as the brushes make intermittent contact with the armature. So this isn't an only-when-you-stop phenomenon; it happens all the time.

Motors catch fire.

Hardware costs money. It takes time to put together. Minor coding issues can lead to costly and dangerous consequences. (OK, often hilarious consequences, too, but that doesn't belong in a list of why I hate motors.) Admitting to your EE that you blew up another FET because you tried to control the motor without disabling the debug UART interrupt, well, I've been there and I feel for you. Work on the very lowest levels first and get a solid base before trying to do fancy motion profiles.

Motor control can be trivially easy or impossibly hard.

Motor control is an entire field of study. If you are lucky, you can afford to buy a good servo motor that will go where commanded with power circuitry to support any necessary movement. If you aren't, well, commutation can make for really pretty oscilloscope traces as you try to determine why it isn't quite right and the FETs keep blowing.

~~Snippy diodes. Snobby diodes.~~ *Snubber diodes. Flyback diodes. Transient suppression diodes (TSDs). Shoot through current. Actually, all of analog electronics.*

Motors use power to turn around, right? What happens when they stop? The power doesn't suddenly disappear; the motor can return a little bit of power to the circuit as it jerks to a halt. This isn't good for the circuit, so electrical engineers put in snubber or flyback diodes to prevent breakage. Note: if you have a motor that goes both directions and are using an H-Bridge, that already has snubber diodes.

In truth, none of electronics really is as instantaneous or clean as we pretend, and motor systems tend to shatter these illusions. It takes time for the FETs to turn on. When you have multiples of them (like with that H-Bridge), sometimes they take time to change states, which can cause them to crowbar—get stuck in a bad position, usually shorting the power to ground and ending the world (for your device).

Only five of these will be related to your motor subsystem.

The word "motor" is like the word "sensor." Sure there are similarities between different types, but there are just as many differences. It isn't sufficient to say "motor" and know what kind of impact that will have on the system. Motors are

---

driven with different mechanisms (PWM, communication, driver chips that do PWM or commutation). Position feedback comes in many forms.

Choosing a motor depends on your application. You'll need to define your goals for torque, speed, accuracy, precision, cost, life-span, and control mechanism. The good news is that you have many options. The bad news is that you have many options.

Further Reading

Adafruit has a motor selection guide (*https://oreil.ly/E0d4V*) that gives pros and cons of each type and follows up with a number of more specific tutorials about running each kind of motor.

Control theory is not for the faint of heart. However, this is an area kids are learning because they need it for FIRST Robotics competitions. So instead of the rigorous and math-heavy tomes I'd usually suggest, I encourage you to look at:

- CTRL ALT FTC (*https://ctrlaltftc.com*) is a complete control theory class for FIRST Tech Challenge. It includes code, diagrams, videos, and exercises. It starts with basic on/off control and builds up to PID controllers, motion profiles, and more advanced topics.
- WPILib's "Advanced Controls" documentation (*https://oreil.ly/x5HWm*) describes how its library works, which is great, but the important information is how all this works together, which is something you can use on your system.

For a more book-based approach to motor control and other control schemes, I like *The Art of Control Engineering* by Ken Dutton, Steve Thompson, and Bill Barraclough (Addison-Wesley). It is a little more math-filled than it needs to be, but still pretty useful for actual implementation.

Many processor vendor application notes have information about using their products to control motors. These can describe libraries already written for you or provide theory. See this book's GitHub repository (*https://github.com/eleciawhite/making-embedded-systems*) for more information from various vendors.

Interview Question: Teach Me

How does an H-Bridge work?

I had a terrible interview at a small company I really wanted to work at. I was well-suited to the job and the senior EE and I hit it off immediately. Then came in a junior EE who asked me about modern C++ language features (ones I was confident their embedded compiler didn't support).

She was very junior (to me, to her EE, to the industry). Preparing for what was probably the first time as an interviewer, she'd looked up questions on the internet, detailed points about C++. But she didn't understand them. She just knew I wasn't giving the answer the internet wanted. And her EE was there, watching and nodding along with me (not her). She felt increasingly frustrated as I essentially belittled her questions in front of her boss.

There are two lessons here.

First, don't be me; I didn't get the job because I was a jerk to her. I should have been looking to help her understand that her questions weren't relevant, possibly suggested different questions for the next interview. Your role as a senior engineer is to help junior engineers.

Second, if you are the interviewer for a position for which you don't have domain knowledge, don't fake it. I'd already established my technical ability for the job, what she should have been looking for was whether we could work together.

Funny enough, it was only a few months later that I was interviewing EE candidates. Other than basic electronics, I couldn't figure out what to ask so that I'd be able to guide them if they got it wrong. I ended up asking about an H-Bridge because I don't understand the circuit for more than about two weeks at a time. It was important that the candidate could explain it to me without making me feel stupid. And after the interview I could look up the answer and make sure the internet agreed it made sense with my new understanding.

Essentially, I used my ignorance to help me find people I could learn from instead of hoping I could fake being an expert.

To that junior EE who has probably gone on to a spectacular career, thank you for helping me realize that one of my goals for being an interviewer is to identify people I do (and don't) want to work with. And I'm still very, very sorry I made you cry.

Index

Symbols

#define declarations, 289, 325

& (bitwise AND) operator, 89, 205
   testing if bit is set in register, 91
   using in clearing bit in a register, 91

<< (bitwise shift left) operator, 91

?: (ternary conditional) operator, 292

^ (XOR) bitwise operator
   using to toggle bit in a register, 91

| (bitwise OR) operator, 89
   setting bit in a register, 91

~ (bitwise NOT) operator, 89
   clearing bit in a register, 91

A

abs function, 118, 290

acceleration, 378
   motion profiles, 382-384

accuracy
   of clock sources, 363
   of different numbers of terms for sine Taylor series, 334
   increased in lookup table with explicit lookup, 344
   versus precision, 323
   resistors associated with, 359
   sine lookup table results, 339

action register, 113

active low pins, 48, 101

active objects, 174-177

actor pattern, 177

actuators, 373

adapter pattern, 25, 100

ADCs (analog-to-digital converters), 127, 195

ADC to DAC data-driven system with multiple pointers into a circular buffer, 209

external ADC example, data ready with SPI, 196-197

external ADC example, SPI and DMA, 200-203

sample frequencies, 229

temperature compensation in ADC input, 345

AES encryption algorithm, 271

Agile development, 43

algorithms
   for addition and multiplication of fake floating-point numbers, lack of precision, 351
   authentication and encryption, security of, 271
   combining strategy and template patterns, 233
   designing and modifying, 332-344
      factor polynomials, 332
      scaling the input, 336
      using lookup tables, 338-344
      using Taylor series, 333-335
   encryption, 271
   implementations, fast or large, 317
   minimum of three variables, implementation example, 292
   stages, pipelines and filters, 233
   strategy pattern, 232
   template pattern, 232
   using an existing algorithm, 329-332

Allen, Charles, 212

analog signals, 227-229
   noise, 230

About the Author

Elecia White is a senior embedded systems consultant at Logical Elegance Inc. She has helped ship many consumer, medical, and industrial products. She is also the cohost of the *Embedded.FM* podcast.

Colophon

The animal on the cover of *Making Embedded Systems* is a great-eared nightjar. Great-eared nightjars are members of the family *Caprimulgidae* and inhabit subtropical or tropical moist lowland forests in Southeast Asia.

Great-eared nightjars are crepuscular, meaning mostly active at dusk and at night, during which time they satisfy their diets of flying insects and moths. Their calls are a distinctive, sharp "tissk," followed by a two-syllable "ba-haw."

These birds have pronounced ear tufts, which, in addition to their average length of 16 inches, make them more conspicuous among nightjars. Their soft gray and brown plumage resembles their preferred habitat, leaf litter and bracken. They lay their eggs either directly on bare ground or in leaf-litter nests on the ground. Nightjar nestlings have been observed to be completely silent and motionless, which, in addition to their leaf-colored plumage, may help protect them from danger while nesting.

The cover illustration is by Karen Montgomery, based on a black-and-white engraving from *Akademie der Wissenschaften*. The series design is by Edie Freedman, Ellie Volckhausen, and Karen Montgomery. The cover fonts are Gilroy Semibold and Guardian Sans. The text font is Adobe Minion Pro; the heading font is Adobe Myriad Condensed; and the code font is Dalton Maag's Ubuntu Mono.

Milton Keynes UK
Ingram Content Group UK Ltd.
UKHW031044011024
449087UK00001B/3

9 781098 151546